Assessing Organizational Behaviors

Magno Oliveira Macambira
Helenides Mendonça
Maria das Graças Torres Paz
Editors

Assessing Organizational Behaviors

A Critical Analysis of Measuring Instruments

Springer

Editors
Magno Oliveira Macambira
Department of Human Sciences & Philosophy
State University of Feira de Santana
Feira de Santana, BA, Brazil

Helenides Mendonça
Department of Psychology
Pontifical Catholic University of Goiás
Goiânia, GO, Brazil

Maria das Graças Torres Paz
Institute of Psychology
University of Brasília
Brasília, DF, Brazil

ISBN 978-3-030-81310-9 ISBN 978-3-030-81311-6 (eBook)
https://doi.org/10.1007/978-3-030-81311-6

This Springer imprint is published by the registered company Springer Nature Switzerland AG
The registered company address is: Gewerbestrasse 11, 6330 Cham, Switzerland

Preface

Organizational and work psychology has been historically marked by huge theoretical, conceptual, and methodological diversity. The number of studies in this field of knowledge increases at the same time when deep changes in the production methods and labor force emerge as a global phenomenon. The twenty-first century – the century of technological revolution that was recently affected by the COVID-19 pandemic – posed drastic changes to civilization in the social and economic fields, making the labor world even more complex and uncertain. This ambivalent and volatile dynamic, rooted in economic development patterns characterized by advances and setbacks, makes the labor world extremely stressing.

The organizations' sustainability is challenged facing the urgent need to review their actions and refocus their strategic decisions. This process may lead to restructuring, mergers, acquisitions, downsizing, off-shoring, outsourcing, and use of temporary labor force, among many other measures. The impacts ensuing from this process are not limited to organizations. Rather, they also affect workers who suffer financial impacts, reduced labor security, decreased job offers, multiple labor demands, and change of work nature and workplace.

In this context, organizational and work psychology, by using measuring instruments built with theoretical and methodological rigor, can contribute to the development of diagnostic analyses to enable organizations to implement the evidence-based changes required for their survival. A wide range of reasons may lead to the need for innovating or reviewing the way organizations function. These reasons may range from different problems experienced by organizations in their attempt to fit into to the new socioeconomic dynamics, or even because when organizations try to change the context they come across the need to change their strategic view and set new objectives that give effect to a multitude of changes.

All these events demand diagnoses based on measuring instruments that allow accessing the organizational and individual variables, as well as the organizational behavior. This would improve the understanding on organizational problems and challenges in the scope of systems, work processes, and behavioral aspects. Specialized literature, however, indicates a wide variety of measuring instruments, many of which susceptible to theoretical or methodological challenging. This entails uncertainties about the use of these instruments by professionals, researchers, and students.

This book fills in a gap in international literature by providing critical reviews on variables of organizational behavior, notably its measuring instruments. What instrument should be used? What instruments present evidence of validity and reliability? Despite the huge effort toward developing measuring instruments, we could not find in the international context any collection that systematically presents to readers a broader overview on variables and their measuring.

Taken together, the chapters of this book were prepared so as to offer readers theoretical reviews followed by technical evaluations of scales internationally linked to measuring the phenomena under review, jointly with a critical analysis that indicates the future of research on the measuring of organizational behavior. The book comprises 12 chapters organized in two parts. The first part is focused on micro-organizational perspectives. It comprises measures on job crafting, reactions to organizational change, psychological well-being at work, bridge employment assessment in the work-retirement transition, resilience at work, and leadership in organizations. The second part of the book, titled Macro-Organizational Measures and Future Perspectives, brings forth state-of-the-art research on the following constructs: quality of life at work, organizational climate for creativity, values and organizations, assessments of organizational support, and contributions by social networks analysis and organizational effectiveness. The last chapter presents a critical discussion about the nature and future of organization behavior measuring.

This book represents our commitment toward critically thinking over instruments to measure organizational behavior. It is expected to be useful both for the academic audience and for market professionals that feel flooded by a list of instruments, missing clear parameters for selection.

Feira de Santana, Brazil — Magno Oliveira Macambira
Goiânia, Brazil — Helenides Mendonça
Brasília, Brazil — Maria das Graças Torres Paz

Acknowledgments

This book is a result of the collective cooperation of a group of Brazilian researchers concerned about the current scenario in the field of organizations and work. We hope that by providing a critical review of some measurements of organizational behavior, readers can properly select the diagnostic instruments that best fit into their organizational reality, or the purpose of their survey. We would like to thank the contributions by each author all over the world who were devoted to developing and validating measuring instruments, sharing them with the scientific community, and allowing research consolidation, science progress, and sound dialogue with the professional practice.

Contents

Contributors

Silvia Miranda Amorim graduated in psychology at the Federal University of Juiz de Fora (UFJF) and specialized in cognitive behavioral therapy at Redentor College. She holds a master's and PhD degree in psychology at Salgado de Oliveira University (UNIVERSO), with emphasis on Social Cognition, Organizations and Work, and a doctoral internship at University of Coimbra (Portugal). Currently, she is an adjunct professor at the Federal University of Minas Gerais (UFMG), working in the area of Organizational and Work Psychology.

Laila Leite Carneiro is an Adjunct Professor at the Institute of Psychology at the Federal University of Bahia. She is a psychologist with a master's and doctoral degree in Organizational and Work Psychology from the Federal University of Bahia. She is member of the Working Group "Organizational Culture and Health at Work" of the National Association of Research and Graduate Studies in Psychology (ANPEPP). She is co-coordinator of the Positive Psychology Laboratory (LAPP). She is dedicated to research on the themes: positive psychology, alternative work arrangements, worker well-being, quality of life at work, organizational commitment, and voice in organizations.

Pedro Afonso Cortez Adjunct Professor in the Postgraduate Program in Health Psychology at the Methodist University of São Paulo (UMESP). Research Professor at the Postgraduate Program in Forensic Psychology at the Tuiuti University of Paraná (UTP). Professor in undergraduate courses of Psychology, Business Management, and Accounting at the Methodist University of São Paulo (UMESP). He is part of the editorial board of the journal Psicologia Teoria e Pesquisa (UNB) in the areas of Social, Labour and Organizational Psychology and Psychometry and Psychological Assessment. Acts as an ad hoc reviewer to the Brazilian Psychological Testing Assessment System (SATEPSI) of the Federal Council of Psychology (CFP).

Ana Carolina Rezende Costa holds a master's degree and PhD in Business Administration (PPGA) from the University of Brasília (UnB), Brazil. Currently, she is a public servant at the University of Brasília Foundation (FUB), Brazil. She works as a researcher in a project funded by National Council for Scientific and Technological Development (CNPq) and she is a member of the Research Group on HR, Customers and Citizens Management (GP2C2) (blog: http://www.gpegpc.blogspot.com/instagram:gp2c2_unb). Her areas of expertise, research and publication are: human resource management, organizational behavior, and strategic planning.

Susiley Correa Costa holds a master's degree in psychology from the Federal University of Uberlândia – UFU and is specialist in business management (UFU/2001). Has experience as a teacher in human resources management. Extensive experience in the corporate environment, working in the area of people and commercial management. Worked in human resources for 10 years in the areas of recruitment and selection, training and development, performance evaluation, positions and salaries, organizational climate management, and internal consulting of HR.

Karla Veloso Coura is a postdoctoral student in Business Administration (PPGA) from the University of Brasília (UnB), Brazil, and holds a PhD in Business Administration from the UnB. Currently, she is a permanent professor in the Department of Administration Sciences and the Center for Applied Social Sciences (CCSA) at the State University of Montes Claros (Unimontes), Brazil. She works as a researcher in a project funded by National Council for Scientific and Technological Development (CNPq) and she is a member of Research Group on HR, Customers and Citizens Management (GP2C2) (blog: http://www.gpegpc.blogspot.com/instagram:gp2c2_unb). Her areas of expertise, research, and publication are: human resource management, organizational behavior, marketing, production and operations management, and operational research.

Elisa Maria Barbosa de Amorim-Ribeiro is a Professor at Salgado de Oliveira University, Niterói, Brazil, where she has been lecturing and advising doctorate and master's candidates. Her main research is focused on Social Network Analysis (SNA) with special interest on work and public policies contexts. She is on the board of the Brazilian Society of Organizational and Work Psychology.

Renata Silva de Carvalho Chinelato Psychologist in the Higher Education Center of Juiz de Fora/MG, Specialist in Human Development from the Federal University of Juiz de Fora (UFJF), Master of Psychology from UFJF, PhD in Psychology from Salgado de Oliveira de Niteroi/RJ. Post-doctoral internship at UFJF. Adjunct Professor in the Department of Psychology at the Federal University of Santa Catarina (UFSC). Coordinator of the Center for Studies and Research on Psychosocial and Health Processes in Organizations and at Work (Neppot/UFSC). Member of the work group Organizational Culture and Health at Work of the National Association for Research and Graduate Studies in Psychology (ANPEPP).

Ranna Carolina dos Santos Cunha has a master's degree in Social Psychology from Salgado de Oliveira University, Niterói, Brasil, and is a specialist in Hospital Psychology and Mental Health Management from Cândido Mendes University. She works as psychologist in public health and social assistance. Her work is focused on the impact of social support at the mental health of professionals who work with victims of violence.

Maria Tereza Tomé de Godoy PhD in Psychology. Master of Strategic Management. Researcher on human behavior with an emphasis on management by competence and teaching by competence. She coordinates and develops studies on adaptive expertise, leadership, human motivation, self-determination, well-being at work, quality of life at work, and worker health. She is a People Management advisor at the Federal University of Goiás (UFG).

Gisela Demo has a postdoctoral degree in Management & Organizations, from Anderson School of Management, University of California, Los Angeles (UCLA), USA, and also holds a PhD in Social, Work and Organizational Psychology from the University of Brasília (UnB), Brazil. Currently, she is an associate professor in the Department of Business Administration (ADM) and in the Graduate Program in Business Administration (PPGA) at UnB. She is a master's, doctoral, and postdoctoral advisor. She is leader of the Research Group on HR, Customers and Citizens Management (GP2C2) (blog: http://www.gpegpc.blogspot.com/instagram:gp2c2_unb) and associate editor of the *Review of Business Management* (RBGN), the journal with the greatest impact factor (JCR) in Latin America. Her areas of research are: human resources management, positive organizational behavior, relationship marketing, brand personality, citizen relationship management, and development and validation of scientific instruments.

Maria Cristina Ferreira is a full professor and the coordinator of the Graduate School of Psychology, Salgado de Oliveira University, Niteroi, Brazil, where she has been teaching and advising master and doctoral students. Her main research interests focus on cross-cultural psychology and positive organizational behavior, with a special interest in Brazilian cultural characteristics, as well as well-being, engagement, job crafting and passion at work. She is a member of the Brazilian Society of Organizational and Work Psychology.

Ronald Fischer holds a doctorate in Social Psychology – Sussex University (2002). He is currently Full Professor-Victoria University of Wellington, New Zealand and Researcher at the D'Or Institute for Research and Education, Sao Paulo, Brazil.

Lucia Helena de Freitas Pinho França holds a PhD in Psychology at the University of Auckland (NZ) and a postdoctoral stage at the University of Aveiro (PT). She works as a full professor in the graduate program in psychology at the University Salgado de Oliveira (BR), supervising master's and doctoral students.

She also worked for 17 years at SESC Nacional, coordinating the elderly area in Brazil. Currently, she has a CNPq Productivity Scholarship and support from FAPERJ in several grants and is a Consultant in Ageing for the organizational and social contexts.

Sharon Glazer is a Professor at The University of Baltimore and President, Healthy Organization, Inc. She has over 25 years of teaching, consulting, and research experience, with expertise in cross-cultural issues in occupational stress and organizational development. Her research has been supported by several grants, including Fulbright, Erasmus Mundus, and NASA Ames Research Center. She has taught and conducted research through visiting professorships in France, Italy, Spain, Portugal, Hungary, and New Zealand. She is a Fellow of the Society for Industrial and Organizational Psychology, the International Academy for Intercultural Research, and the International Association of Applied Psychology. In April 2021 she was awarded the university's highest honor, President's Faculty Award and the Yale Gordon College of Arts & Sciences Distinguished Scholar Award.

Diogo Freitas Pereira Gomes holds a master's degree in Psychology from the Federal University of Uberlândia – UFU, an MBA in Strategic People Management from the Faculty of Business Management – FAGEN/UFU and a degree in Psychology from the Centro Universitário do Triângulo – UNITRI. He is currently a professor of the Psychology Course at Centro Universitário do Triângulo and manager in the Human Resources, with generalist experience in the HR subsystems.

Sinésio Gomide Júnior holds a PhD in psychology from the University of Brasília (1999). He is currently a full professor at the Federal University of Uberlândia. He is a member of the Working Group on Organizational Culture and Health at Work of the National Association of Graduate Studies in Psychology (ANPEPP). He has experience in the area of psychology, with emphasis on WOP (organizational behavior, psychometrics, well-being at work, and human resources management).

Nivaldo Sales Galvão Junior holds a degree in business administration from Universidade Santa Cecilia (Unisanta), specialized in Integrated Logistics from fundação Instituto de Administração/Universidade de São Paulo (FIA/USP). He holds a master's degree in Health Psychology from the Metodist University of São Paulo (UNIMESP). He is currently regional distribution manager in Rio Grande do Sul by Correios and professor at Universidade Paulista (Unip) in the area of Logistics and Human Resources

Johannes Alfons Karl holds BA Business Psychology from FhaM, Germany, and an MSc in Cross-Cultural Psychology from Victoria University of Wellington. Currently, he is doing his PhD in Victoria University of Wellington (Supervisor: Professor Ronald Fischer). His areas of interest are rituals, mindfulness, stress, nature connectedness, values, personality, and research methods.

Magno Oliveira Macambira holds a PHD in psychology from the Federal University of Bahia. He is a professor at the State University of Feira de Santana and develops studies in the area of psychology with a focus on organizational behavior and social netword analysis in work context. He is a member of the Working Group on Organizational Culture and Health at Work of the National Association of Graduate Studies in Psychology (ANPEPP).

Leonardo Fernandes Martins is a Professor at Universidade Salgado de Oliveira (Universo Niterói), Brazil. He has been lecturing and advising doctorate and master's candidates at Universo-Niterói. His work focuses on training health professionals to reduce social stigma related to people who use alcohol and other drugs. He is a member of Latin American Network about Drugs and Stigma and member of the Association for Contextual Behavioral Science.

Elaine Rabelo Neiva holds a bachelor's, master's, and doctoral degree in Psychology at University of Brasilia and PhD – Doctorate Felowship at Complutense University of Madrid. Currently she is a professor at University of Brasilia. She has experience in Psychology, with emphasis on the following topics: organizational change, intervention for change, evaluation of change, organizational power, and organizational analysis. She is a postdoc in the Graduate Program in Social and Organizational Psychology at Columbia University at New York, Teachers College.

Aurea de Fátima Oliveira obtained her PhD in Psychology from the University of Brasília (1999). She is a Full Professor at the Federal University of Uberlândia and a member of the Working Group Organizational Culture and Health at Work of the National Association of Graduate Studies in Psychology (ANPEPP). She has experience in Work and Organizational Psychology, with emphasis on organizational behavior, organization culture and values, psychometrics, well-being at work, and human resources management.

Maria das Graças Torres Paz holds a PhD in Psychology from São Paulo University, Brazil, and a postdoctorate in social psychology from Complutense University of Madri. She is associate researcher at the social, work, and organizational Psychology postgraduate program os University of Brasília. She is a supervisor of master's and doctorate courses. She develops researcher about culture, management, quality of organizational life, and personnel well-being.

Juliana Seidl is a psychologist, holds a master's degree in Work, Organizational and Personnel Psychology (Erasmus Mundus WOP-P) from the University of Coimbra (mobility period at the University of Barcelona) and a PhD in Social, Work, and Organizational Psychology at the University of Brasilia (mobility period at the University of Florida). She is the founder and CEO of Longeva, working specially with career counseling, age diversity management practices and retirement planning programs for organizations.

Rose Helen Shimabuku is a Psychologist. She has a master's degree and PhD in Psychology from the Pontifical Catholic University of Goiás (PUC-Go), she works at the Federal Institute of Education, Science and Technology of Goiás – IFG. Specialist in People Management and in Higher Education Teaching, she has training in Quality of Life at Work, Stress Management, Psychopathology, and Psychopharmacology. She is also a postgraduate professor and researcher on topics such as organizational and work psychology, presenteeism, mental health at work, positive psychology, stress management, conflict mediation, emotional intelligence, and related topics.

Bruna Luise Silva is a psychologist, with a master's degree in Education at the Federal University of Mato Grosso, Brazil, a PhD student in Psychology at the Pontifical Catholic University of Goiás, Brazil, dedicated to the themes of job crafting and well-being at work. She works in the area of occupational health and human development in the Government of the state of Mato Grosso, Brazil.

Juliany Gonçalves Guimarães Silva is assistant professor, manager, and consultant in Social and Work Psychology. Graduated in Psychology at Pontifical Catholic University of Goiás (PUC Goiás) (2000), Master of Psychology from PUC Goiás (2003), and doctoral degree at University of Brasília UNB (2017), with experience in Psychology, with emphasis on Group and Communication Processes, and Organizational and Work Psychology, working mainly on the following themes: mental health at work, organizational diagnosis, human resources implementation, leadership development, and positive psychology.

Louise Cristine Santos Sobral PhD in progress – 2017– Federal University of Bahia (research line: individual and work: micro-organizational processes; Master of Psychology – Federal University of Bahia – 2010 with Fapesb institutional scholarship; undergraduate degree in psychology, Universidade Tiradentes – SE (2006). Member of the research group Emotions, Feeling and Affections-emotrab (http://emotrab.ufba.br/). University professor, experience in extension projects, management and consultancy in people management. ORCID: https://orcid.org/0000-0003-3900-903.

Cláudio V. Torres is a professor at the Department of Basic Psychological Processes at the University of Brasilia, Brazil. He obtained his PhD in Psychology at the California School of Professional Psychology (1999) in San Diego – California (USA), investigating cross-cultural preferences between Americans and Brazilians employees on leadership. Since then, he has spent his sabbaticals at the Griffith University, Australia (2004), University of Sussex, UK (2009), and the Hebrew University of Jerusalem, Israel (2013 and 2018), always developing cross-cultural research. His main interests include basic human values, cultural values, consumer behavior, and political psychology. Participated in previous research projects that included studies on indigenous approaches to achieve informal influence in organizations, the validity of the basic values in the refined value theory, political consumerism and core political values, among others. Dr. Torres has published over 90 articles and book chapters on the above related content, and has supervised about 50 MSc theses and PhD dissertations. He lectures courses on Cross-cultural Psychology, Consumer Behavior, Social Psychology, and Cultural Diversity and Inclusion.

Heila Magali da Silva Veiga Professor of work and organizational psychology at Federal University of Uberlandia, Brazil. She received her PhD in Organizational and Social Psychology from University of Brasilia. Her principal research profile is: entrepreneurship, organizational creativity, and well-being at work.

Part I
Micro-organizational Aspects

Chapter 1
Job Crafting Measures

Maria Cristina Ferreira, Renata Silva de Carvalho Chinelato, and Helenides Mendonça

1.1 Introduction

For some time, studies aimed at identifying the experiences and the meanings that employees attributed to their jobs were developed from work design theories, such as that of Hackman and Oldham (1980). These theories were dedicated to describing the main characteristics of the tasks and roles assigned to employees and the ways in which they impact individuals, groups, and organizations. The assumption was that the organization should be primarily responsible for structuring and modifying these characteristics, as the employee was seen as a passive recipient of external influences related to the task itself and the context in which it is performed (Grant & Parker, 2009).

Investigations guided by these approaches have accumulated abundant empirical evidence on positive (such as job motivation, well-being at work, effective work performance, among others) and negative effects (such as stress, burnout and absenteeism, among others) of various characteristics of the work (Grant & Parker, 2009). Their objective was to contribute to the improvement of the roles and tasks specific to each position and, consequently, to stimulate positive attitudes and behaviors in relation to work and organizational productivity (Leana et al., 2009).

However, the nature of work has changed considerably in recent decades, driven mainly by the strong development observed worldwide in the areas of information and communication technologies and in the services sector, which has led

M. C. Ferreira (✉)
Salgado de Oliveira University, Niterói, RJ, Brazil
e-mail: mcris@centroin.com.br

R. S. de Carvalho Chinelato
Federal University of Santa Catarina, Florianópolis, SC, Brazil

H. Mendonça
Pontifical Catholic University of Goiás, Goiânia, GO, Brazil

M. O. Macambira et al. (eds.), *Assessing Organizational Behaviors*,
https://doi.org/10.1007/978-3-030-81311-6_1

individuals to experience new forms of work (Grant & Parker, 2009). The current world of work has seen the advent of teleworking, with virtual and self-managed work teams, which work in a collaborative, interdependent, autonomous, and flexible way to achieve common goals, transcending geographical and cultural boundaries and disregarding the face-to-face interaction (Griffin et al., 2007). Furthermore, competitive pressures have led to the need for tasks to be completed at an increasingly faster pace and have amplified the uncertainty inherent in the work context (Grant & Parker, 2009). Furthermore, the nature of the workforce has also changed, with employees becoming seen as primarily responsible for their own careers. In this context, they tend to remain in a single job or organization for less time, seeking to gain positions that allow them to achieve their personal and professional goals more quickly (Grant & Parker, 2009). In summary, the increased complexity of the work promoted by technological advances has meant that currently functions are generally formed by a specific set of dynamic working conditions and subjected to constant changes (Demerouti & Bakker, 2014).

All of these changes have therefore become incompatible with the passive performance of formally described tasks and roles, which aim to achieve pre-established performance standards, as this context no longer fulfills the requirements of the current world of work and the needs of employees. In other words, job performance comes to be seen as a result mainly linked to the employees' skills in adapting to change, introducing the methods that are most appropriate for the efficient execution of their tasks and the satisfaction of their needs (Griffin et al., 2007).

As a result, new theoretical perspectives on work design began to emerge in the literature in the organizational area, supported by the premise that the employee must be active and personally involved in the process of reconfiguring their own work (Demerouti, 2014). These approaches, called bottom-up, therefore, complement the traditional perspectives (referred to as top-down), which focused only on making changes in tasks and in the work environment from initiatives developed by the organization (Wrzesniewski & Dutton, 2001; Demerouti, 2014).

Among these new theoretical approaches, the job crafting perspective should be highlighted (Tims & Bakker, 2010; Wrzesniewski & Dutton, 2001), this being dedicated to the study of the ways in which employees act proactively in their work context, in order to identify the problems and solve them (even if this implies changing routines). The aim is to adjust activities to personal preferences and needs (Tims et al., 2013) and to adapt the organization to its external environment (Ghitulescu, 2006).

The first studies on job crafting were predominantly of a theoretical (Wrzesniewski & Dutton, 2001) or qualitative nature (Berg et al., 2010). Subsequently, however, different measures of the construct emerged, which made it possible not only to increase the studies on the prediction of the phenomenon but also to expand its nomological network (Schachler et al., 2019).

Accordingly, the purpose of this chapter is to carry out a review and critical analysis of the main measurement instruments for the operationalization of job crafting. For this, initially we present the two main theoretical perspectives that have dominated the literature on this construct for some time, namely, that of

Wrzesniewski and Dutton (2001) and the other based on the Job Demands and Resources Model (JD-R; Tims & Bakker, 2010), as well as the main instruments developed to operationalize the construct, in the context of each of these initial approaches. Following this, we describe the theoretical models that have emerged more recently, in order to refine and/or integrate these initial approaches, as well as the instruments developed or improved, based on these proposed new models. In the final considerations, we critically evaluate the revised instruments and suggest new paths for research, which may prove to be potentially capable of contributing further to the adequate operationalization of job crafting.

1.2 Job Crafting and Its Measurement from the Perspective of Wrzesniewski and Dutton (2001)

According to Wrzesniewski and Dutton (2001), work tasks and the resulting interactions – what individuals do at work and with whom they interact – constitute important raw materials that individuals use to shape their professional activities. Accordingly, the authors introduced the term job crafting into the literature of the organizational area to characterize the process by which employees shape their work, making physical and cognitive changes directed toward tasks and interpersonal relationships at work.

Physical changes relate to changes in the form, content, number, and type of work activities, such as performing usual tasks in new ways. Cognitive changes refer to changes in the perception of tasks, such as when a worker realizes that their activity contributes to society. Finally, changes in work relationships are related to changes in the quality and quantity of interactions maintained with co-workers, as in offering colleagues help. By altering any of these elements, the individual alters the design of their work and the social environment in which they are inserted (Demerouti & Bakker, 2014; Wrzesniewski & Dutton, 2001). To these three initial types of job crafting, Wrzesniewski and colleagues (Wrzesniewski et al., 2012) more recently added the job crafting of skills, which refers to the changes that the worker implements in their skills in order to better carry out their work.

From this perspective, job crafting is associated with self-initiated changes, which employees engage in order to adjust their work activities to their preferences, motivations, and passions (Berg et al., 2008). When they obtain greater satisfaction of their basic needs through work, they review their identities and strengthen the meaning that work has for them (Lichtenthaler & Fischbach, 2019; Zhang & Parker, 2019). Wrzesniewski and Dutton's (2001) theory has been called role-based job crafting, as the changes it advocates relate to changes made specifically in the job roles (Bruning & Campion, 2018).

Several instruments have been developed to evaluate job crafting according to this theoretical perspective. One of the first endeavors in this direction was made by Ghitulescu (2006), who constructed scales to assess task, relational and cognitive crafting in industry workers and in special education teachers, containing specific items for these different samples.

This instrument, however, was not shown to be suitable for research with samples of workers in general (Slemp & Vella-Brodrick, 2013), which led other researchers to propose or adapt instruments for measuring job crafting, using the theory of Wrzesniewski and Dutton (2001) as the reference. Among them, the Job Crafting Questionnaire (JCQ; Slemp & Vella-Brodrick, 2013), the Job Crafting Scale developed by Niessen et al. (2016), and the Individual and Collaborative Crafting Scale (Leana et al., 2009) can be highlighted.

The Job Crafting Questionnaire (JCQ; Slemp & Vella-Brodrick, 2013), in its initial version, after qualitative analysis of the items, consisted of 21 items, distributed equally across the 3 dimensions proposed by Wrzesniewski and Dutton (2001), these being task, relational, and cognitive crafting. The instrument was applied in a sample of 334 Australian workers and exploratory factor analyses, performed with a subsample of 151 randomly selected participants, revealed the presence of 3 factors, with 7 items in the task and relational dimensions, and 5 items in the cognitive dimension. Confirmatory factor analyses, conducted with the other subsample, led to the removal of four more items from the original scale, providing a three-factor model with good fit to the data. The reliability analyses of the final version of the scale, calculated through Cronbach's Alpha, indicated high internal consistency.

In the convergent validation, the JCQ correlated positively with proactive behaviors, such as the behaviors of organizational citizenship and the use of strengths and intrinsically motivated goals at work. The instrument also showed positive correlations with satisfaction, contentment, enthusiasm, and positive affects at work. The JCQ correlated negatively with negative affects, with the exception of the relational dimension, which did not present statistical significance, despite the negative direction. In addition, the negative relationships, although mostly significant, were weaker than the positive ones.

The final version of the JCQ was, therefore, composed of 15 items, distributed equally across its 3 dimensions. The instrument begins with a brief explanation about job crafting, informing the respondent about the opportunities for change that the individual can engage in their work to make it more appealing. Then the participants are asked to indicate the extent to which they engage in different behaviors, on a six-point Likert-type scale, ranging from 1 (hardly ever) to 6 (very often). Examples of items: "Introduce new work tasks that you think better suit your skills or interests" (task crafting); "Think about how your job gives your life purpose" (cognitive crafting); and "Make an effort to get to know people well at work" (relational crafting).

The JCQ has also been validated in several other cultural contexts. Accordingly, Schachler et al. (2019) evaluated the psychometric properties of the JCQ, in its 15-item version, however, with a 5-point response scale, in 482 German workers. In the confirmatory factor analyses, the original three-factor internal structure was the one that best fitted the data, thus corroborating the study by Slemp and Vella-Brodrick (2013). The reliability analyses carried out through Cronbach's Alpha were also shown to be adequate, although smaller than the original study. In addition, crafting behaviors were positively correlated with personal initiative, autonomy, creative self-efficacy, vigor, and job satisfaction. The instrument's invariance between German and Australian samples was also observed.

Letona-Ibañez et al. (2019) analyzed the psychometric characteristics of the Spanish version of the JCQ, in a sample of 768 employees. Exploratory and confirmatory factor analyses demonstrated that the original three-factor structure of the scale obtained good fit indexes. The composite reliability indexes were considered adequate. In the convergent validation, the three scales showed positive correlations with engagement at work and negative correlations with burnout.

Pimenta de Devotto and Machado (2020), in turn, evaluated the psychometric properties of the JCQ, in its version with 15 items and a 6-point response scale, in 2 independent samples, composed, respectively, of 261 (sample 1) and 152 (sample 2) Brazilian workers. The results of the exploratory (sample 1) and confirmatory (sample 2) factor analyses indicated that the original three-dimensional structure of the scale presented good fit indexes. The instrument also showed adequate internal consistency indexes in the two samples, calculated through Cronbach's alpha coefficient.

Unlike previous studies, Geldenhuys et al. (2020) performed a validation of the 15-item version of the JCQ through diary studies. The sample consisted of 134 South African employees that participated in a 3-week diary study, with the instruments completed on Fridays. Multilevel confirmatory analyses attested to the instrument's original three-dimensional structure, with good fit indexes. It was also observed that intra-role performance was influenced by task crafting and cognitive crafting, while extra-role performance was influenced by cognitive and relational crafting.

Another scale designed to assess job crafting in the context of Wrzesniewski and Dutton's theory (2001) was developed by Niessen et al. (2016). The initial version of the scale consisted of 12 items, distributed over the 3 dimensions recommended in the typology of Wrzesniewski and Dutton (2001), and was tested with a total sample of 466 German workers.

Exploratory factor analyses conducted with one of the subsamples (233 respondents), as well as confirmatory factor analyses performed with the other subsample (233 respondents), resulted in a three-dimensional job crafting structure that presented good fit indexes, after the elimination of three items. The internal consistency of the general measure, calculated through Cronbach's Alpha, as well as that of the subscales, proved to be adequate. In the convergent validation, the results confirmed the hypotheses of positive correlations between the three dimensions of job crafting and personal initiative and the behavior of organizational citizenship. In a second study with 118 workers, measured in 2 stages over a 2-week interval, the structure of the scale was confirmed.

This led to the final version of the scale, composed of nine items, distributed equally across its three dimensions. Participants are instructed to rate the crafting activities based on the question "So that the job I do suits me...", according to a five-point Likert-type scale, ranging from 1 (not at all) to 5 (absolutely). Examples of items: "I concentrate on specific work tasks" (task crafting); "I find personal meaning in my tasks and responsibilities at work" (cognitive crafting); and "I invest in the relationships with people whom I get along with the best" (relational crafting).

Still considering Wrzesniewski and Dutton's (2001) theory, but extending the original job crafting concept, which is of an individual nature, Leana et al. (2009) developed a scale designed to assess individual crafting (proactive behaviors that alter the work) and collaborative crafting (joint efforts made by employees to change their work). The instrument contains 12 items, equally distributed between the 2 subscales, and was validated in a sample of 232 North American teachers, having presented good internal consistency indexes.

Participants are asked to indicate the frequency with which they engaged in some job crafting behaviors on their own or in collaboration with coworkers, on six-point Likert-type scales, ranging from 1 (never) to 5 (every day). Examples of items: "Introduce new approaches on your own to improve your work in the classroom" (individual crafting) and "Work together with your coworkers to introduce new approaches to improve your work in the classroom" (collaborative crafting).

The scale by Leana et al. (2009), similarly to the scale of Ghitulescu (2006), received criticism for containing items that were very specific to the study sample, which prevented its use with samples of workers in general (Slemp & Vella-Brodrick, 2013). However, it has been validated in other cultural contexts, in studies in which its original items have been adapted, in order to be answered by workers in general.

Llorente-Alonso and Topa (2019) adapted and validated the scale with a sample of 302 Spanish workers, having confirmed the instrument's two-dimensional structure with good fit indexes and good reliability indexes, with both dimensions of the scale correlating positively with job engagement. Di Fabio (2020) also confirmed that the scale's two-dimensional structure presented good fit indexes, by adopting confirmatory factor analysis procedures, in the validation for a sample of 237 Italian workers. The internal consistency indexes were very good, and the two scales correlated positively with acceptance of change and job satisfaction.

1.3 Job Crafting and Its Measurement from the Perspective of the Job Demands and Resources Model

Inspired by the perspective of Wrzesniewski and Dutton (2001), but aiming to not be restricted to only the modification of tasks and relationships, Tims and collaborators (Tims & Bakker, 2010; Tims et al., 2012) developed a typology of job crafting theoretically supported by the Job Demands and Resources Model (JD-R; Bakker & Demerouti, 2017). The aim was to link the construct to a greater number of aspects of the work and occupations context.

According to the JD-R Model, all the characteristics inherent to the work context can be allocated to two categories: job demands and job resources. Job demands relate to the characteristics of the work context (physical, psychological, social, and organizational) that require physical or psychological (cognitive and emotional) efforts from the worker and, consequently, imply physiological and psychological costs. Work overload and difficult interactions with customers are examples of these work demands. Job resources, in turn, refer to characteristics of work situations that reduce job demands and the costs associated with them, being functional for achieving goals and stimulating learning and personal development. These resources can be found in the organization (e.g., career opportunities, safety at work), in the interpersonal environment of the worker (e.g., support from colleagues, supervisors), in the work organization (e.g., clarity of roles, participation in decision-making) and in the task context (e.g., autonomy, variety of skills) (Bakker & Demerouti, 2017).

In an extension of the JD-R Model, some authors (Crawford et al., 2010) also distinguish between challenging demands and hindrance demands. Challenging demands (such as work overload and time pressure) relate to characteristics of the work context that require extra effort in their execution but contribute to the employee's development, which is why they are perceived as positive. Hindrance or obstacle demands, however, hinder the development of the employee and obstruct the achievement of their objectives, being therefore perceived as negative.

Based on the JD-R model, Tims and Bakker (2010) proposed that job crafting concerns proactive and self-initiated changes that employees make in their work context, in order to obtain a balance between the demands and resources of their work and their personal needs and skills. In this sense, they seek to decrease the demands and increase the resources of the job, as a way of achieving better adaptation to it (person-work fit) and greater motivation to achieve their work goals.

According to Petrou et al. (2012), job crafting manifests itself in daily and non-episodic actions, which can be performed in any occupational situation, including very stable environments with clearly described work procedures. According to the authors, even in these environments, employees need to adopt job crafting, as a way to make adjustments in their work context that are more appropriate to their preferences and, therefore, make them more motivated and healthier.

In summary, from the perspective of the JD-R Model, job crafting consists of changes that employees make in their job demands and resources, based on their abilities and needs, to make work more rewarding and fitting to them (Demerouti & Bakker, 2014; Tims & Bakker, 2010; Tims et al., 2012). This perspective has been designated as resource-based job crafting, as its main goal is to restore the balance between the person and their work, by manipulating the underlying resources and demands (Bruning & Campion, 2018).

Tims et al. (2012) consider that job crafting behaviors are characterized by four dimensions: increasing structural job resources, increasing social job resources, increasing challenging job demands, and decreasing hindering job demands. The increase in structural resources is associated with changes in aspects intrinsic to the design of the job, such as requests for more autonomy, while the increase in social resources refers to changes in aspects of the social context in which the work is carried out, such as requests for more feedback from colleagues and supervisors. The increase in challenging demands, in turn, focuses on the effort so that difficult goals are maximized, as in the case of seeking inclusion in new projects, while the decrease in hindering demands includes attempts to reduce tasks that prevent the achievement of goals, such as, for example, seeking to reduce the emotional overload inherent in the tasks performed.

Among the job crafting scales that adopt the Job Demands and Resources Model as a theoretical reference, the Job Crafting Scale (JCS), developed by Tims et al. (2012) should be highlighted, as well as the adaptations which it has undergone. In its initial version, the scale contained 42 items and was validated in three different studies, which involved 1181 Dutch workers. Although the authors initially tested a three-dimensional model (increasing job resources, increasing challenging demands, decreasing hindering demands), successively carried out exploratory and confirmatory factor analyses led to the elimination of several items and indicated that the best fit indexes were obtained through a structure composed of four factors: increasing structural resources, increasing social resources, increasing challenging demands, and decreasing hindering demands. The internal consistency of these factors, calculated through Cronbach's Alpha, presented adequate results.

In the convergent validation, positive correlations were observed between the four job crafting dimensions and the proactive personality, as well as between three of the job crafting dimensions and personal initiative. Negative correlations were found between cynicism and three of the job crafting dimensions. Additionally, in support of criterion validity, the results indicated that the self-reports on job crafting correlated positively with the reports of colleagues on the subject.

The instrument by Tims et al. (2012) contains 21 items. It asks respondents to reflect on the way they behave in relation to work and, then, indicate the frequency with which they perform these behaviors, according to a five-point Likert-type scale, varying from 1 (never) to 5 (often). Examples of items: "I try to develop my capabilities" (increasing structural job resources); "I look to my supervisor for inspiration" (increasing social job resources); "When an interesting project comes along, I offer myself proactively as project co-worker" (increasing challenging job demands); and "I make sure that my work is mentally less intense" (decreasing hindering job demands).

The original version of the Job Crafting Scale (JCS; Tims et al., 2012) has been validated in several other cultural contexts, although its original four-factor structure has not always been confirmed. The study by Akin et al. (2014), carried out with a sample of 364 Turkish workers; that of Lichtenthaler and Fischbach (2016), conducted with a sample of 412 German workers; that of Peral and Geldenhuys (2019), involving a sample of 318 South African workers and adopting the Item Response Theory (Rasch model) to examine the internal structure of the scale; and the study of Bakker et al. (2018), carried out with a sample of 896 Spanish workers, confirmed the original four-factor structure of the scale, with their dimensions presenting good internal consistency indexes.

However, the validation of the scale in a Brazilian sample of 491 workers (Chinelato et al., 2015) found that the results obtained in the confirmatory factor analyses did not allow the full reproduction of the original structure of the scale. The final version had 14 items, distributed in 3 first-order factors (increasing structural job resources, increasing social job resources, increasing challenging job demands), with a general second-order factor (job crafting), which presented adequate internal consistency indexes.

Similarly, Cenciotti et al. (2016) adapted the JCS to the Italian context, using a sample of 721 workers, but considered only the three positive dimensions of the job crafting behaviors. The exploratory and confirmatory factor analyses showed that the final model of 13 items, distributed in 3 factors (increasing structural resources, increasing social resources, increasing challenging demands), was the one that presented the best fit indexes, in addition to adequate internal consistency indexes.

A version of the JCS was also validated with a sample of 470 South African workers, divided into 2 different samples (De Beer et al., 2016). The results obtained revealed a three-dimensional structure, with 21 items, as the best solution for the scale. This version obtained good internal consistency indexes but proved to be different from the structure obtained in the two previous studies, by combining the increasing structural job resources and the increasing challenging job demands into a single factor.

Contrary to previous studies, in which the best solution implied the reduction of the four original factors of the JCS, Eguchi et al. (2016), when validating the scale in a sample of 972 Japanese workers, found that the best solution obtained was that of 5 factors, with 21 items. Therefore, the dimension of decreasing hindering demands was divided into two (decreasing emotional demands and decreasing cognitive demands), with all dimensions showing good internal consistency indexes.

Other studies involving the Job Crafting Scale (JCS; Tims et al., 2012) have aimed to make adaptations to it, through the proposition and testing of reformulated instruments, which sometimes expand and sometimes reduce the dimensions originally proposed for the scale. Petrou et al. (2012), adopting a slightly different perspective from that previously proposed by Tims and Bakker (2010), but still referring theoretically to the Job Demands and Resources Model, conceptualized job crafting behaviors as voluntary actions initiated by employees, which aim to seek resources, to seek challenges, and to reduce demands. Therefore, the categories of increasing structural resources and increasing social resources, of the typology proposed by Tims and Bakker (2010), were combined into a single category, called seeking resources.

Based on this typology, Petrou et al. (2012) reformulated the JCS (Tims et al., 2012), aiming to obtain an instrument that could be used to measure job crafting as a trait (general measure) and as a state (daily measure). The scale was applied in a sample of 95 Dutch workers, who completed the general questionnaire and then answered it daily, for another 5 days. The results of the confirmatory factor analyses supported the three-factor structure proposed by the authors, with good fit indexes, both for the general version (with 13 items) and the version of the scale for diary studies (with 10 items). The internal consistency indexes of the three dimensions, in both versions, proved to be reasonable. There were also positive correlations at the daily level between seeking challenges and engagement at work, as well as negative correlations between reducing demands and engagement. In some later studies (Petrou, Demerouti, & Schaufeli, 2015; Petrou, Demerouti, & Schaufeli, 2018), the version of the scale for general measurement was reduced to 11 items, with the elimination of 2 items, the factor loadings of which were below .40, in the original study by Petrou et al. (2012).

The job crafting measurement instrument by Petrou et al. (2012) invites the participant to indicate how often they engage in some behaviors during the past 3 months (general measure) or in the past day (daily), on a five-point Likert-type scale, ranging from 1 (never) to 5 (often). Item examples: "I ask others for feedback on my performance" (seeking resources); "I ask for more responsibilities" (seeking challenges); and "I try to ensure that my work is less physically intense" (reducing demands).

Another review of the JCS was proposed by Nielsen and Abildgaard (2012), as they considered that some of the items on the scale were not appropriate to the work context of blue collar employees. Based on interviews with these workers, the authors then chose to review and add items to the JCS, producing an initial version with 22 items, of which only 9 originally belonged to the scale. This version was adopted in a longitudinal two-wave study (*N*T1 = 362; *N*T2 = 408), with an interval of 1 year, carried out with Danish employees that worked in postal delivery services.

Exploratory and confirmatory factor analyses indicated that the best structure of the scale, after excluding seven items, was associated with a five-factor solution (increasing challenging job demands, increasing social job resources, increasing quantitative job demands, decreasing social job demands, decreasing hindering job demands), which obtained adequate internal consistency indexes. However, the decreasing hindering job demands dimension was left with only two items, and its internal consistency was not assessed. The different dimensions of the scale also presented positive relationships with work engagement and job satisfaction, and negative, with burnout.

The scale proposed by Nielsen and Abildgaard (2012) was therefore composed of 15 items, to be answered on a 5-point Likert-type scale, ranging from 1 (never) to 5 (very often), according to the frequency with which the respondents present each of the individual job crafting behaviors. Examples of items: "When a new task comes up I sign up for it" (increasing challenging job demands); "I ask for feedback on my performance from my customers" (increasing social job resources); "When there isn't much to do I offer my help to colleagues" (increasing quantitative job demands); "I try to avoid emotionally challenging situations with my customers" (decreasing social job demands); and "I ensure that my work is the least burdening/straining" (decreasing hindering job demands).

Nielsen et al. (2017) named the instrument proposed by Nielsen and Abildgaard (2012) the Job Crafting Questionnaire (JCRQ) and examined its psychometric properties using data collected in a diary study with 164 Spanish workers, a longitudinal study in three waves with 191 Spanish workers and a cross-cultural study with samples from Spain (N = 164), the United Kingdom (N = 109), China (N = 170), and Taiwan (N = 165). The results obtained confirmed the five-factor structure proposed by Nielsen and Abildgaard (2012), with a version of the scale composed of 14 items (reduction of 1 item in the increasing challenging job demands dimension). This version was replicated in the four countries and presented adequate indexes of test-retest reliability, as well as criterion validity throughout the different studies, through positive relationships of the scales with well-being and performance measures. Similarly, the study by Ghadi (2019) confirmed the factorial structure of the Job Crafting Questionnaire, with 15 items (JCQR-15), in a sample of 513 Jordanian workers, as well as its convergent validity, when obtaining positive correlations of the different scales with affective commitment and performance, and negative correlations with loneliness at work, stress, anxiety, and depression.

A revision of the original version of the Job Crafting Scale (JCS; Tims et al., 2012) was also proposed by Sora et al. (2018), in order to validate a shorter version of the instrument. For this, the authors selected, from each of the dimensions of the instrument, the three items that best represented the conceptual meaning of the dimension and that, in previous studies, had presented factor loadings above .60. This reduced version, made up of 12 items, was applied in a sample of 1647 Spanish workers. The confirmatory factor analyses supported the four-factor structure of this version, with good fit indexes. The four dimensions of the scale also presented reasonable internal consistency indexes, as well as positive correlations with work performance and personal growth.

Yen et al. (2018) also developed a scale based on the model by Tims et al. (2012), specifically aimed at evaluating job crafting in tour guides. Based on some items from previously developed scales (Leana et al., 2009; Slemp & Vella-Brodrick, 2013; Tims et al., 2012), as well as the analysis of interviews from focus groups, the authors came up with an initial version of the scale composed of 36 items. The instrument was tested on two different samples of Thai tourist guides ($N1 = 268$; $N2 = 253$), who were asked to give their answers on five-point Likert-type scales, ranging from 1 (strongly disagree) to 5 (strongly agree). Exploratory and confirmatory factor analyses led to a final version of 30 items, distributed over four dimensions (increasing structural job resources, increasing social job resources, increasing challenging job demands, decreasing hindering job demands), which presented good structural fit indexes and high internal consistency indexes. It was also observed that the four dimensions of the scale presented positive correlations with a person-job fit scale.

In summary, the Job Crafting Scale (JCS), originally developed by Tims et al. (2012), as well as its adaptations and reformulations, has been widely adopted in studies focusing on the job crafting, from the perspective of the Job Demands and Resources Model (Pimenta de Devotto & Machado, 2017). These studies have been carried out in different cultural and occupational contexts and have focused on the investigation of the construct's nomological network, as attested by two recent meta-analyses (Lichtenthaler & Fischbach, 2019; Rudolph et al., 2017), as well as on carrying out interventions aimed at stimulating it (Oprea et al., 2019). Therefore, they are increasingly contributing to the dissemination of the JD-R model as the theoretical support for investigations on job crafting (Bakker & Demerouti, 2017).

1.4 Comparison, Refinement, and Integration of the Role-Based and Resource-Based Job Crafting Perspectives and Their Measurement

The perspectives of Wrzesniewski and Dutton (2001) and those referring to the Job Demands and Resources Model (Tims et al., 2012) show certain similarities, but also some differences. Both focus on the description of strategies aimed at reconfiguring work situations, by facing problems and seeking better solutions (Demerouti, 2014). Furthermore, both focus on the content of the crafting, that is, on certain aspects of the work that are crafted (Hu et al., 2020), with the crafting being beneficial for the employee, by contributing to facilitate their job motivation (Lichtenthaler & Fischbach, 2019).

Despite these similarities, the two theories differ in that, from the perspective of Wrzesniewski and Dutton (2001), job crafting is entirely motivational in nature, since its objective is only to increase the meaning of the job and the identification with it. The approach of Tims and colleagues (Tims & Bakker, 2010; Tims et al., 2012) focuses not only on motivational aspects but also on occupational health aspects, considering that job crafting is characterized as a way to balance resources with demands, in order to obtain a better fit between the person and their job and, as a consequence, avoid stress at work and protect the employee's health (Bruning & Campion, 2018; Niessen et al., 2016).

Add to this the fact that the model of Tims and colleagues (Tims & Bakker, 2010; Tims et al., 2012) refers only to changes in tangible aspects of the job (characteristics of work associated with demands or resources), while that of Wrzesniewski and Dutton (2001) concerns changes in tangible (tasks and relationships) and intangible aspects (cognitive alterations) of the job (Lichtenthaler & Fischbach, 2019). Therefore, the two theories differ in terms of the specific content of the job crafting strategies, with the first addressing changes in work characteristics, and the second, changes in tasks, relationships, and cognition about the job itself (Zhang & Parker, 2019). Even so, some authors (Demerouti, 2014; Rudolph et al., 2017) consider that the changes in tasks, proposed by Wrzesniewski and Dutton (2001), bear conceptual similarity with the changes in the job demands (increasing challenging demands and decreasing hindrance demands), proposed by Tims and Bakker (2010), whereas the relational changes resemble the changes in the social job resources.

These divergences meant that, for some time, studies on job crafting adopted only one of these two traditional perspectives on the construct. Consequently, only the crafting strategies contained within these theories were measured. More recently, however, there have been several proposals in the literature to refine these initial approaches and their measurement, which seek to associate the different job crafting strategies (crafting content) with the way in which this phenomenon occurs (crafting form).

In characterizing the job crafting forms, researchers have used several terms that, in the final analysis, can be seen as synonyms, and which represent two general motivational trends of action, associated with approach/promotion/expansion or avoidance/prevention/contraction (Hu et al., 2020). In this sense, job crafting oriented to the first perspective leads the employee to expand the elements of their work, while job crafting oriented to the second perspective leads the employee to make changes aimed at preventing negative results from occurring (Bindl et al., 2019).

Taking into account the theory of Wrzesniewski and Dutton (2001), Laurence (2010) formulated one of the first proposals on these forms of crafting, distinguishing between job crafting oriented to expansion or contraction, associated, respectively, with the increase or decrease in the number or complexity of tasks and interactions at work. Later, Weseler and Niessen (2016) adopted this concept in the refinement of the questionnaire proposed by Niessen et al. (2016), previously mentioned. For this, they added five items to the original instrument, so that it also contained items related to the reduction of tasks and the reduction of relationships. This version, containing 14 items, with a 5-point Likert-type response scale ranging from 1 (disagree) to 5 (agree), was validated with two different samples, the first consisting of 138 German workers, and the second, of 131 dyads of German employees and their supervisors.

The confirmatory factor analyses carried out on the two samples showed that the five-factor model (crafting by extending task boundaries, crafting by reducing task boundaries, crafting by extending relational boundaries, crafting by reducing relational boundaries, cognitive crafting of task boundaries) was the one with the best fit indexes. The internal consistency indexes of these factors, in the two samples, proved to be adequate. It was also verified that crafting by extending tasks correlated positively with the self- and peer-rated performance, while crafting by extending relationships presented positive correlations only with the self-rated performance. The crafting by reducing tasks was negatively correlated with self-rated performance, while crafting by reducing relationships was negatively correlated with self- and peer-rated performance.

Also restricting itself to the theory of Wrzesniewski and Dutton (2001), but articulating this with the needs of individuals and with the motivational theory of regulatory focus (Higgins, 1997), Bindl et al. (2019) argue that the individual needs of employees motivate them to adopt different strategies for changes in their work, which differ in terms of focus on promotion or prevention. The authors defined eight types of job crafting strategies, associated with promoting or preventing changes in job tasks, relationships, skills, and cognitions.

For the operationalization of their model, Bindl et al. (2019) developed a questionnaire initially containing 33 items, adapted from scales previously developed or specifically constructed for the study. The instrument was validated in three different samples (N = 421-cross-sectional study; N = 144-diary study; N = 388-three-wave study), composed of workers from the United States and the United Kingdom. Adopting exploratory and confirmatory factor analysis procedures, the authors obtained results that supported the initially proposed model, composed of eight dimensions, with the elimination of five items, which showed good internal consistency indexes. The hypotheses regarding the positive relationships between promotion-oriented strategies and innovation were also proven. The final version of the scale therefore consisted of 28 items, to be answered on a 5-point Likert-type scale, ranging from 1 (not at all) to 5 (a great deal). Participants are asked to indicate the extent to which they have engaged in the different job crafting strategies highlighted in each item, over the past week.

Regarding the refinement of the job crafting model based on the JD-R, Costantini et al. (2021) proposed a multidimensional and hierarchical job crafting model of a behavioral nature (superordinate construct), which unfolds as a second level, formed by the dimensions of expansion and contraction, which differ in a third level, in which the strategies of seeking resources and seeking challenges reflect the expansion dimension, and the strategies of decreasing demands and optimizing demands reflect the contraction dimension. In this way, the authors add to the types of crafting based on the JD-R model (Tims et al., 2012; Petrou et al., 2012), the demand optimization strategy. This strategy was introduced by Demerouti and Peeters (2018), and although it is associated with the demands reduction dimension, it nevertheless implies an active performance regarding obstacles, in order to eliminate them and, consequently, make work processes more efficient, unlike the demand reduction strategy, which relates to the passive removal of obstacles that hinder the development of work processes and generate stress.

To test the validity of the hierarchical behavioral job crafting model, Costantini et al. (2021) conducted a cross-sectional study ($N = 936$), a diary study ($N = 199$), and a longitudinal study ($N = 226$) with Italian workers. In the operationalization of the model, the authors adopted a questionnaire composed by the scale of Petrou et al. (2012), previously mentioned, which measures seeking resources, seeking challenges, and reducing demands, as well as the scale of Demerouti and Peeters (2018), which measures the optimization of demands. The instrument was composed of 13 items, to be answered on a 5-point Likert-type scale, ranging from 1 (never) to 5 (often), according to the frequency of engagement in the described behaviors, in the past 3 months.

The exploratory and confirmatory factor analyses showed that the four-factor structure was the one that produced the best fit indexes for the instrument to the data. It was also found that the internal consistency indexes for the four factors were good. Additionally, the general construct of behavioral crafting was positively related to job engagement and, negatively, to exhaustion.

Bruning and Campion (2018) went on to develop one of the first taxonomies integrating the approach of Wrzesniewski and Dutton (2001), which they called the role perspective, with the one based on the JD-R Model (Tims et al., 2012), which they called the resource perspective, in addition to articulating them with the motivational theory of approach and avoidance (Elliot, 1999), in a model that they called the "role-resource approach-avoidance model of job crafting." According to the authors, approach crafting is characterized by activities motivated and focused on the problem, which seek to increase resources and accept challenges, aiming to improve the work experience. Avoidance crafting is intended to reduce or eliminate parts of the job itself. In this way, they propose four general categories of job crafting: approach role crafting, approach resource crafting, avoidance role crafting, and avoidance resource crafting.

Based on this taxonomy and adopting qualitative research methods (interviews), Bruning and Campion (2018) arrived at the characterization of seven types of job crafting strategies: work-role expansion and social expansion (approach role crafting) and work-role reduction (avoidance role crafting); work resource organization, work resource adoption, and work resource metacognition (approach resource crafting); and work withdrawal (avoidance resource crafting). Next, the authors developed a questionnaire that was validated in a second study, including a sample of 323 American workers. Confirmatory factor analyses confirmed the seven-factor structure of the instrument, with good fit indexes, which obtained adequate internal consistency indexes. In the convergent validation of the instrument, its different dimensions correlated, in the directions expected, with work enrichment, engagement, performance, strain, and work disinvestment. The instrument consists of 30 items, to be answered on a 5-point Likert-type scale, ranging from 1 (never) to 5 (all the time).

Lichtenthaler and Fischbach (2019) also integrated the role and resources perspective, articulating them with the regulatory focus theory (according to the previous proposal by Bindl et al., 2019). For the authors, therefore, job crafting is associated with changes in the limits and perceptions of the job roles, as a way to obtain gains (promotion-focused job crafting) or to avoid losses (prevention-focused job crafting) in motivation, health, and performance. In this sense, they define five types of promotion-focused job crafting: increasing job resources, increasing challenging job demands, expansion-oriented task crafting, expansion-oriented relational crafting, and expansion-oriented cognitive crafting. Regarding prevention-focused job crafting, three types are defined: decreasing hindering job demands, contraction-oriented task crafting, and contraction-oriented relational crafting. The model proposed by the authors was tested in a meta-analysis that involved studies on job crafting carried out from the role and resources perspective and confirmed the predictions about the beneficial and harmful effects of different types of job crafting on the well-being of the employee.

Seeking to advance in relation to the previous typologies, which articulate only two levels of job crafting (form and content), Zhang and Parker (2019) proposed that the referred construct can be characterized though a three-level hierarchical structure. The first level is defined by the approach or avoidance orientation; the second, by the behavioral or cognitive form; and the third, by the content based on resources or demands. The combination of the three levels gives rise to eight types of job crafting: seeking job resources (approach resources crafting of a behavioral nature), increasing challenging job demands or addressing hindering job demands (approach demands crafting of a behavioral nature), reframing mentally one's job to perceive more positive aspects of the work (approach resources crafting of a cognitive nature), reappraising mentally one's demands to view them as more challenging or less hindrance (approach demands crafting of a cognitive nature), avoiding jobs with few positive resources (avoidance resources crafting of a behavioral nature), avoiding jobs with few challenging demands or many hindering demands (avoidance demands crafting of a behavioral nature), reframing mentally one's job to avoid that aspects with few positive resources (avoidance resources crafting of a cognitive nature), and reframing mentally one's job to avoid the experience of demands (avoidance demands crafting of a cognitive nature) (Zhang & Parker, 2019).

In summary, the most recent theorizing regarding job crafting, which integrated the role and resources theories with the approach/promotion/expansion and avoidance/prevention/contraction perspectives, starts from the assumption that job crafting concerns the use of self-initiated strategies by employees (Tims & Parker, 2020). When adopting them, employees can, however, choose to expand the resources, boundaries, and meaning of their job, so that it starts to have more positive characteristics, or to reduce or limit them, as a way to prevent the negative aspects involved in their work (Costantini et al., 2021; Tims & Parker, 2020). Therefore, the motivations for the employee to engage in job crafting strategies can be proactive, when the individual seeks to expand resources to achieve a certain objective, or reactive, when they reduce their resources to face the adverse aspects of their work (Lazazzara et al., 2020).

It should be emphasized, however, that the concept that the avoidance strategy is reactive, rather than proactive, is not yet consensual in the literature, since theoretically it concerns active changes aimed at avoiding the negative aspects of the job. These changes could characterize it as a proactive strategy with positive consequences for the employee, like other types of crafting (Tims & Bakker, 2010; Zhang & Parker, 2019). However, meta-analyses (Lichtenthaler & Fischbach, 2019; Rudolph et al., 2017) and recent literature reviews (Lazazzara et al., 2020; Zhang & Parker, 2019) have highlighted that job crafting aimed at expansion of the scope of the job has been shown to be beneficial to the employee, whereas crafting aimed at reducing the scope of the job is detrimental to the employee.

With regard to the operationalization of the multiple job crafting strategies advocated by the different theoretical perspectives of the construct, Hu et al. (2020) developed one of the first studies aimed at verifying the similarities and differences between these diverse operationalizations. For this, they compared the JCQ (Slemp & Vella-Brodrick, 2013), which measures task, relational and cognitive crafting; the JCS (Tims et al., 2012), which measures increasing structural resources, increasing social resources, increasing challenging demands, and decreasing hindering demands; the instrument developed by Weseler and Niessen (2016), which they called the Job Crafting Measure (JCM), which measures task and relational crafting by expansion and contraction, as well as cognitive crafting; the Overarching Job Crafting Scale (OJCS; Hu et al., 2019) which is unified and emphasizes changes in the job to optimize well-being; and the Combined Job Crafting Scale (CJCS; Bizzi, 2017), which consists of a revised version of the scale by Leana et al. (2009) and is also unifactorial, thus providing a global score related to crafting behaviors aimed at changes in the structure of tasks.

The study comprised two samples, with a total of 364 Chinese workers. The results of the exploratory factor analysis showed the three scales of the JCQ, the four scales of the JCS, the two scales of the JCM (cognitive crafting and task expansion), the OJCS and the CJCS loaded in a first factor (approach crafting), while the scales of reducing tasks, reducing relationships, and expanding relationships of the JCM loaded in a second factor (avoidance crafting), which reflects an active coping strategy.

Accordingly, the behavioral and cognitive crafting strategies overlapped in some way, as they loaded in the same approach crafting factor. In addition, approach crafting demonstrated greater predictive strength in work engagement and innovation behavior, when compared to avoidance crafting. Hu et al. (2020), therefore, shed light on the importance of job crafting and self-regulation, by demonstrating that the emission of positive attitudes to the detriment of passive attitudes of behavior avoidance leads to greater work engagement. Passive attitudes of behavior avoidance, however, are detrimental to work engagement, being characterized as dysfunctional self-regulation. The authors concluded that behavioral crafting, composed of approach behaviors and active coping behaviors, is the one that best fulfills the characterization of the construct as an adaptive behavior that leads to the best fit between the person and their job.

1.5 Final Considerations

This chapter described the characteristics of the main instruments developed for measuring job crafting, contextualizing them according to the theoretical perspective(s) adopted in their construction process, with a synthesis of these instruments being presented in Table 1.1. The review highlights the fact that the most recent efforts to theorize about job crafting, which have sought to integrate the different perspectives regarding the construct, have not yet been accompanied, in the same proportion, by instruments specifically developed for its operationalization.

In this sense, the questionnaire proposed by Weseler and Niessen (2016) only focuses on the integration of the expansion versus contraction perspective with role theory (Wrzesniewski & Dutton, 2001), while the questionnaire proposed by Costantini et al. (2021) refers only to the integration of the expansion versus reduction dimension with resources theory (Tims et al., 2012). Regarding the integration of role and resource theories with the perspective of expansion versus contraction, the only instrument available to date is the one developed by Bruning and Campion (2018), which, however, does not adopt the job content crafting categories advocated by role and resources theories.

It would therefore be interesting to develop new measurement instruments and/or to refine the existing measurement instruments, with the support of the theoretical model of Zhang and Parker (2019), which can be seen as one of the most complete regarding the integration of job crafting theories. These measures should seek to evaluate, independently or in combination, all the crafting strategies proposed by the authors. An initiative in this direction was recently carried out by Constantini et al. (2021), but these authors only focused on measuring behavioral job crafting, not considering the part of the model associated with cognitive crafting. Therefore, the operationalization of cognitive crafting, according to the proposal of Zhang and Parker (2019), has yet to be carried out.

Regarding cognitive crafting, it is also worth mentioning the fact that its theorization and measurement have caused debates in the literature. The cognitive crafting strategy is considered vital to the concept and measurement of job crafting from the role crafting perspective, in order to promote the fit of the employee to their environment, by redefining the meaning of their work (Wrzesniewski & Dutton, 2001; Niessen et al., 2016). However, this strategy is not included in the characterization and measurement of job crafting from the resources crafting perspective, as it is argued that this type of strategy does not imply an active change in the

Table 1.1 Scales developed and/or adapted to measure job crafting

Theoretical perspective	Authors	Country and sample	Dimensions and number of items	Reliability (α)	Subsequent validations with replication of the original structure
Role theory (Wrzesniewski & Dutton, 2001)					
	Slemp and Vella-Brodrick (2013)	Australia ($N = 334$)	Task crafting (5 items)	$\alpha = .87$	Schachler et al. (2019): Germany ($N = 482$) Letona-Ibañez et al. (2019): Spain ($N = 768$) Pimenta de Devotto and Machado (2020): Brazil ($N = 413$) Geldenhuys et al. (2020): South Africa ($N = 134$)
			Relational crafting (5 items)	$\alpha = .83$	
			Cognitive crafting (5 items)	$\alpha = .89$	
			General measure (15 items)	$\alpha = .91$	
	Niessen et al. (2016)	Germany ($N1 = 466$; $N2 = 118$)	Task crafting (3 items)	$\alpha = .79$	
			Relational crafting (3 items)	$\alpha = .75$	
			Cognitive crafting (3 items)	$\alpha = .81$	
			General measure (9 items)	$\alpha = .86$	
	Leana et al. (2009)	The United States ($N = 232$)	Individual crafting	$\alpha = .79$	Llorente-Alonso and Topa (2019): Spain ($N = 302$) Di Fabio (2020): Italy ($N = 237$)
			Collaborative crafting	$\alpha = .89$	
Resources theory (Tims et al., 2012)					
	Tims et al. (2012)	Netherlands ($N1 = 375$; $N2 = 616$; $N3 = 190$)	Increasing structural job resources (5 items)	$\alpha = .82$	Akin et al. (2014): Turkey ($N = 364$) Lichtenthaler and Fischbach (2016): Germany ($N = 412$) De Beer et al. (2016): South Africa ($N = 318$) Bakker et al. (2018): Spain ($N = 896$)
			Increasing social job resources (5 items)	$\alpha = .77$	
			Increasing challenging job demands (5 items)	$\alpha = .75$	
			Decreasing hindering job demands (6 items)	$\alpha = .79$	

Validations of the scale of Tims et al. (2012) in other cultural contexts					
	Chinelato et al. (2015)	Brazil ($N = 491$)	Increasing structural job resources (4 items)	$\alpha = .71$	
			Increasing social job resources (5 items)	$\alpha = .78$	
			Increasing challenging job demands (5 items)	$\alpha = .77$	
	Cenciotti et al. (2016)	Italy ($N = 721$)	Increasing structural job resources (4 items)	$\alpha = .81$	
			Increasing social job resources (4 items)	$\alpha = .74$	
			Increasing challenging job demands (5 items)	$\alpha = .78$	
	De Beer et al. (2016)	South Africa ($N1 = 260$; $N2 = 210$)	Increasing structural job resources and challenging job demands (10 items)	$\alpha = .77/.83$	
			Increasing social job resources (5 items)	$\alpha = .73/.79$	
			Decreasing hindering job demands (6 items)	$\alpha = .77/.80$	
	Eguchi et al. (2016)	Japan ($N = 972$)	Increasing structural job resources (5 items)	$\alpha = .90$	
			Increasing social job resources (5 items)	$\alpha = .76$	
			Increasing challenging job demands (5 items)	$\alpha = .84$	
			Decreasing emotional job demands (3 items)	NR	
			Decreasing cognitive job demands (3 items)	NR	

(continued)

Table 1.1 (continued)

Theoretical perspective	Authors	Country and sample	Dimensions and number of items	Reliability (α)	Subsequent validations with replication of the original structure
Reformulations of the scale of Tims et al. (2012)					
	Petrou et al. (2012)	Netherlands ($N = 95$)	Seeking resources (6 items)	$\alpha = .70$	
			Seeking challenges (3 items)	$\alpha = .76$	
			Reducing demands (4 items)	$\alpha = .69$	
	Nielsen and Abildgaard (2012)	Denmark ($NT1 = 362$; $NT2 = 408$)	Increasing challenging job demands (4 items)	$\alpha = .85$	Nielsen et al. (2017): Spain ($N = 164/N = 191$); United Kingdom ($N = 109$); China ($N = 170$); Taiwan ($N = 165$) Ghadi (2019): Jordan ($N = 513$)
			Increasing social job resources (3 items)	$\alpha = .75$	
			Increasing quantitative job demands (3 items)	$\alpha = .74$	
			Decreasing social job demands (3 items)	$\alpha = .76$	
			Decreasing hindering job demands (2 items)	NR	
	Sora et al. (2018)	Spain ($N = 1647$)	Increasing structural job resources (3 items)	$\alpha = .75$	
			Increasing social job resources (3 items)	$\alpha = .78$	
			Increasing challenging job demands (3 items)	$\alpha = .77$	
			Decreasing hindering job demands (3 items)	$\alpha = .64$	

	Yen et al. (2018)	Taiwan ($N1 = 268$; $N2 = 253$)	Increasing structural job resources (9 items)	$\alpha = .90/.94$	
			Increasing social job resources (8 items)	$\alpha = .90/.90$	
			Increasing challenging job demands (7 items)	$\alpha = .88/.95$	
			Decreasing hindering job demands (6 items)	$\alpha = .91/.94$	
Role theory vs. approach/promotion-avoidance/prevention theory					
	Weseler and Niessen et al. (2016)	Germany ($N1 = 138$; $N2 = 131$)	Crafting by extending task boundaries (3 items)	.73/.66	
			Crafting by reducing task boundaries (3 items)	.67/.79	
			Crafting by extending relational boundaries (2 items)	.77/.79	
			Crafting by reducing relational boundaries (3 items)	.74/.79	
			Cognitive crafting of task boundaries (3 items)	.83/.82	
	Bindl et al. (2019)	The United States ($N1 = 421$) The United Kingdom ($N2 = 144$; $N3 = 388$)	Promotion-oriented task crafting (4 items)	.90/.89**	
			Prevention-oriented task crafting (3 items)	.82/.82	
			Promotion-oriented relational crafting (4 items)	.92/.91	
			Prevention-oriented relational crafting (3 items)	.81/.77	

(continued)

Table 1.1 (continued)

Theoretical perspective	Authors	Country and sample	Dimensions and number of items	Reliability (α)	Subsequent validations with replication of the original structure
			Promotion-oriented skills crafting (4 items)	.95/.95	
			Prevention-oriented skills crafting (3 items)	.82/.83	
			Promotion-oriented cognitive crafting (4 items)	.83/.83	
			Prevention-oriented cognitive crafting (3 items)	.70/.68	
Resource theory X approach/promotion-avoidance/prevention					
	Constantini et al. (2021)	Italy (*N*1 = 936; *N*2 = 199; *N*3 = 226)	Seeking resources (6 items)	.85***	
			Seeking challenges (3 items)	.87	
			Reducing demands (3 items)	.86	
			Optimizing demands (6 items)	.90	
Role theory X resource theory X approach/promotion-avoidance/prevention					
	Bruning and Campion (2018)	The United States (*N* = 323)	Work role expansion (5 items)	.83	
			Social expansion (4 items)	.85	
			Work role reduction (4 items)	.83	
			Work resource organization (4 items)	.79	
			Work resource adoption (5 items)	.88	
			Work resource metacognition (5 items)	.84	
			Work withdrawal (3 items)	.72	

NR not reported
Note: * Study 1; ** Studies 1 and 3; *** Study 3, Time 1

characteristics of the job, but only a passive adjustment of the needs and preferences to the working conditions (Tims & Bakker, 2010).

With this, the scales were developed, with the support of one or the other of these positions, and, consequently, measuring or not cognitive crafting. It is only more recently that initiatives to compare these instruments have started to emerge (Hu et al., 2020), especially with regard to the real role played by cognitive crafting in measuring job crafting. It would therefore be interesting if new studies were developed to compare the instruments based on role theory and resources theory, with aggregation of the dimension of expansion and contraction, in order to consider, in a more complete way, the different job crafting strategies predicted by these theories. These studies should include cognitive crafting by expansion and by contraction, similar to the procedure adopted by Bindl et al. (2019), since, in the study by Hu et al. (2020), none of the instruments included simultaneously measured these two types of cognitive crafting.

It is still worth to mention that the most adequate internal structure to describe the Job Crafting Scale (JCS; Tims et al., 2012) has been the subject of divergences, although this scale is one of the most frequently adopted in studies focused on job crafting (Pimenta de Devotto & Machado, 2017; Rudolph et al., 2017). Among the scale adaptation studies reviewed here, some have confirmed the original four-factor structure (Bakker et al., 2018; Lichtenthaler & Fischbach, 2016), while others have indicated a three-factor (Cenciotti et al., 2016; Chinelato et al., 2015) or five-factor structure (Eguchi et al., 2016). Therefore, it is necessary to carry out further studies on the scale, in diverse occupational and cultural contexts, in order to reach a consensus on the best structure of the JCS.

In summary, the literature in the area of job crafting, specifically with regard to the instruments aimed at its operationalization, still needs to evolve in order to deepen the knowledge about the different measurement possibilities of the various strategies that characterize the construct. The development and/or adaptation and validation of instruments in this direction will certainly further contribute to the expansion of the nomological network of the construct, especially with regard to the antecedents, mechanisms, and consequences of the experiences of the employees that adopt each one of the various job crafting strategies.

References

Akin, A., Sariçam, H., Kaya, C., & Demir, T. (2014). Turkish version of Job Crafting Scale (JCS): The validity and reliability study. *International Journal of Educational Researchers, 5*(1), 10–15. http://ijer.eab.org.tr/media/volume5/issue1/a_akin.pdf

Bakker, A. B., & Demerouti, E. (2017). Job demands–resources theory: Taking stock and looking forward. *Journal of Occupational Health Psychology, 22*(3), 273–285. https://doi.org/10.1037/ocp0000056

Bakker, A. B., Ficapal-Cusí, P., Torrent-Sellens, J., Boada-Grau, J., & Hontangas-Beltrán, P. (2018). The Spanish version of the Job Crafting Scale. *Psicothema, 30*(1), 136–142. https://doi.org/10.7334/psicothema2016.293

Berg, J. M., Dutton, J. E., & Wrzesniewski, A. (2008). *What is job crafting and why does it matter?* Michigan Ross School of Business. https://positiveorgs.bus.umich.edu/wp-content/uploads/What-is-Job-Crafting-and-Why-Does-it-Matter1.pdf

Berg, J. M., Wrzesniewski, A., & Dutton, J. E. (2010). Perceiving and responding to challenges in job crafting at different ranks: When proactivity requires adaptivity. *Journal of Organizational Behavior, 31*(2–3), 158–186. https://doi.org/10.1002/job.645

Bindl, U. K., Unsworth, K. L., Gibson, C. B., & Stride, C. B. (2019). Job crafting revisited: Implications of an extended framework for active changes at work. *Journal of Applied Psychology, 104*(5), 605–628. https://doi.org/10.1037/apl0000362

Bizzi, L. (2017). Network characteristics: When an individual's job crafting depends on the jobs of others. *Human Relations, 70*(4), 436–460. https://doi.org/10.1177/0018726716658963

Bruning, P. F., & Campion, M. A. (2018). A role–resource approach–avoidance model of job crafting: A multimethod integration and extension of job crafting theory. *Academy of Management Journal, 61*(2), 499–522. https://doi.org/10.5465/amj.2015.0604

Cenciotti, R., Borgogni, L., Callea, A., Colombo, L., Cortese, C. G., Ingusci, E., … Zito, M. (2016). The Italian version of the job crafting scale (JCS). *Applied Psychology Bulletin, 44*(277), 28–36. https://www.giuntipsy.it/catalogo/rivista/bollettino-di-psicologia-applicata

Chinelato, R. S. D. C., Ferreira, M. C., & Valentini, F. (2015). Evidence of validity of the job crafting behaviors scale. *Paidéia, 25*(62), 325–332. https://doi.org/10.1590/1982-43272562201506

Costantini, A., Demerouti, E., Ceschi, A., & Sartori, R. (2021). Evidence on the hierarchical, multidimensional nature of behavioural job crafting. *Applied Psychology, 70*(1), 311–341. https://doi.org/10.1111/apps.12232

Crawford, E. R., LePine, J. A., & Rich, B. L. (2010). Linking job demands and resources to employee engagement and burnout: A theoretical extension and meta-analytic test. *Journal of Applied Psychology, 95*(5), 834–848. https://doi.org/10.1037/a0019364

De Beer, L. T., Tims, M., & Bakker, A. B. (2016). Job crafting and its impact on work engagement and job satisfaction in mining and manufacturing. *South African Journal of Economic and Management Sciences, 19*(3), 400–412. https://doi.org/10.17159/2222-3436/2016/v19n3a7

Demerouti, E. (2014). Design your own job through job crafting. *European Psychologist, 19*(4), 237–247. https://doi.org/10.1027/1016-9040/a000188

Demerouti, E., & Bakker, A. B. (2014). Job crafting. In M. C. W. Peeters, J. de Jonge, & T. W. Taris (Eds.), *An introduction to contemporary work psychology* (pp. 414–433). Wiley-Blackwell.

Demerouti, E., & Peeters, M. C. W. (2018). Transmission of reduction-oriented crafting among colleagues: A diary study on the moderating role of working conditions. *Journal of Occupational and Organizational Psychology, 91*(2), 209–234. https://doi.org/10.1111/joop.12196

Di Fabio, A. (2020). Job Crafting Scale: Proprietà psicometriche della versione italiana [Job Crafting Scale: Psychometric properties of the Italian version]. *Counseling: Giornale Italiano di Ricerca e Applicazioni, 13*(1), 105–113. https://doi.org/10.14605/CS1312007

Eguchi, H., Shimazu, A., Bakker, A. B., Tims, M., Kamiyama, K., Hara, Y., … Kawakami, N. (2016). Validation of the Japanese version of the job crafting scale. *Journal of Occupational Health Psychology, 58*(3), 231–240. https://doi.org/10.1539/joh.15-0173-OA

Elliot, A. J. (1999). Approach and avoidance motivation and achievement goals. *Educational Psychologist, 34*(3), 169–189. https://doi.org/10.1207/s15326985ep3403_3

Geldenhuys, M., Bakker, A., & Demerouti, E. (2020). How task, relational and cognitive crafting relate to job performance: A weekly diary study on the role of meaningfulness. *European Journal of Work and Organizational Psychology*. Advance online publication. https://doi.org/10.1080/1359432X.2020.1825378

Ghadi, M. Y. (2019). A psychometric evaluation of the job crafting questionnaire (JCRQ) among employees working in Jordanian universities. *International Journal of Organizational Analysis, 27*(1), 36–50. https://doi.org/10.1108/IJOA-05-2017-1173

Ghitulescu, B. E. (2006). *Shaping tasks and relationships at work: Examining the antecedents and consequences of employee job crafting* (Unpublished doctoral dissertation). University of Pittsburgh.

Grant, A. M., & Parker, S. K. (2009). Redesigning work design theories: The rise of relational and proactive perspectives. *The Academy of Management Annals, 3*(1), 317–375. https://doi.org/10.1080/19416520903047327

Griffin, M. A., Neal, A., & Parker, S. K. (2007). A new model of work role performance: Positive behavior in uncertain and interdependent contexts. *Academy of Management Journal, 50*(2), 327–347. https://doi.org/10.5465/AMJ.2007.24634438

Hackman, J. R., & Oldham, G. R. (1980). *Work redesign*. Addison-Wesley.

Higgins, E. T. (1997). Beyond pleasure and pain. *American Psychologist, 52*(12), 1280–1300. https://doi.org/10.1037/0003-066X.52.12.1280

Hu, Q., Schaufeli, W. B., Taris, T. W., Shimazu, A., & Dollard, M. F. (2019). Resource crafting: Is it really 'resource' crafting—or just crafting? *Frontiers in Psychology, 10*, Article 614. https://doi.org/10.3389/fpsyg.2019.00614

Hu, Q., Taris, T. W., Dollard, M. F., & Schaufeli, W. B. (2020). An exploration of the component validity of job crafting. *European Journal of Work and Organizational Psychology, 29*(5), 776–793. https://doi.org/10.1080/1359432X.2020.1756262

Laurence, G. A. (2010). *Workaholism and expansion and contraction oriented job crafting: The moderating effects of individual and contextual factors* (Unpublished doctoral dissertation). The Graduate School Syracuse University.

Lazazzara, A., Tims, M., & De Gennaro, D. (2020). The process of reinventing a job: A meta–synthesis of qualitative job crafting research. *Journal of Vocational Behavior, 116*, Article 103267. https://doi.org/10.1016/j.jvb.2019.01.001

Leana, C., Appelbaum, E., & Shevchuk, I. (2009). Work process and quality of care in early childhood education: The role of job crafting. *Academy of Management Journal, 52*(6), 1169–1192. https://doi.org/10.5465/AMJ.2009.47084651

Letona-Ibañez, O., Carrasco, M., Martinez-Rodriguez, S., Amillano, A., & Ortiz-Marques, N. (2019). Cognitive, relational and task crafting: Spanish adaptation and analysis of psychometric properties of the Job Crafting Questionnaire. *PLoS One, 14*(10), Article e0223539. https://doi.org/10.1371/journal.pone.0223539

Lichtenthaler, P. W., & Fischbach, A. (2019). A meta-analysis on promotion-and prevention-focused job crafting. *European Journal of Work and Organizational Psychology, 28*(1), 30–50. https://doi.org/10.1080/1359432X.2018.1527767

Lichtenthaler, P. W., & Fischbach, A. (2016). The conceptualization and measurement of job crafting. Validation of a German version of the Job Crafting Scale. *Zeitschrift für Arbeits- und Organisationspsychologie, 60*(4), 173–186. https://doi.org/10.1026/0932-4089/a000219

Llorente-Alonso, M., & Topa, G. (2019). Individual crafting, collaborative crafting, and job satisfaction: The mediator role of engagement. *Journal of Work and Organizational Psychology, 35*(3), 217–226. https://doi.org/10.5093/jwop2019a23

Nielsen, K., & Abildgaard, J. S. (2012). The development and validation of a job crafting measure for use with blue-collar workers. *Work & Stress, 26*(4), 365–384. https://doi.org/10.1080/02678373.2012.733543

Nielsen, K., Antino, M., Sanz-Vergel, A., & Rodríguez-Muñoz, A. (2017). Validating the Job Crafting Questionnaire (JCRQ): A multi-method and multi-sample study. *Work & Stress, 31*(1), 82–99. https://doi.org/10.1080/02678373.2017.1293752

Niessen, C., Weseler, D., & Kostova, P. (2016). When and why do individuals craft their jobs? The role of individual motivation and work characteristics for job crafting. *Human Relations, 69*(6), 1287–1313. https://doi.org/10.1177/0018726715610642

Oprea, B. T., Barzin, L., Vîrgă, D., Iliescu, D., & Rusu, A. (2019). Effectiveness of job crafting interventions: A meta-analysis and utility analysis. *European Journal of Work and Organizational Psychology, 28*(6), 723–741. https://doi.org/10.1080/1359432X.2019.1646728

Peral, S. L., & Geldenhuys, M. (2019). A Rasch analysis of the Tims, Bakker, and Derks (2012) Job Crafting Scale. *Journal of Career Assessment, 27*(4), 579–593. https://doi.org/10.1177/1069072718788787

Petrou, P., Demerouti, E., Peeters, M. C. W., Schaufeli, W. B., & Hetland, J. (2012). Crafting a job on a daily basis: Contextual antecedents and the effect of work engagement. *Journal of Organizational Behavior, 33*(8), 1120–1141. https://doi.org/10.1002/job.1783

Pimenta de Devotto, R., & Machado, W. L. (2017). *Job Crafting*: Uma revisão da produção científica internacional [Job Crafting: A review of international scientific production]. *Psico-USF, 22*(3), 413–423. https://doi.org/10.1590/1413-82712017220303

Pimenta de Devotto, R., & Machado, W. L. (2020). Evidências de validade da versão brasileira do *Job Crafting Questionnaire* [validity evidences of the Brazilian version of the Job Crafting Questionnaire]. *Psico-USF, 21*(1), 39–49. https://doi.org/10.1590/1413-82712020250104

Petrou, P., Demerouti, E., & Schaufeli, W. B. (2015). Job crafting in changing organizations: Antecedents and implications for exhaustion and performance. *Journal of Occupational Health Psychology, 20*(4), 470–480. https://doi.org/10.1037/a0039003

Petrou P, Demerouti E, Schaufeli WB. Crafting the Change: The Role of Employee Job Crafting Behaviors for Successful Organizational Change (2018). *Journal of Management, 44*(5),1766-1792. https://doi.org/10.1177/0149206315624961

Rudolph, C. W., Katz, I. M., Lavigne, K. N., & Zacher, H. (2017). Job crafting: A meta-analysis of relationships with individual differences, job characteristics, and work outcomes. *Journal of Vocational Behavior, 102*, 112–138. https://doi.org/10.1016/j.jvb.2017.05.008

Schachler, V., Epple, S. D., Clauss, E., Hoppe, A., Slemp, G. R., … Ziegler, M. (2019). Measuring job crafting across cultures: Lessons learned from comparing a German and an Australian sample. *Frontiers in Psychology, 10*, Article 991. https://doi.org/10.3389/fpsyg.2019.00991

Slemp, G. R., & Vella-Brodrick, D. A. (2013). The Job Crafting Questionnaire: A new scale to measure the extent to which employees engage in job crafting. *International Journal of Wellbeing, 3*(2), 126–146. https://doi.org/10.5502/ijw.v3i2.1

Sora, B., Caballer, A., & García-Buades, E. (2018). Validation of a short form of Job Crafting Scale in a Spanish sample. *The Spanish Journal of Psychology, 21*, Article E51. https://doi.org/10.1017/sjp.2018.52

Tims, M., & Bakker, A. B. (2010). Job crafting: Towards a new model of individual job redesign. *South African Journal of Industrial Psychology, 36*(2), Article 841. https://doi.org/10.4102/sajip.v36i2.841

Tims, M., Bakker, A. B., & Derks, D. (2012). Development and validation of the job crafting scale. *Journal of Vocational Behavior, 80*(1), 173–186. https://doi.org/10.1016/j.jvb.2011.05.009

Tims, M., Bakker, A. B., & Derks, D. (2013). The impact of job crafting on job demands, job resources, and well-being. *Journal of Occupational Health Psychology, 18*(2), 230–240. https://doi.org/10.1037/a0032141

Tims, M., & Parker, S. K. (2020). How coworkers attribute, react to, and shape job crafting. *Organizational Psychology Review, 10*(1), 29–54. https://doi.org/10.1177/2041386619896087

Weseler, D., & Niessen, C. (2016). How job crafting relates to task performance. *Journal of Managerial Psychology, 31*(3), 672–685. https://doi.org/10.1108/JMP-09-2014-0269

Wrzesniewski, A., Berg, J. M., Grant, A. M., Kurkoski, J., & Welle, B. (2012, August). *Job crafting in motion: Achieving sustainable gains in happiness and performance* [Conference presentation]. Annual Meeting of the Academy of Management, Boston, MA, United States.

Wrzesniewski, A., & Dutton, J. E. (2001). Crafting a job: Revisioning employees as active crafters of their work. *Academy of Management Review, 26*(2), 179–201. http://www.jstor.org/stable/259118

Yen, C. H., Tsaur, S. H., & Tsai, C. H. (2018). Tour leaders' job crafting: Scale development. *Tourism Management, 69*, 52–61. https://doi.org/10.1016/j.tourman.2018.05.017

Zhang, F., & Parker, S. K. (2019). Reorienting job crafting research: A hierarchical structure of job crafting concepts and integrative review. *Journal of Organizational Behavior, 40*(2), 126–146. https://doi.org/10.1002/job.2332

Chapter 2
Employee Reactions to Organizational Change: The Main Models and Measures

Elaine Rabelo Neiva, Elisa Amorim-Ribeiro, and Magno Oliveira Macambira

2.1 Introduction

Organizational change, defined as actions that impact an organization's members or outcomes, is conceived as a continuous process inherent to organizational routines (Neiva & Paz, 2012). Cognitive, affective, and behavioral factors are potential components of individuals' responses to organizational changes and may have a positive or negative valence or yet be ambivalent (Piderit, 2000). In general, organizational change elicits a range of emotions and responses ranging from optimism to fear, possibly including anxiety, resistance, enthusiasm, inability, motivation, or pessimism (Bordia et al., 2011; Bortolotti, 2010).

In the last two decades, research on organizational behavior has focused on organizational change (OC). Such an interest unfolded in a larger number of constructs studied in the field, measurement instruments, and, consequently, demands new models to explain OC. Thus, studies addressing OC face the challenge to review the constructs considered to be reactions to change, assess the operationalization and description of the mechanisms involved, promote a debate regarding the relevance of measures of attitudes and/or behavior, and balance emphases on analyses at the individual level compared to the relational, organizational, and macro-social level.

A review addressing papers published in 67 years (1940 to 2007; Oreg et al., 2011) proposed a model to understand the phenomenon of organizational change (OC), including elements such as (a) individuals' reactions and/or responses to

E. R. Neiva (✉)
University of Brasília, Brasília, DF, Brazil

E. Amorim-Ribeiro
Salgado de Oliveira University, Niterói, RJ, Brazil

M. O. Macambira
State University of Feira de Santana, Feira de Santana, BA, Brazil

M. O. Macambira et al. (eds.), *Assessing Organizational Behaviors*,
https://doi.org/10.1007/978-3-030-81311-6_2

change, (b) pre-change antecedents or the change itself, and (c) consequences for workers. The model includes constructs directly focused on organizational change and others comprising the entire spectrum of constructs in the field of organizations and labor (e.g., job satisfaction).

Analysis of the state-of-the-art literature in the field of OC, considering Oreg et al. (2011), shows an emphasis on resistance to change and understanding these processes from an attitudinal perspective. An important set of phenomena often unrelated to organizational change (e.g., job satisfaction and organizational commitment) is considered individual responses to organizational change processes. Hence, in the context of reactions to organizational change, we need to review a myriad of constructs considered reactions but not limited to organizational change processes.

An assessment of the literature also indicates the emergence of measurement approaches that advance from the individual to the relational and group levels, with an emphasis on understanding the role of collective behavior in OC processes or organizational readiness for change (Rafferty et al., 2013; Vakola, 2013; Weiner et al., 2020). There are also advancements in understanding the role of management in responses to OC. Coupled with these are behavioral measures that present relevant results and support interventions in change processes focusing on worker well-being (Lines, 2005; Nery et al., 2020).

In order to improve understanding regarding the issues surrounding the current context, its obstacles, and advances, this chapter covers OC studies, including the analysis of behaviors toward change and constructs traditionally studied, resistance to change, change-supportive behavior, instruments used to measure attitudinal and/or behavioral constructs, and considerations and conclusions regarding measures and constructs.

2.2 Attitudinal Constructs Traditionally Addressed in Organizational Change Processes and Respective Measures

Whenever individuals are told about an organizational change, they question how such a change will impact their jobs and how likely it is to succeed (Vakola, 2016). The literature shows that some concepts are important indicators of responses to organizational change (Bouckenooghe, 2010; Choi, 2011; Neiva et al., 2005), such as openness to change (Wanberg & Banas, 2000), commitment to change (Herold et al., 2007, 2008; Herscovitch & Meyer, 2002; Meyer et al., 2007), cynicism toward change (DeCelles et al., 2013; Reichers et al., 1997; Wanous et al., 2000), readiness to change (Cunningham et al., 2002; Holt et al., 2007; Rafferty et al., 2013; Weiner et al., 2020), and resistance to organizational change (Oreg et al., 2008).

A common factor among attitudes toward change, i.e., commitment, cynicism, readiness to change (Cunningham et al., 2002; Holt et al., 2007; Rafferty et al.,

2013; Weiner et al., 2020), and resistance to organizational change (Oreg et al., 2008), is that these present a primarily individual attitudinal nature. An individual's attitudes are based on his/her assessment of a subset of characteristics of an attitudinal object (Lines, 2005). Attitudes involve cognitive, affective, and behavioral aspects and can be difficult to change because they are built and consolidated throughout life (Ajzen, 1991; Eagly & Chaiken, 1993; Fishbein & Ajzen, 1974). The cognitive component is composed of information regarding an attitude object based on what this individual believes to be true. The affective component consists of an individual's feelings regarding an object of assessment and, in general, is expressed as liking or disliking that attitude object. Finally, the behavioral component consists of how a person intends to behave toward an attitude object (Lines, 2005). Henceforward, this chapter will present an analysis of the primary attitudinal constructs concerning reactions to organizational change.

The use of organizational and worker performance indicators predominated for a long time as objective criteria to assess the implementation and consolidation of organizational change processes (Neiva & Paz, 2012). However, how individuals respond to change has attracted the interest of researchers, given the impact of these responses on change processes (Bordia et al., 2011; Oreg et al., 2011; Vakola et al., 2013; Vakola, 2016). A myriad of scales and measures are used to assess individuals' responses to organizational change, and the main ones reported in the literature are presented and discussed in this chapter. The measures are classified according to the level of analysis and dimensions of the constructs addressed. Table 2.2 presents a summary of these measures.

2.3 Attitudes Toward Change

There is much interest in attitudes toward change (Bouckenooghe, 2010), concerning the process in which attitudes are formed (Lau & Woodman, 1995), how attitudes are investigated (Lines, 2005; Vakola et al., 2004), and the factors that impact attitudes (Van den Heuvel et al., 2017). According to Vakola and Nikolaou (2005: 162), "attitudes toward change in general consist of a person's cognitions about change, affective reactions to change, and a behavioral tendency toward change." Therefore, change can be received with excitement and happiness or anger and fear, while employee responses may range from supportive, positive intentions to opposing, negative intentions. Within organizations, individuals may have a general attitude toward change while simultaneously having different attitudes toward different change initiatives (Choi, 2011). Acceptance attitudes portray an assessment of the beliefs and predisposition of organizational members to express positive behaviors toward change processes. Fearful attitudes portray the organizational members' fear of losing power, benefits, or reflect uncertainty regarding changes. Skeptical attitudes, in turn, comprise beliefs and predisposition to negative behavior toward changes, with an emphasis on disbelief and non-collaborative attitudes toward change programs (Neiva et al., 2005). An individual's attitudes toward organizational change are based on a positive or negative assessment regarding an organization's initiatives to change (Lines, 2005) and are critical to the success of organizational change because attitudes predispose individuals to act in a certain way (Lines, 2005; Vakola, 2016; Vakola et al., 2004).

Attitudes toward change may include assessments of any episode of change (general attitudes, any change) or directed to a specific change process (specific attitudes such as changes in the board of top managers, for instance). Specific attitudes predict behaviors toward change processes (Vakola et al., 2013) and explain the cognitive schemes mediating attitudes toward generic changes and attitudes toward specific changes (Lau & Woodman, 1995).

The most important implication of studies addressing reactions to organizational change based on attitudes toward change is that attitudes involve positive and negative aspects, while a significant portion of the literature focuses on negative responses to change – i.e., resistance (Lines, 2005). When employees have a strong and positive attitude toward change, they are more likely to support and facilitate changes (Lines, 2005). On the other hand, individuals with negative attitudes toward change are likely to resist and even sabotage attempts of change (Lines, 2005).

The oldest instrument measuring attitudes toward organizational change was proposed by Dunham et al. (1989). It is an 18-item instrument consisting of three dimensions: cognitive, affective, and behavioral intent, each containing six items. Examples of items included in the cognitive subscale are: "I do not like changes" and "I usually resist new ideas." Examples of the items included in the affective dimension are: "Organizations usually benefit from change" and "Most of my co-workers benefit from changes." Examples of the items included in the behavioral dimension are: "I am looking forward to changes at work"; "I am inclined to try new ideas." The items are rated on a seven-point scale ranging from 1 (completely disagree) to 7 (completely agree). The subscales are scored separately. The internal consistency (Cronbach's alpha) of the cognitive, affective, and behavioral subscales was 0.92, 0.89, and 0.95, respectively. Other researchers used this instrument and obtained satisfactory validity indexes (see Elias, 2009; Yousef, 2000, 2017).

The Attitudes Toward Change Questionnaire (ACQ) was developed by Vakola et al. (2004). This 29-item instrument (14 positive and 15 negative items) assesses the extent to which the participants agree with each item, rated on a 5-point scale that ranges from (1) completely disagree to (5) completely agree. A typical item in the positive attitude scale is "I am looking forward to changes in my work environment," and an example of a negative item is: "when a new organizational change program starts, I emphatically show my disagreement." The negatively stated items are reversed so that high scores indicate positive attitudes toward organizational changes (Vakola & Nikolaou, 2005). The Change Recipients' Reactions (CRRE) Scale is a self-reported scale similar to the one previously mentioned. Tsaousis and Vakola (2018) designed this 21-item scale to address three attitudinal components (cognitive, affective, and behavioral) rated on a 5-point Likert scale (1 – very unfavorable to 5 – very favorable). Examples of items include "This change is unpleasant for me," and "I feel uncomfortable with the change they are trying to implement."

Another instrument, *Reaction to Specific Changes at Work Scale* (Giauque, 2015), was proposed to measure employees' perceptions of organizational changes and how these impact the daily life of the population under study. The items were designed to measure the extent to which the respondents consider organizational transformations to be favorable or unfavorable in the various aspects of their jobs. In other words, this measure captures the interviewees' favorable or unfavorable perceptions regarding the impact of recent organizational changes on their working conditions. Therefore, this instrument does not measure positive attitudes toward changes in general but the reactions of individuals toward specific organizational changes. Individual reactions to various changes contribute to feelings and/or a general assessment of changes. The items in this specific measure are rated on a five-point Likert scale ranging from (1) very favorable to (5) very unfavorable. The scores obtained in the six items are summed to result in a six-item general measure of attitudes toward change (reliability of the general scale was alpha = 0.91).

The scale *Attitudes Towards Organizational Change* (Neiva et al., 2005) presents good validity indexes and comprises three factors – skepticism, fears, and acceptance, with the following reliability indexes, 0.90, 0.88, and 0.85, respectively. These factors represent the typical attitudes individuals present toward organizational changes. The scale was submitted to parallel analysis and exploratory and confirmatory factor analyses; the latter was performed with the structural equation modeling technique, presenting satisfactory validity evidence. The items for this specific measure were established using a five-point Likert scale ranging from (1) completely disagree to (5) completely agree. Examples of items include "People are afraid because of the uncertainty generated by the new way of working," "This organization does not plan processes of change – they just happen," and "The changes bring gains for the organization." This scale was adopted in other Brazilian studies and presented consistent validity evidence (Machado & Neiva, 2017; Nery & Neiva, 2015; Franco et al., 2016).

Kin and Karrem (2017) developed the Teacher Attitudes Towards Change Scale (TATCS) to measure the general attitudes of teachers toward changes. The scale's validity was assessed using exploratory factor analysis to identify underlying factors, while confirmatory factor analysis was used to test the measurement models, from which three factors emerged: (a) cognitive, (b) behavioral, and (c) affective reaction to change. Psychometric analyses provided evidence of convergent validity, discriminant validity, and construct reliability. A six-point Likert scale, ranging from (1) completely disagree to (6) completely agree, was used. Examples of items include "Most changes at my school are pleasing," "Change frustrates me," and "I often suggest changes for my school."

The literature shows that most of the measures of attitudes toward organizational change comprise three widely interconnected dimensions: (1) cognitive, assessing change-related beliefs; (2) affective, identifying associated feelings; and (3) behavioral, considering the extent to which individuals take measures to support or sabotage changes (Piderit, 2000). Positive and negative items are distributed in each of these dimensions (Elias, 2009; Giauque, 2015; Van den Heuvel et al., 2017; Policarpo et al., 2018; Vakola & Nikolaou, 2005; Vakola et al., 2004). Regarding levels of analysis, the measures mentioned here present analyses at the individual level; however, the instruments that include, in addition to individual perceptions, organizations' items, co-workers, and work team offer the possibility to improve understanding regarding OC at the middle and macro levels.

2.4 Commitment to Change

Organizational changes are costly endeavors that often fail to produce the expected results. The literature proposes that affective commitment to change is vital, especially in turbulent contexts, characterized by multiple and continuous episodes of change that demand continuous support from employees (Herscovitch & Meyer, 2002; Meyer et al., 2007). Such bond is shaped by beliefs concerning the need and legitimacy of organizational change and its leaders (Morin et al., 2016). A significant discussion regarding the construct affective commitment with change refers to the specificity of commitment to organizational change and its differentiation in terms of measure and concept with the construct organizational commitment and its affective, normative, and calculative bases.

Organizational commitment refers to an individual's identification and involvement with a given organization. Organizational commitment is defined as (1) a strong belief and acceptance of the companies' values, (2) a willingness to use skills and effort in favor of the organization, and (3) an intense disposition to remain in the organization. The word commitment can be conceptualized as an employee attachment at various levels, such as the entire organization, an organizational subunit, supervisor, or even a change program (Herscovitch & Meyer, 2002). Commitment to change was defined as "a force (mindset) that binds an individual to a course of action of relevance to one or more targets" (Herscovitch & Meyer, 2002, p.475). Herscovitch and Meyer (2002) presented a three-component model of commitment to organizational change based on the general model of organizational commitment. They were also the first researchers to test this model of commitment to organizational change empirically. The components of commitment to change were described as (i) affective commitment, that is, commitment based on the realization of the inherent benefits of change; (ii) normative commitment that is based on a sense of obligation; and (iii) continuance commitment that is based on an attempt to avoid costs for not complying with the purposes of change. Finally, commitment to organizational change involves the individual being engaged with actions in the organizational change process. Organizational changes are costly endeavors that often fail to produce the expected results. The literature proposes that affective commitment to change is vital, especially in turbulent contexts, characterized by multiple and continuous episodes of change that demand continuous support from employees (Herscovitch & Meyer, 2002; Meyer et al., 2007). Such bond is shaped by beliefs concerning the need and legitimacy of organizational change and its leaders (Morin et al., 2016). A significant discussion regarding the construct affective commitment with change refers to the specificity of commitment to organizational change and its differentiation in terms of measure and concept with the construct organizational commitment and its affective, normative, and calculative bases.

Jansen (2004) developed a measure of commitment to change that consists of eight items assessing agreement among the organization's members and willingness to work toward change goals. The measure showed high reliability (alpha = 0.93). Confirmatory factor analysis provided evidence that commitment with change was distinguishable and presented satisfactory goodness of fit (c2 = 399.88; df = 149; RMSEA =0.08; CFI = 0.92; NFI = 0.90).

Finally, Herscovitch and Meyer (2002) developed a measure of commitment to organizational change. It is a 22-item distributed into 3 commitment subscales: affective (i.e., wants to change), continuance (i.e., have to change), and normative (e.g., must change). The three subscales presented high reliability (alpha = 0.94, 0.94, and 0.96), and the confirmatory factor analysis confirmed three distinguishable subscales. The three subscales performed consistently with the one-item measure of commitment to change but were empirically distinguishable from a similar three-component scale of organizational commitment. Commitment to change predicted behavioral responses to change (e.g., conformity, cooperation, and defense). Additionally, the instrument differentiated groups of employees according to these different behavioral responses. The confirmatory factor analysis showed three factors with satisfactory goodness of fit (c2 = 239.87; df = 132; RMSEA = 0.07; CFI = 0.92).

The commitment to organizational change scale (Cinite & Duxbury) addresses the behavioral dimension, one dimension with six items rated on a seven-point Likert scale ((1) completely disagree to 7 (completely agree)). An example of item is "I introduce changes in my daily work to help the organization achieve its change goals." The exploratory and confirmatory factor analyses presented satisfactory goodness of fit, with a Cronbach's alpha = 0.80 and internal consistency = 0.87 (Fornell and Larcker criterion), indicating that the scale is reliable and all the items measure the same underlying dimension. This measure also showed high convergent and discriminant validity. AVE was equal to 0.57 and higher than the square of the correlation coefficient between the two subscales (r2 = 0.462). Chi-square was equal to 406.168 (degree of freedom [df] = 239 $p < 0.001$), residual mean square root (RMR) was 0.034 (the closer to 0 the better), and all the other indexes were above 0.9, showing goodness of fit: comparative goodness of fit index (CFI) = 0.977, adequacy index (GFI) = 0.944, adjusted adequacy index (AGFI) = 0.930, and normed fit index (NFI) = 0.947. The mean squared error of approximation (RMSEA) was equal to 0.035 and did not reach the common accepted upper limit of 0.05, with a 90% confidence interval between 0.029 and 0.040, $p = 1.000$.

2.5 Cynicism Toward Organizational Change

Resistance to organizational change may be expressed in the form of specific cynicism toward change, a phenomenon defined as employees' belief that the organization lacks the integrity to implement specific projects (DeCelles et al., 2013).

Cynicism toward organizational change is similar to the organizational cynicism construct. It is a multidimensional construct that may emerge as employees' defense strategy (Naus et al., 2007; Schmitz et al., 2018) to deal with an organizational change (Nguyen et al., 2018), for believing there will be losses for the organization itself (Fauzan, 2019). A change process is a disturbing event that impacts and influences the workers' belief systems (Mitchell & Lee, 2001). In this context, cynicism may function as a protective mechanism against manipulation and questioning the *status quo* to verify the validity of what is being proposed (Thundiyil et al., 2015). Additionally, it may reflect ideas concerning management problems and the implementation of change, so that a cynical attitude is an individual attempt to make sense of the changes proposed (Bergström et al., 2014).

Because this construct is derived from the organizational context, specific cynicism toward change is conceived as disbelief on the part of managers or collaborators regarding the stated or implicit reasons for specific organizational changes. Employee cynicism results from a lack of trust in the leaders' explicit or stated motives for decisions or actions in general. Dispositional cynicism refers to disbelief in people's explicit or stated motives in general regarding decisions or actions (Stanley et al., 2005). Cynicism about organizational change is often considered an essential factor that influences whether employees will accept changes. There are culturally adapted instruments to assess this phenomenon (e.g., Change-Specific Cynicism Scale, Grama & Todericiu, 2016); however, cynicism has been compared to some similar constructs – organizational trust, resistance to change, and organizational cynicism – with little conceptual or empirical differentiation. For this reason, researchers insist there is a need to improve and refine the conceptualization of cynicism (Thundiyil et al., 2015).

Cynicism toward organizational change can be defined as "a pessimistic viewpoint about change efforts being successful" (Wanous et al., 2000; p. 133). The authors proposed the Cynicism About Organizational Change – CAOC (Wanous et al., 2000) with two dimensions: pessimism regarding the potential success of changes and negative dispositional attributions about those responsible for successfully implementing changes. Examples of items include "Most of the programs that are supposed to solve problems around here will not do much good" and "Plans for future improvements will not amount to much." The dispositional include items such as "The people responsible for solving problems around here do not care enough about their jobs" and "The people responsible for making improvements do not know enough about what they are doing." Other studies submitted the scale to an expert panel, exploratory and confirmatory factor analysis (Wanous et al., 2000, 2004; Albrecht, 2008). Cynicism toward change was measured through eight items in which employees were asked to rate their level of agreement with change-related statements on a scale ranging from (1) strongly disagree to (7) strongly agree. Lower scores suggest less cynicism toward change. Wanous et al. (2004) reported that the Cronbach's alpha for the total scale ranged from $\alpha = 0.75$ to $\alpha = 0.82$ and from $\alpha = 0.72$ to $\alpha = 0.86$ across a range of occupational groupings.

2.6 Readiness for Organizational Change

Readiness is undoubtedly one of the most critical factors involved in initial support to change (Armenakis et al., 1993; Armenakis et al., 1999). For changes to occur in the direction top leadership desires, conflicts must be resolved so that the beliefs and cognitions of the organization's members are aligned to those of its leaders, which implies that a state of readiness must be established (Holt et al., 2007).

A review conducted by Bouckenooghe (2010) in 58 papers published between 1993 and 2007 addressing attitudes toward organizational change identified that out of the 21 studies included in the review, Armenakis et al. (1993) most frequently mentioned organizational readiness. The authors defined readiness to change as "beliefs, attitudes, and intentions regarding the extent to which changes are needed and the organization's capacity to successfully undertake those changes" (Bouckenooghe, 2010, p. 681).

In summary, the concepts of attitudes toward organizational change, commitment to change, readiness to change, cynicism toward change are relatively traditional constructs regarding employee responses to organizational change. Generally, they involve cognitive and affective assessments of change processes and often include behavioral aspects. Traditionally, these constructs are measured and delimited at the individual level, though there are attempts to address them at a collective level: collective attitudes toward organizational change (Nery et al., 2018; Vakola, 2016) and cynicism and readiness toward change as multilevel phenomena with origin at the individual level (DeCelles et al., 2013; Weiner et al., 2020). In terms of valence, the attitude toward organizational change includes positive and negative valence, commitment and readiness toward change have a positive valence, and cynicism has only a negative valence.

The literature is full of terms that characterize positive attitudes such as acceptance, readiness to change, openness, adaptation, coping with change, commitment to change, and negative attitudes such as resistance and cynicism (Bouckenooghe, 2010). This traditional view has been discussed using ambivalence in the context of organizational change (Vakola et al., 2020). Ambivalence, inherent to organizational life (Rothman et al., 2017), is defined as a contradictory attitude encompassing positive and negative reactions toward an object (Kaplan, 1972; Oreg & Sverdlik, 2011; van Harreveld et al., 2009). In this sense, leaders and employees need to balance demands daily such as competition and cooperation, excellence and cost reduction, organizational and personal agendas, stability and change, structural change and flexibility, and tradition and innovation (Gibson & Birkinshaw, 2004; Rothman et al., 2017).

Various studies recognize that the attitudes of recipients of change strongly influence the way employees adapt to change (Oreg et al., 2011; Van Dam et al., 2008). However, these studies failed to acknowledge that attitudes toward change are not clear-cut (Vakola, 2016; Vakola et al., 2020); instead, attitudes may be ambivalent, involving both positive and negative cognitions, emotional reactions, and simultaneously favorable and unfavorable assessments of change (Oreg et al., 2018; Piderit,

2000). Failing to consider the existence of conflicting views on the change in question can reduce the precision and validity of results and confuse workers in the process (Oreg & Sverdlik, 2011; Vakola et al., 2020).

The literature suggests that attitudes toward organizational change facilitate the implementation of changes (Nery & Neiva, 2015) and should be used to indicate how favorable organizational changes are. Some authors (Schwarz & Bouckenooghe, 2017) have recently focused on collective attitudes, proposing multilevel models for organizational change. Authors propose a more direct model for collective attitude toward change, identifying mechanisms in which collective attitudes change, as well as the circumstances and contingencies from which new collective attitudes emerge, which do not necessarily reflect individual attitudes (Schwarz & Bouckenooghe, 2017).

Assessing readiness before introducing changes is encouraged, and various instruments were designed with this purpose (Cunningham et al., 2002; Jones et al., 2005). Instruments are intended to measure readiness from a perspective of the change process: based on change content, change context, or the individual attributes of those participating in the change process (Holt et al., 2007). There are instruments such as scales or inventories addressing readiness toward change. The Survey Lay of the Land (Burke et al., 1996) captures readiness by assessing the general perceptions of an organization's members regarding the environment where change is taking place without considering a specific initiative. Another instrument, the University of Rhode Island Change Assessment Scale (McConnaughy et al., 1983), assesses readiness toward specific initiatives, though irrelevant from an organizational perspective, such as an individual effort to quit smoking or lose weight. Later, this instrument was adapted to be used in an organizational setting (Cunningham et al., 2002), though it still lacks validity evidence.

The Readiness for Organizational Change Scale was developed and assessed using a systematic framework (i.e., item development, questionnaire administration, item reduction, scale assessment, and replication). It was designed to measure readiness toward organizational change at an individual level. More than 900 members from public and private organizations participated in the study's different phases, and it was tested in different organizations. Data analysis (25 items) showed that readiness toward change is a multidimensional construct influenced by the employees' beliefs that (a) they are capable of implementing changes (i.e., specific change self-efficacy; (b) change is appropriate for the organization (i.e., adequacy); (c) the leaders are committed to change (i.e., management support); and (d) that change will benefit the organization's members (i.e., personal valence) (Holt et al., 2007). Thus far, this is the most successful instrument available to assess the construct readiness toward organizational change, and from it, other instruments emerged (Weiner et al., 2008; Weiner et al., 2020). This scale was based on the dimensions reported in the literature and was submitted to an expert panel and exploratory factor analysis. The items include *I think the organization will benefit from this change*; *It does not make much sense for us to initiate this change*; *There are legitimate reasons for us to make this change*; *This change will improve our organization's overall efficiency*; and *This change makes my job easier.* The 25-item instrument captured four readiness dimensions: appropriateness, management support, change efficacy, and personal benefit. The confirmatory factor analysis performed with the initial sample and its replication supported the instrument's four-factor structure. The instrument also showed convergent, discriminant, concurrent, and predictive validity. Specifically, the readiness subscale showed (a) positive associations with measures of locus of control and general attitudes toward change, (b) negative association with rebelliousness and negative affect, (c) discriminant validity between groups at different levels of readiness, and (d) predictive validity with job satisfaction and affective commitment. In both the initial sample and replication, reliability estimates for three of the four readiness dimensions exceeded 0.70. In both samples, the personal valence dimension (i.e., perceived personal benefits) presented reliability alphas equal to 0.65 and 0.66, respectively. The instrument was designed to measure readiness at the individual level and, later, was submitted to confirmatory factor analysis (Vakola, 2014).

The literature has shown the relevance of using behavioral and affective responses such as resistance and supportive behaviors as criteria to infer the success of changes (Bordia et al., 2011). However, the construct most frequently investigated has been resistance toward organizational change (Piderit, 2000), which is addressed next.

2.7 Behavioral Responses to Organizational Change Processes and Measurement

Despite its relevance, few measures address behavioral responses to change (Bortolotti, 2010), and none of the existing measures address the two dimensions: supportive behavior and resistance. Organizational changes can incite emotions and reactions that range from optimism to fear, possibly including anxiety, resistance, excitement, inability, motivation, or pessimism (Bortolotti, 2010). In general, the phenomenon involves a range of positive and negative reactions, which can be placed on a continuum beginning at the individual level and resulting in a collective response, configuring group patterns (Nery & Neiva, 2015). The phenomenon of behavioral reactions toward change has been frequently analyzed at the individual level (Choi, 2011). However, this phenomenon may also be observed from a collective perspective and is characterized by behavioral patterns presented by a group of individuals (Bouckenooghe, 2010; Choi, 2011; George & Jones, 2001), often resulting from organizational inertia. In this sense, inertia would manifest or originate at the individual level and resistance at a group level (George & Jones, 2001).

Phenomena originating at the individual level can lead to attributes at the macro or middle level (emersion phenomenon, to emerge) based on different processes of composition or structuring attributes (Klein & Kozlowski, 2000). Over time, as people work under the influence of the same events, they start sharing perceptions regarding phenomena in their organizational environment. Even though interpretation is an individual cognitive process, it is socially constructed based on social benchmarks (collective interpretations). Additionally, individuals may develop behavioral patterns associated with these interpretations, using social mechanisms, often called contagion (Wiltermuth & Heath, 2009).

Change-supportive behaviors and resistance to change emerge at the individual level but may become collective as behavioral patterns that most (perhaps all) organizational members manifest in response to events within the organization (George & Jones, 2001; Nery & Neiva, 2015). Despite emersion processes, one way to access a phenomenon is still through individual assessment (Hox, 2010).

2.8 Resistance to Organizational Change

The psychologist Kurt Lewin first used the expression "resistance to change" as a metaphor in physical sciences (Bortolotti, 2010). Since then, resistance is a prominent theme because it is a critical factor, listed as one of the main barriers to the success of organizational transformations (Neiva & Paz, 2012; Piderit, 2000). The reason is that resistance to change delays the implementation of changes, generates costs, and results in unexpected instability, unforeseen inefficiency, procrastination, and efforts to sabotage the change process (Franco et al., 2016).

The concept of resistance to change is rooted in Lewin's (1947) theory, unfreeze, change and refreeze organizational model of change, which states that there are driving forces that seek to cause or resist change. Studies addressing resistance to change generally describe it at an individual level through three dimensions: cognitive, affective, and behavioral (Erwin & Garman, 2010; Isabella, 1990). The cognitive dimension refers to what employees think about change, including their perception of being efficacious to occupy new positions (Giangreco & Peccei, 2005). The affective dimension is defined as the employees' emotional and psychological responses toward changes (Denhardt et al., 2009). The behavioral dimension refers to resistance in terms of actions, considering that the two first dimensions are frequently seen as the sources or causes of resistance. The behavioral dimension includes the actual manifestation of resistance as behaviors, acts, and observable events (Fiedler, 2010; Giangreco & Peccei, 2005; Lines et al., 2014). Some measures exclusively focus on behavioral resistance to change because this is the only dimension directly observable. Twelve specific types of resistant behavior (Table 2.1) were found based on the definitions provided in the literature (Bovey & Hede, 2001; Emiliani & Stec, 2004; Fiedler, 2010; Giangreco & Peccei, 2005; Mishra & Spreitzer, 1998; Van de Ven & Poole, 1995) (Table 2.2).

There is a profusion of approaches addressing resistance to change, from the conception of the phenomenon as a dispositional trait (Oreg, 2003; Oreg et al., 2008) up to approaches that consider the phenomenon to be a political movement in the relational context (Thomas & Hardy, 2011; Mumby, 2005). From a primarily collective and group perspective, negotiating the meaning is inevitably imbued with power-resistance relations. Traditionally, power and resistance have been treated separately, while the exercise of power is seen as domination, and resistance

Table 2.1 Types of resistant behaviors

Types of resistant behaviors	Definitions
Reluctant compliance	Doing the minimum required, lack of enthusiasm, caution, and doubt
Delaying	Expressing verbal agreement but not following through, obstruction, procrastination
Lack of transparency	Hiding or omitting useful information during implementation
Restricting communication	Avoiding or restricting the dissemination of change message
Arguing and open criticism	Expressing opposition verbally and/or finding fault with the implementation of change
Obstruction and subversion	Openly sabotaging, blocking, and undermining the implementation of change
Disseminating a negative word	Disseminating negative opinion and rumors, encouraging fear in resistance
Termination	Voluntarily or involuntarily withdrawing from a project or the organization
Reversion	Changing back to traditional practices during the implementation of change
Misguided application	Changing the implementation beyond the stated process, goals, and methods
Forcing change	Struggling for perfection at the expense of implementation efforts
External influence	Behavior in response to negative feedback from external sources

constitutes actions taken to challenge it (Hardy & Clegg, 1996). Authors of this approach also argue that there is a harmful dichotomy in the literature between a positive and a negative view of resistance (Thomas & Hardy, 2011).

Even though a scale was not designed, a typology of resistant behaviors was developed based on observations and interviews (Lines et al., 2014). This typology characterizes behaviors (Table 2.1) as delay in meeting deadlines, omitting information, obstruction, argumentation and open criticisms to change, etc. The study's significant contribution lies in the operational description of the behaviors that qualify resistance to change.

Most papers addressing resistance to change provide their own conceptual definitions (Bouckenooghe, 2010), which are different, though consider the intentional/behavioral component as an opposing force that impedes the successful implementation of change, supporting the *status quo* (Nery & Neiva, 2015). The literature also shows that resistance is the most frequent response to organizational change (Piderit, 2000; Bouckenooghe, 2010) and, for this reason, should be seen as an element that is inherent to individual and collective cognitive transformations that occur during change processes (George & Jones, 2001).

In 2003, Oreg proposed a scale to directly assess the dispositional component that contributes to individual resistance to change, called the Resistance to Change Scale (RTC). This scale is composed of 44 items rated on a 6-point Likert scale. The validation process indicated four factors: routine seeking, emotional reaction to

Table 2.2 Measures to Assess Employee Reactions to Organizational Change

OC construct	Instrument and author	Sphere (attitudinal/ value/ behavioral/ hybrid)	Factors	No de Items	Level of analysis de (individual, group, organization)	Scale	Example of item
Attitude	Attitudes Toward Change in General-Initial Instrument (Dunham et al., 1989)	Attitudinal	Three dimensions: affective, cognitive, and behavioral intent	18	Individuals report about themselves, other workers, and the organization	7-point Likert scale (1 – totally disagree to 7 – totally agree)	"I do not like changes" "Most of my co-workers benefit from change" "Change usually benefits the organization"
Attitude	*Attitudes Toward Change Questionnaire* (ACQ) Vakola et al. (2004)	Attitudinal	14 positive factors and 14 negative factors	29	Individual self-report	5-point Likert scale (1 – totally disagree to 5 – totally agree)	"I am looking forward to changes within my work environment" "When a new organizational change program is initiated, I emphatically show my disagreement"
Reactions to specific work changes	Attitudes Toward Change (Giauque, 2015)	Attitudinal	One dimension: all the items concern specific job aspects	6	Individual self-report	5-point Likert scale (1 – very unfavorable to 5 – very favorable)	Organizational changes had a favorable or unfavorable impact on your job regarding "management of uncertainties"
Reactions to organizational change	Change Recipients' Reactions (CRRE) Scale Tsaousis and Vakola (2018)	Attitudinal	Three-factor model (cognitive, emotional, and behavioral)	21	Individual self-report	5-point Likert scale (1 – strongly disagree to 5 – strongly agree)	I feel uncomfortable with the change that they are trying to implement

Typical attitudes	Attitudes Toward Organizational Change (Neiva et al., 2005)	Attitudinal	Three factors: skepticism, fear and acceptance of changes	36	Individuals report about themselves, other workers, and organization	5-point Likert scale (1 – strongly disagree to 5 – strongly agree)	"People are afraid because of the uncertainty generated by the new way of working" "This organization does not plan processes of change – they just happen"
Teachers' attitudes	Teacher Attitudes Toward Change Scale (TATCS) (Kin & Karrem, 2017)	Attitudinal	Three factors: cognitive, behavioral, and affective reaction to change (positive and negative) Four quadrants: acceptance, embracing, resistance, and indifference	9	Individuals report about themselves, other workers, and the organization	6-point Likert scale (1 – totally disagree to 6 – totally agree)	Most changes at my school are pleasing Change frustrates me I often suggest changes for my school
Readiness	*Readiness for Organizational Change Scale* (Holt et al., 2007)	Attitudinal	Four dimensions: (1) change-specific efficacy, (2) appropriateness, (3) management support, and (4) personal valence	25	Individual	7-point Likert scale (1 – totally disagree to 7 – totally agree)	There are legitimate reasons for us to make this change Our organization's top decision-makers have put all their support behind this change effort When we implement this change, I feel I can handle it with ease My future in this job will be limited because of this change

(continued)

Table 2.2 (continued)

OC construct	Instrument and author	Sphere (attitudinal/ value/ behavioral/ hybrid)	Factors	No de Items	Level of analysis de (individual, group, organization)	Scale	Example of item
Resistance	*Resistance to Change Scale* (RTC) (Oreg, 2003)	Attitudinal	Cognitive, affective, and behavioral aspects distributed into four factors: (a) routine seeking, (b) emotional reaction to imposed change, (c) short-term focus, and (d) cognitive rigidity	16	Individual	6-point Likert scale (1 – totally disagree to 6 – totally agree)	I'd rather be bored than surprised. When I am informed of a change of plans, I tense up a bit Changing plans seems like a real hassle to me My views are very consistent over time
Resistance	*Escala de Resistência à Mudança* (RAM) [Change Resistance Scale] (Bortolotti, 2010)	Hybrid: attitudinal and behavioral	Three levels: acceptance, indifference, and resistance to change	52	Individual	4-point Likert scale (1 – totally disagree to 4 – totally agree)	Change is positive to employees I am indifferent and not surprised by changes When they talk about changes, I pretend it has nothing to do with me

Commitment to change	*Commitment to change* (Herscovitch & Meyer, 2002)	Behavioral	Three dimensions: affective, continuity, normative commitment	22	Individual	Items were rated on a 7-point Likert scale, ranging from 1 (strongly disagree) to 7 (strongly agree)	Twenty-two items were written to measure commitment to change: seven items assessed affective commitment (e.g., "I believe in the value of this change"), seven items assessed continuance commitment (e.g., "I have no choice but to go along with this change"), and eight items assessed normative commitment (e.g., "I would feel guilty about opposing this change")
Openness to change	*Change-Related Commitment* (Jansen, 2004)	Behavioral	One dimension	8	Individual	Eight items assessed the participants' agreement with and willingness to work toward the goal (= 0.93)	It is hard for me to take this change seriously; the principles of this change effort are good goals to shoot for; it is unrealistic to expect that I will adopt this change
Commitment to change	*Commitment to organizational change scale (Cinite & Duxbury)*	Behavioral	One dimension	6	Individual	7-point Likert scale (1 – totally disagree to 4 – totally agree)	I introduce changes in my daily work to help the organization achieve its change goals
Openness to change	Individual-level openness to the process of change (Randall, Nielsen, & Tvedt, 2009)	Attitudinal	One dimension	3	Individual	Agreement	"I have high expectations that the workshops can improve my skills in using ICT in my daily work

(continued)

Table 2.2 (continued)

OC construct	Instrument and author	Sphere (attitudinal/ value/ behavioral/ hybrid)	Factors	No de Items	Level of analysis de (individual, group, organization)	Scale	Example of item
Openness to change	Individual-level openness to the content of change (Davis, 1989; Davis, Bagozzi, & Warshaw, 1989)	Attitudinal	One dimension	8	Individual	Agreement	"The use of ICT gives me more control over my job"
Openness to change	Group-level openness to the content of change 9 Augustsson et al., 2017)	Attitudinal	One dimension	Um item	Group	Agreement with aggregation at the group level	("At my workplace, we are positive towards the use of ICT")
Resistance	Resistance to organizational change scale (Cinite & Duxbury, 2018)	Behavioral	One dimension	4	Individual	7-point Likert scale (1 – totally disagree to 7 – totally agree)	I provide constructive suggestions to people who are in a position to influence the change
Change-supportive behavior	*Change-supportive behavior* (Kim et al., 2011)	Behavioral	One dimension	3	Individual	5-point scale ranging from 1 – not at all to 5 – to a very great extent	I have made suggestions to be addressed in the councils

Change-supportive behavior/resistance to change	*Escala de Respostas Comportamentais à Mudança Organizacional* [Scale of Behavioral Responses to Change]	Behavioral	Two dimensions: change-supportive behavior and resistance to change	19	Individual and collective versions	11-point Likert scale (0 – totally disagree to 10 – totally agree). The scale was developed considering factors that portray change-supportive behavior and resistance to change, which have been addressed in the literature (Choi, 2011; Kim et al., 2011)	Individual version I declare that I am in favor of the changes that have occurred I seek information about change I ridicule those responsible for the change I disobey the new rules introduced by the change Collective version The employees declare to be in favor of the changes that have occurred The employees ridicule change agents The employees actively participate in the change process The employees deny that change is happening
Cynicism About Organizational Change	*Cynicism About Organizational Change*	Attitudinal	Two dimensions	8	Individual	Employees were asked to indicate their agreement with change-related statements on a scale ranging from 1 – strongly disagree to 7 – strongly agree. Lower scores suggest less cynicism toward change	"Suggestions on how to solve problems will not produce much real change," "plans for future improvements will not amount to much," and "the people responsible for making changes here do not have the skills needed to do their jobs"

imposed change, cognitive rigidity, and short-term focus. It became the primary measure addressing resistance to organizational change and presents data and convergent validity with samples from various countries (Oreg et al., 2008). The authors sought individual differences in the structure, with validity evidence from different cultures, and also tried to associate the structure of values to dispositional resistance to change. Schwartz's (1992) theory of personal values was used as a framework to assess the validity of the measure between cultures. Assuming that dispositional resistance shares its meaning across cultures, openness to change was negatively correlated to conservative values and positively correlated with resistance scores in all the countries included in the sample (Oreg et al., 2008). Other results also indicated that idealistic values and organizational climate explained resistance to organizational change, predicting self-perceived performance (Freires et al., 2014). The importance of the dispositional resistance approach is that it predisposes individuals to see the change from a particular perspective, whether negative or positive. However, the level of resistance toward a specific event of change will be influenced by other factors such as the organizational context and how changes are implemented. Consequently, the importance of dispositional resistance lies in its ability to influence organizational readiness to change and identify the level of resistance managers can expect to find, and therefore, which approach should be adopted (Michel et al., 2013).

In 2010, Bortolotti created a measure of resistance to change (RAM) based on the Item-Response Theory (IRT), using cause variables, individual variables, context, and result variables. The one-dimension scale contains 52 items and obtained a Cronbach's alpha equal to 0.75. The split model was adopted due to its precision in estimating the respondent's level in the latent trait resistance to change. With this statement, "Resistance to change is a latent trait or a latent variable," Bortolotti (2010 p. 28) highlights that its characteristics cannot be directly measured. Therefore, the following definition was adopted to develop the dimension "Resistance to organizational change" of the scale behavioral response to change: a manifestation of stated or implicit opposition to change (Kim et al., 2011).

Recent studies address how employees express resistance to change, such as the resistance to organizational change scale proposed by Cinite and Duxbury (2018). This scale was based on the frequency of resistance using exploratory and confirmatory factor analyses. Findings suggest that employees resist "expressing their concerns regarding changes," and only employees committed to change tend to "express their concerns" to those higher in the hierarchy. Four items were found to typify the behavior of employees who resist organizational change. Cronbach's alpha was 0.77. Other tests determined that the measure presented high convergent and discriminant validity (AVE was 0.58 and greater than the square correlation between the two subscales). Chi-square was 406.168 (degrees of freedom [df] = 239, $p < 0.001$), root mean square residual (RMR) was 0.034 (the closer to 0 the better), and all the other goodness of fit indexes were satisfactory, above 0.9; comparative fit index (CFI) = 0.977, goodness of fit index (GFI) = 0.944, adjusted goodness of fit index (AGFI) = 0.930, and normed fit index (NFI) = 0.947. Root mean squared error of approximation (RMSEA) = 0.035 did not reach the commonly accepted upper limit of 0.05, with a 90% confidence interval between 0.029 and 0.040, $p = 1.000$.

2.9 Change-Supportive Behavior: The Relevance of Studying and Measuring Behavior Toward Organizational Change

Many authors recently defended that emphasizing current behavior toward organizational change, active support, and collective actions produces more consistent results than emphasizing psychological states and individual and passive responses. Change-supportive behavior – such as expressing active behavior toward changes, participatory behavior – facilitates and promotes changes (Kim et al., 2011). In this sense, Kim et al. (2011) define "change-supportive behavior as actions employees engage in to actively participate, facilitate, and contribute to a planned change." This definition seems very appropriate to assess the responses of individuals to change.

This definition contains three elements that differ from other constructs: (a) it focuses on visible behavior instead of psychological states toward organizational change, such, for instance, behavioral intentions or attitudes; (b) it emphasizes active support to change, adapting, or dealing with changes; and (c) it implies collective support to a planned change process, instead of individual effort (Bordia et al., 2011; Oreg et al., 2011; Vakola et al., 2013; Vakola, 2016).

The studies conducted in the last 15 years were reviewed to list the instruments used to measure positive behavioral responses to organizational change (Kim et al., 2011). In 2011, Kim et al. advanced knowledge by developing a scale to address change-supportive employee behavior. By taking into account the following constructs: commitment to change, readiness to change, attitudes toward organizational change, and openness to change, the authors developed the Change-Supportive Employee Behavior scale, composed of three items rated on a five-point Likert scale ranging from 1 (not at all) to 5 (to a very great extent). This measure explicitly addresses the positive and active role employees can play in supporting organizational change. Change-supportive behavior is defined as actions employees actively engage in to facilitate and contribute to a change proposed by an organization, or more precisely, by the organization's management. This definition contains three elements that differ from the constructs previously studied: (a) it focuses on actual behavior, instead of change-related psychological states such as behavioral intentions or attitudes; (a) it emphasizes active support to change, instead of passive responses such as merely agreeing, adapting, or coping with change; and (c) it involves collective planned effort instead of individual effort. The instrument addresses active contributions (proactive behavior) beyond mere adaptive behavior, such as planned organizational change. Three items operationalize the main change-supportive actions: "I have made suggestions to be addressed in the Councils" and "I have discussed issues with co-workers." Internal consistency was 0.85 (T1) and

0.91 (T2). A five-point Likert scale (1 = not at all to 5 = to a large extent) was used in all the measures. The scale obtained internal consistency equal to 0.85 and 0.91 at different points in time.

The *Escala de Respostas Comportamentais à Mudança Organizacional* [Behavioral Responses to Organizational Change Scale] was designed and tested, including content validity (expert panel), construct validity (exploratory and confirmatory factor analyses), and convergent validity (Nery et al., 2020). The 19-item scale ($R^2 = 58.46\%$) is based on a two-latent factor structure. The items are rated on an 11-point Likert scale ((0) totally disagree to (10) totally agree). The scale considers factors addressed in the literature and which portray change-supportive responses and resistance to change (Choi, 2011; Kim et al., 2011). The scale comprises the individual and collective dimensions (two versions with similar validity evidence) and two factors: support to change (9 items) assesses behaviors that support change processes, such as flexibility, openness to change, defense of change ($a = 0.91$), and resistance to change with ten items that assess opposition to organizational change ($a = 0.90$). The confirmatory factor analysis confirmed the bi-factor structure for the collective and individual versions, with satisfactory goodness of fit (individual version, c2 = 182.35; df = 88; RMSEA = 0.05; CFI = 0.93; TLI = 0.94; collective version, c2 = 86.91; df = 42; RMSEA = 0.05; CFI = 0.96; TLI = 0.97).

The responses of individuals to organizational change involve their reactions expressed during change programs and which may present positive or negative valence or be ambivalent (Piderit, 2000). Despite its relevance, there are few instruments with validity evidence to measure behavioral response to change (Bortolotti, 2010), and among the existing measures, none simultaneously address change-supportive behavior and resistance to change. Organizational change may elicit different emotions and reactions that range from optimism to fear, possibly including anxiety, resistance, enthusiasm, inability, motivation, or pessimism (Bortolotti, 2010).

Additionally, there is great emphasis on negative responses to organizational change, given the many studies addressing resistance to organizational change (Kim et al., 2011). Few studies assess positive responses to organizational change programs such as supportive behavior and commitment to change (Kim et al., 2011). Another issue to be considered is that few studies consider these responses to belong to a support-to-resistance spectrum (Lines, 2005; Piderit, 2000). Finally, the level of analysis was expanded from the individual to the middle level. In this sense, Nery and Neiva (2015) argue that the phenomenon may involve a range of positive and negative reactions that can be placed on a continuum, from the individual to the collective level, when it becomes a group behavior pattern.

2.10 Conclusions and Recommendations

The state-of-the-art literature indicates the emergence of measures that advanced from the individual to the relational and collective level, attempting to understand the role of collective attitudes toward OC. There is also an improved understanding of the management's role in responses to OC. Additionally, behavioral measures present relevant results to support interventions in change processes intending to improve worker wellbeing.

Traditionally, responses to organizational change predominantly involve cognitive and affective aspects and potentially behavioral intention. Additionally, there is great emphasis on negative responses to organizational change, given the many studies addressing resistance to organizational change (Kim et al., 2011). Few studies consider the possibility of responses/reactions belonging to a support-resistance continuum (Lines, 2005; Piderit, 2000). In general, the phenomenon involves a spectrum of positive and negative reactions that can be structured on a continuum, starting at the individual level and reaching the collective level, configuring a group behavior pattern (Nery & Neiva, 2015).

Despite the various factors considered by studies addressing responses to change, there are gaps concerning how the construct is defined and measured, along with problems that hinder comparing and integrating the findings of different studies. There is significant inconsistency in how the terms are used in studies addressing responses to change. Authors should be clear about the distinction between (previous or contextual) antecedents of change, explicit responses, and consequences of change. Additionally, authors need to specify the names given to variables. For instance, variables such as organizational commitment and job satisfaction may be considered both pre-change antecedents and a consequence of responses to change.

Even though the definitions involve cognitive, affective, and behavioral components, authors should note which component is addressed. Studies should focus on behavioral responses considering that the measurement of behavioral responses has been more successful. Another aspect to be considered refers to the progression of theories and approaches that include cognitive and affective assessments as specific objects of study and require methods and theories to advance in the Theory of Planned Behavior (Ajzen, 1991).

Many studies report explicit responses as a result or consequence of change processes. Explicit responses are often different from consequences of changes, which are diverse and may vary in terms of the organizational levels in which they occur. As more results concerning the responses of recipients of change are reported, more specific studies are needed to investigate whether explicit responses differ from the consequences of changes and in which circumstances.

The recipients of change are naturally concerned with personal impacts. If perceived risks/costs outweigh the benefits, collaborators will naturally resist changes. Managers do not always foresee how the recipients of change will respond to change and do not consider their perspectives. Global and local change agents need to be clear from the outset about the precise ramifications the program will result for the recipients of change. More importantly, however, change agents should pay attention to these ramifications and attempt to understand and incorporate the viewpoint of the recipients of change when planning organizational changes. In practice, they should carefully plan interventions and make an effort to explain how threats can be addressed and, at the same time, present and highlight how such a change can personally benefit the employees, in addition to its importance for the organization.

References

Ajzen, I. (1991). The theory of planned behavior. *Organizational Behavior and Human Decision Processes, 50*(2), 179–211. https://doi.org/10.1016/0749-5978(91)90020-T

Albrecht, S. (2008). Measuring cynicism toward organizational change one dimension or two? *Journal of Applied Measurement, 9*(4), 374–386. https://www.researchgate.net/publication/23673276_Measuring_cynicism_toward_organizational_change_-_One_dimension_or_two

Armenakis, A. A., Harris, S. G., & Feild, H. S. (1999). Making change permanent: A model for institutionalizing change interventions. In W. A. Pasmore & R. W. Woodman (Eds.), *Research in organizational change and development* (Vol. 12, pp. 97–128).

Armenakis, A. A., Harris, S. G., & Mossholder, K. W. (1993). Creating readiness for organizational change. *Human Relations, 46*(6), 681–703. https://doi.org/10.1177/001872679304600601

Augustsson, H., Richter, A., Hasson, H., & von Thiele Schwarz, U. (2017). The need for dual openness to change: A longitudinal study evaluating the impact of employees' openness to organizational change content and process on intervention outcomes. *Journal of Applied Behavioral Science, 53*, 349–368. https://doi.org/10.1177/0021886317691930

Bergström, O., Styhre, A., & Thilander, P. (2014). Paradoxifying organizational change: Cynicism and resistance in the Swedish armed forces. *Journal of Change Management, 14*(3), 384–404. https://doi.org/10.1080/14697017.2014.938096

Bovey, W., & Hede, A. (2001). Resistance to organizational change: The role of cognitive and affective processes. *Leadership and Organization Development Journal, 22*(8), 372–382. https://www.emerald.com/insight/content/doi/10.1108/01437730110410099/full/html

Bordia, P., Restubog, S. L. D., Jimmieson, N., & Irmer, B. (2011). Haunted by the past: Effects of poor change management history on employee attitudes and turnover. *Group & Organization Management, 36*(2), 191–222. https://doi.org/10.1177/1059601110392990

Bortolotti, S. L. V. (2010). *Resistência à mudança organizacional: Medida de avaliação por meio da Teoria da Resposta ao Item*. Universidade Federal de Santa Catarina.

Bouckenooghe, D. (2010). Positioning change recipients' attitudes toward change in the organizational change literature. *The Journal of Applied Behavioral Science, 46*(4), 500–531. https://doi.org/10.1177/0021886310367944

Burke, W. W., Coruzzi, C. A., & Church, A. H. (1996). The organizational survey as an intervention for change. In A. I. Kraut (Org.) (Ed.), *Organizational surveys: Tools for assessment and change* (pp. 41–66). Jossey-Bass.

Choi, M. (2011). Employees' attitudes toward organizational change: A literature review. *Human Resource Management, 50*(4), 479–500. https://doi.org/10.1002/hrm.20434

Cinite, I., & Duxbury, L. E. (2018). Measuring the behavioral properties of commitment and resistance to organizational change. *The Journal of Applied Behavioral Science, 54*(2), 113–139. https://doi.org/10.1177/0021886318757997

Hardy, C., & Clegg, S. (1996). Some dare call it power. In S. Clegg, C. Hardy, & W. Nord (Eds.), *Handbook of organization studies*. SAGE Publications.

Hox, J. J. (2010). *Multilevel analysis. Techniques and applications* (2nd ed.). Routledge.

Cunningham, C. E., Woodward, C. A., Shannon, H. S., MacIntosh, J., Lendrum, B., Rosenbloom, D., & Brown, J. (2002). Readiness for organizational change: A longitudinal study of workplace, psychological and behavioral correlates. *Journal of Occupational and Organizational Psychology, 75*, 377–392. http://safewellwork.com/readiness_for_organizationa.pdf

DeCelles, K. A., Tesluk, P. E., & Taxman, F. S. (2013). A field investigation of multilevel cynicism toward change. *Organization Science, 24*(1), 154–171. https://doi.org/10.1287/orsc.1110.0735

Denhardt, R., Denhard, J., & Aristigueta, M. (2009). *Managing human behavior in public and nonprofit organizations*. Sage Publications.

Eagly, A. H., & Chaiken, S. (1993). *The psychology of attitudes*. Harcourt Brace Jovanovich College Publishers.

Elias, S. M. (2009). Employee commitment in times of change: Assessing the importance of attitudes toward organizational change. *Journal of Management, 35*, 37–55. https://doi.org/10.1177/0149206307308910

Emiliani, M. L., & Stec, D. J. (2004). Leaders lost in translation. *Leadership and Organization Development Journal, 26*(5), 370–387. https://www.researchgate.net/publication/255630468_Leaders_lost_in_transformation

Erwin, D. G., & Garman, A. N. (2010). Resistance to organizational change: Linking research and practice. *Leadership & Organizational Development Journal, 31*(1), 39–56. https://www.cin.ufpe.br/~llfj/Emerald/Resistance%20to%20organizational%20change%20-%20linking%20research%20and%20practice.pdf

Fauzan, R. (2019). Upgrading at work: Employee disposition and cynicism about organizational changes. *International Journal of Organizational Analysis, 28*(3), 677–697. https://doi.org/10.1108/IJOA-07-2019-1826

Fiedler, S. (2010). Managing resistance in an organizational transformation: A case study from a mobile operator company. *International Journal of Project Management, 28*, 370–383. https://doi.org/10.1016/j.ijproman.2010.02.004

Fishbein, M., & Ajzen, I. (1974). Attitudes toward objects as predictors of single and multiple behavioral criteria. *Psychological Review, 81*, 59–74. https://doi.org/10.1037/h0035872

Franco, K. S., Neiva, E. R., Nery, V. F., & Demo, G. (2016). The relationship between context, attitudes and well-being in organizational change. *Psicologia: Teoria e Pesquisa, 32*, 1–10. https://doi.org/10.1590/0102-3772e32ne219

Freires, D. A. N., Golveia, V. V., Bortolotti, S. L. V., & Ribas, F. T. T. (2014). Resistência à Mudança Organizacional: Perspectiva Valorativa e Organizacional. *Psico, 45*(4), 513–523. https://doi.org/10.15448/1980-8623.2014.4.16220

Grama, B. S., & Todericiu, R. (2016). Change, resistance to change and organizational cynicism. *Studies in Business and Economics, 11*, 47–54. https://doi.org/10.1515/sbe-2016-0034

George, J. M., & Jones, G. R. (2001). Towards a process model of individual change in organization. *Human Relations, 54*(4), 419–444. https://doi.org/10.1177/0018726701544002

Giauque, D. (2015). Attitudes toward organizational change among public middle managers. *Public Personnel Management, 44*, 70–98. https://doi.org/10.1177/0091026014556512

Giangreco, A., & Peccei, R. (2005). The nature and antecedents of middle manager resistance to change: Evidence from an Italian context. *The International Journal of Human Resource Management, 16*, 1812–1829. https://doi.org/10.1080/09585190500298404

Gibson, C. B., & Birkinshaw, J. (2004). The antecedents, consequences, and mediating role of organizational ambidexterity. *Academy of Management Journal, 47*(2), 209–226. https://doi.org/10.5465/20159573

Herold, D. M., Fedor, D. S., & Caldwell, D. (2007). Beyond change management: A multilevel investigation of contextual and personal influences on employees' commitment to change. *Journal of Applied Psychology, 92*(4), 942–951. https://doi.org/10.1037/0021-9010.92.4.942

Herold, D. M., Fedor, S., Caldwell, & Liu, Y. (2008). The effects of transformational and change leadership on employees' commitment to a change: A multilevel study. *Journal of Applied Psychology, 93*(2), 346–357. https://doi.org/10.1037/0021-9010.93.2.346

Herscovitch, L., & Meyer, J. P. (2002). Commitment to organizational change: Extension of a three-component model. *Journal of Applied Psychology, 87*(3), 474–487. https://doi.org/10.1037/0021-9010.87.3.474

Holt, D. T., Armenakis, A. A., Field, H. S., & Harris, S. G. (2007). Readiness for organizational change: The systematic development of a scale. *The Journal of Applied Behavioral Science., 43*(2), 232–255. https://doi.org/10.1177/0021886306295295

Isabella, L. A. (1990). Evolving interpretations as a change unfolds: How managers construe key organizational events. *Academy of Management Journal, 33*, 7–41. https://doi.org/10.5465/256350

Jansen, K. J. (2004). From persistence to pursuit: A longitudinal examination of momentum during the early stages of strategic change. *Organization Science, 15*(3), 276–294. https://www.jstor.org/stable/30034733

Jones, R. A., Jimmieson, N. L., & Griffiths, A. (2005). The impact of organizational culture and reshaping capabilities on change implementation success: The mediating role of readiness for change. *Journal of Management Studies, 42*(2), 361–386. https://doi.org/10.1111/j.1467-6486.2005.00500.x

Kaplan, K. J. (1972). On the ambivalence–indifference problem in attitude theory and measurement: A suggested modification of the semantic differential technique. *Psychological Bulletin, 77*(5), 361–372. https://doi.org/10.1037/h0032590

Kim, T. G., Hornung, S., & Rousseau, D. M. (2011). Change-supportive employee behavior: Antecedents and the moderating role of time. *Journal of Management, 37*(6), 1664–1693. https://doi.org/10.1177/0149206310364243

Klein, K., & Kozlowski, S. (2000). *Multilevel theory, research and methods in organizations.* Jossey-Bass.

Lau, C.-M., & Woodman, R. W. (1995). Understanding organizational change: A schematic perspective. *Academy of Management Journal, 38*(2), 537–554. https://doi.org/10.2307/256692

Lewin, K. (1947). Group decision and social change. In T. M. Newcomb & E. L. Hartley (Eds.), *Readings in social psychology* (pp. 330–344). Henry Holt.

Lines, R. (2005). The structure and function of attitudes toward organizational change. *Human Resource Development Review, 4*(1), 8–32. https://doi.org/10.1177/1534484304273818

Lines, B., Sullivan, K., & Smithwick, J. (2014). *An action research approach to implementation of APDMs within AEC owner organizations: Overcoming resistance through education* (pp. 2084–2095). ASCE Construction Research Congress. https://doi.org/10.1061/9780784413517.212

Machado, L. C. P., & Neiva, E. R. (2017). Práticas de gestão da mudança: Impacto nas atitudes e nos resultados percebidos. *Revista Psicologia: Organizações e Trabalho, 17*(1), 22–29. https://doi.org/10.17652/rpot/2017.1.12157

McConnaughy, E. A., Prochaska, J. O., & Velicer, W. F. (1983). Stages of change in psychotherapy: Measurement and sample profiles. *Psychotherapy: Theory, Research & Practice, 20*(3), 368–375. https://doi.org/10.1037/h0090198

Meyer, J. P., Srinivas, E. S., Lal, J. B., & Topolnytsky, L. (2007). Employee commitment and support for an organizational change: Test of the three-component model in two cultures. *Journal of Occupational and Organizational Psychology, 80*(2), 185–211. https://doi.org/10.1348/096317906X118685

Michel, A., Todnem By, R., & Burnes, B. (2013). The limitations of dispositional resistance in relation to organizational change. *Management Decision, 51*(4), 761–780. https://doi.org/10.1108/00251741311326554

Mitchell, T. R., & Lee, T. W. (2001). The unfolding model of voluntary turnover and job embeddedness: Foundations for a comprehensive theory of attachment. *Research in Organizational Behavior, 23*, 189–246. https://doi.org/10.1016/S0191-3085(01)23006-8

Mishra, A. K., & Spreitzer, G. M. (1998). Explaining how survivors respond to downsizing: The roles of trust, empowerment, justice and work redesign. *The Academy of Management Review, 23*, 567–588. https://doi.org/10.2307/259295

Morin, A. J., Meyer, J. P., Bélanger, É., Boudrias, J.-S., Gagné, M., & Parker, P. D. (2016). Longitudinal associations between employees' beliefs about the quality of the change management process, affective commitment to change and psychological empowerment. *Human Relations, 69*(3), 839–867. https://doi.org/10.1177/0018726715602046

Mumby, D. K. (2005). Theorizing resistance in organization studies: A dialectical approach. *Management Communication Quarterly, 19*(1), 19–44.

Naus, F., van Iterson, A., & Roe, R. (2007). Organizational cynicism: Extending the exit, voice, loyalty, and neglect model of employees' responses to adverse conditions in the workplace. *Human Relations, 60*(5), 683–718. https://doi.org/10.1177/0018726707079198

Neiva, E. R., Ros, M., & Paz, M. G. T. (2005). Attitudes towards organizational change: Validation of a scale. *Psychology in Spain, 9*(1), 81–90. https://www.researchgate.net/publication/28106122_Attitudes_towards_organizational_change_validation_of_a_scale
Neiva, E. R., & Paz, M. T. (2012). Percepção de mudança individual e organizacional: O papel das atitudes, dos valores, do poder e da capacidade organizacional. *Revista de Administração, 47*(1), 22–37. https://doi.org/10.5700/rausp1023
Nery, V. F., & Neiva, E. R. (2015). Variáveis de contexto e respostas à mudança organizacional: Testando o papel mediador das atitudes. *Psicologia: Teoria e Pesquisa, 31*(2), 259–268. https://doi.org/10.1590/0102-37722015021968259268
Nery, V. F., Neiva, E. R., & Franco, K. S. (2018). Estrutura fatorial da escala de respostas comportamentais à mudança organizacional. *Avaliação Psicológica, 17*(1), 79–91. https://doi.org/10.15689/ap.2017.1701.09.13327
Nery, V. F., Franco, K. S., & Neiva, E. R. (2020). Attributes of the organizational change and its influence on attitudes toward organizational change and well-being at work: A longitudinal study. *The Journal of Applied Behavioral Science, 56*(2), 216–236. https://doi.org/10.1177/0021886319848125
Nguyen, D. T. N., Teo, S. T. T., Pick, D., & Jemai, M. (2018). Cynicism about change, work engagement, and job satisfaction of public sector nurses. *Australian Journal of Public Administration, 77*(2), 172–186. https://doi.org/10.1111/1467-8500.12270
Oreg, S. (2003). Resistance to change: Developing an individual differences measure. *Journal of Applied Psychology, 88*(4), 680–693. https://doi.org/10.1037/0021-9010.88.4.680
Oreg, S., Bayazit, M., Vakola, M., Arciniega, L., Armenakis, A., Barkauskiene, R., Bozionelos, N., Fujimoto, Y., González, L., Han, J., Hřebíčková, M., Jimmieson, N., Kordačová, J., Mitsuhashi, H., Mlačić, B., Ferić, I., Topić, M. K., Ohly, S., Saksvik, P. Ø., & van Dam, K. (2008). Dispositional resistance to change: Measurement equivalence and the link to personal values across 17 nations. *Journal of Applied Psychology, 93*(4), 935–944. https://doi.org/10.1037/0021-9010.93.4.935
Oreg, S., Vakola, M., & Armenakis, A. (2011). Change recipients' reactions to organizational change: A 60-year review of quantitative studies. *Journal of Applied Behavioral Science, 20*(10), 1–64. https://doi.org/10.1177/0021886310396550
Oreg, S., & Sverdlik, N. (2011). Ambivalence toward imposed change: The conflict between dispositional resistance to change and the orientation toward the change agent. *Journal of Applied Psychology, 96*(2), 337–349. https://doi.org/10.1037/a0021100
Oreg, S., Bartunek, J. M., Lee, G., & Do, B. (2018). An affect-based model of recipients' responses to organizational change events. *Academy of Management Review, 43*(1), 65–86. https://doi.org/10.5465/amr.2014.0335
Piderit, S. K. (2000). Rethinking resistance and recognizing ambivalence: A multidimensional view of attitudes toward an organizational change. *Academy of Management Review, 25*(4), 783–794. https://doi.org/10.5465/amr.2000.3707722
Policarpo, R. V. S., Borges, R. S. G., & Almada, L. (2018). Liderança e reações individuais à mudança organizacional. *Revista Ciências Administrativas, 24*(2), 1–19. https://doi.org/10.5020/2318-0722.2018.7197
Rafferty, A. E., Jimmieson, N. L., & Armenakis, A. A. (2013). Change readiness: A multilevel review. *Journal of Management., 39*(1), 110–135. https://doi.org/10.1177/0149206312457417
Rafferty, A. E., & Jimmieson, N. L. (2017). Subjective perceptions of organizational change and employee resistance to change: Direct and mediated relationships with employee well-being. *British Journal of Management, 28*(2), 248–264. https://doi.org/10.1111/1467-8551.12200
Reichers, A. E., Wanous, J. P., & Austin, J. T. (1997). Understanding and managing cynicism about organizational change. *Academy of Management Executive, 11*(1), 48–59. https://www.jstor.org/stable/4165371
Rothman, N. B., Pratt, M., Rees, L., & Vogus, T. (2017). *Understanding the dual nature of ambivalence: Why and when ambivalence leads to good and bad outcomes.*

Stanley, D. J., Meyer, J. P., & Topolnytsky, L. (2005). Employee cynicism and resistance to organizational change. *Journal of Business Psychology, 19*, 429–459. https://doi.org/10.1007/s10869-005-4518-2

Schwarz, Gavin M., & Bouckenooghe, D. (2017). *A collective action process model for attitudes to organizational change*. Proceedings. https://doi.org/10.5465/AMBPP.2017.332

Tsaousis, I., & Vakola, M. (2018). *Measuring change recipients' reactions: The development and psychometric evaluation of the CRRE scale*. https://doi.org/10.4324/9781315386102.

Thomas, R., & Hardy, C. (2011). Reframing resistance to organizational change. *Scandinavian Journal of Management, 27*(3), 322–331. https://doi.org/10.1016/j.scaman.2011.05.004

Thundiyil, T. G., Chiaburu, D. S., Oh, I. S., Banks, G. C., & Peng, A. C. (2015). Cynical about change? A preliminary meta-analysis and future research agenda. *The Journal of Applied Behavioral Science, 51*, 429–450. https://journals.sagepub.com/doi/10.1177/0021886315603122

Vakola, M., Tsaousis, I., & Nikolaou, I. (2004). The role of emotional intelligence and personality variables on attitudes toward organizational change. *Journal of Managerial Psychology, 19*(1), 88–110. https://doi.org/10.1108/02683940410526082

Vakola, M., & Nikolaou, I. (2005). Attitudes towards organizational change: What is the role of employees' stress and commitment? *Employee Relations, 27*(2), 160–174. https://www.emerald.com/insight/content/doi/10.1108/01425450510572685/full/html

Vakola, M. (2013). Multilevel readiness to organizational change: A conceptual approach. *Journal of Change Management, 13*, 96–109. https://doi.org/10.1080/14697017.2013.768436

Vakola, M., Armenakis, A., & Oreg, S. (2013). Reactions to organizational change from an individual differences perspective: A review of empirical research. In S. Oreg, A. Michel, & R. T. By (Eds.), *The psychology of organizational change: Viewing change from the employee's perspective* (pp. 95–122). Cambridge University Press. https://doi.org/10.1017/CBO9781139096690.008

Vakola, M. (2014). What's in there for me? Individual readiness to change and the perceived impact of organizational change. *Leadership & Organization Development Journal, 35*(3), 195–209. https://doi.org/10.1108/LODJ-05-2012-0064

Vakola, M. (2016). The reasons behind change recipients' behavioral reactions: A longitudinal investigation. *Journal of Managerial Psychology, 31*(1), 202–215. https://doi.org/10.1108/JMP-02-2013-0058

Van Dam, K., Oreg, S., & Schyns, B. (2008). Daily work contexts and resistance to organ- isational change: The role of leader–member exchange, development climate, and change process characteristics. *Applied Psychology, 57*(2), 313–334. https://doi.org/10.1111/j.1464-0597.2007.00311.x

Van Harreveld, F., Van der Pligt, J., & de Liver, Y. N. (2009). The agony of ambivalence and ways to resolve it: Introducing the MAID model. *Personality and Social Psychology Review, 13*(1), 45–61. https://doi.org/10.1177/1088868308324518

Van de Ven, A., & Poole, M. S. (1995). Explaining development and change in organizations. *The Academy of Management Journal, 20*(3), 510–540. https://doi.org/10.2307/258786

Van den Heuvel, S., Freese, C., Schalk, R., & van Assen, M. (2017). How change information influences attitudes toward change and turnover intention: The role of engagement, psychological contract fulfillment, and trust. *Leadership & Organization Development Journal, 38*(3), 398–418. https://doi.org/10.1108/LODJ-03-2015-0052

Wanberg, C. R., & Banas, J. T. (2000). Predictors and outcomes of openness to changes in a reorganizing workplace. *Journal of Applied Psychology, 85*(1), 132–142. https://doi.org/10.1037/0021-9010.85.1.132

Wanous, J. P., Reichers, A. E., & Austin, J. T. (2000). Cynicism about organizational change: Measurement, antecedents, and correlates. *Group Organizacional Management, 25*(2), 132–153. https://doi.org/10.1177/1059601100252003

Wanous, J. P., Reichers, A. E., & Austin, J. T. (2004). Cynicism about organizational change: An attribution process perspective. *Psychological Reports, 94*, 1421–1434. https://doi.org/10.2466/pr0.94.3c.1421-1434

Weiner, B. J., Amick, H., & Lee, S. Y. (2008). Conceptualization and measurement of organizational readiness for change: A review of the literature in health services research and other fields. *Medical care research and review: MCRR, 65*(4), 379–436. https://doi.org/10.1177/1077558708317802

Weiner, B. J., Clary, A. S., Klaman, S. L., Turner, K., & Alishahi-Tabriz, A. (2020). Organizational readiness for change: What we know, what we think we know, and what we need to know. In B. Albers, A. Shlonsky, & R. Mildon (Eds.), *Implementation Science 3.0*. Springer. https://doi.org/10.1007/978-3-030-03874-8_5

Wiltermuth, S. S., & Heath, C. (2009). Synchrony and cooperation. *Psychological Science, 20*(1), 1–5. https://doi.org/10.1111/j.1467-9280.2008.02253.x

Yousef, D. A. (2017). Organizational commitment, job satisfaction and attitudes toward organizational change: A study in the local government. *International Journal of Public Administration, 40*(1), 77–88. https://doi.org/10.1080/01900692.2015.1072217

Yousef, D. A. (2000). Organizational commitment and job satisfaction as predictors of attitudes toward organizational change in a non-western setting. *Personnel Review, 29*, 567–592. http://doi.org/c8r

Chapter 3
Psychological Well-Being at Work Measures

Helenides Mendonça, Bruna Luise Silva, Juliany Gonçalves Guimarães Silva, and Maria Cristina Ferreira

3.1 Introduction

The concept of well-being has been linked to the concept of health, since the World Health Organization, in 1947, defined health as the complete biological, psychological, and social well-being and not as the absence of illness. Thus, a new definition of health was born based on the biopsychosocial model that is structured as a multidimensional concept associated with the well-being experiences (e.g., Keyes, 2005).

Nevertheless, another important milestone in the evolution of the well-being concept has been the advent of positive psychology (Seligman & Csikszentmihalyi, 2000), from which the positive aspects of human experience, as well as the positive psychological states related to such experience's strengths and virtues, have gained prominence in the literature. The emergence of positive psychology, combined with the movement of positive organizational behavior (Luthans, 2002), became the object of study by organizational and work psychologists within the framework in which the actual work relationships change dramatically.

In recent years, researchers have endeavored to condense existing knowledge about psychological well-being (e.g., Fredrickson, 2013; Ryan & Deci, 2001), but the understanding of the concept varies widely (Bartels et al., 2019; Dagenais-Desmarais & Savoie, 2012; Ilies et al., 2015). As a consequence, a wide range of conceptual models emerged simultaneously, often based on theoretical assumptions that were implicit or not verified empirically (Ryan & Deci, 2001). In most cases, it is only by examining the measures chosen in a given study that one can deduce

H. Mendonça (✉) · B. L. Silva · J. G. G. Silva
Pontifical Catholic University of Goiás, Goiânia, GO, Brazil

M. C. Ferreira
Salgado de Oliveira University, Niterói, RJ, Brazil

M. O. Macambira et al. (eds.), *Assessing Organizational Behaviors*,
https://doi.org/10.1007/978-3-030-81311-6_3

which is the concept adopted by the scholars (Diener, 1994; Dagenais-Desmarais & Savoie, 2012). Despite these deficiencies, conceptual proposals on the nature of psychological well-being, in general or in the specific field of work, have been developed around two independent but related research perspectives – hedonic well-being and eudaimonic well-being.

The general purpose of this chapter is to carry out a review and critical analysis of the main measures to obtain psychological well-being at work. To this end, the hedonic and eudaimonic perspectives of well-being and the differences between general well-being and well-being in the workplace context are addressed. Three measures recently developed, addressing the existing gaps in the concept and often in the measurement of the psychological well-being at work (PWBW), are described, and the main measures used in studies on psychological well-being at work published in the last 5 years are critically described.

3.2 Psychological Well-Being: The Hedonic and Eudaimonic Perspectives

Well-being, positive emotions, and happiness have been the object of study since ancient philosophy. In Nicomachean Ethics, Aristóteles (1973) establishes that happiness is the greatest of all human assets that can be obtained based on a virtuous life. Virtue, in turn, is related to the best in each person. In this sense, seeking pleasure and satisfaction of desires emerges as an important condition for obtaining an optimal state of existence and experiencing a healthy and prosperous life. The understanding of this perspective became possible since Epicurus (1997). Taken together, these definitions emerge from the hedonic and eudaimonic philosophical perspectives.

The hedonic perspective, also known as the subjective dimension of well-being, consists of the prevalence of positive emotions over negative ones, and the subjective assessment of life satisfaction or job satisfaction (e.g., Diener, 1984; Diener et al., 2002; Warr, 1990). The main reference in this approach is Ed Diener, who in the 1980s disseminated the use of the term subjective well-being to describe this emerging field of study, using it interchangeably with the term happiness. Well-being, in this perspective, involves high levels of positive affects and low levels of negative affects, as well as the cognitive assessment of satisfaction with one's own life (Diener et al., 1999).

In the wake of the concepts of subjective well-being, considering the hedonic perspective and focusing on the work context, Warr (1990) developed a measure that aggregates the well-being at work affective and cognitive dimensions when considering affects, and personal assessment about positive functioning at work. The author correlates well-being in the workplace with general well-being. Warr's measure is structured in three bipolar axes that present enthusiasm, pleasure, and contentment on one side and anxiety, displeasure, and depression on the other side.

Although this is an important measure, widely used in the workplace and validated in different countries, it covers only the facets of subjective well-being linked to affection and cognition; in this sense, it is incomplete to help understand the complexity of psychological well-being at work.

In a later study, Diener and Biswas-Diener (2008) indicate that the subjective well-being emerges under certain conditions, as in front of positive social relationships but that these conditions alone are not able to lead the individual to well-being and to happiness, bringing the cognitive perspective that involves subjective evaluations related to different domains of life, such as work. The author makes it clear, however, that there is no single or characteristic condition that accounts for the complexity that encompasses well-being as a psychological construct.

Different measures that give access to pleasure and displeasure are described in the literature, and, probably, the one most used is the positive and negative affects scale (PANAS), developed by Watson et al. (1988). When justifying the need to develop a new subjective measure of well-being that includes positive and negative affects, Diener et al. (2009) points out PANAS' severe limitations claiming that this measure has adjectives that are often not related to feelings, both in positive and negative affects. The author adds that the measure includes characteristics such as "strong," "alert," "active," and "determined," which are adjectives and cannot be considered as feelings or affections. These characteristics are motivational states and not necessarily something pleasurable or desirable. For example, a person may be "determined" because of some discontent, anger, or desire for revenge and not because of a feeling of pleasure or some purpose focused on a dimension of positivity. In addition, the PANAS list of negative emotions excludes "sadness" and "depression," for example, which are important feelings to be considered on a scale of negative emotions.

Considering that PANAS presents a restricted definition of positive and negative feelings according to Diener et al. (2009), those authors developed the Scale of Positive and Negative Experience (SPANE), composed of 12 items, 6 of which associated with positive emotions (cheerful, well, pleasant, happy, content, positive) and the other 6 related to negative emotions (furious, bad, unpleasant, sad, afraid, negative). Respondents are asked to answer on a scale of 1 (rarely) to 5 (very often) the frequency with which each of these feelings has been felt. When applied to the work context, the respondent is encouraged to "think about what he has done and experienced in the work environment in recent weeks and tell how often he has experienced each of these feelings."

In seeking to refine the concept of psychological well-being, the hedonic and eudaimonic perspectives have come under severe criticism. Critics of the hedonic perspective consider it to be a limited approach, because it takes into account exclusively well-being in its cognitive and affective aspects (Lent, 2004). Scholars also consider that well-being in a hedonic perspective aims to maximize individual happiness disregarding autonomy, competence, and social affiliation (Ryan & Deci, 2001; Fisher, 2014) or the meaning of life (McGregor & Little, 1998).

Despite advances in research and consensus that both perspectives are important for understanding the general well-being of the individuals, the debate on the well-being hedonic and eudaimonic dimensions has not settled. Studies demonstrate, for example, that the hedonic and eudaimonic perspectives are differently related to activities that allow individuals to materialize their potential (Waterman, 1993), with prosocial behaviors (Kiziah, 2003) and with creative performance (Mendonça et al., 2018). While much has been investigated about the hedonic components of well-being at work, such as positive emotions and affections, happiness, and job satisfaction, little is known about the eudaimonic perspective of well-being at work.

When considering that well-being goes beyond positive affects and satisfaction with life, Carol Ryff (1995) dedicates to better understand the eudaimonic perspective of well-being, labeled as psychological well-being. To this end, she seeks to describe a set of experiences, reasons, and modes of operation that are related to a balanced and well-lived life (Ryan et al., 2008). From there arises a model of general psychological well-being, also known as eudaimonic well-being, associated with the purpose and meaning of life, with personal growth and fulfillment, as well as with the development of human potential and its self-determination (Ryff, 1995). This perspective contemplates the individuals' axiological priorities when establishing that the experience of well-being is related to living according to oneself, with own beliefs and values.

The model developed by Ryff (1995) has its theoretical grounds in the social cognitive theory (Bandura, 1986) and in the theory of motivational needs (Maslow, 1968) and is composed of six dimensions: (1) self-acceptance, positive attitude about oneself; (2) positive relationships with others, interpersonal relationships of trust; (3) autonomy, a sense of freedom in connection with social norms; (4) environment mastery, ability to control the environment; (5) purpose in life, sense of purpose, steering, and intentionality; and (6) personal growth, continuous development of human potential. These six dimensions represent the perspective of psychological or eudaimonic well-being. Based on this model and on the theory of self-determination (Ryan & Deci, 2001), Diener et al. (2009) developed a measure of thriving in life composed of eight items that, taken together, express that thriving is achieved when people experience a high degree of purpose, perceive life with a meaning, are optimistic about the future, and have a sense of competence and satisfaction with life itself. This measure was adapted to the workplace context by Mendonça et al. (2014) and will be described in detail in the PWBW measures further in this chapter.

The definitions and the operationalization of psychological well-being are marked by this great conceptual variety, which demonstrates the lack of consensus on the dimensions that constitute it (Diener et al., 2016; der Kinderen & Khapova, 2020). In summary, psychological well-being is defined as a complex multidimensional construct that covers affective, cognitive experiences and satisfaction with life – hedonic perspective – but also encompasses self-acceptance, positive relationships with others, autonomy, environment control, the meaning and purpose of life, as well as personal growth and fulfillment – eudaimonic perspective (Ryff, 1995; Ryan & Deci, 2001; Diener et al., 2009; Fisher, 2014).

Advances in understanding psychological well-being at work were achieved by Keyes (2002, 2005, 2007). He defined well-being in a unified way between positive feelings and positive functioning. Keyes (2005) tested his hypotheses with 3032 middle-class individuals in the United States of America, aged from 25 to 74 years. The author validates a model that includes four variables associated with the integral health of people: (1) positive affects (e.g., happy, calm, at peace, content, tranquil); (2) satisfaction with life (satisfaction with life in general); (3) psychological well-being (self-acceptance, positive relationship with others, personal growth, purpose of life, environmental mastery, and autonomy); (4) social well-being (acceptance, cooperation, coherence, and social integration). The studies developed by Keyes are based on theoretical conceptions that consider happiness as a positive state of mind that involves the experiences of life and, therefore, emerges from the effort of people to maximize pleasure and minimize suffering (Waterman, 1993).

This model includes the dimensions of personal fulfillment, self-actualization, and self-determination in the concept of psychological well-being (Maslow, 1968; Ryan & Deci, 2001). The results of the confirmatory factor analysis demonstrated a better fit when the variables related to mental health and mental illness were reviewed separately, despite the factors being negatively correlated ($r = -.53$). This result demonstrates that the positive and negative factors are not in opposition in a bipolar axis, as previously hypothesized. Based on the results obtained in these studies, Keyes concludes that the hedonic and eudaimonic perspectives are related. However, its integrative proposition has not yet been sufficiently investigated and lacks research that would demonstrate its validity.

Considering that these different approaches can influence attitudes and behaviors in different ways, research that considers hedonic and eudaimonic well-being as interchangeable should consider the risk of being biased, since the levels of happiness or satisfaction with life do not necessarily imply the feeling of being able, competent, and optimistic about the future. Likewise, it does not necessarily mean that this person has environmental mastery. Therefore, the importance of understanding psychological well-being in a specific domain of life, as in the case of the workplace, is emphasized.

3.3 Psychological Well-Being at Work (PWBW) Model: Adapted by Mendonça et al. (2014)

Psychological well-being may vary depending on the context and on the different situations experienced. Studies show that there is a moderate to strong link between general psychological well-being and psychological well-being in specific life domains, such as work (Warr, 1990; Diener, 1994; Mendonça et al., 2014).

PWBW, with its specific characteristics, is a potentially powerful tool for the optimal performance of individuals and organizations. At the individual level, workers with a higher level of psychological well-being demonstrate better performance at work, are more creative, and are more likely to exhibit prosocial behaviors (Lyubomirsky et al., 2005b). At the organizational level, meta-analysis studies have shown that optimal employee's mental health leads to increased organizational performance, greater customer satisfaction, improved employee retention, as well as more financial benefits (Harter et al., 2002; Lyubomirsky et al., 2005a). The first PWBW models found in the literature integrate positive and negative components associated with affections and satisfactions in life in general. As an example, in the model by Danna and Griffin (1999), physical and psychological symptoms associated with work (attachment and job satisfaction) are used, as well as general experience in life. Subsequently, Daniels (2000) is based on Warr's model (1990) to conceptualize PWBW in affective terms and defines it as a construct composed of five bipolar axes: anxiety, comfort; depression, pleasure; boredom, enthusiasm; tiredness, vigor; and anger, placidity. The heuristic model of organizational health developed by Cotton and Hart (2003), on the other hand, includes an axiological dimension, and emotional states arising from excessive stress, as well as the personal assessment made in relation to the work experience. In general, as shown by Dagenais et al. (2008), the authors define psychological well-being at work as a combination of morale, distress, and job satisfaction.

Later studies have sought to integrate the hedonic and eudaimonic perspectives of well-being, covering subjective, emotional, and psychological aspects related to PWBW. For example, for Medzo-M'Engone and Sima (2021), psychological well-being at work does not reflect the reality itself, but rather elements perceived by the worker and which are associated with the reality of the work context. These elements include worker-perceived autonomy, meaning, workload, feeling of capacity, opportunities, cooperation between colleagues, social recognition, among others.

The lack of consensus on well-being definition has given rise to competing models, many of which do not present their reference theory, so that the conceptual basis on which they are grounded can be deduced by examining the measures chosen by the researchers. While investigations on the hedonic components of well-being at work are advanced, specifically with what concerns positive emotions and job satisfaction, little is known about eudaimonic well-being, its dimensions and its influence on workers' attitudes and behaviors, as well as on organizational effectiveness (der Kinderen & Khapova, 2020).

Thus, in view of the enormous range of measures being used to operationalize psychological well-being at work and the priority focus of studies being on the hedonic perspective, this chapter will highlight three eudaimonic measures. The choice of these measures was made because they were developed based on theoretical models widely disseminated in the specialized literature (Ryff, 1995; Diener et al., 2009), in addition to the methodological consistency used in their development. They include thriving scale developed by Diener et al. (2010) adapted to the work context by Mendonça et al. (2014), the psychological work well-being index developed by Dagenais-Desmarais and Savoie (2012), and, subsequently, the eudaimonic well-being scale developed by Bartels et al. (2019). These measures were developed in order to fill the gaps observed in previous studies, and, despite exhibiting differences in their structure and conceptual basis, they have in common the focus on the work context and the definition of psychological well-being at work as being the assessment that the worker has on his ability to achieve optimal functioning at work. These three approaches to psychological well-being at work will be discussed below, as well as their psychometric characteristics.

3.4 Thriving-at-Work Scale (TAWS): An Integrated Perspective of Psychological Well-Being at Work

Thriving at work was initially understood as linked to experience of vigor, enthusiasm, and learning (Spreitzer et al., 2005). Later studies claim that this perspective is incomplete and suggest that thriving is also related to prosperity, happiness, engagement, self-motivation, and success (Bono et al., 2011).

In the search for the development of a new psychological well-being measure that includes the eudaimonic perspective and not just the hedonic one, at the same time that it answered criticisms related to its subjective well-being model, Diener et al. (2009) developed a thriving measure. Humanistic theories about universal human needs and the optimal functioning of people are the theoretical grounds that materialized this model. It is a short measure, developed using the deductive method (top down) and is composed of eight items.

According to Diener et al. (2009), each of the proposed items was based on specific theoretical concepts developed by important authors in this field of knowledge, namely, meaning and purpose of life (Ryff, 1995; Seligman, 2008), support and reward relationships (Ryff, 1995; Ryan & Deci, 2000), engagement and interest (Csikszentmihalyi, 1990; Ryff, 1995; Seligman, 2008), contributing to the well-being of others (Maslow, 1968; Ryff, 1995; Ryan & Deci, 2000), feeling of competence (Ryff, 1995; Ryan & Deci, 2000), self-acceptance (Maslow, 1968; Ryff, 1995), optimism (Seligman, 2008), and being respected (Maslow, 1968; Ryff, 1995). In summary, thriving is achieved when people experience a high degree of purpose, meaning, optimism, competence, and satisfaction with their own life (Diener et al., 2009, 2010).

The thriving measure developed by Diener et al. (2009) has been adapted and validated for the workplace context by Mendonça et al. (2014), who consider thriving at work to be a perspective of psychological well-being related to the self-image that the worker has regarding his/her skills, involvement, and contribution to the development of work activities. The measure encompasses the feeling of being respected for the activity developed and the perception that his/her work helps the worker be a better person and have a satisfactory life. Well-being in this perspective also involves interpersonal relationships with colleagues, professional competence, and optimism about the professional future. This measure, initially applied to a sample of 536 workers, is unifactorial and consists of 8 items that encompass the positive functioning of the worker. The results of the factor analysis indicated a unifactorial structure, with factor loads ranging from .40 to .75, explaining 50.54%

of the total variance of the responses and Cronbach's alpha coefficient of .85. The thriving at work scale (TAWS) has been used in several studies and is associated with dispositional forgiveness of others and emotional support (Chaves et al., 2019), used as a mediator in the relationship between mindfulness and creativity (Mendonça et al., 2018), correlated with perceptions of justice in a context of change (Nery et al., 2016), among others. In all of these studies, TAWS is used to operationalize psychological well-being at work.

3.5 Index of Psychological Well-Being at Work (IPWBW): The Model Developed by Dagenais-Desmarais and Savoie (2012)

Dagenais-Desmarais and Savoie (2012) argue that among the different domains of life, the context of work has very specific characteristics and distinct from any other, be it in hierarchical relationships, or in the interpersonal relationship established with colleagues, in the capacity that the worker believes he has to develop his work well or even in his involvement with work. Thus, using an inductive and ethno-semantic methodology, they performed a survey in which the participants were asked to report incidents that caused them to experience well-being at work, according to the following instruction: "Describe a recent situation in which you experienced psychological well-being at work." After submitting the responses to analysis regarding their content, the authors reached 80 manifestations of PWBW, from which they worked on a bottom-up approach and arrived at a measurement instrument composed of 25 items, which was applied to 1080 workers from different organizations in context-free psychological well-being measures such as distress, positive and negative affects, and life satisfaction. The 25 items were structured in 5 dimensions, each consisting of 5 items. The first dimension is interpersonal fit at work and is associated with the employee's perception that he/she is experiencing positive relationships with colleagues and interacting in the work context. An example of an item in this dimension is: "I value the people I work with." The second dimension is thriving at work – it is associated with the perception that the person is doing a job that allows him/her a sense of fulfillment as a person. An example is the item: "I find meaning in my work." The third dimension is feeling of competency – this dimension is associated with the perception that you have the necessary skills to do your job efficiently and master the tasks to be performed. An example of an item of this dimension is: "I know that I am capable of doing my job." The fourth dimension is perceived recognition at work – this dimension is associated with the perception of being valued in the organization for your work and personality. An example of an item in this dimension is: "I feel that my work is recognized." The fifth dimension is the desire for involvement at work – it is associated with being involved with the organization and contributing to its smooth functioning and success. An example of an item in this dimension is: "I want to take the initiative in my

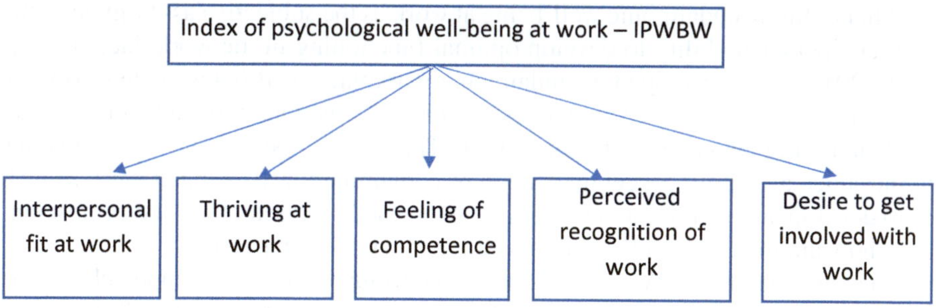

Source: Figure constructed by the authors of this chapter based on the model developed by Dagenais-Desmarais and Savoie (2012).

Fig. 3.1 IPWBW graphical representation. (Source: Figure constructed by the authors of this chapter based on the model developed by Dagenais-Desmarais and Savoie (2012)

work." These dimensions can be grouped into a single second-order factor (see graphical representation of the model in Fig. 3.1).

The IPWBW presented adequate adjustment indices in the confirmatory factor analysis (CFA) for the model with the five dimensions ($\chi 2 = 1982.354$; CFI = .906; RMSEA = .077 [low CI = .074; high CI = .080]; SRMSR = .0628), as well as strong internal consistency in the general factor ($\alpha = .964$). At the level of dimensions, the Cronbach Alphas ranged from .920 to .833.

The model developed by Dagenais-Desmarais and Savoie (2012) is promising, since in addition to be structured as theoretically predicted and having good psychometric indices, it presents an integrated perspective, besides having been validated in India (Medzo-M'engone & Sima, 2020) and Gabon (Medzo-M'Engone & Sima, 2021), and the validation of the measure in Brazil is in an advanced process phase. Another characteristic of IPWBW is the fact that it considers psychological well-being at work not only as a trait but also as a transitory state, which is influenced by socio-organizational dynamics and interpersonal relationships faced in the work context.

3.6 Eudaimonic Workplace Well-Being Scale (EWWS): The Model Proposed by Bartels et al. (2019)

Bartels et al. (2019) argue that the eudaimonic perspective, when considering the optimal functioning of individuals and their personal growth, is related to the activities they perform and to authentic mental states, based on deeply held beliefs and values. For these authors, the hedonic perspective is not sufficient to cover the complexity of the psychological well-being in the workplace construct, being restricted to the subjective aspects of well-being. Another argument used to justify the study is the fact that although research on eudaimonic well-being is moving swiftly, the focus is not on the specific context of work.

After defining eudaimonic well-being at work as the subjective assessment of the worker's personal ability to develop optimal functioning in the workplace, Bartels et al. (2019) have developed an eudaimonic workplace well-being scale (EWWS). This optimal functioning encompasses two dimensions: interpersonal well-being at work and intrapersonal well-being at work. The authors specify that the study aims to introduce a specific conceptualization of eudaimonic well-being at work as well as to develop and validate a new measure to be used by researchers and professionals who want to access well-being beyond the hedonic perspective.

The items on the EWWS scale were created using the deductive approach and the analysis of judges. To that effect, constructs associated with general well-being and those similar to eudaimonic well-being were considered, namely, subjective well-being, psychological well-being, burnout, irritation, self-assessment of anxiety, vitality, focus on job promotions, engagement, belonging, trust, communion with others, perception of kindness in others, and social integration. The items listed were adapted to the work context and subsequently underwent an assessment by a wellness expert to categorize them into the intrapersonal (25 items) and interpersonal (11 items) dimensions. The intrapersonal dimension includes items with a focus on energy, purpose, growth, and ability to contribute to the work environment. An example of an item of this dimension is: "I feel that I have a purpose in my work." The items in the interpersonal dimension are focused on comfort, the ability to have reciprocity and establish relationships with co-workers. An example of an item of this dimension is: "Among the people I work with, I feel that there is a sense of brotherhood" (see Fig. 3.2).

The content validation of the EWWS was carried out with 44 judges, and the questionnaire was further applied to 120 MBA students. The factor analysis resulted in 8 retained items, 4 for each of the dimensions – intrapersonal and interpersonal. To test the 8-item measure, the study included 5 different samples, totaling 1226 participants. The final EWWS convergent, discriminant, and predictive validation study included measures of psychological well-being, work engagement, life satisfaction, social fragility, leader-member exchange, creativity, turnover intention, absenteeism, job satisfaction, behavior organizational citizenship, and popularity scale. Confirmatory factor analyses were applied to all seven samples included in the

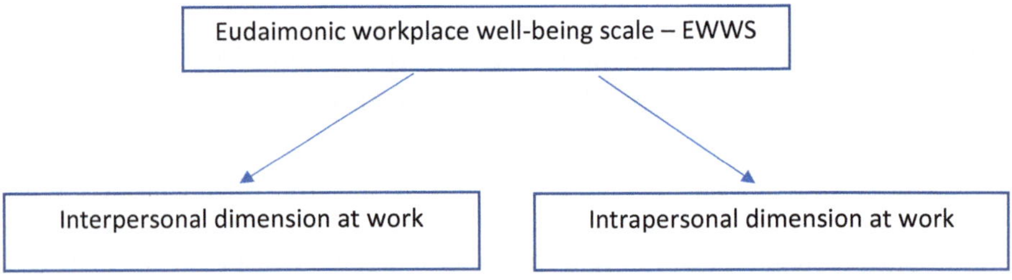

Source: Figure constructed by the authors of this chapter based on the model developed by Bartels et al. (2019)

Fig. 3.2 Graphical representation of the eudaimonic well-being scale at work. (Source: Figure constructed by the authors of this chapter based on the model developed by Bartels et al. (2019))

study, showing good fit rates for the hypothetical model that eudaimonic well-being at work is a latent construct of a higher order composed of two first-order factors – intrapersonal and interpersonal. The adjustment indices of the two-factor model were adequate for all samples, with CFI ranging from .96 to .99 and SRMR ranging from .025 to .077. The authors also tested a three-dimensional model by including job satisfaction, a subjective measure from a hedonic perspective. The three-dimensional model had a better fit than the two-dimensional model, which led the authors to conclude that a more complete photograph of psychological well-being at work involves the combination of the hedonic and eudaimonic perspectives.

The reliability coefficients, measured by the Cronbach's alpha, ranged from .54 to .86 for the interpersonal dimension and from .70 to .96 for the intrapersonal dimension of eudaimonic well-being at work. The convergent and discriminant validity of the measure was proven by correlating the EWWS with general psychological well-being ($r = .44$, $p \leq .01$), employee engagement ($r = .49$, $p \leq .01$), satisfaction with life ($r = .49$, $p \leq .01$), social weakening ($r = -.32$, $p \leq .01$), and leader-member exchange ($r = .49$, $p \leq .01$). Among the measures used to achieve competing and discriminating validity, only engagement and leader-member exchange are measures related to the work environment. The measures of psychological well-being, social weakening, and satisfaction with life are general measures, free from any specific context, such as work. Predictive validity was analyzed by the impact of EWWS on creativity (significant and positive relationship), turnover (significant and negative relationship), and absenteeism (no significant relationship).

This study shed light on the importance of adding interpersonal aspects to well-being at work, besides emphasizing that well-being extends beyond the affective dimension, but that job satisfaction must be considered. One aspect to note, however, is the fact that the authors use the terms eudaimonic well-being and psychological well-being as synonyms. In fact, previous studies have established that the hedonic perspective of well-being is called subjective well-being (Diener, 1994) and the eudaimonic perspective psychological well-being (Ryff, 1995).

3.7 Similarities and Differences Between TAWS, IPWBW, and EWWS

The detailed description of the three measures of psychological well-being at work highlighted the conceptual and methodological similarities and differences between them. The first aspect to be considered is that the TAWS and the EWWS were developed using the deductive methodology (top-down), so that the items were raised from the reference theories. On the other hand, the items of the IPWBW were developed in an inductive perspective (bottom-up), starting from the experience of the workers themselves on the psychological well-being experienced in the workplace environment, to further arrive at the constitutive and operational definitions. When reviewing the items and dimensions of each of these measures, it can be seen that despite having used different methodologies, they are anchored on the same theoretical bases, as shown in Table 3.1.

Table 3.1 PWBW measurements analyzed, dimensions investigated, and theoretical reference bases for each of the measurement items

	Measures reviewed and number of items that cover each PWBW aspect			
Aspects of *psychological well-being at work* covered in the three measures analyzed	*Thriving at work* Unifactorial – 8 items	*Index of psychological well-being at work* Five factors – 25 items Each factor composed of 5 items	*Eudaimonic workplace well-being* Bifactorial – 8 items Each of the factors composed of 4 items	Ryff (1995), Diener et al. (2009, 2010), Dagenais-Desmarais and Savoie (2012), and Bartels et al. (2019)
1. Meaning and purpose	1 item	5 items that make up the *thriving at work* factor	2 items that make up the *intrapersonal dimension*	Ryff (1995) and Seligman (2008).
2. Supporting and reward interpersonal relationship	1 item	5 items that make up the *interpersonal fit at work* dimension	4 items that make up the *interpersonal dimension*	Ryff (1995) and Ryan and Deci (2000)
3. Involvement, engagement, Vigor, and energy at work	1 item	5 items that make up the *desire to be involved in work* dimension	1 item that make up the *intrapersonal dimension*	Ryff (1995), Csikszentmihalyi (1990), and Schaufeli and Bakker (2004)
4. Contribute to the welfare of others	1 item	Aspect not covered	Aspect not covered	Ryff (1995), Maslow (1968), and Ryan and Deci (2000)
5. Sense of competence	1 item	5 items that make up the *feeling of competence at work*	Aspect not covered	Ryff (1995) and Ryan and Deci (2000)
6. Growth as a person	1 item	Aspect not covered	1 item that makes up the *intrapersonal dimension*	Ryff (1995) and Maslow (1968)
7. Be respected and considered	1 item	5 items that make up the *perceived recognition at work* dimension	Aspect not covered	Ryff (1995) and Maslow (1968)
8. Optimism	1 item	Aspect not covered	Aspect not covered	Seligman (2008) and Diener et al. (2009)

Source: Table built by the authors of this chapter

The first aspect that stands out in the analysis of the measures described is that the measures items are included in the theory of Carol Ryff (1995), having emerged from the theories, as in the case of TAWS and EWWS, or from the experiences of workers, as in the case of IPWBW. In addition, in terms of theoretical basis, some measurement items are based on the theory of basic human needs (Maslow, 1968), on conceptions of positive psychology (Csikszentmihalyi, 1990; Seligman, 2008), on the subjective perspectives of psychological well-being (Diener et al., 2009) and in the theory of self-determination (Ryan & Deci, 2000).

Among the three studies analyzed, the IPWBW is the only model of psychological well-being that was developed using the inductive approach to reflect the subjective experience of workers about psychological well-being at work. The results obtained constituted innovative contributions in the theoretical and methodological field for the specialized literature; however, the model does not capture the hedonic aspects of psychological well-being at work.

According to Dagenais-Desmarais and Savoie (2012), psychological well-being at work must be conceptualized based on a specific model that considers the work context since, despite the similarities, there are differences in relation to well-being in specific and general contexts. When advancing in studies on well-being, Diener (1994) stated in this regard that well-being can vary depending on the specific domain of life in which it is investigated. Thus, considering the fact that in an organizational context it is intended to analyze and predict variables related to the organizational environment and the behavior of workers, the measures of psychological well-being at work must also be specific to this domain.

3.8 Psychological Well-Being at Work: A Phenomenon with Multiple Measures

The main criticism related to studies on psychological well-being at work is that the variables have been studied in different ways, using different measures and, many times, without the authors clarifying the theoretical basis used (Dagenais-Desmarais et al., 2018). Thus, in order to better understand how this construct has been operationalized in scientific articles, a literature review was carried out in order to identify the main measures of psychological well-being at work used in the last 5 years.

The articles were extracted simultaneously by two investigators, with access to several databases (see Appendix), through the Brazilian virtual library "Portal of the Coordination for the Improvement of Higher Education Personnel Journals" – CAPES. The keywords used were "*eudaimonic workplace well-being*" in the "any" field, the Boolean operator "OR," and again in the "any" field "*hedonic workplace well-being*," the Boolean operator "OR," followed by the keyword "*well-being at work*."

The search included empirical and peer-reviewed articles, published in the English language from 2016 to 2021, refined according to the topics *well-being at work* and *well-being*, totaling 91 articles. Articles indicating that instruments to measure the construct were not used were excluded. Based on abstracts review, ten articles that were in other languages were excluded as well as 06 articles that did not refer to the search topic, 05 because they were literature reviews or theoretical articles, 04 because they did not use welfare measures, and 03 because they were duplicate articles. Finally, 63 articles were selected for full reading and review. The results were summarized considering the theoretical perspectives used about well-being at work and the measures used, in addition to descriptive data, such as year of publication, country, sample group, journal, and databases.

Among the 63 articles reviewed, 58 different measures of well-being at work were identified, which demonstrate that there is a wide variety of instruments used to operationalize the construct. In addition, some studies have presented new measures (Barbieri et al., 2019; Nery et al., 2019; Nislin et al., 2016; Olawale et al., 2017; Steffgen et al., 2020) and seven of them accessed the construct by means of a single question to be answered on a five-point Likert scale (1 = little; 5 = a lot). Table 3.2 shows the number of times that each measure of psychological well-being at work was used in scientific articles, identifying the measure and the referenced source by the author.

Taken together, these studies demonstrate that PWBW conceptions encompass negative dimensions such as worker's fatigue, stress, burnout syndrome, anxiety traits, and suicidal ideas; dimensions with focus on organizational identity and on the vigor and meaning of work, such as commitment and engagement at work; and positive dimensions such as indices of ability to work, affections, emotions, and satisfaction with life. Some studies used integrated perspectives of psychological well-being at work, through measures that include hedonic and eudaimonic well-being at work or context-free (Dose et al., 2019; Sandilya & Shahnawaz, 2018; Van Rensburg et al., 2017); there are also those studies that selected more than one measure of well-being to assess both aspects of psychological well-being – hedonic and eudaimonic (Puigmitja et al., 2019; Turban & Yan, 2016).

The diversity of measures used in the investigations is associated with a variety of conceptions about psychological well-being at work and with the lack of consensus on their dimensions and theoretical guiding concepts. With regard to the theoretical scope that anchors the conceptual bases on well-being, it is noteworthy that not all studies have brought clear definitions about the psychological well-being at work construct, having the same been evaluated through context-free measures or single-item questions (Buruck et al., 2016; Haapakangas et al., 2018; McCunn & Frey, 2020; Platsidou & Agaliotis, 2017). The review of the theoretical construct underlying the measures used in the articles surveyed confirms the conceptual multiplicity in the operationalization of PWBW, as can be seen in Table 3.3.

In the studies surveyed, there is a prevalence of research that uses the hedonic perspective of well-being (positive affects and satisfaction with life), although measures that are context-free are often used. The view of psychological well-being at work conceived from the relationship between engagement and burnout (Schaufeli & Bakker, 2004) has also been widespread, especially in European studies, demonstrating focus on eudaimonic well-being. There is also a considerable percentage of

Table 3.2 Measures used to operationalize psychological well-being at work, their references, and the number of studies that used them

N	Measure used to operationalize the PWBW	References	Frequency
1	UWES-9	Schaufeli et al. (2006)	11
2	Maslach Burnout Inventory	Maslach and Jackson (1981) and Maslach et al. (1996)	7
3	PANAS	Watson et al. (1988)	4
4	Satisfaction with Life Scale	Diener et al. (1985)	3
5	Copenhagen Psychosocial Questionnaire II	Pejtersen et al. (2010)	3
6	PERMA Scale	Kern et al. (2014)	2
7	Four items each drawn from the circumplex model	Feldman Barrett and Russell (1998)	2
8	Scale of psychological well-being	Ryff (1989)	2
9	Index of Psychological Well-Being at Work (IPWBW)	Dagenais-Desmarais and Savoie (2012)	2
10	Psychosomatic complaints scale	Spector and Jex (1998)	2
11	Job satisfaction	Brayfield and Rothe's (1951)	2
12	Job-related well-being measure	Warr (1990)	2
13	Well-being at work scale	Paschoal and Tamayo (2008)	1
14	WHO-Five	Bech et al. (2003)	2
15	Tokyo Occupational Mental Health well-being scale	Komase et al. (2020)	2
16	SPANE Scales	Diener et al. (2010)	1
17	Elevation and Moral Virtue M. B. Oliver et al. openness to change (e.g., an exciting life). In line with Haidt's (2003) notion that elevation results from witnessing moral excellence, altruistic values resembled the idea of moral human virtues most closely because they were inherently linked to interpersonal and, thus, truly moral behavior. Elevation and Moral Virtue M. B. Oliver et al. openness to change (e.g., an exciting life). In line with Haidt's (2003) notion that elevation results from witnessing moral excellence, altruistic values resembled the idea of moral human virtues most closely because they were inherently linked to interpersonal and, thus, truly moral behavior. Affective responses indicative of elevation	Oliver et al. (2012)	1
18	Affect checklist	Kessler and Staudinger's (2009)	1
19	Well-Being at Work Scale	Demo and Paschoal (2013)	
20	PERMA scale	Positive Psychology Center (2013)	1

(continued)

Table 3.2 (continued)

N	Measure used to operationalize the PWBW	References	Frequency
21	The relatedness subscale from the basic psychological needs at work scale	Baard et al. (2004)	1
22	The Shirom-Melamed Burnout Measure (SMBM)	Shirom and Melamed (2006)	1
23	The tiredness subscale of the Activation-Deactivation-Checklist	Thayer (1989)	1
24	Job-Related Affective Well-being scale	Katwyk et al. (2000) and Basińska et al. (2014)	1
25	Subjective Happiness Scale	Lyubomirsky and Lepper (1999)	1
26	Hedonia measure	Waterman (1993) and Huta and Ryan (2010)	1
27	Flourishing (Thriving) Scale	Diener et al.'s (2010)	1
28	Inventory of Job-Related Stress Factors (IJRSF)	Platsidou and Agaliotis (2008)	1
29	The Work and Meaning Inventory (WAMI)	Steger et al. (2012)	1
30	Appreciative Management Scale	Harmoinen (2014)	1
31	Work Values Survey and one item from	Cable and Edwards's (2004)	1
32	Task significance scale	Hackman and Oldham's (1976)	1
33	4 Dimension Mood Scale	Gregg and Shepherd (2009)	1
34	Employee well-being (Workaholism and Burnout items)	Hakanen et al. (2018)	1
35	Job satisfaction	Farrell and Rusbult (1981)	1
36	Flourishing (Thriving) index	VanderWeele (2017)	1
37	General Health Questionnaire	Mullola et al. (2019)	1
38	Jenkins' Sleep Problems Scale and Suicidal Ideation	Jenkins et al. (1988)	1
39	Psychological symptoms scale	Lehto and Sutela (2008)	1
40	Subjective vitality scale	Ryan and Frederick's (1997)	1
41	The "engagement" questionnaire	May et al. (2004)	1
42	The Brief Index of Affective Job Satisfaction-Spanish version (BIAJS)	Fernández-Muñoz and Topa (2018)	1
43	The Daniels five-factor measure of affective well-being (D-FAW)	Daniels (2000)	1
44	The Educational Flow questionnaire (EduFlow)	Heutte et al. (2016)	1
45	The employee's well-being scale	Zheng et al. (2015)	1
46	The Flourishing-at-Work Scale (FAWS)	Rautenbach (2015)	1
47	The Organizational Commitment Questionnaire (OCQ)	Mowday et al. (1979)	1

(continued)

Table 3.2 (continued)

N	Measure used to operationalize the PWBW	References	Frequency
48	The short (6-item) Spielberger State-Trait Anxiety Inventory	Marteau and Bekker (1992)	1
49	The work and meaning inventory	Steger et al. (2012)	1
50	Work Ability Index	El Fassi et al. (2013)	1
51	Work Exhaustion (burnout)	Wharton (1993)	1
52	Related Job Satisfaction	Nislin et al. (2016)	1
53	Questions relating to the ability of the subjects to handle day-to-day demands and stress	Olawale et al. (2017)	1
54	One-factor instrument designed according to information from the work	Van Horn et al. (2004) and Nery et al. (2019)	1
55	SATJOB. Satisfaction with the current job environment and SATTEACH. Satisfaction with teaching profession	Barbieri et al. (2019)	1
56	Three-item work satisfaction scale	Steffgen et al. (2020)	1
57	Occupational Satisfaction Scale (SOS); The Scale of Involvement with Work (SIW); Affective Organizational Engagement Scale (SAOE),	Polizzi and Claro (2019)	1
58	Measure of somatic symptoms	Adapted from Derogatis et al. (1974)	1
59	Single-item measurements (satisfaction, well-being, exhaustion)	Craig and Kuykendall (2019), Framke et al. (2016), Gil-Beltrán et al. (2020), Haapakangas et al. (2018), Jonsdottir et al. (2020), Lloren and Parini (2017), and McCunn and Frey (2020)	07

Table 3.3 Different perspectives of well-being presented in the studies

Theoretical construct used in PWBW measurements	%
Hedonic well-being	22%
Engagement/burnout	18%
Eudaimonic well-being	17%
Stress/health impairment	17%
Job satisfaction	13%
Work well-being	8%
PERMA model	3%
Positive energy	1%
Mental well-being	1%
General well-being	1%

studies (17%) that consider the negative results of well-being at work, such as stress or damage to the worker's health, disregarding the positive dimensions of work in the constitution of the PWBW.

Therefore, these studies demonstrate that the lack of conceptual theoretical consensus has given rise to competing models on psychological well-being at work, and many of them do not present their reference theory, making it often necessary to deduce what is the conceptual basis used by examining the measures chosen by the researchers.

3.9 Final Considerations

In this chapter, we carried out a review and critical analysis of the main measures of psychological well-being at work; we discussed the conceptual differences in the hedonic and eudaimonic perspectives of well-being and characterized the specifics of psychological well-being at work in relation to the general well-being. Free of context, three well-being measures developed recently were described. These measures were compared in theoretical and methodological perspectives, and a critical review was drawn of the multiplicity of measures used in the literature to operationalize psychological well-being at work.

In this connection, it was possible to observe that the studies that analyze the impact of psychological well-being at work, for the most part, do not use measures that have a specific conceptual structure for the work context, besides presenting serious limitations in the theoretical and methodological field. For example, many studies focus on only one facet of psychological well-being at work and do not use a measure adapted to the specific work situation. By using measures of well-being out of the specific context, they establish that well-being is a stable trait in all domains of life (e.g., Dagenais-Desmarais et al., 2018), which constitutes an issue. Another aspect to be considered is that most studies focus essentially on the hedonic components of psychological well-being at work, in addition to those that access well-being through variables such as stress, burnout, and engagement. In addition, the same richness of research is not observed when it comes to eudaimonic well-being at work.

In view of the important benefits for both organizations and individuals, it is crucial that further studies carry out a theoretical cleanup in order to refine the concept of psychological well-being at work and avoid bias in research and in understanding what this construct is. The use of different theoretical perspectives in the operationalization of the construct may give the impression that well-being is everything and at the same time nothing, since multiple and even inconsistent definitions lead to conceptual uncertainty and to the risk of inducing investigators and professionals to serious errors in the investigation and practical intervention processes.

To better illustrate this point, one of the measures widely used to operationalize psychological well-being at work has been engagement (17% among the studies reviewed). However, it seems to be incomplete to conceive both psychological well-being at work exclusively from the perspective of affections and satisfaction and from the perspective of engagement and burnout. For example, highly engaged people may be sick and be present in the workplace precisely because they are engaged (see Watanabe & Yamauchi, 2018). Thus, engagement does not seem to be synonymous of psychological well-being at work, as highly engaged people tend to be present and work even if they feel sick. It should be noted that the actual concept of general health has also been used as an indicator of well-being at work. Given the above, it seems to be reckless to operationalize psychological well-being at work without a clear conceptual background about its hedonic and eudaimonic dimensions, without considering the context in which it emerges, and without knowing how this construct influences attitudes and behaviors in the workplace. Thus, the analysis of the measures used to evaluate the PWBW, combined with the understanding of their psychometric characteristics, their heuristic power, as well as their antecedents and consequences, should be encouraged.

The literature review of this chapter shows that research on the hedonic components of well-being at work is advanced, specifically in the form of positive emotions and job satisfaction. However, in a study by Dagenais-Demarais (2012), it was evident that the hedonic components of psychological well-being did not emerge when using the bottom-up methodological perspective to access the construct. This empirical evidence is important, but it is suggested that studies be conducted in other sample groups that start from the workers' well-being experience.

Despite little knowledge being available about eudaimonic well-being, its dimensions and its influences on workers' attitudes and behaviors, as well as organizational effectiveness (der Kinderen & Khapova, 2020), this perspective seems to be useful for managers in the sense that it gives direction to the development of intervention programs focusing on the workers' well-being and health.

In summary, the literature in the field of psychological well-being at work, specifically with regard to the measures used for the operationalization of the construct, highlights the need to advance in its theoretical and methodological aspects, corroborating toward the understanding of what psychological well-being at work represents.

References

Aristóteles. (1973). Ética a Nicômaco. Tradução de Leonel Vallandro e Gerd Bornheim da versão inglesa de W. D. Ross. In *Os Pensadores* (v. 4). Nova Cultural.

Baard, P. P., Deci, E. L., & Ryan, R. M. (2004). Intrinsic need satisfaction: A motivational basis of performance and wellbeing in two work settings. *Journal of Applied Social Psychology, 34*(10), 2045–2068.

Bandura, A. (1986). *Social foundations of thought and action: A social cognitive theory.* Prentice-Hall.

Barbieri, B., Sulis, I., Porcu, M., & Toland, M. D. (2019). Italian teachers' well-being within the high school context: Evidence from a large scale survey. *Frontiers in Psychology, 10*, 1926. https://doi.org/10.3389/fpsyg.2019.01926

Bartels, A. L., Peterson, S. J., & Reina, C. S. (2019). Understanding wellbeing at work: Development and validation of the eudaimonic workplace well-being scale. *PLoS One, 14*(4), e0215957. https://doi.org/10.1371/journal.pone.0215957

Basińska, B. A., Gruszczyńska, E., & Schaufeli, W. B. (2014, December). Psychometric properties of the polish version of the Job-related Affective Well-being Scale. *International Journal of Occupational Medicine and Environmental Health, 27*(6), 993–1004. https://doi.org/10.2478/s13382-014-0329-x

Bech, P., Olsen, L. R., Kjoller, M., & Rasmussen, N. K. (2003). Measuring well-being rather than the absence of distress symptoms: A comparison of the SF-36 mental health subscale and the WHO-five well-being scale. *International Journal of Methods in Psychiatric Research, 12*, 85–91. https://doi.org/10.1002/mpr.145

Bono, J., Davies, S., & Rasch, R. (2011). Some traits associated with flourishing at work. In K. Cameron & G. Spreitzer (Orgs.), *The Oxford handbook of positive organizational scholarship* (pp. 125–137). Oxford University Press. https://doi.org/10.1093/oxfordhb/9780199734610.013.0010

Brayfield, A. H., & Rothe, H. F. (1951). An index of job satisfaction. *Journal of Applied Psychology, 35*(5), 307–311. https://doi.org/10.1037/h0055617

Buruck, G., Dörfel, D., Kugler, J., & Brom, S. S. (2016). Enhancing well-being at work: The role of emotion regulation skills as personal resources. *Journal of Occupational Health Psychology, 21*(4), 480–493. https://doi.org/10.1037/ocp0000023

Cable, D. M., & Edwards, J. R. (2004). Complementary and supplementary fit: A theoretical and empirical integration. *Journal of Applied Psychology, 89*(5), 822–834. https://doi.org/10.1037/0021-9010.89.5.822

Chaves, S. M. D. S., Ferreira, M. C., Pereira, M. M., & Freitas, C. P. P. D. (2019). Florescimento no Trabalho: Impacto do Perdão Disposicional e do Suporte Social Emocional. *Psicologia: Ciência e Profissão, 39*, e184816. Epub July 29, 2019. https://doi.org/10.1590/1982-3703003184816

Cotton, P., & Hart, P. M. (2003). Occupational wellbeing and performance: A review of organisational health research. *Australian Psychologist, 38*(2), 118–127.

Craig, L., & Kuykendall, L. (2019). Examining the role of friendship for employee well-being. *Journal of Vocational Behavior, 115*, 103313. https://doi.org/10.1016/j.jvb.2019.06.001

Csikszentmihalyi, M. (1990). *Flow: The psychology of optimal experience*. Harper & Row.

der Kinderen, S., & Khapova, S. N. (2020). Positive psychological well-being at work: The role of Eudaimonia. In S. Dhiman (Ed.), *The Palgrave handbook of workplace Well-being*. Palgrave Macmillan. https://doi.org/10.1007/978-3-030-02470-3_79-1

Dagenais, S., Caro, J., & Haldeman, S. (2008, January–February). A systematic review of low back pain cost of illness studies in the United States and internationally. *Spine Journal, 8*(1), 8–20. https://doi.org/10.1016/j.spinee.2007.10.005. PMID: 18164449.

Dagenais-Desmarais, V., & Savoie, A. (2012). What is psychological well-being, really? A grassroots approach from the organizational sciences. *Journal of Happiness Studies, 13*, 659–684. https://doi.org/10.1007/s10902-011-9285-3

Dagenais-Desmarais, V., Leclerc, J. S., & Londei-Shortall, J. (2018). The relationship between employee motivation and psychological health at work: A chicken-and-egg situation? *Work & Stress, 32*, 147–167.

Daniels, K. (2000). Measures of five aspects of affective well-being at work. *Human Relations, 53*(2), 275–294.

Danna, K., & Griffin, R. W. (1999). Health and well-being in the workplace: A review and synthesis of the literature. *Journal of Management, 25*(3), 357–384.

Demo, G., & Paschoal, T. (2013). Well-being at work scale: Exploratory and confirmatory validation in the United States comprising affective and cognitive components. *Encontro da ANPAD*. Rio de Janeiro, RJ, Brasil, 37.

Derogatis, L. R., Lipman, R. S., Rickels, K., Uhlenhuth, E. H., & Covi, L. (1974). The Hopkins Symptom Checklist (HSCL): A self-report symptom inventory. *Behavioral Science, 19*(1), 1–15.

Diener, E. (1984). Subjective well-being. *Psychological Bulletin, 95*(3), 542–575.

Diener, E. (1994). Assessing subjective well-being: Progress and opportunities. *Social Indicators Research, 31*, 103–157.
Diener, E., & Biswas-Diener, R. (2008). *Happiness: Unlocking the mysteries of psychological wealth*. Blackwell Publishing.
Diener, E., Emmons, R. A., Larsen, R. J., & Griffin, S. (1985). The satisfaction with life scale. *Journal of Personality Assessment, 49*(1), 71–75. https://doi.org/10.1207/s15327752jpa4901_13
Diener, E., Suh, E. M., Lucas, R. E., & Smith, H. L. (1999). Subjective well-being: Three decades of progress. *Psychological Bulletin, 125*(2), 276–302. https://doi.org/10.1037/0033-2909.125.2.276
Diener, E., Lucas, R. E., & Oishi, S. (2002). Subjective well-being: The science of happiness and life satisfaction. In C. R. Snyder & S. J. Lopez (Eds.), *Handbook of positive psychology* (pp. 463–473). Oxford University Press.
Diener, E., Wirtz, D., Biswas-Diener, R., Tov, W., Kim-Prieto, C., & Choi, D.-w., & Oishi, S. (2009). New measures of well-being. In E. Diener (Ed.), *Assessing well-being: The collected works of Ed Diener, social indicators research series. 39* (pp. 247–266). Springer.
Diener, E., Wirtz, D., Tov, W., Kim-Prieto, C., Choi, D. W., Oishi, S., & Biswas-Diener, R. (2010). New well-being measures: Short scales to assess flourishing and positive and negative feelings. *Social Indicators Research, 97*(2), 143–156.
Diener, E., Heintzelman, S. J., Kushlev, K., Tay, L., Wirtz, D., Lutes, L. D., & Oishi, S. (2016). Findings all psychologists should know from the new science on subjective well being. *Canadian Psychology/Psychologie Canadienne*. Advance online publication. https://doi.org/10.1037/cap0000063
Dose, P. E., Desrumaux, P., Bernaud, J.-L., & Hellemans, C. (2019). What makes happy counselors? From self-esteem and leader-member exchange to well-being at work: The mediating role of need satisfaction. *Europe's Journal of Psychology, 15*(4), 823–842. https://doi.org/10.5964/ejop.v15i4.1881
El Fassi, M., Bocquet, V., Majery, N., Lair, M. L., Couffignal, S., & Mairiaux, P. (2013, April 8). Work ability assessment in a worker population: Comparison and determinants of work ability index and work ability score. *BMC Public Health, 13*, 305. https://doi.org/10.1186/1471-2458-13-305
Epicuro. (1997). *Carta sobre a felicidade* (p. 1997). UNESP.
Farrell, D., & Rusbult, C. E. (1981). Exchange variables as predictors of job satisfaction, job commitment, and turnover: The impact of rewards, costs, alternatives, and investments. *Organizational Behavior & Human Performance, 28*(1), 78–95. https://doi.org/10.1016/0030-5073(81)90016-7
Feldman Barrett, L., & Russell, J. A. (1998). Independence and bipolarity in the structure of current affect. *Journal of Personality and Social Psychology, 74*(4), 967–984. https://doi.org/10.1037/0022-3514.74.4.967
Fernández-Muñoz, J. J., & Topa, G. (2018, June 8). Older workers and affective job satisfaction: Gender invariance in Spain. *Frontiers in Psychology, 9*(930). https://doi.org/10.3389/fpsyg.2018.00930
Fisher, C. D. (2014). Conceptualizing and measuring wellbeing at work. In P. Y. Chen & C. L. Cooper (Eds.), *Wellbeing: A complete reference guide, work and wellbeing* (Vol. III, pp. 9–33). Wiley.
Framke, E., Sørensen, O. H., & Pedersen, J. (2016). Effect of a participatory organizational-level occupational health intervention on job satisfaction, exhaustion and sleep disturbances: Results of a cluster randomized controlled trial. *BMC Public Health, 16*, 1210. https://doi.org/10.1186/s12889-016-3871-6
Fredrickson, B. L. (2013). Updated thinking on positivity ratios. *American Psychologist, 68*(9), 814–822.
Gil-Beltrán, E., Meneghel, I., Llorens, S., & Salanova, M. (2020). Get vigorous with physical exercise and improve your well-being at work! *International Journal of Environmental Research and Public Health, 17*(17), 6384. https://doi.org/10.3390/ijerph17176384

Gregg, V. H., & Shepherd, A. J. (2009). Factor structure of scores on the state version of the four dimension mood scale. *Educational and Psychological Measurement, 69*(1), 146–156. https://doi.org/10.1177/0013164408322002

Haapakangas, A., Hallman, D. M., Mathiassen, S. E., & Jahncke, H. (2018). Self-rated productivity and employee well-being in activity-based offices: The role of environmental perceptions and workspace use. *Building and Environment, 145*, 115–124.

Hackman, J. R., & Oldham, G. R. (1976). Motivation through the design of work: Test of a theory. *Organizational Behavior and Human Performance, 16*, 250–279.

Hakanen, J. J., Peeters, M. C. W., & Schaufeli, W. B. (2018, April). Different types of employee well-being across time and their relationships with job crafting. *Journal of Occupational Health Psychology, 23*(2), 289–301. https://doi.org/10.1037/ocp0000081

Harmoinen, M. (2014). *Arvostava johtaminen terveydenhuollossa [Appreciative management in health care]* (PhD Thesis). University of Tampere, Finland. English abstract. Available at: https://tampub.uta.fi/bitstream/handle/10024/96359/978-951-44-9668-4.pdf?sequence=1

Harter, J. K., Schmidt, F. L., & Hayes, T. L. (2002). Business-unit-level relationship between employee satisfaction, employee engagement, and business outcomes: A meta-analysis. *Journal of Applied Psychology, 87*(2), 268–279.

Heutte, J., Fenouillet, F., Martin-Krumm, C., Boniwell, I., Csikszentmihalyi, M. (2016). Proposal for a conceptual evolution of the flow in education (EduFlow) model. In *8th European conference on positive psychology (ECPP 2016)*, Jun 2016, Angers, France ⟨hal-01470857⟩.

Huta, V., & Ryan, R. M. (2010). Pursuing pleasure or virtue: The differential and overlapping well-being benefits of hedonic and eudaimonic motives. *Journal of Happiness Studies: An Interdisciplinary Forum on Subjective Well-Being, 11*(6), 735–762. https://doi.org/10.1007/s10902-009-9171-4

Haidt, J. (2003). Elevation and the positive psychology of morality. In C. L. M. Keyes & J. Haidt (Eds.), Flourishing: Positive psychology and the life well-lived (pp. 275–289). American Psychological Association.https://doi.org/10.1037/10594-012

Ilies, R., Aw, S. S., & Pluut, H. (2015). Intraindividual models of employee well-being: What have we learned and where do we go from here? *European Journal of Work and Organizational Psychology, 24*(6), 827–838.

Jenkins, C. D., Stanton, B. A., Niemcryk, S. J., & Rose, R. M. (1988). A scale for the estimation of sleep problems in clinical research. *Journal of Clinical Epidemiology, 41*(4), 313–321.

Jonsdottir, I. J., Rafnsdottir, G. L., & Ólafsdóttir, T. (2020). Job strain, gender and well-being at work: A case study of public sector line managers. *International Journal of Workplace Health Management, 13*(4), 445–460. https://doi.org/10.1108/IJWHM-10-2019-0134

Katwyk, V., Paul, T., Fox, S., Spector, P. E., & Kelloway, E. K. (2000). Using the job-related affective well-being scale (JAWS) to investigate affective responses to work stressors. *Psychology Faculty Publications*, 678.

Kern, M. L., Waters, L., White, M., & Adler, A. (2014). Assessing employee wellbeing in schools using a multifaceted approach: Associations with physical health, life satisfaction, and professional thriving. *Psychology, 5*, 500–513. https://doi.org/10.4236/psych.2014.56060

Kessler, E.-M., & Staudinger, U. M. (2009). Affective experience in adulthood and old age: The role of affective arousal and perceived affect regulation. *Psychology and Aging, 24*(2), 349–362. https://doi.org/10.1037/a0015352

Keyes, C. L. M. (2002). The mental health continuum: From languishing to flourishing in life. *Journal of Health and Social Behavior, 43*, 207–222. https://doi.org/10.2307/3090197

Keyes, C. L. M. (2005). Mental illness and/or mental health? Investigating axioms of the complete state model of health. *Journal of Consulting and Clinical Psychology, 73*, 539–548. https://doi.org/10.1037/0022-006X.73.3.539

Keyes, C. L. M. (2007). Promoting and protecting mental health as flourishing: A complementary strategy for improving national mental health. *American Psychologist, 62*(2), 95–108. https://doi.org/10.1037/0003-066X.62.2.95

Kiziah, J. E. (2003). Job satisfation vs. work fulfillment: Exploring positive experience at work. *Dissertation Abstracts International, 64*(10), 5261. (UMI n. 3107643).
Komase, Y., Watanabe, K., Sasaki, N., & Kawakami, N. (2020). Reliability and validity of the Japanese version of the Gratitude at Work Scale (GAWS). *Journal of Occupational Health, 62*(1), e12185. https://doi.org/10.1002/1348-9585.12185
Lehto, A. M., & Sutela, H. (2008). *Työolojen kolme vuosikymmentä: työolotutkimusten tuloksia 1977–2008*. Helsinki.
Lent, R. W. (2004). Toward a unifying theoretical and practical perspective on well-being and psychosocial adjustment. *Journal of Counseling Psychology, 51*(4), 482–509.
Lloren, A., & Parini, L. (2017). How LGBT-supportive workplace policies shape the experience of lesbian, gay men, and bisexual employees. *Sexuality Research & Social Policy, 14*, 289–299. https://doi.org/10.1007/s13178-016-0253-x
Luthans, F. (2002). The need for and meaning of positive organizational behavior. *Journal of Organizational Behavior, 23*(6), 695–706. https://doi.org/10.1002/job.165
Lyubomirsky, S., & Lepper, H. S. (1999). A measure of subjective happiness: Preliminary reliability and construct validation. *Social Indicators Research, 46*(2), 137–155. https://doi.org/10.1023/A:1006824100041
Lyubomirsky, S., King, L., & Diener, E. (2005a). The benefits of frequent positive affect: Does happiness lead to success? *Psychological Bulletin, 131*(6), 803.
Lyubomirsky, S., Sheldon, K. M., & Schkade, D. (2005b). Pursuing happiness: The architecture of sustainable change. *Review of General Psychology, 9*(2), 111–131.
Marteau, T. M., & Bekker, H. (1992). Development of a six item short form of the state scale of the Spielberger State-Trait Inventory (STAI). *British Journal of Clinical Psychology, 31*, 301–306.
Maslach, C., & Jackson, S. E. (1981). The measurement of experienced burnout. *Journal of Occupational Behavior, 2*(2), 99–113.
Maslach, C., Jackson, S. E., & Leiter, M. P. (1996). *The Maslach burnout inventory: Test manual* (3rd ed.). Consulting Psycologist Press.
Maslow, A. H. (1968). *Toward a psychology of being* (2nd ed.). VanNostrand.
May, D. R., Gilson, R. L., & Harter, L. M. (2004). The psychological conditions of meaningfulness, safety and availability and the engagement of the human spirit at work. *Journal of Occupational and Organizational Psychology, 77*, 11–37.
McCunn, L., & Frey, C. (2020). Impacts of large-scale interior murals on hospital employees: A pharmacy department case study. *Journal of Facilities Management, 18*(1), 53–70. https://doi.org/10.1108/JFM-10-2019-0053
McGregor, I., & Little, B. R. (1998). Personal projects, happiness, and meaning: On doing well and being yourself. *Journal of Personality and Social Psychology, 74*(2), 494–512.
Medzo-M'engone, J., & Sima, M. (2020). Psychometric properties of the psychological well-being at work scale in Gabonese public administration. *Journal of Evidence-Based Social Work, 18*, 1–14. https://doi.org/10.1080/26408066.2020.1808551
Medzo-M'Engone, J., & Sima, M. (2021). Psychometric properties of the psychological well-being at work scale in Gabonese public administration. *Journal of Evidence-Based Social Work, 18*(1), 101–115. https://doi.org/10.1080/26408066.2020.1808551
Mendonça, H., Caetano, A., Ferreira, M. C., Sousa, I. F., & Junça-Silva, A. (2014). Florescimento no trabalho. In M. M. M. Siqueira (Ed.), *Novas medidas do comportamento organizacional* (pp. 172–177). Artmed.
Mendonça, H., Junça-Silva, A., & Ferreira, M. C. (2018). Présenceattentive et créativitéautravail: examen du rôlemédiateur du bien-être et de l'auto-efficacitécréative. *Psychologie du Travail et des Organisations, 3*, 1–10.
Mowday, R. T., Steers, R. M., & Porter, L. W. (1979). The measurement of organizational commitment. *Journal of Vocational Behavior, 14*(2), 224–247. https://doi.org/10.1016/0001-8791(79)90072-1
Mullola, S., Hakulinen, C., Gimeno Ruiz de Porras, D., Presseau, J., Jokela, M., Vänskä, J., Paunio, T., & Elovainio, M. (2019). Medical specialty choice and well-being at work: Physician's per-

sonality as a moderator. *Archives of Environmental and Occupational Health, 74*(3), 115–129. https://doi.org/10.1080/19338244.2018.1448355

Nery, V. F., Neiva, E. R., & Mendonça, H. (2016). The changing context and the organizational justice impact on the employee well-being. *Paidéia* (USP. Online), *26*, 317–324.

Nery, V. D. F., Franco, K. S., & Neiva, E. R. (2019). Attributes of the organizational change and its influence on attitudes toward organizational change and well-being at work: A longitudinal study. *The Journal of Applied Behavioral Science, 55*(4), 477–496. https://doi.org/10.1177/0021886319848125

Nislin, M., Paananen, M., Repo, L., Sajaniemi, N., & Sims, M. (2016). Working with children with special needs in Finnish kindergartens: Professionals and/or specialists? *South African Journal of Childhood Education, 5*(3). https://doi.org/10.4102/sajce.v5i3.368

Olawale, O. O., Taiwo, O. A., & Hesham, A. (2017, July–September). Quality of sleep and well-being of health workers in Najran, Saudi Arabia. *Indian Journal of Psychiatry, 59*(3):347–351. https://doi.org/10.4103/psychiatry.IndianJPsychiatry_241_16. PMID: 29085095; PMCID: PMC5659086.

Oliver, M. B., Hartmann, T., & Woolley, J. K. (2012). Elevation in response to entertainment portrayals of moral virtue. *Human Communication Research, 38*(3), 360–378. https://doi.org/10.1111/j.1468-2958.2012.01427.x

Paschoal, T., & Tamayo, A. (2008). Construção e validação da Escala de bem-estar no trabalho. *Avaliação Psicológica, 7*(1), 11–22. Recuperado em 10 de maio de 2021, de http://pepsic.bvsalud.org/scielo.php?script=sci_arttext&pid=S1677-04712008000100004&lng=pt&tlng=pt

Platsidou, M., & Agaliotis, I. (2008). Burnout, job satisfaction and instructional assignment-related sources of stress in Greek special education teachers. *International Journal of Disability, Development and Education, 55*(1), 61–76.

Platsidou, M., & Agaliotis, I. (2017). Does empathy predict instructional assignment-related stress? A study in special and general education teachers. *International Journal of Disability, Development and Education, 64*(1), 57–75. https://doi.org/10.1080/1034912X.2016.1174191

Polizzi, F. A., & Claro, J. A. C. S. (2019). O Impacto de Bem-Estar o Trabalho e Capital Psicológico sobre Intenção de Rotatividade: Um Estudo com Professores. *RAM, Revista de Administração Mackenzie* [online], *20*(2). https://doi.org/10.1590/1678-6971/eramg19006

Puigmitja, I., Robledo, E., & Topa, G. (2019). Cross-cultural validity and psychometric properties of the ISC Intrapreneurial Self-Capital Scale in Spain. *Personality and Individual Differences, 151*, 109296. https://doi.org/10.1016/j.paid.2019.02.040

Pejtersen, J. H., Kristensen, T. S., Borg, V., & Bjorner, J. B. (2010). The second version of the Copenhagen Psychosocial Questionnaire. *Scandinavian journal of public health, 38*(3_suppl), 8–24. https://doi.org/10.1177/1403494809349858

Positive Psychology Center. (2013). Web Page. https://www.authentichappiness.sas.upenn.edu/questionnaires/perma

Rautenbach, C. (2015). *Flourishing of employees in a fast-moving consumable goods environment* (Unpublished doctoral thesis). North-West University, Vanderbijlpark, South Africa.

Ryan, R. M., & Deci, E. (2000). Self-determination theory and the facilitation of intrinsic motivation, social development, and wellbeing. *American Psychologist, Washington, 55*(1), 68–78.

Ryan, R. M., & Deci, E. L. (2001). On happiness and human potentials: A review of research on hedonic and eudaimonic well-being. *Annual Review of Psychology, 52*, 141–166.

Ryan, R. M., & Frederick, C. M. (1997). On energy, personality and health: Subjective vitality as a dynamic reflection of well-being. *Journal of Personality, 65*, 529–565.

Ryan, R., Huta, V., & Deci, E. L. (2008). Living well: A self-determination theory perspective on eudaimonia. *Journal of Happiness Studies, 9*, 139–170. https://doi.org/10.1007/s10902-006-9023-4

Ryff, C. D. (1989). Happiness is everything, or is it? Explorations on the meaning of psychological well-being. *Journal of Personality and Social Psychology, 57*(6), 1069–1081.

Ryff, C. D. (1995). Psychological well-being in adult life. *Current Directions in Psychological Science, 4*(4), 99–104. https://doi.org/10.1111/1467-8721.ep10772395

Sandilya, G., & Shahnawaz, G. (2018). Index of psychological well-being at work—validation of tool in the Indian organizational context. *Vision: The Journal of Business Perspective, 22*, 097226291876613. https://doi.org/10.1177/0972262918766134

Schaufeli, W. B., & Bakker, A. B. (2004). Job demands, job resources, and their relationship with burnout and engagement: A multi-sample study. *Journal of Organizational Behavior, 25*, 293–315.

Schaufeli, W. B., Bakker, A. B., & Salanova, M. (2006). The measurement of work engagement with a short questionnaire: A cross-national study. *Educational and Psychological Measurement., 66*(4), 701–716. https://doi.org/10.1177/0013164405282471

Seligman, M. E. (2008). Positive health. *Applied Psychology: An International Review, 57*(1), 3–18.

Seligman, M. E., & Csikszentmihalyi, M. (2000). Positive psychology: An introduction. *American Psychologist, 55*(1), 5–14.

Shirom, A., & Melamed, S. (2006). A comparison of the construct validity of two burnout measures in two groups of professionals. *International Journal of Stress Management, 13*(2), 176–200. https://doi.org/10.1037/1072-5245.13.2.176

Spector, P. E., & Jex, S. M. (1998). Development of four self-report measures of job stressors and strain: Interpersonal conflict at work scale, organizational constraints scale, quantitative workload inventory, and physical symptoms inventory. *Journal of Occupational Health Psychology, 3*(4), 356–367. https://doi.org/10.1037/1076-8998.3.4.356

Spreitzer, G. M., Sutcliffe, K., Dutton, J., Sonenshein, S., & Grant, A. M. (2005). A socially embedded model of thriving at work. *Organization Science, 16*(5), 537–549.

Steffgen, G., Sischka, P. E., & de Henestrosa, M. F. (2020). The quality of work index and the quality of employment index: A multidimensional approach of job quality and its links to well-being at work. *International Journal of Environmental Research and Public Health, 17*(21), 1–30. https://doi.org/10.3390/ijerph17217777

Steger, M. F., Dik, B. J., & Duffy, R. D. (2012). Measuring meaningful work: The work and meaning inventory (WAMI). *Journal of Career Assessment, 20*(3), 322–337. https://doi.org/10.1177/1069072711436160

Thayer, R. E. (1989). *The biopsychology of mood and arousal*. Oxford University Press.

Turban, D. B., & Yan, W. (2016). Relationship of eudaimonia and hedonia with work outcomes. *Journal of Managerial Psychology, 31*(6), 1006–1020. https://doi.org/10.1108/JMP-07-2015-0271

Van Horn, J. E., Taris, T. W., Schaufeli, W. B., & Scheurs, P. J. G. (2004). The structure of occupational well-being: A study among Dutch teachers. *Journal of Occupational and Organizational Psychology, 77*, 365–375.

VanderWeele, T. J. (2017). Religious communities and human flourishing. *Current Directions in Psychological Science, 26*(5), 476–481. https://doi.org/10.1177/0963721417721526

Van Rensburg, C., Rothmann, S., & Diedericks, E. (2017). Person-environment fit, flourishing and intention to leavein universities of technology in South Africa. *SA Journal of Industrial Psychology, 43*, 10 pages.https://doi.org/10.4102/sajip.v43i0.1422

Warr, P. (1990). The measurement of well-being and other aspects of mental health. *Journal of Occupational Psychology, 63*(3), 193–210.

Watanabe, M., & Yamauchi, K. (2018). The effect of quality of overtime work on nurses' mental health and work engagement. *Journal of Nursing Management, 26*(6), 679–688. https://doi.org/10.1111/jonm.12595

Waterman, A. S. (1993). Two conceptions of happiness: Contrasts of personal expressiveness (eudaimonia) and hedonic enjoyment. *Journal of Personality and Social Psychology, 64*(4), 678–691.

Watson, D., Clark, L. A., & Tellegen, A. (1988). Development and validation of brief measures of positive and negative affect: The PANAS scales. *Journal of Personality and Social Psychology, 54*, 1063–1070.

Wharton, A. S. (1993). The affective consequences of service work: Managing emotions on the job. *Work and Occupations, 20*(2), 205–232. https://doi.org/10.1177/0730888493020002004

Zheng, X., Zhu, W., Zhao, H., & Zhang, C. (2015). Employee well-being in organizations: Theoretical model, scale development, and cross-cultural validation. *Journal of Organizational Behavior, 36*(5), 621–644.

Chapter 4
Measurement Scales About Retirement Decision-Making

Silvia Miranda Amorim, Juliana Seidl, and Lucia Helena de Freitas Pinho França

4.1 Introduction

The increase in life expectancy among populations around the world has brought different perspectives on aging and retirement, including the fact that not all retirees are old, and not all old people are retired. There has been a significant increase in the number of people who continue to work into their later years, whether because they are not eligible for retirement or because many of those who are eligible cannot maintain their standard of living on their pension benefits alone (Beehr & Bennett, 2015).

In addition, with all of the global economic challenges that arose in the past century, approximately 55 developed and developing countries have already raised the minimum age for retirement, including Germany, the United States, Australia, Greece, India, and Chile.[1] In the case of Brazil, constitutional amendment n° 103 of November 12, 2019, consolidated a fiscal agenda that had been debated for years and implemented a reform of the retirement system. Since then, the minimum retirement age at the federal level has been 62 for women and 65 for men (Brazil, 2019).

[1] https://economia.uol.com.br/noticias/redacao/2019/03/01/previdencia-idade-minima-reforma.htm

S. M. Amorim (✉)
Federal University of Minas Gerais, Belo Horizonte, MG, Brazil
e-mail: silvia-amorim@ufmg.br

J. Seidl
Empresa Longeva – Maturidades e Oportunidades, Brasília, DF, Brazil
e-mail: juliana@longevapsi.com.br

L. H. de F. P. França
University Salgado de Oliveira, Niterói, RJ, Brazil

M. O. Macambira et al. (eds.), *Assessing Organizational Behaviors*,
https://doi.org/10.1007/978-3-030-81311-6_4

At the end of 2019, when the retirement reform was approved, approximately 90,000 federal employees met the requirements for voluntary retirement. In March 2021, data available from the Brazilian Open Data Portal[2] indicated that 78,000 employees who were already eligible for retirement continued to work, meaning they were earning a bonus to continue working past retirement age. In this context, human resource managers, coordinators, and facilitators of retirement education programs and scholars in this field have asked what motives lead workers to remain in the labor market and postpone retirement other than financial gains (in that they are no longer obliged to contribute to their retirement accounts) (Amorim & França, 2019; França et al., 2013; Menezes & França, 2012; Seidl et al., 2020).

Despite a significant increase in research on the topic over the past 20 years, the decision about retirement is still a phenomenon on which there is little agreement in a world of work that has become increasingly volatile, uncertain, and precarious. Workers who dedicate years to the same company or career and then retire, never more to return to the labor market, are increasingly rare. Just as there are a great many ways to organize and design work, there are also different manners, types, and meanings of retirement, which can no longer be described as simply a definitive exit from work (Jex & Grosch, 2012; Shultz & Wang, 2011).

Changes in demographics and the world of work mean researchers and professionals must define the meaning of retirement and work before beginning a study of the subject or launching a retirement-preparation program (RPP), for example. In this chapter, we adopt the concept presented by Shultz and Wang (2011) that retirement refers to the behavioral and psychological distancing of an individual from work. Among several models available in the literature, the one proposed by these authors (Fig. 4.1) represents how retirement has been considered a multilevel and multicausal process. Similarly, the decision to retire can be voluntary or involuntary and may involve few or many phases before the definitive transition and adaptation to retirement (Jex & Grosch, 2012).

To deepen our understanding of the model, it is necessary to discuss the concept of work and its implications for retirement in various contexts. Work can be conceptualized as a set of human activities, paid or unpaid, of a productive and creative nature that allows one to obtain, produce, or supply certain goods, products, or services. In this activity, a person contributes energy, skills, knowledge, and other resources to obtain some material, psychological, and/or social compensation (Peiró, 1985). The Marxist definition considers work an essentially human activity that transforms reality (Marx, 1980), based on which Yamamoto (2015) highlights a person's work occupation as a central category of the social being and human existence. According to the definition cited above, one can generally say that people who have chosen to postpone retirement, people who engage in bridge employment, and people who retire completely may all be said to be working. However, in Brazil, postponing retirement or engaging in bridge employment is considered paid work, whether it is done out of necessity, lack of alternatives or interest, and whether or

[2] https://dados.gov.br/dataset/gastos-pessoal-abono-permanencia

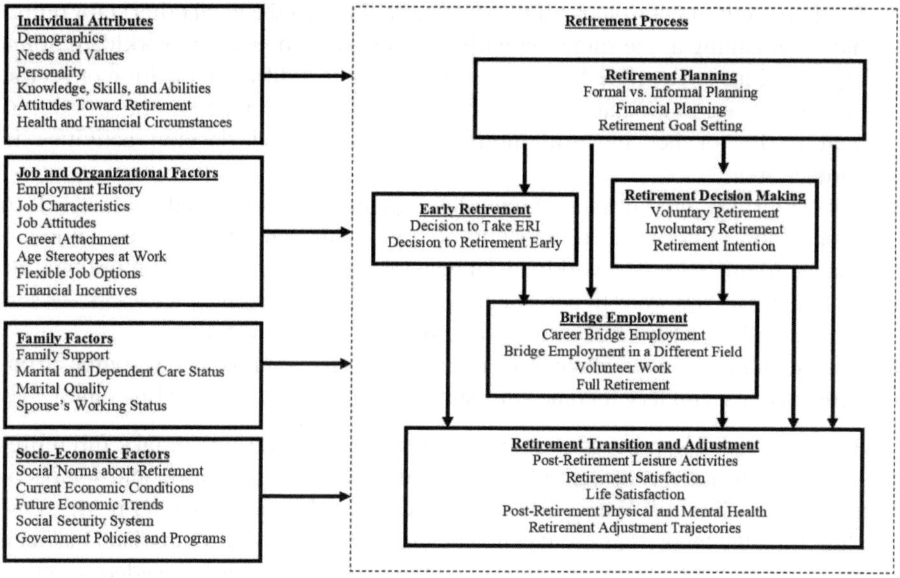

Fig. 4.1 Longitudinal progression of the retirement process and potential impact factors (Shultz & Wang, 2011)

not one also receives the pension to which retirees are legally entitled. Models such as Shultz and Wang (2011) may therefore classify volunteer work as a type of bridge employment, but this is based on the structure of voluntary work in developed countries such as the United States and Canada, where volunteer opportunities often require a defined work day and offer benefits in return; in countries like Brazil, this is rarely the case.

In this discussion, it is worth presenting the difference between financial autonomy and financial independence (Pimenta, 2014). A financially autonomous person has income that exceeds his or her expenses; that is, he or she does not rely on the help of third parties or institutions to pay his or her bills. Financial independence is a condition that is similar to autonomy but dispenses with the need to work. Retirement benefits should be sufficient to promote financial independence, but, unfortunately, this is rarely the case. On the other hand, those who – through savings, regular investment, or inheritance – have managed to generate an income that exceeds their expenses can achieve financial independence prior to retirement (Pimenta, 2014). Thus, the small proportion of Brazilians who achieve financial independence usually choose to retire completely and then engage in activities that are not necessarily remunerated. The others continue working full or part time for many years.

Based on this theoretical view, three options for retirement decisions have been highlighted (Beehr & Bennett, 2015; Menezes & França, 2012):

1. Postpone retirement (*late retirement*) after having met the legal criteria for retirement, remaining at the same job with the same work hours and workload. Some organizations have offered the option of moving to a different position or sector, in order to accommodate the physical and cognitive changes in the worker, as well as his or her intrinsic motivation to learn and develop activities in another area.
2. Choose *bridge employment*, leaving one's primary career to dedicate oneself to another job or position, in the same field or a different one, with or without a change to one's former workload. In general, these people choose more flexible jobs; that is, they want to act as entrepreneurs, independent contractors, or service providers, with a lighter and more flexible work schedule.
3. Choose *full retirement*, leaving the job market to live on financial resources from pensions or secondary income (investments, inheritance, or rental income).

Thus, the decision process about whether to continue working or take full retirement entails an analysis of individual, familial, organizational, work, and socioeconomic factors (Shultz & Wang, 2011; Wang & Shi, 2014), as shown in Fig. 4.1. One can highlight the theory of rational choice, which considers the comparison between one's accumulated financial resources and the financial resources needed to retire. From this theoretical perspective, workers will end their employment only when they feel that their accumulated and future financial resources permit them to meet their living expenses in retirement (Wang & Shi, 2014). This view matches recent empirical studies, which have highlighted financial circumstances as one of the main factors of well-being in retirement, together with health (Amorim & França, 2020; Hershey et al., 2017; Vogelsang et al., 2018). This is why preparation/education/counseling programs for retirement are so strongly recommended. On the other hand, a large number of workers are compelled to retire against their will by early retirement programs imposed by organizations or to continue working for individual, family, social, organizational, or economic reasons.

Menezes and França (2012) carried out a study with 148 public employees at a technology company that focused on their retirement decisions. The authors did not create a predictive instrument at that time but used seven predictors that had been partially tested in the literature: (i) subjective life expectancy; (ii) age; (iii) perceived health; (iv) perception of work – involvement and satisfaction; (v) flexibility of schedule; (vi) commitment to their career; and (vii) control of their work. These predictors were correlated with a dependent variable consisting of a single question that contained the three main options for retirement decisions. Hierarchical regressions identified the predictors for each of the options: (i) age and perception of work favored the option to postpone the age of retirement; (ii) flexibility of schedule, control of work, and perception of work predicted bridge employment; and (iii) perceived health was the main predictor for full retirement (Menezes & França, 2012).

Accurate measurement of the motives or predictors that lead people to retire or continue working is an important issue that must be investigated so that organizations can address the different interests of older workers with regard to this career transition and plan not only for the well-being of their workers but also for the composition and needs of their workforce. In light of this need, this chapter aims to highlight instruments related to perceptions of the decision about whether to take early retirement, seek bridgework, or continue to work after retirement, as well as measures of the factors that influence this decision.

To this end, it contains a narrative review of the literature on instruments related to the decision about retirement that have been developed in doctoral theses or published in peer-reviewed journals. It focuses on instruments that undertake psychometric analyses to explore and confirm the structure of the measure, emphasizing instruments that have proven valid and consistent in testing at least one sample (Table 4.1). It also compiles a list of the dimensions addressed by decision-predicting instruments (Table 4.2) and, finally, includes other items developed by authors in their studies to measure decisions about retirement (Table 4.3). The instruments are therefore presented in two groups: the first refers to intentions or motives for retirement, and the second refers to attitudes and predictors of the retirement decision, followed by other measurement items. Measures of attitudes were included in the set of predictor scales because the theory of planned behavior considers them antecedents of the decision (Ajzen, 1991).

4.2 Measures

Instruments That Assess Intention and Interests in Retirement

Scale of Interest in Bridge Employment and Phased Retirement

The Scale of Interest in Bridge Employment and Phased Retirement was developed by Kalokerinos et al. (2015) to measure older workers' interest in engaging in bridge employment currently or in the future. The instrument consisted of four items and two dimensions: one dimension related to phased retirement, with questions about reducing work hours and working from home for a period leading up to retirement, and another dimension related to intermediate employment, with questions about working as an independent contractor after retirement and working on specific tasks or for a specific time after retirement.

At the time, it was developed with a sample of 609 Australian workers aged 50 or older, and the instrument showed good psychometric characteristics (CFI = 0.99, RMSEA = 0.03) based on confirmatory factor analysis. No translations of the instrument were found, nor cases of its application in other studies.

Retirement Intention Scale (RIS)

The Retirement Intention Scale (RIS) was developed by De Vos and Segers (2013) to measure workers' intention to continue working until the official age of retirement. The instrument has four Likert items (a 5-point scale according to degree of agreement) organized in a single factor. The items are (i) I intend to stop working before my official retirement age (reversed scoring); (ii) I can easily continue working until my official retirement age; (iii) I plan to stop working as soon as I can

Table 4.1 Measurement instruments included in the narrative review and their features

Measure	Instrument name (authors, year)	Country (original language)	Number of factors (number of items)	Type of response scale	Reliability indices	Application in other countries (authors)
Intention and interests in retirement	Scale of Interest in Bridge Employment and Phased Retirement (Kalokerinos et al., 2015)	Australia (English)	2 factors (4 items)	Likert, 5 points (interest)	CFI = 0.99; RMSEA = 0.03	–
	Retirement Intention Scale (RIS) (De Vos & Segers, 2013)	Belgium (Dutch)	1 factor (4 items)	Likert, 5 points (agreement)	Cronbach's alpha of 0.81	–
Predictors of decisions	Escala de Actitudes Hacia la Jubilacíon (Rodríguez, 2007)	Argentina (Spanish)	3 factors (40 items)	Thurstone, 7 points (favorability)	Cronbach's alpha of 0.81	–
	Executives' Perceived Gains in Retirement (EPGR) and Executives' Perceived Losses in Retirement (EPLR) (França, 2004)	New Zealand (English)	Scale of gains (positive attitudes): 5 factors (19 items); scale of losses (negative attitudes): 4 factors (19 items)	Likert, 4 points (perceived importance)	Cronbach's alpha of sub-scales: 0.78 and 0.92	Brazil (França & Vaughan, 2008; Pissinati et al., 2016)
	Older Workers' Intentions to Continue Working (OWICW) (Shacklock & Brunetto, 2011)	Australia (English)	7 factors (41 items)	Likert, 7 points (agreement)	Cronbach's alpha of factors: 0.79; 0.69; 0.81; 0.87; 0.89; 0.76; 0.85	Brazil (Macêdo et al., 2020)
	Reasons for Entrepreneurs' Retirement Decision Inventory (RERDI) (Chevalier et al., 2013)	France (French)	4 factors (16 items)	Likert, 5 points (clarity)	CFI = 0.96; IFI = 0.96; RMSEA = 0.06. Cronbach's alpha of factors: 0.86; 0.87, 0.80 and 0.73	–
	Reasons for Retirement Scale (RFR) (Floyd et al., 1992)	The United States (English)	4 factors (15 items)	Likert, 6 points (importance)	Cronbach's alpha of factors: 0.80; 0.79; 0.66; 0.61. Factor load of the items above 0.42	France (Fouquereau et al., 1999), Spanish (Muñoz et al., 2011) and Brazil (Amorim & França, 2019)

	Scale of Factors Influencing the Post-career Employment Decision (Kerr & Armstrong-Stassen, 2011)	Canada (English)	Sub-scale of engagement with entrepreneurship: 4 factors (18 items) Sub-scale of transition from paid employment: 5 factors (22 items)	Likert, 5 points (importance)	Cronbach's alpha of factors: 0.85; 0.84; 0.78; 0.60; 0.81; 0.84; 0.73; 0.74; 0.76. Factor load of items above 0.61	–
	Escala de motivos para continuar trabalhando na aposentadoria (EMCTA) (Souza & França, 2020)	Brazil (Portuguese)	7 factors (44 items)	Likert, 5 points (influence)	χ^2 (gl) = 1178,20 (881); CFI = 0,96; TLI = 0,95; RMSEA = 0,03. Cronbach's alpha of factors: 0.86; 0.92; 0.90; 0.81; 0.93; 0.94 e 0.93	–
	Workers' Retirement Motivations Inventory (WRMI) (Fouquereau et al., 1999)	France (French)	4 factors (20 items)	Likert, 10 points (importance)	B-Sχ2 = 189.14, df = 164, B-Sχ2/df = 1.15; CFI = 0.90; TLI = 0.90; SRMR = 0.06; RMSEA = 0.06, AIC = 410.382; MECVI = 1.163	–

Table 4.2 Dimensions covered by the instruments about retirement decision-making predictors

Category	Dimension	Instrument
Individual factors	Personal satisfaction	Scale of Factors Influencing the Post-career Employment Decision (Kerr & Armstrong-Stassen, 2011)
	Search for other interests	Escala de Actitudes Hacia la Jubilación (Rodríguez, 2007) Older Workers' Intentions to Continue Working (OWICW) (Shacklock & Brunetto, 2011) Reasons for Entrepreneurs' Retirement Decision Inventory (RERDI) (Chevalier et al., 2013) Reasons for Retirement Scale (RFR) (Floyd et al., 1992) Workers' Retirement Motivations Inventory (WRMI) (Fouquereau et al., 1999)
	Independence	Executives' Perception of Gains in Retirement (EPGR) (França, 2004) Reasons for Entrepreneurs' Retirement Decision Inventory (RERDI) (Chevalier et al., 2013) Scale of Factors Influencing the Post-career Employment Decision (Kerr & Armstrong-Stassen, 2011) Workers' Retirement Motivations Inventory (WRMI) (Fouquereau et al., 1999)
	New experiences	Executives' Perception of Gains in Retirement (EPGR) (França, 2004) Scale of Factors Influencing the Post-career Employment Decision (Kerr & Armstrong-Stassen, 2011)
	Physical condition	Escala de Motivos para Continuar Trabalhando na Aposentadoria (Souza & França, 2020)
	Financial circumstances	Escala de Motivos para Continuar Trabalhando na Aposentadoria (Souza & França, 2020) Escala de Actitudes Hacia la Jubilación (Rodríguez, 2007) Executives' Perception of Losses in Retirement Scale (EPLR) (França, 2004) Scale of Factors Influencing the Post-career Employment Decision (Kerr & Armstrong-Stassen, 2011)
	Intellectual development	Escala de Motivos para Continuar Trabalhando na Aposentadoria (Souza & França, 2020) Reasons for Entrepreneurs' Retirement Decision Inventory (RERDI) (Chevalier et al., 2013)
Social/family factors	Time for friends and family	Escala de Actitudes Hacia la Jubilación (Rodríguez, 2007) Executives' Perception of Gains in Retirement (EPGR) (França, 2004) Workers' Retirement Motivations Inventory (WRMI) (Fouquereau et al., 1999)
	Time for cultural and leisure activities	Escala de Actitudes Hacia la Jubilación (Rodríguez, 2007) Executives' Perception of Gains in Retirement (EPGR) (França, 2004)
	Family circumstances	Reasons for Retirement Scale (RFR) (Floyd et al., 1992)

Work and organization factors	Ties with work	Escala de Actitudes Hacia la Jubilación (Rodríguez, 2007) Executives' Perception of Losses in Retirement Scale (EPLR) (França, 2004) Older Workers' Intentions to Continue Working (OWICW) (Shacklock & Brunetto, 2011) Reasons for Entrepreneurs' Retirement Decision Inventory (RERDI) (Chevalier et al., 2013) Workers' Retirement Motivations Inventory (WRMI) (Fouquereau et al., 1999)
	Importance of work to the individual	Escala de Motivos para Continuar Trabalhando na Aposentadoria (Souza & França, 2020) Older Workers' Intentions to Continue Working (OWICW) (Shacklock & Brunetto, 2011) Workers' Retirement Motivations Inventory (WRMI) (Fouquereau et al., 1999)
	Life-work balance	Scale of Factors Influencing the Post-career Employment Decision (Kerr & Armstrong-Stassen, 2011)
	Perception of autonomy	Older Workers' Intentions to Continue Working (OWICW) (Shacklock & Brunetto, 2011)
	Flexible work arrangements	Older Workers' Intentions to Continue Working (OWICW) (Shacklock & Brunetto, 2011)
	Job-related stress	Reasons for Entrepreneurs' Retirement Decision Inventory (RERDI) (Chevalier et al., 2013) Reasons for Retirement Scale (RFR) (Floyd et al., 1992) Workers' Retirement Motivations Inventory (WRMI) (Fouquereau et al., 1999)
	Satisfaction and motivation at work	Reasons for Entrepreneurs' Retirement Decision Inventory (RERDI) (Chevalier et al., 2013) Workers' Retirement Motivations Inventory (WRMI) (Fouquereau et al., 1999)
	Management	Older Workers' Intentions to Continue Working (OWICW) (Shacklock & Brunetto, 2011)
	Pressure from employer	Reasons for Retirement Scale (RFR) (Floyd et al., 1992) Workers' Retirement Motivations Inventory (WRMI) (Fouquereau et al., 1999)
	Working conditions	Escala de motivos para continuar trabalhando na aposentadoria (Souza & França, 2020) Workers' Retirement Motivations Inventory (WRMI) (Fouquereau et al., 1999)
	Relationship with the organization	Escala de Motivos para Continuar Trabalhando na Aposentadoria (Souza & França, 2020) Executive' Perception of Losses in Retirement Scale (EPLR) (França, 2004);
	Relationships at work	Escala de Actitudes Hacia la Jubilación (Rodríguez, 2007) Escala de Motivos para Continuar Trabalhando na Aposentadoria (Souza & França, 2020) Older Workers' Intentions to Continue Working (OWICW) (Shacklock & Brunetto, 2011) Reasons for Entrepreneurs' Retirement Decision Inventory (RERDI) (Chevalier et al., 2013) Scale of Factors Influencing the Post-career Employment Decision (Kerr & Armstrong-Stassen, 2011)
Socioeconomic factors	Association of retirement with inactivity/old age/death	Escala de Actitudes Hacia la Jubilación (Rodríguez, 2007)

Table 4.3 Compilation of the items developed by the authors

Dimension	Items
Intention to retire early	I'd like to retire earlier, if I can
	I'd like to stop working as soon as possible
	I hope to take early retirement in the near future
	I intend to stop working before age 65
	I have considered retiring before reaching the legal age of retirement
	I'd like to retire earlier if my financial circumstances permit it
Intention to continue working/ return to work	Personally, I have no problem with postponing retirement
	It's important to me to continue working past the age of retirement
	Unless something unexpected happened, I'd remain in this organization indefinitely
	I'd like to work for my current employer after retiring
	I'd like to work for another employer after retiring
	I'd like to become an independent contractor after retiring
	Even when I'm eligible for retirement, I intend to keep working
	I believe if I retire at the age at which I'm eligible for retirement, I'll still want to return to work
	I don't see any way I'll be able to retire in the near future
	In light of my circumstances, there's no way I can stop working
Intention to retire early	I don't see myself continuing in my current job much longer
	I hope to start drawing a pension in the near future
	I intend to retire in the near future
	As soon as I can retire, I'm going to stop working altogether
	In my opinion, work and retirement don't go well together
	I don't intend to do any sort of work at all during my retirement
Intention to engage in bridge employment	I don't consider working half time during my retirement a disadvantage
	I would consider coming back to work part time in my current field during my retirement
	Even after I'm eligible for retirement, I'm going to keep working part time
	Even after I'm eligible for retirement, I'm going to keep working in a different type of work.
	As soon as I'm eligible for retirement, I intend to work for myself
	As soon as I'm eligible for retirement, I intend to work in a new job
	I'm interested in taking a temporary job until I fully retire

(reverse scoring); and (iv) I intend to work as long as possible. Its application to a sample of 265 Belgian workers over the age of 45 showed good internal consistency ($\alpha = 0.81$).

Instruments for Predicting Decisions

Escala de Actitudes Hacia la Jubilación [Attitudes Toward Retirement Scale]
The *Escala de Actitudes Hacia la Jubilación* [Attitudes Toward Retirement Scale] was developed by Rodríguez (2007) to measure favorable, unfavorable, or neutral attitudes toward retirement. Using Thurston' method of equal appearing intervals, participants were asked to assign a value between 1 and 7 to each item, in which 1 indicated an extremely unfavorable opinion, 4 a neutral opinion and 7 an extremely favorable opinion, and the participant's score was calculated by the arithmetic average of these values. At the time, it was developed with a sample of 300 pre-retirees and retirees in Argentina; it had a structure of 3 dimensions and 40 items (14 favorable, 16 unfavorable, and 10 neutral), with good psychometric characteristics ($\alpha = 0.81$).

Executives' Perception of Gains in Retirement (EPGR) and Executives' Perception of Losses in Retirement Scale (EPLR)
The Executives' Perception of Gains in Retirement (EPGR) and Executives' Perception of Losses in Retirement (EPLR*)* scales were developed by França (2004) to measure positive attitudes (perceived gains) and negative attitudes (perceived losses) toward retirement. The instruments were developed on a 4-point Likert scale that indicated degree of importance (with 1 being very important and 4 unimportant), with the EPGE composed of 19 items and 5 factors (autonomy at work, relationships, a new beginning, cultural and leisure activities, and investments) and the EPLR composed of 19 items and 4 factors (losses of an emotional nature, losses of a material nature, relationship with the company. and salary and/or benefits).

Used with a sample of 517 Brazilian and New Zealand executives, the experimental factor analyses showed good rates of internal consistency. The EPGE showed total explained variation of 60%, with internal consistency indices ranging from 0.51 to 0.83 ($\alpha = 0.83$; 0.77; 0.58; 0.51) and factor loads of the items between 0.25 and 0.86. The EPLR showed a total explained variation of 63%, with internal consistency indices ranging from 0.69 to 0.90 ($\alpha = 0.90$; 0.82; 0.88; 0.69) and factor loads of the items between 0.44 and 0.88.

In 2016, the scale was applied by Pissinati et al. (2016) in Brazil, as originally proposed (França, 2004; França & Vaughan, 2008). In this application with a sample of 164 workers at a public university, the authors found that the older the workers were, the lower their perception of total gains in retirement, and the less value they placed on time for relationships and a new beginning after retirement. However, those with partners considered the time they would have for relationships after retirement more important. In addition, the more educated the respondent, the greater the value placed on retirement as a new beginning. Participants with the highest salaries gave less importance to having time for cultural and leisure activities or for investment. Finally, the longer the respondent had been employed, the more acute was the feeling of loss in general, and especially the material aspects of employment. With regard to the types of work at the university, those who were teachers attributed greater importance to losses related to the emotional aspects of work and to salaries and benefits (Pissinati et al., 2016).

Older Workers' Intentions to Continue Working (OWICW)
The Older Workers' Intentions to Continue Working (OWICW) instrument was developed by Shacklock and Brunetto (2011) for Australian workers. In this instrument, respondents used a 7-point Likert scale (with 1 indicating complete disagreement and 7 indicating complete agreement) to indicate their view on 41 items and 7 dimensions (connection with work, importance of work to the individual, personal relationships at work, perception of autonomy, flexible work arrangements, management and organizational factors, and interests outside work), as well as statements about health, financial circumstances, and sociodemographic data. At the time, it was developed and applied to a sample of 379 workers over the age of 50, and the scale showed adequate psychometric properties ($\alpha \geq 0.70$) in its initial structure. The scale was recently adapted for use in the Brazilian context (Macêdo et al., 2020) and found to have a structure similar to the original, suggesting its adequacy and applicability to other contexts.

Reasons for Entrepreneurs' Retirement Decision Inventory (RERDI)
The Reasons for Entrepreneurs' Retirement Decision Inventory (RERDI) was developed by Chevalier et al. (2013) to access the structure of the reasons underlying the retirement decision process among entrepreneurs, using the push and pull view previously employed by Shultz et al. (1998) to analyze the variables that could retain a worker (pull) or push him or her out of the organization (push). Chevalier et al. (2013) proposed an instrument composed of four sub-scales related to push (negative aspects of the entrepreneur's current situation that contribute to the end of his or her career), pull (positive perceptions of post-professional life), anti-push (positive assessments of the entrepreneur's present life), and anti-pull (negative aspects of retirement), each composed of four items. In a sample of 500 entrepreneurs aged 52 to 69, confirmatory factor analyses showed a tool with good psychometric characteristics for the four-factor model (CFI = 0.96; IFI = 0.96; RMSEA = 0.06) with adequate internal consistency indices (0.86; 0.87, 0.80, and 0.73).

Reasons for Retirement Scale (RFR)
The Reasons for Retirement Scale was developed by Floyd et al. (1992) in the United States to form the Retirement Satisfaction Inventory (RSI). It is a Likert instrument composed of 15 items distributed into 4 factors (job stress, pressure from the employer, pursuit of one's own interests, and retirement due to circumstances). At the time it was developed, the instrument was applied to 402 American retirees, with factor loads higher than 0.42 for the items and Cronbach's alpha ranging from

0.61 to 0.80 for the factors. The instrument was adapted for use with French retirees (Fouquereau et al., 1999) in the 1990s, and more recently for use with Spanish retirees (Muñoz et al., 2011) and Brazilians (Amorim & França, 2019), showing good evidence of validity in all three cases.

Scale of Factors Influencing the Post-Career Employment Decision
The Scale of Factors Influencing Post-Career Employment Decisions was developed by Kerr and Armstrong-Stassen (2011) using a sample of Canadian employees and entrepreneurs over the age of 50 to identify factors that favor or discourage the decision to engage in post-retirement work. Based on the literature, two sub-scales were developed: the first related to the decision about engaging in entrepreneurship, composed of 18 items and 4 factors (personal satisfaction, independence, financial necessity, and life-work balance); the second related to the decision to engage in paid employment, composed of 22 items and 5 factors (work connection, continuous contribution, financial necessity, life-work balance, and new experiences).

Its development with a sample of 282 respondents showed good psychometric characteristics, with the first sub-scale showing items with factor loads above 0.75 and alpha ranging from 0.60 to 0.85, and the second sub-scale showing items with factor loads above 0.67 and alphas ranging from 0.73 to 0.81. No additional applications or translations of this instrument for other contexts were identified (Kerr & Armstrong-Stassen, 2011).

Escala de Motivos para Continuar Trabalhando na Aposentadoria [Scale of Reasons for Continuing to Work in Retirement]
The *Escala de Motivos para Continuar Trabalhando na Aposentadoria* [Scale of Reasons for Continuing to Work in Retirement] was developed by Souza and França (2020) in Brazil to measure the motives that lead retirees to make this decision. This is a 5-point Likert instrument in which respondents indicate the degree to which their decision was influenced by 44 items distributed into 7 factors: economic circumstances, physical conditions, working conditions, importance of work, relationships at work, relationships with the organization, and intellectual development. Analyses based on a sample of 511 workers age 45 or older showed that the instrument had good psychometric qualities (χ^2 (gl) = 1178.20 (881); CFI = 0.96; TLI = 0.95; RMSEA = 0.03), with internal consistency of the factors, measured by Cronbach's alpha, ranging from 0.81 to 0.94.

Workers' Retirement Motivations Inventory (WRMI)
The Workers' Retirement Motivations Inventory (WRMI) was developed by Fouquereau et al. (1999) based on interviews with French workers using the push/pull/anti-push/anti-pull model. This is a Likert instrument with a scale ranging from 1 to 10 in importance, with 20 items distributed into 4 dimensions: (i) push (reasons to stop working); (ii) pull (aspects of life that make retirement attractive); (iii) anti-push (reasons to continue working); and (iv) anti-pull (concerns about retirement).

Its development entailed six successive analyses using different samples that totaled 1854 participating French workers. With an initial sample of 251 workers between 45 and 62 years of age, exploratory factor analyses indicated the extraction of 4 factors that explained 53.78% of the variance. Next, confirmatory factor analyses were conducted using a sample of 375 workers between the ages of 49 and 61, and the model of 4 factors and 20 items showed good fit indices (B-Sχ2 = 189.14, df = 164, B-Sχ2/df = 1.15; CFI = 0.90; TLI = 0.90; SRMR = 0.06; RMSEA = 0.06, AIC = 410,382; MECVI = 1163). Additional tests performed on a sample of 108 workers between 50 and 65 years of age showed temporal stability of the instrument's factors [*r* (CCI) = 0.54; 0.62; 0.54; 0.84.) and nonsignificant correlations with the Marlowe-Crowne Social Desirability Scale (*r* ranging from −0.11 to 0.18) (Fouquereau et al., 1999).

In a fifth analysis, invariance analyses were conducted using a sample of 433 workers between 50 and 66 years old, which showed invariance in models of gender, marital status, employment contract, age, and possessions (nonsignificant increase in the qui-square and minimal differences of CFI and RMSEA for all models). Finally, to verify evidence of predictive validity, Latent Profile Analyses (LPA) were conducted with a sample of 687 workers between the ages of 50 and 66, and these indicated 3 profiles and participants, namely, (i) determined elderly people, who showed a medium level of push, a high level of pull and low levels of anti-push and anti-pull; (ii) hesitant elderly people, who reported low levels of push and pull and medium levels of anti-push and anti-pull; and (iii) ambivalent elderly people who attributed great importance to all 4 factors (Wilk's Λ = 0.123, $F(8, 1340) = 309.383$, $p < 0.001$, partial $\eta^2 = 0.649$) (Fouquereau et al., 1999).

Dimension of the Decision-Predicting Instruments

Considering the large number of instruments that attempt to measure predictors of the retirement decision, we compiled the dimensions and items covered by these instruments. As shown in Table 4.3, the eight instruments dealt with four categories: (i) individual factors related to pursuit of interests outside work, independence and new experiences, personal satisfaction, and physical, financial, and intellectual conditions; (ii) social and family factors related to time for friends and family, time for cultural and leisure activities, and family circumstances; (iii) factors having to do with work and the organization, related to the bonds and importance attributed to work, to life-work balance and flexible arrangements, to perception of autonomy, stress, satisfaction, and motivation at work, to the type of management, to working conditions and pressure from the employer, and to relationships with colleagues and with the organization; and (iv) socioeconomic factors related to social norms that associate retirement with inactivity, age, or death.

Other Items Used as Measurements

In addition to the instruments presented, it is worth noting that the narrative review found a significant number of studies that did not use previously validated instruments but rather measured decisions about retirement using items developed by the authors of these or previous studies. These are items related to the intention to retire before reaching retirement age (Gaillard & Desmette, 2008, 2010; van Dam et al., 2009; Topa & Alcover, 2015), the intention to continue working or return to work after retirement (Dordoni et al., 2017; Menezes & França, 2012; Rodrigues, 2016; Seidl et al., 2020; Stuer et al., 2019; Topa & Alcover, 2015), the intention to engage in bridge employment or engage in a different type of work (Dordoni et al., 2017; Menezes & França, 2012; Lahlouh et al., 2019; Seidl et al., 2020; Topa & Alcover, 2015), or the intention to take full retirement (Adams et al., 2002; Dordoni et al., 2017; Lahlouh et al., 2019; Menezes & França, 2012; Prakash et al., 2019; Seidl et al., 2020; Topa & Alcover, 2015), with four studies measuring more than one of these possibilities (Dordoni et al., 2017; Menezes & França, 2012; Seidl et al., 2020; Topa & Alcover, 2015). The authors used between two and eight items as measures, which were not described as validated instruments but showed indices of validity and reliability.

The items used by these authors were compiled and are shown in Table 4.3. The compilation was organized into four groups called behavioral intentions for retirement, namely, (i) intention to retire early; (ii) intention to continue working or return to work; (iii) intention to take full retirement; and (iv) intention to engage in bridge employment.

4.3 Final Considerations

To highlight instruments that attempt to measure perceptions and predictors of retirement decisions, this chapter carried out a narrative review of the literature on instruments that are valid and consistent in psychometric terms. Ten instruments were presented, two of which refer to intentions or interests in retirement and eight of which refer to predictors of retirement decisions.

This narrative review of the instruments allows us to assess the available measures, highlighting both their potential and the remaining gaps and limitations in the literature on retirement-related decisions. In addition to being more numerous, the instruments related to reasons for retirement appear to have greater theoretical consistency, in light of the majority of factors addressed by Shultz and Wang (2011) in the longitudinal model of the retirement process and its potential impact factors. Of the four factors considered by the model (individual attributes, social and family factors, work and organizational factors, and socioeconomic factors), it was observed that only the fourth factor was not taken fully into account by the instruments available in the literature, as no factors or items were identified that related to future economic trends, the social security system, or government programs and policies. Considering this gap in the instruments, future studies could develop measures to incorporate these aspects.

Among the available instruments related to predictors, we highlight the instruments based on the push and pull model, which are relevant to consideration not only of the reasons for ending a career or promoting retirement but also of the reasons for continuing to work and factors that raise concerns over retirement (Chevalier et al., 2013; Fouquereau et al., 1999). We also highlight the recent development and validation of an instrument that addresses the various dimensions of reasons for continuing to work (Souza & França, 2020), which is essential in the current context in which many workers want or need to stay in the labor market even after retirement, while it also addresses and improves the dimensions highlighted by previously developed instruments (Menezes & França, 2012; Shacklock & Brunetto, 2011).

While the instruments related to predictors appear to be in theoretical agreement, the instruments related to decisions address specific directions, such as bridge employment (Kalokerinos et al., 2015) and full retirement (De Vos & Segers, 2013). The finding that researchers often create items and measurements seems to corroborate the lack of instruments, as this is the way they can assess the decision-making process surrounding retirement in the absence of a measure that considers its complexity.

We conclude that an instrument has not yet been developed that covers all the possibilities and interests related to behavior and engagement in activities surrounding retirement and the social context in which we find ourselves. We therefore suggest that instruments be developed, applied, validated, and employed in this sense and that studies be undertaken that relate the intentions of decisions with the reasons for retirement.

Changes caused by longevity, together with different work arrangements in the contemporary world, have led to increasingly different ways of experiencing retirement. In conducting studies and activities on the topic, it is therefore important that researchers and professionals pay attention to what concept of retirement is being used: if it is seen as the end of a long career, as the receipt of social security payments, as a self-image (the individual identifies as a retired person), or as a combination of these criteria (Jex & Grosch, 2012).

It is also important to emphasize that the way individuals assess their retirement decision can be related to the experiences they have had, or are having, following their decision to retire (Shultz et al., 1998), and this is part of the transition process, as shown in Shultz and Wang's model (2011). For this reason, longitudinal studies are needed to assess the retirement decision, or even the entire decision-making process (attitudes, predictors, planning, decision, retirement, adjustment, well-being), which is not often linear. This means that individuals can have attitudes toward retirement based on individual, social, and/or organizational predictors, or their attitudes can be reinforced by these predictors. Similarly, they may have to face their retirement decision and choose an option without previous planning.

We hope that the instruments described in this chapter offer a range of possibilities for assessing workers' decision-making processes with regard to retirement.

This will contribute to better understanding the circumstances workers face and promoting the implementation of practices that favor their well-being and satisfaction.

References

Adams, G. A., Prescher, J., Beehr, T. A., & Lepisto, L. (2002). Applying work-role attachment theory to retirement decision-making. *The International Journal of Aging and Human Development, 54*(2), 125–137.

Ajzen, I. (1991). The theory of planned behavior. *Organizational Behavior and Human Decision Processes, 50*, 179–211. https://doi.org/10.1016/0749-5978(91)90020-T

Amorim, S. M., & França, L. H. (2019). Reasons for retirement and retirement satisfaction. *Psicologia: Teoria e Pesquisa, 35*, e3558. https://doi.org/10.1590/0102.3772e3558

Amorim, S. M., & França, L. H. D. F. P. (2020). Health, financial and social resources as mediators to the relationship between planning and satisfaction in retirement. *Current Psychology*, 1–15. https://doi.org/10.1007/s12144-020-00836-8

Beehr, T. A., & Bennett, M. M. (2015). Working after retirement: Features of bridge employment and research directions. *Work, Aging and Retirement, 1*(1), 112–128. https://doi.org/10.1093/workar/wau007

Brasil. (2019). *Emenda Constitucional n° 103 de 12 de novembro de 2019.* Altera o sistema de previdência social e estabelece regras de transição e disposições transitórias. http://www.planalto.gov.br/ccivil_03/Constituicao/Emendas/Emc/emc103.htm

Chevalier, S., Fouquereau, E., Gillet, N., & Demulier, V. (2013). Development of the reasons for Entrepreneurs' retirement decision inventory (RERDI) and preliminary evidence of its psychometric properties in a French sample. *Journal of Career Assessment, 21*(4), 572–586. https://doi.org/10.1177/1069072712475288

De Vos, A., & Segers, J. (2013). Self directed career attitude and retirement intentions. *Career Development International, 18*(2), 155–172. https://doi.org/10.1108/CDI-04-2012-0041

Dordoni, P., Van der Heijden, B., Peters, P., Kraus-Hoogeveen, S., & Argentero, P. (2017). Keep up the good work! Age-moderated mediation model on intention to retire. *Frontiers in Psychology, 8*, 1717. https://doi.org/10.3389/fpsyg.2017.01717

Floyd, F. J., Haynes, S. N., Doll, E. R., Winemiller, D., Lemsky, C., Burgy, T. M., Werle, M., & Heilman, N. (1992). Assessing retirement satisfaction and perceptions of retirement experiences. *Psychology and Aging, 7*(4), 609–621. https://doi.org/10.1037/0882-7974.7.4.609

Fouquereau, E., Fernández, A., & Mullet, E. (1999). The retirement satisfactory inventory: Factor structure in a French sample. *European Journal of Psychological Assessment, 15*(1), 49–56. https://doi.org/10.1027/1015-5759.15.1.49

França, L. H. (2004). *Attitudes towards retirement: a cross-cultural study between New Zealand and Brazilian executives* (PhD Thesis). Psychology Department, The University of Auckland, New Zealand. https://doi.org/10.13140/RG.2.1.1302.6401

França, L. H. F. P., & Vaughan, G. (2008). Ganhos e perdas: atitudes dos executivos brasileiros e neozelandeses frente à aposentadoria. *Psicologia em Estudo, 13*(2), 207–216. https://doi.org/10.1590/S1413-73722008000200002

França, L., Menezes, G., Bendasolli, P., & Macêdo, L. (2013). Aposentar-se ou continuar trabalhando? O que influencia essa decisão? *Psicologia: Ciência e Profissão, 33*(3), 548–563. https://doi.org/10.1590/S1414-98932013000300004

Gaillard, M., & Desmette, D. (2008). Intergroup predictors of older workers' attitudes towards work and early exit. *European Journal of Work and Organizational Psychology, 17*(4), 450–481. https://doi.org/10.1080/13594320801908564

Gaillard, M., & Desmette, D. (2010). (In)validating stereotypes about older workers influences their intentions to retire early and to learn and develop. *Basic and Applied Social Psychology, 32*(1), 86–98. https://doi.org/10.1080/01973530903435763

Hershey, D. A., van Dalen, H. P., Conen, W., & Henkens, K. (2017). Are "voluntary" self-employed better prepared for retirement than "forced" self-employed? *Work, Aging and Retirement, 3*(3), 243–256. https://doi.org/10.1093/workar/wax008

Jex, S. M., & Grosch, J. (2012). Retirement decision making. In M. Wang (Ed.), *The Oxford handbook of retirement* (pp. 267–279). Oxford University Press.

Kalokerinos, E. K., von Hippel, C., & Henry, J. D. (2015). Job attitudes are differentially associated with bridge employment and phased retirement among older Australian employees. *Work, Aging and Retirement, 1*(2), 190–201. https://doi.org/10.1093/workar/wau014

Kerr, G., & Armstrong-Stassen, M. (2011). The bridge to retirement: Older workers' engagement in post-career entrepreneurship and wage-and-salary employment. *The Journal of Entrepreneurship, 20*(1), 55–76. https://doi.org/10.1177/097135571002000103

Lahlouh, K., Lacaze, D., & Huaman-Ramirez, R. (2019). Bridge employment and full retirement intentions: The role of person-environment fit. *Personnel Review, 48*(6), 1469–1490. https://doi.org/10.1108/PR-02-2018-0067

Macêdo, L. S. S., Bendassolli, P. F., Torres, T. D. L., & França, L. H. D. F. P. (2020). Adaptação e validação brasileira da Escala older workers' intentions to continue working. *Psico-USF, 25*(1), 127–138. https://doi.org/10.1590/1413-82712020250111

Marx, K. (1980). O capital (crítica da economia política). In *Livro 1: O processo de produção do capital* (Vol 1., 5ª edição). Civilização Brasileira.

Menezes, G. S., & França, L. H. F. (2012). Preditores da decisão da aposentadoria em servidores públicos federais. *Revista Psicologia: Organizações e Trabalho, 12*(3), 315–328.

Muñoz, J. J. F., Díaz, A. C., & la Hela, C. M. A. (2011). La transición hacia el retiro: Adaptación en una muestra de prejubilados espanoles de la escala Retirement Satisfaction Inventory. *Revista Española de Geriatría y Gerontología, 46*(3), 139–146. https://doi.org/10.1016/j.regg.2010.11.009

Peiró, J. M. (1985). Some perspectives of work and organizational psychology in Spain. *Occupational Psychology Newsletter, 18*, 27–47.

Pimenta, M. (2014). Autonomia financeira na aposentadoria. In S. G. Murta, C. Leandro-França, & J. Seidl (Eds.), *Programas de educação para aposentadoria: Como planejar, implementar e avaliar* (pp. 210–226). Sinopsys Editora.

Pissinati, P. S. C., Haddad, M. F., Dalmas, J. C., & Birolim, M. M. (2016). Fatores sociodemográficos e ocupacionais associados aos ganhos e perdas percebidos por trabalhadores de uma universidade pública frente à proximidade da aposentadoria. *Cadernos de Saúde Pública, 32*(9), e00141415. https://doi.org/10.1590/0102-311x00141415

Prakash, K. C., Oakman, J., Nygård, C., Siukola, A., Lumme-Sandt, K., Nikander, P., & Neupane, S. (2019). Intention to retire in employees over 50 years. What is the role of work ability and work life satisfaction? *International Journal of Environmental Research Public Health, 16*, 14–25. https://doi.org/10.3390/ijerph16142500

Rodrigues, A. R. C. S. (2016). *Trabalhadores seniores: estudo dos fatores que favorecem a intenção de permanecer no mercado de trabalho* (Dissertação de Mestrado). Instituto Politécnico do Porto. Recuperado de https://core.ac.uk/reader/83044181

Rodríguez, N. (2007). Actitudes hacia la jubilación. *Interdisciplinaria, 24*(1), 5–42. http://www.redalyc.org/articulo.oa?id=18024101

Seidl, J., Neiva, E. R., & Murta, S. G. (2020). Planning and reasons for retirement: Focus groups with Brazilian workers. *Trends in Psychology, 29*(1), 1–18. https://doi.org/10.1007/s43076-021-00063-5

Shacklock, K., & Brunetto, Y. (2011). A model of older workers' intentions to continue working. *Personnel Review, 40*(2), 252–274. https://doi.org/10.1108/00483481111106110

Shultz, K. S., & Wang, M. (2011). Psychological perspectives on the changing nature of retirement. *American Psychological Association, 66*(3), 170–179. https://doi.org/10.1037/a0022411

Shultz, K. S., Morton, K., & Werckerle, J. R. (1998). The influence of push and pull factors on voluntary early retirees, retirement decision and adjustment. *Journal of Vocational Behavior, 53*(1), 45–57.

Souza, A. P., & França, L. H. F. P. (2020). Construção e evidências de validade da escala de motivos para continuar trabalhando na aposentadoria. *Ciências Psicológicas, 14*(2), e2261. https://doi.org/10.22235/cp.v14i2.2256

Stuer, D., De Vos, A., Van der Heijden, B. I., & Akkermans, J. (2019). A sustainable career perspective of work ability: The importance of resources across the lifespan. *International Journal of Environmental Research and Public Health, 16*(14), 2572. https://doi.org/10.3390/ijerph16142572

Topa, G., & Alcover, C. M. (2015). Psychosocial factors in retirement intentions and adjustment: A multi-sample study. *Career Development International, 20*(4), 384–408. https://doi.org/10.1108/CDI-09-2014-0129

van Dam, K., van der Vorst, J. D. M., & van der Heijden, B. I. J. M. (2009). Employees' intentions to retire early: A case of planned behavior and anticipated work conditions. *Journal of Career Development, 35*(3), 265–289. https://doi.org/10.1177/0894845308327274

Vogelsang, E. M., Shultz, K. S., & Oslon, D. A. (2018). Emotional well-being following a later life career change: The roles of agency and resources. *The International Journal of Aging and Human Development, 87*(4). https://doi.org/10.1177/0091415017745972

Wang, M., & Shi, J. (2014). Psychological research on retirement. *Annual Review of Psychology, 65*, 209–233. https://doi.org/10.1146/annurev-psych-010213-115131

Yamamoto, O. H. (2015). Trabalho. In P. F. Bendassolli & J. E. Borges-Andrade (Eds.), *Dicionário de Psicologia do Trabalho e das Organizações* (pp. 641–647). Casa do Psicólogo.

Chapter 5
Resilience at Work: Research Itineraries, a Critical Review of Measures and a Proposal for Measurement of the Construct for Organizational Diagnosis

Gisela Demo, Ana Carolina Rezende Costa, Karla Veloso Coura, Áurea de Fátima Oliveira, and Sinésio Gomide Júnior

5.1 Introduction

The theoretical movement of positive organizational studies has gained prominence in the last decade as a line of investigation aimed at improving organizations, using their internal forces (Cunha et al., 2013). Based on health as opposed to disease, positive psychology aims to comprehend human qualities, virtues, potentialities, and abilities, seeking to support people for a happier, healthier, and more productive life in work organizations (Taboada et al., 2006; Scorsolini-Comin et al., 2013).

In this context, the contemporary organizational environment requires the employee to be flexible and able to adapt to new demands, challenges, and difficulties, that is, to be a resilient worker (Ribeiro et al., 2011). The authors point out that with regard to comprehending the resilience process in organizational contexts, it is important to highlight the role of social support that allows employees to overcome adverse conditions and to live with the uncertainty inherent in the current, dynamic, and globalized organizational environment.

Resilience is one of the processes that explain the overcoming of crises and adversities in individuals, groups, and organizations (Alvarez et al., 1998; Campanella, 2006; Cecconello, 2003; Yunes, 2003). Furthermore, resilience has

G. Demo (✉) · A. C. R. Costa
University of Brasília, Brasília, DF, Brazil
e-mail: giselademo@unb.br

K. V. Coura
State University of Montes Claros, Montes Claros, MG, Brazil

Á. de. F. Oliveira · S. Gomide Júnior
Federal University of Uberlândia, Uberlândia, MG, Brazil
e-mail: aurea.oliveira@ufu.br

M. O. Macambira et al. (eds.), *Assessing Organizational Behaviors*,
https://doi.org/10.1007/978-3-030-81311-6_5

been identified as an important predictor of adaptation to adverse conditions of life and work, happiness, and recovery from traumatic situations (Batista & Oliveira, 2008).

Models for measuring organizational constructs, also known as instruments, scales, and measures, translate the perceptions that people have about attitudes and behaviors in the work environment, so that by evaluating these perceptions, the effectiveness of organizational strategies, policies, and practices can be identified. Therefore, the main aim of this chapter is to present a review of the international scientific literature on the theoretical development and empirical studies concerning the resilience at work construct, with a special focus on the proposed measurement models. Accordingly, in the first instance, the resilience at work construct will be presented, followed by a systematic review of the theoretical development and of the instruments elaborated, as well as a critical analysis of the instruments available in the literature. Finally, we end the chapter by proposing a resilience measure for organizational diagnosis and its application instructions.

In view of the strategic character of resilience at work for contemporary people management in organizations, the systematic review of the current high-impact international scientific productions proposed contributes to mapping the state of the art on the topic. In this way, research itineraries will be unveiled, as well as gaps in the literature, that shed light on new possibilities to rethink and encourage resilience at work, producing healthier work environments, which will contribute to the optimization of results at individual and organizational levels.

5.2 Resilience: Its Origins, Assumptions, and Definitions

Since the late 1970s, the concept of resilience, a word originally from the Latin *resiliens* (Pinheiro, 2004), began to be studied more carefully by psychiatry and developmental psychology (Lopes & Martins, 2011). However, the concept of resilience is an old one, and its use is common in the field of physics and engineering, having been used for the first time by the Englishman Thomas Young, in 1807, to refer to the capacity of a material to receive impact energy without suffering permanent deformation (Barlach et al., 2008; Oliveira et al., 2008).

In the field of human sciences, the concept of resilience began to be used at the end of the twentieth century to characterize individuals that were immune to any adversity (Emílio & Martins, 2012). In Brazil, studies on resilience are recent, since the first works published in this area can be found only from the end of the 1990s (Lopes & Martins, 2011), with resilience having only been present in international psychology congresses from the 2000s onward (Batista, 2010).

In principle, the term resilience was understood as a synonym for invulnerability (Luthar et al., 2000). This understanding brought influences on the way of thinking about the construct in the psychological field, which for decades considered resilience as a fixed and innate characteristic of the individual (Emílio & Martins, 2012).

For this reason, the focus of the research was initially concentrated on certain personality traits (Ribeiro et al., 2011).

However, with the evolution of research on the topic, people began to be vulnerable to adverse situations, with resilient people being those that managed to recover and present healthy development in adulthood (Souza & Cerveny, 2006). The development of resilience in individuals also started to be considered, which was not possible when it was conceived as a personality trait (Ribeiro et al., 2011).

Resilient individuals would be those that did not experience stress or did not feel threatened by adversity or risk (Poletto et al., 2004). For Rutter (1993), resilience is a concept widely used to explain differences in the effects that the same level of stress has on different individuals. However, Brandão et al. (2011), when studying the concepts and origins of resilience in a comprehensive way, realized that, in general, in relation to the concepts adopted on the theme, English and North American researchers understand resilience as resistance to stress, while Brazilian and Latin-speaking researchers have a concept that comprehends resilience, sometimes as resistance to stress and sometimes as being associated with processes of recovery and overcoming emotional upheavals caused by stress.

Furthermore, resilience is considered a process that allows adversity to be faced through the interaction of social and intrapsychic aspects (characteristics and capabilities of each individual) with the environment (Alvarez et al., 1998; Cecconello, 2003; Yunes, 2003). For Lazarus and Folkman (1984), a way to manage and extinguish stress is by coping, which refers to the ways in which one tries to change circumstances, or the way they are interpreted, in order to make them more favorable and less threatening. Coping can also be defined as the set of strategies that people use to adapt to the adverse events that happen (Antoniazzi et al., 1998).

Along these lines, Hockenbury and Hockenbury (2003) described two ways to manage stress: coping strategies focused on the problem and those focused on emotion. In the first form, efforts are directed at managing or changing a threatening or harmful stressor. In the second, efforts are directed to regulating or alleviating the emotional impact of the stressful situation.

Although closely correlated, resilience and coping are distinct concepts. Resilience corresponds to the totality of the subject's experience in the sense of adapting and overcoming adversity, and coping with the strategies for an appropriate solution to a situation of tension (Taboada et al., 2006). Among the mechanisms that mediate resilience, personal coping strategies may be included (Rutter, 2007). Therefore, among the variables that contribute to greater resilience, coping strategies stand out (Busnello et al., 2009).

However, the complexity of resilience is not limited to the existence of diverse aspects that can influence the individual's adaptation process, or to the countless forms and proportions in which these aspects can be combined (Reppold et al., 2012). Masten (2001), and Luthar et al. (2000) treated resilience as a dynamic, multidimensional, or ecosystemic process. Waller (2001) added that resilience is comprehended in a systemic way, based on the individual-context relationship, which will be discussed in the next section.

5.3 Resilience at Work

The modern work scenario requires the worker to be flexible, adaptable to changes, and able to constantly adjust to the new demands, challenges, and difficulties faced daily (Ribeiro et al., 2011; Taboada et al., 2006). Concepts and methods employed by organizations are able to encourage workers to have attitudes desired by the organization. However, in some cases, an obscure movement between the attitude required by the organization and the attitude desired by the workers puts their resilience to the test, that is, creates in them attitudes that make them adapt to the work, in order to achieve positive results even in an adverse context (Cimbalista, 2006).

According to Job (2003), the sphere of work is probably the main source of meaning and order in human life. Therefore, it is important to investigate the way of being a subject in the globalized work environment and the ways in which the individual is resilient in the face of adversity, as knowing how to face difficult situations can be the difference between adequate and inadequate performance and between staying healthy and becoming sick (Emílio & Martins, 2012). From this perspective, Taboada et al. (2006) pointed out that it is necessary to study the potentials and skills of people in order to comprehend their mental health and not concentrate only on studies focused on pathologies, mental illnesses, and human deficiencies, thus advocating positive psychology. Accordingly, there seems to be a tendency to incorporate stress management intervention programs from positive psychology into the workplace (Tetrick & Winslow, 2015). For the authors, these programs are fundamental for promoting the health of employees.

When it comes to understanding the resilience process in organizational contexts, it is important to highlight the risk and protective factors that allow employees to overcome adverse conditions and live with the uncertainty inherent in the current organizational environment (Ribeiro et al., 2011). Barlach, Limongi-França, and Malvezzi, in 2008, coined the term "resilience at work" when they investigated stress and coping in executives and students of continuing education courses, highlighting that resilience at work stems from the individual's ability to reframe adverse situations (Gomide Jr. et al., 2015). In addition to risk and protection factors, coping strategies have also been important in understanding an individual's resilience (Oliveira et al., 2008).

Risk factors are tensions originating from multiple stressful events or from a variety of other factors, namely, the pressure and responsibility of the work, lack of family time, lack of support from peers or superiors, limited freedom of creation, lack of autonomy in activities, fear of losing a job, obligations of having to make cuts in the workforce, and moral harassment (Job, 2003). When exposed to risk factors, individuals are more likely to acquire a disease (Sapienza & Pedromônico, 2005). Protection factors, on the other hand, help to overcome difficulties (Eisenstein & de Souza, 1993; Ralha-Simões, 2001). Autonomy, self-esteem, respect, recognition, participation of family and friends, and the support of peers and superiors can be cited as protective factors for a worker within the context of adverse work (Job, 2003).

When considering the importance of risk factors and protective factors to understand the phenomenon of resilience, it is important to highlight that, in the organizational context, the resources available to workers to face adversity are not only present in their field of work but also in other aspects of their lives (Ribeiro et al., 2011). For this reason, although there is empirical evidence that a large part of the existing diversity among individual adaptation patterns may result from the combination of the effects of risk and protection factors, the study of resilience should not be limited to the investigation of these elements (Reppold et al., 2012).

Resilience tends to be particularly important and often essential in times of transition, change, and uncertainty, which commonly produce a high level of stress in individuals (Ribeiro et al., 2011), especially when faced with crises, such as the COVID-19 pandemic, a reality present worldwide that affects organizations in a particular way. Therefore, the investigation of resilience in workers is emerging in the management literature, being of paramount importance for managers, as it is a promising subject for understanding the behavior, human perception, and performance of the worker, especially in times of crisis. However, it is still the subject of a limited number of studies, especially with regard to organizational interventions to promote resilience (Angst, 2009), which constitutes an important gap in the scientific literature (Emílio & Martins, 2012; Farsen et al., 2018).

Since resilience in the organizational sphere refers to the existence or construction of adaptive resources that preserve the healthy relationship between the individual and their work (Barlach et al., 2008), the professionals that deal with these relationships need to understand and perform actions to protect the employee's health in the work context (Ribeiro et al., 2011). For Batista and Oliveira (2012), understanding resilience as human potentiality can be an indicator capable of influencing attitudes and behaviors at work.

5.4 Systematic Review of Resilience at Work

To achieve the objective of mapping the state of the art of recent scientific production on resilience at work, a systematic review of the literature was carried out in the Web of Science (WoS) database. This database is considered one of the most reliable research databases, being one of the most comprehensive, in temporal terms. With it founded in 1964, it contains publications from the beginning of the twentieth century until today, mainly, favoring high-impact international journals, giving relevance and quality to the review (Birkle et al., 2020; Chadegani et al., 2013).

The systematic review was based on the protocol proposed by Cronin et al. (2008), formed by the following steps: (a) formulation of the research question, (b) definition of inclusion and exclusion criteria, (c) assessment of the quality of the literature, (d) assessment of relevance, and (e) assessment of eligibility. To analyze the included results, bibliometric, bibliographic coupling, co-quotation, and co-occurrence analyses were carried out, using the VOSviewer 1.6.10 software, which performs bibliographic mapping through the identification of groups of associated publications (van Eck & Waltman, 2017). This bibliometric analysis highlights the behavior and development of an area of knowledge, while it identifies theoretical and empirical gaps in scientific production (Araújo & Alvarenga, 2011), and is therefore consistent with the objectives proposed in this chapter.

The first step (a) referred to the research problem, which was to identify the current scenario of scientific publications related to resilience at work and new research possibilities for the construct.

Then, in step (b) of the protocol, an investigation of the publications on the Web of Science database was carried out in May 2020. First, the search proceeded through the keywords "*resilience at work*," "*organi*ational resilience*," or "*psychological resilience*" in titles, abstracts, keywords, or keywords plus, providing a total of 1550 publications. It should be highlighted that the use of the asterisk in the term "organi*ational" allows it to cover articles with variations in the spelling of the word, with the "s" being used in British English and the "z" in American English. Then, the "article" document type and the time period of the previous 5 years (January 2016 to May 2020) were delimited, with the purpose of portraying the state of the art of the subject. The results were also filtered by areas of research knowledge, namely, *business economics*, *psychology*, and *public administration*, as they are areas similar to the researched construct. With the adoption of these inclusion and exclusion criteria, 331 articles were selected.

To achieve step (c), there was the identification of journals indexed by the Journal Citation Report (JCR), seeking to distinguish the works published in high impact journals. It should be mentioned that the impact factor considered was that of 2018 because the 2019 index had not been published at the time of the search. After this sorting, the number of articles totaled 266.

In step (d), it was verified whether the title, the abstract, or the keywords were relevant or not to the context of resilience at work. With this, 176 works were removed, resulting in 90 articles.

Finally, in step (e), the articles were analyzed in full, in order to verify whether they were eligible or not for inclusion considering the topic in question. This analysis resulted in 31 articles, which made up the corpus of the present work. Figure 5.1 presents the steps of the systematic literature review.

Initially, the demographic profile of the scientific production on the topic and the evolution of the number of publications per year were analyzed. It was found that 65% of the articles had been published in the previous 18 months (from January 2019 to May 2020, the moment of data collection in the Web of Science), which may suggest that the production of the area has an increasing trend. Although the number of publications was low from 2016 to 2018, in 2019, there was a significant increase in the interest of researchers in relation to resilience at work. Figure 5.2 illustrates the evolution of publications over the previous 5 years.

Regarding the journals that published the most, the International Journal of Human Resource Management predominated, with four publications, followed by Applied Psychology an International Review (three publications); Frontiers in Psychology (two publications); International Journal of Entrepreneurial Behavior Research (two publications); Journal of Nursing Management (two publications); and *Revista Argentina de Clinica Psicologica* (two publications).

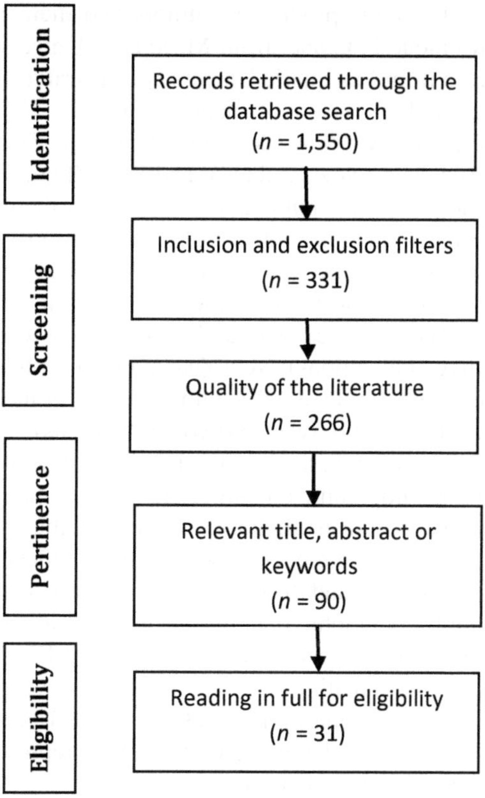

Source: prepared by the authors, 2021.

Fig. 5.1 Search strategy flow diagram. (Source: Prepared by the authors, 2021)

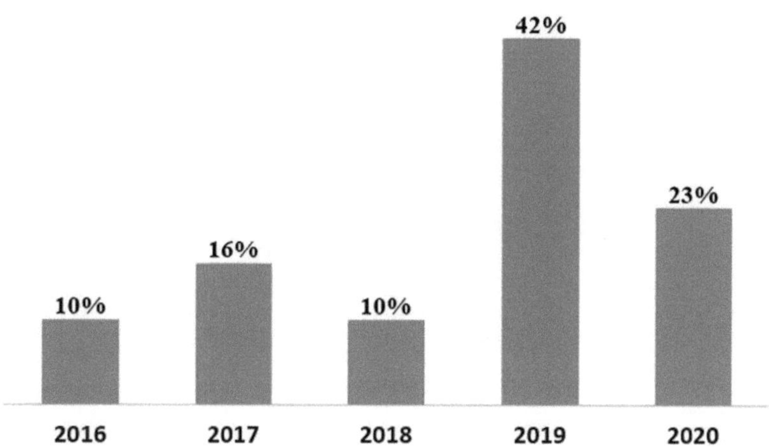

Source: prepared by the authors, 2021.

Fig. 5.2 Percentage of publications per year. (Source: Prepared by the authors, 2021)

The most productive authors and their corresponding professional links were Monique F. Crane, from Macquarie University (Australia); Layla Jayne Branicki, also from Macquarie University (Australia); Sanna Malinen, from the University of Canterbury (New Zealand); Katharina Näswall, also from the University of Canterbury (New Zealand); Bridgette Sullivan-Taylor, from the University of Auckland (New Zealand); and Wen Zhou, from Central South University (China), each with two publications. Although there is a dispersion of researchers on the subject, there is evidence of a specialist group on the subject in New Zealand, represented by the universities of Auckland and Canterbury. The other authors published only once during the analysis period.

The countries that published the most were China (eight publications), Australia (five publications), New Zealand (four publications), the United States (four publications), England (three publications), France (three publications), Brazil (two publications), and Sweden (two publications).

Considering the initial relational analysis of the references of the articles, that is, the bibliographic coupling, this aims to map the thematic proximity, whether theoretical and/or methodological, among the articles (Marshakova, 1981). For Grácio (2016), the reference list of an article reflects the researcher's knowledge construction process and the conversation established by them with their peers. Therefore, in the bibliographic coupling analysis, it is possible to identify groups of associated publications (van Eck & Waltman, 2017), with higher numbers of references in common equating to stronger linkage between the articles (Egghe & Rousseau, 2002).

In this scenario, Fig. 5.3 shows the 14 articles with the strongest links between them, subdivided into 3 clusters, here represented by groups of publications associated with their themes.

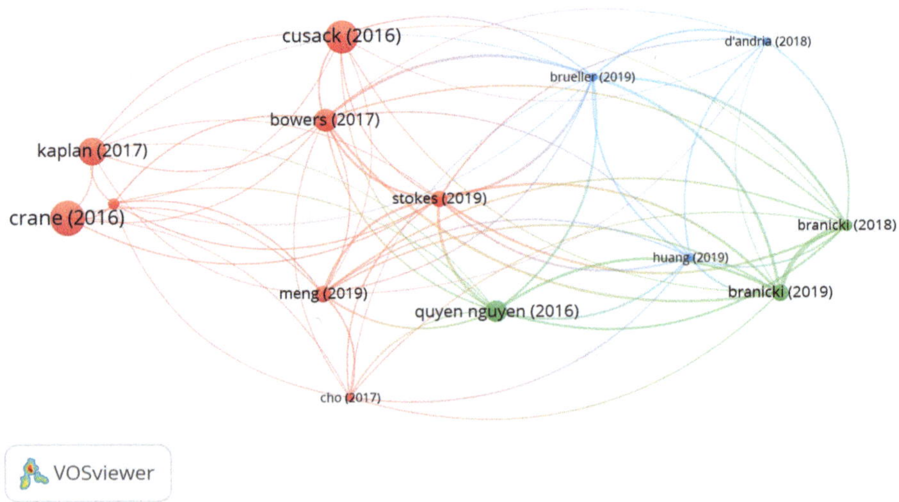

Source: elaborated by the authors through *VOSviewer*, 2021.

Fig. 5.3 Bibliographic coupling. (Source: Elaborated by the authors through *VOSviewer*, 2021)

A central theme that can be extracted from the articles categorized in the cluster represented by the color red is that of psychological resilience in professional exhaustion. To cite some of the studies, Crane and Searle (2016) researched the positive and negative points of the types of stressors in psychological resilience and the role of resilience in the moderation between hindrances and strain in the workplace. Kaplan et al. (2017), in turn, examined the mechanistic role of psychological resilience in worker exhaustion. The results indicated that an increase in mindfulness was related to an increase in resilience, which in turn was related to a decrease in burnout. From this perspective, Meng et al. (2019) discussed the role of the social exchange in the relationship of resilience with organizational commitment and professional exhaustion. The study provided information on the mechanisms of resilience in the workplace, from the perspective of social exchange, and also emphasized the importance of reciprocity between supervisors and subordinates in the practice of human management.

The green cluster addresses studies regarding the association between individual and organizational resilience, such as the work of Branicki et al. (2019), which inductively theorizes the links between these types of resilience. The reports of this study reveal the microprocesses involved in the production of resilient organizations and highlight the challenges faced in resilience work in large organizations, with implications for how human resource management interventions can help promote individual and also organizational resilience. In this sense, when affirming that there is a limited understanding of the individual and contextual factors that promote resilient behaviors in organizations, Nguyen et al. (2016) dedicated their study to the relationships between dispositional variables (proactive personality and optimism), leadership styles (empowering and contingent reward leadership), and employee resilience. The results highlight the importance of measuring employee resilience as a contextualized behavioral capacity, taking into account the interaction of organizational facilitators and dispositional variables. Another study classified in this cluster, that of Branicki et al. (2018), aimed to investigate how the entrepreneurial behaviors of employees support the resilience of small- and medium-sized companies. According to the authors, the findings indicate that companies should pay more attention to developing capacities to deal with uncertainty, activating the ability to think creatively in response to crises, and generating and leveraging personal relationships.

Finally, the blue cluster covers studies that deal with resilience in adverse and uncertain environments. Brueller et al. (2019) conducted their study in the context of a declining company. For the authors, the working relationships constructed between employees can help a declining organization to deal with setbacks and difficulties. The authors also highlighted the coping and adaptive qualities for the company. From this perspective, D'Andria et al. (2018) investigated how resilience can support entrepreneurs in uncertain environments by identifying forms of resilience during the business acquisition process, which helped the entrepreneur to overcome adversity and succeed. For this, the researchers proposed a different approach to the study of entrepreneurial resilience, analyzing it in relation to the logic of action (causation/effectuation). Huang et al. (2019), when addressing aspects of employee well-being, resilience, and gender, claimed that organizational resilience can be promoted through human resource management practices that improve the well-being of employees and their ability to deal with adversity.

The co-citation analysis highlights the fundamental and most influential works in the studied theme (Small, 1973), as it presents the relationship between two articles in relation to the number of publications in which they appear cited concurrently (Grácio, 2016). The scientific community establishes the proximity and interlocution of two studies as this forms connections in the process of producing new knowledge (Grácio, 2016). Accordingly, the articles with the highest number of co-citations were those of Bonanno (2004), Shin et al. (2012), and Luthar et al. (2000).

Next, the most frequent keywords were identified in the 31 articles through the co-occurrence network, presented in Fig. 5.4.

From the keywords found, it appears that *psychological resilience* had the highest number of occurrences, appearing 16 times. In the second position, the term *resilience* stands out with 15 citations. The words *performance* and *workplace* appear with the same number of occurrences: 12. In addition to these, sequentially, the most cited were *work* (nine occurrences), *stress* (eight occurrences), *positive emotions* (six occurrences), *resources*, *management*, *mental health* (five occurrences each), and *organizational resilience* (three occurrences), revealing the influence of variables such as the work environment, management, resources, mental health, and positive emotions on resilience at work.

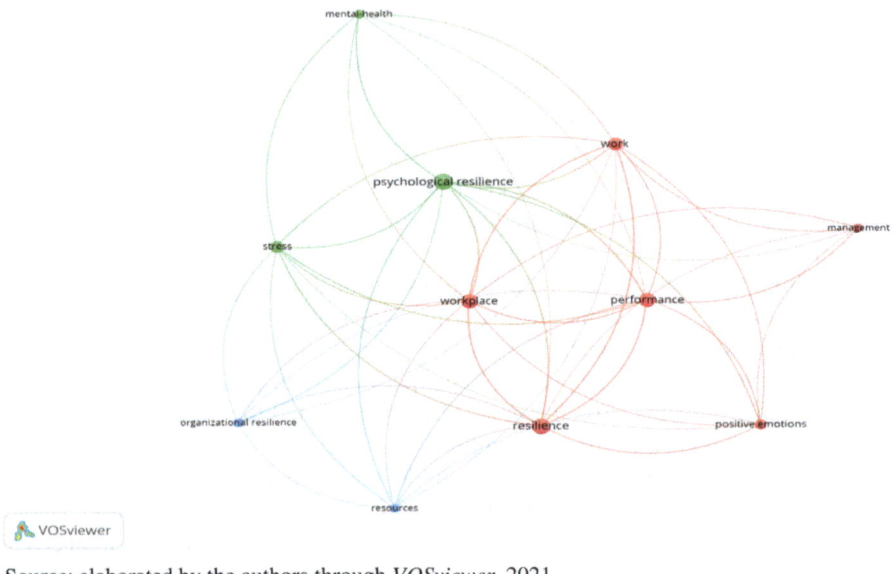

Source: elaborated by the authors through *VOSviewer*, 2021.

Fig. 5.4 Co-occurrence of keywords. (Source: Elaborated by the authors through *VOSviewer*, 2021)

5.5 Resilience at Work Measuring Instruments

Studies on resilience in the context of work are still recent (Lopes & Martins, 2011). Furthermore, specific resilience measures for the work environment are rare (Gomide Jr. et al., 2015), and their development has received less research attention than the impact on organizational management (Näswall et al., 2019), constituting a gap in the literature. Therefore, there is a need to expand studies with a focus on resilience measures, providing instruments with evidence of validity and reliability, which can support decisions by organizational managers, constituting one of the main purposes of this chapter. As a starting point, it is necessary to identify the existing models for measuring resilience at work. Only three were identified and will be presented in chronological order, following the evolution and progress of the proposals.

The first model for measuring resilience at work identified in the literature was developed and validated by Winwood et al. (2013). The Resilience at Work (R@W) Scale has 20 items; divided into 7 factors, namely, living authentically, finding one's calling, maintaining perspective, managing stress, interacting cooperatively, staying healthy, and building networks, with Cronbach's alpha of .84. According to the authors, this scale was developed for use in contexts of individual work-related performance and emotional distress. In practice, Walpita and Arambepola (2020) used the Resilience at Work Scale aiming to find out how the level of resilience is related to job performance.

The second model, called the Employee Resilience Scale (EmpRes), proposed by Näswall et al. (2015), was later validated with confirmatory analyses by Senbeto and Hon (2020), with Jöreskog's rho of .90 and 9 items which were designed to reflect the behavioral focus of the employee's resilience construct. The study developed by Senbeto and Hon (2020), which aimed to examine the mediating effect of employee resilience on the relationship between market turbulence and service innovation, and to analyze whether this mediation process was moderated by organizational readiness for change, used the EmpRes to measure employee resilience.

Finally, the measurement model proposed by Costa et al. (2019) is presented. This measure proposed the confirmatory validation, through structural equation modeling, of the *Escala de Resiliência no Trabalho* adapted and validated, through exploratory methods, for the organizational context by Batista and Oliveira (2008), based on the seminal model validated for Brazilian adolescents by Pesce et al. (2005), called the *Escala de Resiliência.*

The model by Costa et al. (2019) has advanced due to providing external validity for the *Escala de Resiliência no Trabalho*, and by obtaining evidence of validity and confirmatory reliability for the scale. The unifactorial structure was maintained, with fewer items (9) compared to the exploratory model that contained 15 items, revealing internal validity (factor loadings ranging from .51 to .78) and good reliability (ρ = .86), in addition to very satisfactory fit indices (χ^2 (25) = 75.492; $p < .001$; NC = 3.0; CFI = .96; RMSEA = .07). This proposal for measuring the construct is the only measure that addresses resilience as a set of beliefs, in line with the assumptions of positive psychology, distinguishing itself from the two other measures presented.

Table 5.1 Psychometric data of the instruments

Authors/year of publication	Construct evaluated	No. of items/ Factors	Reliability	Validation
Batista and Oliveira (2008) and Costa et al. (2019)	*Escala de Resiliência no Trabalho*	9 items/1 factor	.86[a]	Exploratory Factorial (2008) and Confirmatory Factorial (2019) Analyses
Winwood et al. (2013)	Resilience at Work (R@W)	20 items/7 factors	.84[b]	Exploratory and Confirmatory Factorial Analyses
Näswall et al. (2015) and Senbeto and Hon (2020)	Employee Resilience Scale (EmpRes)	9 items/1 factor	.90[a]	Exploratory Factorial (2015) and Confirmatory Factorial (2020) Analyses

Source: Prepared by the authors, 2021
Note:
[a]Jöreskog's rho
[b]Cronbach's alpha

Table 5.1 presents, in chronological order, a synthesis of the characteristics of the reported instruments.

5.6 Critical Analysis of the Instruments for Measuring Resilience at Work

In the field of positive psychology, the virtuous aspects of human beings, their competences, skills, and potentials have gained visibility, having previously been obscured by the pathological view of psychology, focused on the treatment of mental illnesses. This new approach has as its beacon the development, self-realization, and search for the meaning of people's lives, finding a fertile field for thriving in organizational environments. In these settings, positive psychology proposes to support people in seeking a happier and more productive life. On the other hand, modern organizations require greater flexibility from the individual, including the ability to adapt to new demands, challenges, and difficulties. From this configuration, the concept of "resilience at work" appears in the literature.

The concept "resilience" appeared in physics and engineering in the nineteenth century and concerned the ability of materials to maintain their structure after receiving a deformation force. In psychology, the term started to designate those individuals capable of adapting and overcoming adversities, being a dynamic process in which the influences of the environment and the individual interact in a reciprocal relationship, and which, despite the adversity, allow the person to adapt. The definition of resilience, therefore, encompasses an individual's beliefs about their ability to recover from conflicting and adverse situations, maintaining balance and responsibility. In the organizational context, the concept is aimed at the existence or construction of adaptive resources that preserve the healthy relationship between the individual and their work or between the individual and their employing system.

In the midst of the proposal for the use of the concept in work contexts, the problem of its measurement arises. The review work in this chapter identified three measurement models present in the international literature that maintain distinct characteristics.

The first one presented in this chapter (Winwood et al., 2013) used the concept of resilience intrinsically linked to stress. However, as demonstrated throughout this chapter, it is an already outdated link in terms of the concept of the construct. Another characteristic that deserves to be mentioned is the concept of "resilience as behavior" (Senbeto & Hon, 2020) and the definition of resilience as a set of beliefs (Costa et al., 2019). These beliefs refer to the individual's confidence in their ability to recover from conflicting and adverse situations, maintaining balance, responsibility, and the possibility of constructing (or reconstructing) adaptive resources that preserve their health and the health of their relationships with the work and the organization that employs them.

As the authors emphasized (Costa et al., 2019), the model they validated, based on a theoretical reference constructed around beliefs, is at the forefront of the conceptual evolution of resilience at work in line with the assumptions of positive psychology, distinguishing itself from the other two measures described. According to these assumptions, the focus of the theory regarding virtues and competencies lies in the individual's ability to believe in their potential, which would lead them to make efforts toward their own success. Therefore, this measurement model was chosen to be detailed in the following section, as a proposal for a measure of resilience at work, with possibilities for use in organizational diagnosis.

5.7 From Theory to Practice: Proposal of a Resilience at Work Measure to Be Used for Organizational Diagnosis

As reported in the previous section, the measurement model, named *Resilience at Work Scale*, validated by Costa et al. (2019), presents very reliable psychometric indices, being indicated for use in diagnostic evaluation by organizational managers, as well as for application in future studies of relational research models in the areas of People Management and Organizational Behavior. Figure 5.5 presents the application model of the *Resilience at Work Scale*.

For the purposes of organizational diagnosis, the results can be obtained by the simple arithmetic mean, accompanied by the measure of dispersion (e.g., standard deviation), of the items on the scale, remembering that each item can have its value assessed individually as well. Therefore, a value between 1 and 5 (extremes of the scale) will be obtained. The interpretation of the results will occur considering that the higher the value of the arithmetic mean obtained, the more the respondent indicates their agreement with the measurement items.

Please read carefully the 9 statements that illustrate work situations presented below. Then mark how much you agree or disagree with each of the statements, indicating the number from 1 to 5 that best reflects your perception, according to the scale below.

1	2	3	4	5
Completely disagree	**Disagree**	**Do not agree or disagree**	**Agree**	**Completely agree**

In my work....

1	I remain interested in it.	
2	When I'm in a difficult situation, I usually find a way out.	
3	I have enough energy to do what I need to do.	
4	I'm determined.	
5	I can normally look at a situation in several ways.	
6	My work makes sense to me.	
7	I'm proud to have accomplished things.	
8	I'm a person that people can count on in emergency situations.	
9	I'm disciplined.	

Fig. 5.5 *Resilience at Work Scale*. (Source: Prepared by the authors, 2021)

Values between 1 and 2.9 denote disagreement, that is, the respondent does not present resilience at work. Values between 3 and 3.9 indicate the respondent's indifference, and, finally, values between 4 and 5 are indicators of agreement, that is, the respondent presents resilience at work. In practical terms, the higher the mean obtained, the greater the level of resilience in the work presented by the respondent.

Accordingly, when assessing the global mean of the resilience level or the value of each item in a particular way, specific and customized actions can be taken by people managers toward the production of healthier work environments and with greater organizational effectiveness, which is especially desirable in times of crises, pandemics, and changes.

5.8 Conclusion

This chapter provides contributions toward carrying out an extensive systematic review of the literature that exposed the current state of the art in constructing and obtaining evidence of validity of measurement models that deal with the perception of resilience at work, in addition to illustrating the application of one of these models as a diagnostic tool that can be used by organizations, establishing a bridge between theory and practice. Therefore, it represents advances due to proposing an operationally valid and reliable measure, capable of supporting the work of managers because resilience as a state is subject to development, which is one of the strongest characteristics of positive psychology when proposing a construct. From an instrumental point of view, managers can use this model because it allows the planning of actions aimed at the strategic management of people in line with the need for evidence-based management, a prominent object of the contemporary scientific literature.

References

Alvarez, A. S., Moraes, M. C. L., & Rabinovich, E. P. (1998). Resiliência: um estudo com brasileiros institucionalizados. *Revista Brasileira de Crescimento e Desenvolvimento Humano, 8*(1/2), 64–69.

Angst, R. (2009). Psicologia e Resiliência: uma revisão de literatura. *Psicologia Argumento, 27*(58), 253–260.

Antoniazzi, A. D., Dell'Aglio, D. D., & Bandeira, D. R. (1998). O conceito de *coping*: uma revisão teórica. *Estudos de Psicologia, 3*(2), 273–294.

Araújo, R. F., & Alvarenga, L. (2011). A bibliometria na pesquisa científica da pós- graduação brasileira de 1987 a 2007. *Revista Eletrônica de Biblioteconomia, 16*(31), 51–70.

Barlach, L., Limongi-França, A. C., & Malvezzi, S. (2008). O conceito de resiliência aplicado ao trabalho nas organizações. *Revista Interamericana de Psicologia, 42*(1), 101–112.

Batista, R. L. (2010). *Percepção de suporte organizacional, afeto positivo, afeto negativo e resiliência: Antecedentes da confiança do empregado na organização* (Dissertação de mestrado). Universidade Federal de Uberlândia, Uberlândia, MG, Brasil.

Batista, R. L., & Oliveira, A. F. (2008). Validação da escala de resiliência para o contexto organizacional. Sessão de pôster apresentada no *III Congresso Brasileiro de Psicologia Organizacional e do Trabalho*, 3. Florianópolis, Santa Catarina.

Batista, R. L., & Oliveira, A. F. (2012). Antecedentes da confiança do empregado na organização. *Estudos de Psicologia, 17*(2), 247–254.

Birkle, C., Pendlebury, D. A., Schnell, J., & Adams, J. (2020). Web of Science as a data source for research on scientific and scholarly activity. *Quantitative Science Studies, 1*(1), 363–376.

Bonanno, G. A. (2004). Loss, trauma, and human resilience: Have we underestimated the human capacity to thrive after extremely aversive events? *American Psychologist, 59*(1), 20–28.

Brandão, J. M., Mahfoud, M., & Gianordoli-Nascimento, I. F. (2011). A construção do conceito de resiliência em psicologia: discutindo as origens. *Paidéia, 21*(49), 263–271.

Branicki, L. J., Sullivan-Taylor, B., & Livschitz, S. R. (2018). How entrepreneurial resilience generates resilient SMEs. *International Journal of Entrepreneurial Behavior & Research, 24*(7), 1244–1263.

Branicki, L., Steyer, V., & Sullivan-Taylor, B. (2019). Why resilience managers aren't resilient, and what human resource management can do about it. *The International Journal of Human Resource Management, 30*(8), 1261–1286.

Brueller, D., Brueller, N., Brueller, R., & Carmeli, A. (2019). Interorganizational relationships in times of decline: Implications for organizational resilience. *Applied Psychology.* https://doi.org/10.1111/apps.12185

Busnello, F., Schaefer, L., & Kristensen, C. (2009). Eventos estressores e estratégias de *coping* em adolescentes: implicações na aprendizagem. *Revista Semestral da Associação Brasileira de Psicologia Escolar e Educacional, 2*(13), 315–323.

Campanella, T. (2006). Urban resilience and the recovery of New Orleans. *Journal of the American Planning Association, 72*(2), 141–146.

Cecconello, A. M. (2003). *Resiliência e vulnerabilidade em famílias em situação de risco* (Tese de doutorado). Universidade Federal do Rio Grande do Sul, Porto Alegre, RS, Brasil.

Chadegani, A., Salehi, H., Yunus, M., Farhadi, H., Fooladi, M., Farhadi, M., & Ale Ebrahim, N. (2013). A comparison between two main academic literature collections: Web of Science and Scopus databases. *Asian Social Science, 9*(5), 18–26.

Cimbalista, S. (2006). Reflexões sobre o trabalho e a subjetividade de trabalhadores resilientes sob o sistema de produção flexível. *Revista da FAE, 9*(2), 13–28.

Costa, A. C., Demo, G., & Paschoal, T. (2019). Do human resources policies and practices produce resilient public servants? Evidence of the validity of a structural model and measurement models. *Revista Brasileira de Gestão de Negócios, 21*(1), 70–85.

Crane, M. F., & Searle, B. J. (2016). Building resilience through exposure to stressors: The effects of challenges versus hindrances. *Journal of Occupational Health Psychology, 2*(4), 468–479.

Cronin, P., Ryan, F., & Coughlan, M. (2008). Undertaking a literature review: A step-by-step approach. *British Journal of Nursing, 17*(1), 38–43.

Cunha, M. P., Rego, A., & Lopes, M. P. (2013). Comportamento Organizacional Positivo. *Análise Psicológica, 31*(4), 313–328.

D'Andria, A., Gabarret, I., & Vedel, B. (2018). Resilience and effectuation for a successful business takeover. *International Journal of Entrepreneurial Behavior & Research, 24*(7), 1200–1221.

Egghe, L., & Rousseau, R. (2002). Co-citation, bibliographic coupling and a characterization of lattice citation networks. *Scientometrics, 55*(3), 349–361.

Eisenstein, E., & de Souza, R. P. (1993). *Situações de risco à saúde de crianças e adolescentes*. Vozes.

Emílio, E. V., & Martins, M. C. F. (2012). Resiliência e autoconceito profissional em policiais militares: Um estudo descritivo. *Mudanças – Psicologia da Saúde, 20*(1–2), 23–29.

Farsen, T. C., Costa, A. B., & Silva, N. (2018). Resiliência no trabalho no campo da Psicologia: um estudo bibliométrico. *Psicología desde el Caribe, 35*(1), 81–103.

Gomide, S., Jr., Silvestrin, L. H. B., & Oliveira, A. F. (2015). Bem-estar no trabalho: O impacto das satisfações com os suportes organizacionais e o papel mediador da resiliência no trabalho. *Revista Psicologia: Organizações e Trabalho, 15*(1), 19–29.

Grácio, M. C. C. (2016). Acoplamento bibliográfico e análise de cocitação: revisão teórico-conceitual. *Encontros Bibli: Revista Eletrônica de Biblioteconomia e Ciência da Informação, 21*(47), 82–99.

Hockenbury, D. H., & Hockenbury, S. E. (2003). *Descobrindo a Psicologia*. Manole.

Huang, Q., Xing, Y., & Gamble, J. (2019). Job demands–resources: A gender perspective on employee well-being and resilience in retail stores in China. *The International Journal of Human Resource Management, 30*(8), 1323–1341.

Job, F. P. P. (2003). Resiliência na organização: Estudo de caso da medição e avaliação da resiliência de indivíduos em uma organização industrial. *Revista Faculdade de Ciências Médicas de Sorocaba, 5*(1), 33–42.

Kaplan, J. B., Bergman, A. L., Christopher, M., Bowen, S., & Hunsinger, M. (2017). Role of resilience in mindfulness training for first responders. *Mindfulness, 8*(5), 1373–1380.

Lazarus, R. S., & Folkman, S. (1984). *Stress, appraisal, and coping*. Springer.

Lopes, V. R., & Martins, M. C. F. (2011). Validação fatorial da Escala de Resiliência de Connor-Davidson (Cd-Risk-10) para brasileiros. *Revista Psicologia: Organizações e Trabalho, 11*(2), 36–50.

Luthar, S. S., Cicchetti, B., & Becker, B. (2000). The construct of resilience: A critical evaluation and guidelines for future work. *Child Development, 71*(3), 543–562.

Marshakova, I. V. (1981). Citation networks in information science. *Scientometrics, 3*(1), 13–25.

Masten, A. S. (2001). Ordinary magic: Resilience processes in development. *American Psychologist, 56*(3), 227–238.

Meng, H., Luo, Y., Huang, L., Wen, J., Ma, J., & Xi, J. (2019). On the relationships of resilience with organizational commitment and burnout: A social exchange perspective. *The International Journal of Human Resource Management, 30*(15), 2231–2250.

Näswall, K., Kuntz, J., Hodliffe, M., & Malinen, S. (2015). *Employee resilience scale (EmpRes)*. Technical Report. Recuperado de https://ir.canterbury.ac.nz/handle/10092/9469

Näswall, K., Malinen, S., Kuntz, J., & Hodliffe, M. (2019). Employee resilience: Development and validation of a measure. *Journal of Managerial Psychology, 34*(5), 353–367.

Nguyen, Q., Kuntz, J., Näswall, K., & Malinen, S. (2016). Employee resilience and leadership styles: The moderating role of proactive personality and optimism. *New Zealand Journal of Psychology, 45*(2), 13–21.

Oliveira, M. A., Reis, V. L., Zanelato, L. S., & Neme, C. M. B. (2008). Resiliência: Análise das publicações no período de 2000 a 2006. *Psicologia: Ciência e Profissão, 28*(4), 754–766.

Pesce, R. P., Assis, S. G., Avanci, J. Q., Santos, N. C., Malaquias, J. V., & Carvalhaes, R. (2005). Adaptação transcultural, confiabilidade e validade da escala de resiliência. *Cadernos de Saúde Pública, 21*(2), 436–448.

Pinheiro, D. P. N. (2004). A resiliência em discussão. *Psicologia em Estudo, 9*(1), 67–75.

Poletto, M., Wagner, T. M. C., & Koller, S. H. (2004). Resiliência e desenvolvimento infantil de crianças que cuidam de crianças: uma visão em perspectiva. *Psicologia: Teoria e Pesquisa, 20*(3), 241–250.

Ralha-Simões, H. (2001). Resiliência e desenvolvimento pessoal. In J. Tavares (Org.), *Resiliência e Educação* (pp. 95–113). Cortez.

Reppold, C. T., Mayer, J. C., Almeida, L. S., & Hutz, C. S. (2012). Avaliação da resiliência: Controvérsia em torno do uso de escalas. *Psicologia: Reflexão e Crítica, 25*(2), 248–255.

Ribeiro, A. C. A., Mattos, B. M., Antonelli, C. S., Canêo, L. C., & Goulart, E., Jr. (2011). Resiliência no trabalho contemporâneo: Promoção e/ou desgaste da saúde mental. *Estudos em Psicologia, 16*(4), 623–633.

Rutter, M. (1993). Resilience: some conceptual considerations. *Journal of Adolescent Health, 14*(8), 626–631.

Rutter, M. (2007). Resilience, competence and coping. *Child Abuse and Neglect, 31*(3), 205–209.

Sapienza, G., & Pedromônico, M. R. M. (2005). Risco, proteção e resiliência no desenvolvimento da criança e do adolescente. *Psicologia em Estudo, 10*(2), 209–216.

Scorsolini-Comin, F., Fontaine, A. M. G. V., Koller, S. H., & Santos, M. A. (2013). From authentic happiness to well-being: The flourishing of positive psychology. *Psicologia: Reflexão e Crítica, 26*(4), 663–670.

Senbeto, D. L., & Hon, A. H. Y. (2020). Market turbulence and service innovation in hospitality: Examining the underlying mechanisms of employee and organizational resilience. *The Service Industries Journal*, 1–21. https://doi.org/10.1080/02642069.2020.1734573

Shin, J., Taylor, M. S., & Seo, M. G. (2012). Resources for change: The relationships of organizational inducements and psychological resilience to employees' attitudes and behaviors toward organizational change. *Academy of Management Journal, 55*(3), 727–748.

Small, H. (1973). Co-citation in the scientific literature: A new measure of the relationship between two documents. *Journal of the American Society for Information Science, 24*(4), 265–269.

Souza, M. T. S., & Cerveny, C. M. O. (2006). Resiliência psicológica: revisão da literatura e análise da produção científica. *Revista Interamericana de Psicologia, 40*(1), 119–126.

Taboada, N. G., Legal, E. J., & Machado, N. (2006). Resiliência: Em busca de um conceito. *Revista Brasileira de Crescimento e Desenvolvimento Humano, 16*(3), 104–113.

Tetrick, L. E., & Winslow, C. J. (2015). Workplace stress management interventions and health promotion. *Annual Review of Organizational Psychology and Organizational Behavior, 2*(1), 583–603.

van Eck, N. J., & Waltman, L. (2017). Citation-based clustering of publications using CitNetExplorer and VOSviewer. *Scientometrics, 111*(2), 1053–1070.

Waller, M. A. (2001). Resilience in ecosystemic context: Evolution of the concept. *American Journal of Orthopsychiatry, 71*(3), 290–297.

Walpita, Y. N., & Arambepola, C. (2020). High resilience leads to better work performance in nurses: Evidence from South Asia. *Journal of Nursing Management, 28*(2), 342–350.
Winwood, P. C., Colon, R., & McEwen, K. (2013). A practical measure of workplace resilience: Developing the resilience at work scale. *Journal of Occupational and Environmental Medicine, 55*(10), 1205–1212.
Yunes, M. A. M. (2003). Psicologia positiva e resiliência: O foco no indivíduo e na família. *Psicologia em Estudo*, *8*(edição especial), 75–84.

Chapter 6
Leadership in Organizations: State of the Art with Emphasis on Measurement Instruments

Magno Oliveira Macambira, Rose Helen Shimabuku, Maria Tereza Tomé de Godoy, Nivaldo Sales Galvão Junior, and Louise Cristine Santos Sobral

6.1 Introduction

The study on leadership is consolidated in the studies on organizational behavior. This historical scientific effort toward understanding the phenomenon depicts its complexity and results in a field that has deeply developed in how leadership is understood and, thus, measured.

According to Ahlquist and Levi (2011), the colossal literature on leadership over time has produced distinct study drivers such as power and legitimacy, the best ways to achieve goals, and interactions between leaders and subordinates. Throughout its development, leadership has already been defined in terms of traits, behaviors, influence, patterns of interaction, role relationships, and holding an administrative position.

Most definitions of leadership in the organizational context assume that the phenomenon reflects a process by which one person intentionally exerts influence over others to guide, structure, and facilitate activities and relationships in a group or organization (Yukl, 2002).

M. O. Macambira (✉)
State University of Feira de Santana, Feira de Santana, BA, Brazil

R. H. Shimabuku
Federal Institute of Education, Science and Technology of Goiás, Goiânia, GO, Brazil

M. T. T. de Godoy
Federal University of Goiás, Goiânia, GO, Brazil
e-mail: maite_godoy@ufg.br

N. S. Galvão Junior
Universidade Paulista, Santos, SP, Brazil

L. C. S. Sobral
Federal University of Bahia, Salvador, BA, Brazil

M. O. Macambira et al. (eds.), *Assessing Organizational Behaviors*,
https://doi.org/10.1007/978-3-030-81311-6_6

Regarding the many ways of circumscribing the phenomenon that implies the multiple definitions of leadership, Bendassolli et al. (2014) note that some elements are repeated thus making up a common baseline: (1) it is a process that involves the ability to mobilize other people through processes of influence; (2) this influence refers to how the leader affects his/her subordinates and how subordinates, who in turn, affect each other through non-coercive behaviors; (3) it occurs in groups, as there are binding processes, a dynamic of legitimization and mutual recognition; (4) it is the pursuit, both by leaders and subordinates, for actual, effective, substantial, and transforming changes; and (5) it involves the establishment and achievement of objectives understood as mutual, this being the very essence of the exchanges between leaders and subordinates.

Throughout its theoretical development, one can follow the effort to render the field instrumentally, based on measures that allow the identification of types or profiles of leadership, as well as the intensity with which this profile is perceived by the work group members. In this chapter, a set of theories and the instruments developed for its measurement will be presented. In order to know, understand, and compare the theoretical proposals and strategies of measurement, as well as to decide which proposal is more suitable for different objectives, the chapter is organized in two parts. The first one will introduce the historical path of theories, while the second will list the contemporary approaches to leadership. Each section of the chapter reflects moments of development of the literature on leadership in the organizational context. In order to ensure more contemporary usefulness, only the instruments arising from contemporary theories will be described in more detail.

6.2 Trajectory of Theories on Leadership

In order to understand the classical approaches to leadership, Alimo-Metcalfe (2013) organized the area's production into stages, explaining the historical development of studies on leadership. Figure 6.1 shows the approaches and in which stage of development the concept is. Later, Bendassolli et al. (2014) historically classify the main theories into: (1) leader-centered approach, emphasis on leaders; (2) situational or context-centered approach, emphasis on the situation; (3) relationship-centered approach, emphasis on relational and transformational aspects involved in leadership; (4) subordinates-centered approach, emphasis on subordinates; and (5) emerging approaches, emphasis influenced by the positive psychology perspective.

To let you follow the text more easily, we will present theoretical aspects of the leadership phenomenon development based on Alimo-Metcalfe (2013) and the instruments identified in the most relevant approaches in current authors, allowing readers to be instrumented with the valid and reliable range of measurement options.

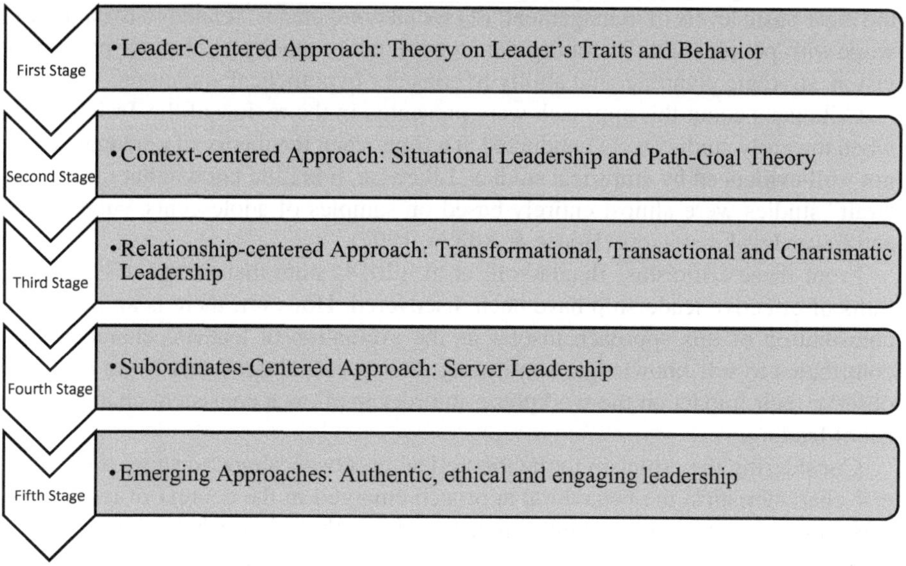

Source: Prepared by the authors

Fig. 6.1 Approaches and development stages of the concept of leadership. (*Source*: Prepared by the authors)

6.3 First Stage: Emphasis on Leader

The leader-centered approach prevailed in the early stage of theoretical proposals on leadership that will seek in the individual qualities that make them a leader. The Trait Theory emerged as the main representative of this stage. In it, the focus is on the identification of personal qualities, as well as personality traits that distinguish leader from subordinates. This theory ranks leadership as innate and does not allow for learning processes, rendering any expectation of leadership development unfeasible. According to Bendassolli et al. (2014), this approach prevailed in the first half of last century and states that traits are the determining factors for the exercise of leadership.

According to Marinho (2006), the theory of traits influenced the scientific thought in the mid-1940s, being reinforced by the psychological personality tests. According to Alimo-Metcalfe (2013), in those tests, traits related to "energy," "dominance," and "intelligence" were presented and absorbed by discussions on leadership as components of the leader.

The major goal of the scholars focused on investigating the sets of traits typical to the leader as such was to determine what characterizes the leaders and how to describe them (Bergamini, 1994). Katiz (1974) was one of the pioneers of this approach and points out three competencies that are not innate and may be developed: (1) technical competence, related to specific knowledge, proficiency, aimed at the most basic levels of management; (2) social competence, related to the ability to work with people; and (3) conceptual competence, capacity of abstract reasoning, vision, strategic planning, and ability to consider hypothetical situations.

Criticisms about this approach were presented in the review of the Trait Theory, when the early studies were conducted at a time when the theory of personality was not well evidenced by empirical studies. Likewise, it is little known that these early "trait" studies were almost entirely based on samples of adolescents, supervisors, and lower-level managers (House & Aditya, 1997).

From these criticisms, Bendassolli et al. (2014) state that no specific defining traits of effective leadership have been discovered. However, there is an important contribution of this approach insofar as the evaluation of leaders' characteristics contributes to self-knowledge, confirming their personal trend and being useful to observe their impact on the workplace, in order to allow a consistent change in the act of leading.

Considering the criticism to the theoretical proposals aimed to suggest the leaders' characteristics, the behavioral approach emerged in the context of research. It was influenced by the growing emphasis of psychology on behavioral aspects, through the so-called Behaviorism school, with a focus on the leader's behavior (Marinho, 2006). The criticism of the 1940s shifts the focus of psychologists from the characteristics of leaders to their behavior and the process of influencing their subordinates (Alimo-Metcalfe, 2013).

That behavior has been described as the "leadership style." Although more than 30 different models have been developed, most of them can be described in 4 styles: (1) concern with task, also called "production-oriented"; (2) concern with people, also called "employee-centered"; (3) directive leadership, also called "authoritarian" or "autocratic"; and (4) participatory, also called "democratic."

Bendassolli et al. (2014) and Marinho (2006) exclude the "production-oriented" style and reaffirm three others: autocratic, democratic, and laissez-faire leadership. The leader's authoritarian style refers to controlling the group and their activities. The democratic style emphasizes group participation and the decision-making of the majority, while the laissez-faire style involves low-level influence by the leader, with the subordinates leading and being responsible for the activities.

6.4 Second Stage: Situation- or Context-Centered Approach

The second stage of the concept evolution comprises the situational and contingency theories, which emphasize the importance of contextual factors on the influence and effectiveness of leadership, such as variables associated with the task or project that are independent of the subordinates (Alimo-Metcalfe, 2013).

The intention was to develop an approach to determine how leadership traits or behaviors related to indicators of leadership effectiveness in different situations. There were aspects that enhanced or nullified the effects of a leader's traits or behaviors. These aspects were called "situation-moderating variables." In this sense, theories that explain leadership effectiveness in terms of situational moderating variables are called "contingency theories" of leadership (Yukl, 2002). In the 1960s, Fred Fiedler pioneered the use of this situational or contingency perspective known as the Contingency Theory or Model (Alimo-Metcalfe, 2013; Bendassolli et al., 2014; Robbins et al., 2010).

For Bendassolli et al. (2014), the theories that embrace this logic propose that leader behavior depends on the circumstances in which they occur. This is consonant with the idea that there is no one effective style for all situations and that different styles can be more effective depending on the situation (Marinho, 2006).

Among the theoretical proposals that excelled in that period is the Situational Leadership Theory, developed by Hersey and Blanchard (1986). It suggests that a person's maturity should be considered in relation to the specific task. The greater the maturity, the greater the leaders' orientation toward relationship and the less authority he/she exercises over the subordinate. Conversely, immaturity should be managed through "strong" use of authority, with little emphasis on relationship.

Another theory that emerged in that context was called the Path-Goal Theory (Evans, 1970), developed to explain how the leader's behavior stimulates subordinates' conduct toward a goal, enhancing satisfaction and performance through subordinate motivation mediated by work variables.

6.5 Third Stage: Relationship-Centered Approach

In the third stage, Alimo-Metcalfe (2013) state that there was a shift in the level of study when situational theories make room to the heroic/charismatic model which grounds the transactional, transformational, and charismatic theories, centered on the relationships between leader and subordinate.

In the 1980s, there was much interest in the emotional and symbolic aspects of leadership, focusing on the ways in which leaders influence subordinates to make sacrifices and put the needs of the mission or organization above their own personal interests. Charismatic, transactional, and transformational leadership theories describe these important aspects of leadership.

Transformational leadership was first conceptualized by Burns in 1978, inspired by the political-social context of the time, and the behavior of great statesmen. The author discussed moral development as a core factor in transformational leadership. For Burns, transformational leadership takes place when leaders and subordinates are engaged at a high level of motivation and morality (Calaça & Vizeu, 2015; Jensen et al., 2019).

Burns (1978) proposed approaching leadership as a dual phenomenon with the proximity between leader and subordinate, and the leader's responsibility for nurturing new leaders. Thus, the transformational leader, in addition to management focused on results of routine activities, is assigned with the task of recognizing the potential of their subordinate, their perspectives, and the encouragement of autonomy in decision-making (Calaça & Vizeu, 2015; Jensen et al., 2019).

Transformational leadership is studied in four dimensions: *charisma* or *idealized influence*, the leader has idealized influence when he or she is considered a role model and arouses admiration, respect, and trust in subordinates; *inspirational motivation*, through symbols and emotion, the leader mobilizes the subordinate to find meaning in their career and to act to achieve results for the organization. *Intellectual stimulation* is the leader's encouragement to the subordinate to rethink their life and career while stimulating new ideas in the workplace. *Individualized consideration*, in turn, stands for the leader's support and attention to the subordinate, understanding the complexity and individuality of each worker (Bass, 1999; Moscon, 2015).

Recent studies have linked transformational leadership to worker's high performance; work practices toward worker engagement (Weller, Süß, Evanschitzky, & Von Wangenheim, 2020); worker empowerment, self-efficacy, and performance (Gao, Murphy & Anderson, 2020); and innovation performance (Sheehan, Garavan, & Morley, 2020).

In 1992, Bass and Avolio developed the leadership inventory (MLQ scale – Multifactor, Leadership Questionnaire Form 6S). For transformational leadership, the authors developed 3 items in 4 dimensions, totaling 12 items. In the latest version, the MLQ (Avolio & Bass, 2004) showed fair goodness-of-fit indexes (CFI = 0.91, GFI = 0.91, AGFI = 0.90, RMSEA = 0.05, Cronbach's alpha ranging from 0.74 to 0.94 for all scale factors). The intention is to administer the inventory to subordinates to assess immediate leadership based on affirmative items on a Likert scale.

The discussion on transactional leadership emerged along with the discussion on transformational leadership held by Burns (1978) and Bass (1999). Transactional leadership refers to the exchanges established in the relationship between leader and subordinates, aimed at catering the interests of both through the use of contingent rewards and sanctions. It is based on the assumption of legitimacy and formal authority of the leader in relation to the subordinate and the use of rules and norms (Bass, 1999; Jensen et al., 2019).

Transactional leadership has been more frequently studied based on two dimensions, namely, *contingent reward* and *exception management*. By contingent reward, we mean the leader's effort to direct the subordinate's behavior toward the results desired by the organization. This dimension refers to the transactional exchange of rewards and recognition of achievements and successful outcomes of subordinates (Bass, 1999; Jensen et al., 2019).

The *management by exception* dimension is related to the use of feedback to the subordinate in the event of errors or problems during the performance of their activities. This dimension is characterized by the establishment of norms, monitoring, search for deviations, rule enforcement, and focus on errors related to crisis intervention (Podsakoff, Bommer, Podsakoff, & MacKenzie, 2006; Jensen et al., 2019).

Transformational and transactional leadership styles converge when we consider the target of attaining organizational goals. The main difference between both styles is that transactional leadership behavior intends to build employees' interest in achieving goals, while transformational leadership is based on encouraging the subordinate.

Empirical studies relate transactional leadership to the achievement of subordinates' performance and organizational goals. However, these same studies point out side effects such as increased conflict within the team and emotional exhaustion of this leadership style, which can damage the established relationship between leader and subordinate (Jensen et al., 2019; Young et al., 2020).

Similarly as for transformational leadership, the assessment of transactional leadership is often through the inventory developed by Avolio and Bass (2004) for leadership, the MLQ. With regard to transactional leadership, the instrument assesses two dimensions (contingent reward and management for exception), making a total of nine items. The instrument assesses transactional leadership, through the perceptions of subordinates, using affirmative items on a Likert scale. As mentioned in transformational leadership, the MLQ (Avolio & Bass, 2004) showed fair goodness-of-fit indexes (CFI = 0.91, GFI = 0.91, AGFI = 0.90, RMSEA = 0.05, Cronbach's alpha ranging from 0.74 to 0.94 for the scale factors).

Charismatic leadership is grounded on the leader's reputation and their values shared with the team and the organization. Literature describes charismatic leaders as capable to formulate and articulate an inspiring vision while fostering similar behaviors in those they lead. These attributes enhance the image of an admirable leader with an extraordinary mission (Cohen & Yoon, 2020; Vlachos, Panagopoulos, & Rapp, 2013; Zehir et al., 2014).

In practice, charismatic leaders can induce change through their vision and impact organizational climate by influencing ethical behavior and inhibiting unethical behavior of the subordinate. Charismatic leaders are considered exceptional, talented, and even heroic people for their devotion and capacity for empathy and resilience (Vlachos, Panagopoulos, & Rapp, 2013; Hamstra et al. 2014; Meslec, Curseu, Fodor, & Kenda, 2020).

Some theorists approach this leadership from the dimension of *charisma* or *idealized influence* stemming from the concept of transformational leadership. Transformational leadership and charismatic leadership are so close to each other that they are sometimes considered synonymous. Thus, one can find studies that use the fragmented transformational leadership scale in order to measure charismatic leadership (Wilderom, Van Den Berg, & Wiersma, 2012; Cohen & Yoon, 2020).

In 1998, Conger and Kanungo developed the charismatic leadership scale that has been used in empirical studies. It consists of 25 items distributed into 6 dimensions, namely, charismatic leadership behavior, sensitivity to the environment, sensitivity to members' needs, strategic vision and articulation, personal risk, unconventional behavior, and status quo. This scale (Cronbach's alpha 0.89) evaluates the leader in affirmative sentences, from the perception of subordinates, on a Likert scale (Vlachos, Panagopoulos & Rapp, 2013; Zehir et al., 2014).

Changes in the workplace characterized by increased employee's autonomy and quick access to information have weakened the centrality of leadership. This context led scholars to delve into understanding the behavior of subordinates who, by virtue of job instability and organizational restructuring, are more skeptical and less susceptible to the role of followers (Bendassolli et al., 2014). In this context emerges the fourth stage entitled Post-Heroic Model. It arises from the dissatisfaction and ethical questionings of the Charismatic leader's heroic capacity.

6.6 Fourth Stage: Subordinates-Centered Approach

Among the theories emerging in the fourth stage, the servant leadership, initially proposed by Robert Greenleaf in the 1970s, refers to a paradigm break when compared to traditional models. It characterizes the leader as someone motivated by the feeling of serving his or her team, detaching from their individual interests on behalf of the collective. This theory relies on intrinsic values of human dignity, reversing the traditional view of leader centrality toward an opposite model (Marinho, 2006).

The Model of Servant Leadership was developed from the 44 dimensions initially identified by Van Dierendonck (2011), with 8 factors: humility, empowerment, authenticity, interpersonal acceptance or forgiveness, accountability, courage, support, and servitude. Although the proposed model was well accepted, the author concluded that most of the scales developed then focused primarily on the servant's profile. In an attempt to fill in the identified gap, Van Dierendonck and Nuijten (2011) validated with a sample of Dutch workers a 30-item scale, composed of 8 factors, with good goodness-of-fit indexes (χ^2(gl) 600.1(397); CFI = 0.94; TLI = 0.93; SRMR = 0.06; RMSEA = 0.05).

Later, the Servant Leadership Scale was translated and validated into other languages such as Spanish (Rodríguez-Carvajal, Rivas, Herrero, Moreno-Jiménez, & Van Dierendonck, 2014), Portuguese from Portugal (Sousa & Van Dierendonck, 2014), and Brazilian Portuguese (Pereira & Ferreira, 2019). In all the studies mentioned, the model maintained its eight factors, supporting the explanatory hypothesis of the proposed model.

6.7 Fifth Stage: Emergent Approaches

Finally, the fifth stage, devoted to emerging perspectives, is focused on the values and integrity of those who lead (Alimo-Metcalfe, 2013). According to Bendassolli et al. (2014), there are also other emerging perspectives that add other references to the study of leadership such as positive psychology (authentic leadership) and psychoanalysis in the psychosocial/psychodynamic approach to leadership. We will next look at three leadership profiles that represent the emerging perspectives, namely, authentic leadership, ethical leadership, and engaging leadership.

6.8 Authentic Leadership

The advancement of leadership studies emphasizes the need to confirm positive behaviors from leaders and subordinates in order to inspire positive impacts and desirable outcomes at different levels of the organization. These studies are largely driven by the emergence of positive psychology, which includes the study of positive emotions, positive traits (strengths, virtues, and skills), positive institutions, and democracy, family and freedom (Seligman, 2009). This new perspective gives rise to authentic leadership (AL) (Avolio & Gardner, 2005; Putra et al., 2020) that comes up not only as a descriptive theory but, above all, as a normative theory, suggesting how the actions and behaviors of the leader should be.

AL is multifactorial, consisting of four components: (1) self-awareness, which refers to the leader's understanding of his or her strengths and limitations as well as their effects on subordinates; (2) transparency of relationships, which indicates openness and willingness of the leader to share his or her true thoughts and feelings with the subordinates; (3) balanced processing, which implies the objectivity, thoughtfulness, and critical analysis that precedes decision-making; and (4) internalized moral perspective, which refers to self-regulation oriented by internal moral values and standards (Walumbwa et al., 2008; Wei et al., 2020).

Authentic leaders tend to be more connected with their limits and potentials based on the self-knowledge process and therefore behave in a transparent, genuine way, effectively becoming authentic (Walumbwa et al., 2008). In this way, they positively influence the proactive, ethical, and autonomous behavior of their subordinates (Cervo et al., 2016; Putra et al., 2020), contributing to make them feel empowered, increasing their levels of well-being, and their performance (Daraba et al., 2021; Pioli et al., 2020).

In order to develop a measure for assessing authentic leadership, Walumbwa, Avolio, Gardner, Wernsing, and Peterson (2008) originally proposed the Authentic Leadership Questionnaire (ALQ). Although the instrument has evidence of validity for construct assessment in several cultural contexts, the ALQ (Walumbwa et al. (2008) is subject to copyrights.

In an attempt to overcome this limitation, Neider and Schriesheim (2011) developed the Authentic Leadership Inventory (ALI), based on the studies of the aforementioned authors. The initial version of the scale comprised 16 items. After initial analyses, it became evident that item 1 (self-knowledge) and item 6 (relational transparency) should be removed to grant more reliability to the instrument. The final version of the scale then comprised 14 items, answered in 5-point Likert-type scales, distributed in the 4 dimensions pointed out in the theoretical definition: balanced processing (4 items), internalized moral perspective (4 items), relational transparency (4 items), and self-awareness (4 items) (Neider & Schriesheim, 2011) that pointed out internal consistency of the scale (Cronbach's alpha) of 0.92 (Daraba et al., 2021).

6.9 Ethical Leadership

Although the description of some leadership styles includes ethical conduct-related aspects (e.g., transformational and authentic leadership), these aspects do not necessarily focus on ethical behaviors. In order to fill in this gap, ethical leadership is presented as a style that highlights the influence of leaders from normatively appropriate conduct, through personal actions and interpersonal relationships (Brown et al., 2005).

The leader's moral behavior inspires his or her subordinates to act proactively (Brown & Treviño, 2006) and fosters a sense of personal obligation, in which workers tend to reciprocate the treatment received from supervisors (Zappalà & Toscano, 2020). By communicating with their subordinates in a direct and transparent manner, spelling out their expectations in relation to them, leaders encourage individuals to be accountable for their behaviors and therefore committed to their obligations (Brown et al. 2005). Thus, ethical leadership is positively related to greater sense of meaning and well-being in the workplace (Avey et al., 2012), work engagement (Ahmad & Gao, 2018) organizational commitment and engagement (Lotfi et al., 2018), job satisfaction (Benevene et al., 2018), and organizational ethical climate (Demirtas & Akdogan). On the other hand, this leadership style is also negatively associated with worker burnout and fatigue (Mo & Shi, 2017).

As with other leadership styles, literature comprises several instruments aimed at measuring ethical leadership. Although most of these instruments are effective tools and have good reliability indexes (Zappalà & Toscano, 2020), the Ethical Leadership Scale (ELS) developed by Brown et al. (2005) stands out for its versatility, since it is brief and fits into various organizational contexts.

The Ethical Leadership Scale is a one-dimension instrument consisting of 10 items, assessed on a 5-point Likert scale. The meta-analysis conducted by Bedi et al. (2015) identified more than 100 studies that used the ELS in different contexts, indicating that it is a reliable tool that achieves Cronbach's alphas near to or above 0.90 (Brown et al., 2005; Walumbwa et al., 2011). A recent study on evidence of the ELS validity for the Italian context suggested that the instrument showed good goodness-of-fit indexes, as follows: $x^2 = 104.67$, $df = 35$, $p < 0.001$; $x^2/df = 2.99$; RMSEA = 0.08, CFI = 0.97 and TLI = 0.95, as well as Cronbach's alpha ranging between 0.94 and 0.95 (Zappalà & Toscano, 2020).

6.10 Engaging Leadership

Analyses on leadership styles have changed over the years. The path taken began in the precursor studies in the 1930s and 1950s, based on Traits Theory, and advanced through the behavioral theories of the 1950s and 1960s, and through the contingent and situational leadership styles of the 1960s and 1970s. More recently, the heroic and visionary leadership profiles that emerged between the 1980s and 1990s were evidenced, mainly defined in the charismatic and transformational styles. Studies developed in the post-heroic era point out to more inclusive leadership styles, which genuinely appraise subordinates and their contributions, thus promoting greater autonomy and engagement (Alimo-Metcalfe et al., 2008). In response to the demands of this new profile, engaging leadership, also called involving leadership, emerges.

Engaging leadership finds support in Self-Determination Theory (SDT; Deci and Ryan, 2000) and refers to the leadership style based on the satisfaction of basic psychological needs, which are crucial to the optimal and healthy functioning of individuals. The theory identifies four basic needs: (1) autonomy (feeling in control over one's own behavior); (2) competence (desire to be effective and achieve goals); (3) relationship (desire to belong to a group and being connected with people); and (4) meaning (involvement in activities that are important and relate to one's values) (Rahmadani & Schaufeli, 2020). This leadership style posits that workers are likely to become engaged (i.e., internalize their tasks and show high levels of energy, concentration, and persistence) as their needs for autonomy, competence, relatedness, and meaning are satisfied (Schaufeli, 2015).

The engaging leader shows concern for the development of the potentials and well-being of his or her subordinates, as well as their integration with other groups, in order to provide a culture permeated by autonomy, critical and strategic thinking. This leader is also inspirational and works to promote connection among team members in order to encourage collaboration and interpersonal links, thus fostering a strong sense of togetherness, comfort, and belonging (Rahmadani & Schaufeli, 2020). The leader's behavior is guided by ethical principles and the desire to co-create and co-possess ways of working with others to achieve a shared vision. Engaging leadership is significantly and positively related to work engagement (Schaufeli, 2015).

The Engaging Leadership Scale was developed by Schaufeli (2015) and consists of 12 items, divided into 4 factors: strengthening, connection, capacity-building, and inspiration, with 3 items each. The items are rated on a 5-point Likert-type scale with higher scores indicating higher levels of engaging leadership, from the perceptions of their subordinates.

Fair goodness-of-fit index was identified, showing Tucker Lewis Index (TLI) = 0.91, Comparative Fit Index (CFI) = 0.94, Root Mean Square Error of Approximation (RMSEA) = 0.08, and Cronbach's alpha for the total scale of 0.86. Positive and significant correlations have been found between engaging leadership and work engagement, satisfaction of basic psychological needs, higher quality in delivery, commitment to work, and performance (Schaufeli, 2015; Rahmadani & Schaufeli, 2020; Rahmadani et al., 2020).

6.11 Conclusions

Measuring the construct of leadership has proven challenging for scholars in the field for many reasons. First, as can already be seen throughout the reading of this chapter, there is a myriad of leadership styles, types, and conditions, which dissipates efforts toward developing or continually improving a scale. The second issue, well described by Crawford and Kelder (2019), reports a split between instruments created by researchers and by management professionals. The main difference is the methodological rigor that results in a series of unsuccessful experiences by the market.

However, it was not the purpose here to exhaust all micro-theories or possibilities. Instead, it presented a chart that reflects the coherent flow of theoretical proposals that have served as grounds for instruments that, despite being dedicated to measuring leadership, operationalize different versions, allowing the identification of that one that best fits what an organization demands.

This choice will take into consideration other contextual and management parameters that can provide good results in the management of workers. There is no sovereign type of leadership, despite an increasing concern for leadership oriented by ethical principles and concerned with the development of the organization, the leaders themselves, and the people they lead. Therefore, it demands assessing, among the possibilities presented, the one that better fits into the specific organizational context and operationalizing it through the scales presented in this chapter.

A complementary point, consonant with the field of emerging approaches, can define a future agenda for the coordination and investigation of leadership in the field of development of socioemotional competencies. Socioemotional competencies work as a path through which other competencies are expressed and developed. Therefore, the classic concept of basic competencies (CHAs) that ensure a level of cross-cutting mastery, which allows workers to mobilize their personal resources, adapting them to the most immediate work context (Abed, 2014; Lee & Shute, 2009) cannot be ruled out.

The mastering of socioemotional competencies plays a core role in the acquisition and development of professional skills, expanding the possibilities of workers' adjustment in their occupations (Gondim, Morais, & Brantes, 2014). Thus, socioemotional competencies are located in the domain of affective-emotional, personal, and interpersonal processes, which are an important exercise in leadership, coordination, supervision, and management occupations.

An important dimension of socioemotional competence is the emotional regulation (ER), which deals with the processes and strategies used to manage emotions (Gross, 2015; Peña-Sarrionandia et al., 2015). According to Sobral (2010), these strategies are necessary for the individual to be able to cope with pressure situations in the work context.

Some studies discuss the emotional component of anger by considering how assertively expressing anger can encourage people beyond what is expected of them. This implies inferring that anger shown by authority seems to motivate members to proactively change in the path of expected performance (Chi & Ho, 2014; Campos, 2017). Definitely, we know that when facing an angry boss, for example, people tend to exhibit avoidance and evasion behavior, avoiding speaking out. In this context, the anger expressed by authority figures seems to demotivate members from initiating possible changes in the achievement of performance (Liu, Wang & Liao, 2021).

The implications of this discussion may result in efforts to construct emotion regulation measures that map the types of emotion regulation strategies used by workers and reflect on the socioemotional competencies needed for a specific occupation in a given context. This perspective contributes to understand the modulation of affect for organizational processes, breaking with a tradition of emphasis on cognition, developing more compatible professional profiles for people management actions, which take into account psychosocial variables and the complexity of factors considering the process of well-being and mental health of leaders and subordinates, the expected performance, and organizational rules.

References

Abed, A. L. Z. (2014). O desenvolvimento das habilidades socioemocionais como caminho para a aprendizagem e o sucesso escolar de alunos da educação básica. *Construção Psicopedagógica, 24*(25), 8–27.

Ahmad, I., & Gao, Y. (2018). Ethical leadership and work engagement. *Management Decision 56*(9), 1991–2005. https://doi.org/10.1108/MD-02-2017-0107

Ahlquist, J. S., & Levi, M. (2011). Leadership: What it means, what it does, and what we want to know about it. *Annual Review of Political Science, 14*, 1–24.

Alimo-Metcalfe, B. (2013). A critical review of leadership. In H. S. Leonard, R. Lewis, A. Freedmam, J. Passmore, & B. Alimo-Metcalfe (Eds.), *The Wiley-Blackwell handbook of the psychology of leadership, change and organizational* (pp. 15–48). John Wiley & Sons.

Alimo-Metcalfe, B., Alban-Metcalfe, J., Bradley, M., Mariathasan, J., & Samele, C. (2008), The impact of engaging leadership on performance, attitudes to work and wellbeing at work: A longitudinal study. *Journal of Health Organization and Management, 22*(6), 586–598. https://doi.org/10.1108/14777260810916560

Avolio, B. J., & Bass, B. M. (2004). Multifactor Leadership Questionnaire. Manual and Sampler Set (3rd ed.). Redwood City, CA: Mindgarden.

Avolio, B. J., & Gardner, W. L. (2005). Authentic leadership development: Getting to the root of positive forms of leadership. *The Leadership Quarterly, 16*(3), 315–338. https://doi.org/10.1016/j.leaqua.2005.03.001

Avey, J. B. Reichard, R. J., Luthans, F., & Mhatre, K. H. (2012). Meta-analysis of the impact of positive psychological capital on employee attitudes, behaviors, and performance. *Human Resource Development Quarterly, 22*(2), 127–152. https://doi.org/10.1002/hrdq.20070

Bendassolli, P. F., Magalhães, M. D., & Malvezzi, S. (2014). Liderança nas Organizações. In J. C. Zanelli, J. E. Borges-Andrade, & A. V. Bastos (Eds.), *Psicologia, Organizações e Trabalho no Brasil* (pp. 413–449). Artmed.

Bergamini, C. W. (1994). *Liderança: Administração do Sentido*. Atlas.

Burns, J. M. (1978). *Leadership*. Harper & How.

Bass, B. M. & Steidlmeier, P. (1999). Ethics, character, and authentic transformational leadership behavior. *Leadership Quarterly, 10*(2), 181–217. https://doi.org/10.1016/S1048-9843(99)00016-8

Bedi, A., Alpaslan, C. M., & Green, S. (2015). A meta-analytic review of ethical leadership outcomes and moderators. *Journal of Business Ethics, 139*(3), 517–536. https://doi.org/10.1007/s10551-015-2625-1

Brown, M. E., & Trevin˜o, L. K. (2006). Ethical leadership: A review and future directions. *The Leadership Quarterly, 17*(6), 595–616. https://doi.org/10.1016/j.leaqua.2006.10.004

Brown, M. E., Treviño, L. K., & Harrison, D. A. (2005). Ethical leadership: A social learning perspective for construct development and testing. *Organizational Behavior and Human Decision Processes, 97*(2), 117–134. https://doi.org/10.1016/j.obhdp.2005.03.002

Benevene, P., Corso, L. D., De Carlo, A., Falco, A., Carluccio, F., & Vecina, M. L. (2018). Ethical leadership as antecedent of job satisfaction, affective organizational commitment and intention to stay among volunteers of non-profit organizations. *Frontiers in Psychology, 9*, 2069. https://doi.org/10.3389/fpsyg.2018.02069

Calaça, P. A., & Vizeu, F. (2015). Revisitando a perspectiva de James MacGregor Burns: qual é a ideia por trás do conceito de liderança transformacional? *Cadernos Ebape. BR, 13*(1), 121–135.

Cervo, C. S., Monico, L. d., dos Santos, N. R. (2016). Authentic Leadership Questionnaire: invariance between samples of Brazilian and Portuguese employees. Psicol. Refl. Crít. 29, 40 (2016). https://doi.org/10.1186/s41155-016-0046-4

Cohen, N. A., & Yoon, J. (2020). Who Makes Whom Charismatic? Leadership Identity Negotiation in Work Teams. *Journal of Leadership & Organizational Studies*, https://doi.org/10.1177/1548051820950372

Chi, N.-w. & Ho, T.-r. (2014). Understanding when leader negative emotional expression enhances follower performance: the moderating roles of follower personality traits and perceived leader power. *Human relations, 67*(9), 1051–1072. https://doi.org/10.1177/0018726714526626

Campos, S. C. & de, C. (2017). Expressões de Raiva, Poder, Traços Pessoais e Desempenho: um estudo das interações entre Líderes e Liderados. Dissertação de Mestrado. Programa de Pós-Graduação de Psicologia. Universidade Federal da Bahia.

Crawford, J. A., & Kelder, J. (2019). Do we measure leadership effectively? Articulating and evaluating scale T development psychometrics for best practice. *The Leadership Quarterly, 30*, 133–144. https://doi.org/10.1016/j.leaqua.2018.07.001

Deci, E. L., & Ryan, R. M. (2000). The "what" and "why" of goal pursuits: Human needs and the self-determination of behavior. *Psychological Inquiry, 11*(4), 227–268. https://doi.org/10.1207/S15327965PLI1104_01

Evans, M. G. (1970). The effects of supervisory behavior on the path-goal relationship. *Organizational Behavior and Human Performance, 5*, 277–298.

Greenleaf, R. K. (1977). *Servant leadership*. Paulist Press.

Gondim, S. M. G., Morais, F. A., & Brantes, C. A. A. (2014). Competências socioemocionais: fator-chave no desenvolvimento de competências para o trabalho. Revista Psicologia Organizações e Trabalho, 14(4), 394-406. Recuperado em 20 de setembro de 2021, de http://pepsic.bvsalud.org/scielo.php?script=sci_arttext&pid=S1984-66572014000400006&lng=pt&tlng=pt.

Gross, J. J. (2015). Emotion regulation: Current status and future prospects. *Psychological Inquiry, 26*(1), 1–26. https://doi.org/10.1080/104784X.2014.940781

Hersey, P., & Blanchard, K. (1986). *Psicologia para administradores: a teoria e as técnicas da liderança situacional*. EPU.

House, R. J., & Aditya, R. N. (1997). The social scientific study of leadership: Quo vadis? *Journal of Management, 23*(3), 409–473.

Hamstra, M. R., Van Yperen, N. W., Wisse, B., & Sassenberg, K. (2014). Transformational and transactional leadership and followers' achievement goals. *Journal of Business and Psychology, 29*(3), 413-425. https://doi.org/10.1007/s10869-013-9322-9

Jensen, U. T., Andersen, L. B., Bro, L. L., Bøllingtoft, A., Eriksen, T. L. M., Holten, A. L., ... & Würtz, A. (2019). Conceptualizing and measuring transformational and transactional leadership. *Administration & Society, 51*(1), 3-33. https://doi.org/10.1177/0095399716667157

Katiz, R. L. (1974). *Skills of an effective administrator* (pp. 90–102). Harvard Buiness Review.

Lotfi, Z., Atashzadeh-Shoorideh, F., Mohtashami, J., & Nasiri, M. (2018). Relationship between ethical leadership and organisational com mitment of nurses with perception of patient safety culture. *Journal of Nursing Management, 26*(6), 726–734. https://doi.org/10.1111/jonm.12607

Liu, W., Wang, F., & Liao, Z. (2021). Leader's Anger and Employee Upward Voice. In: Peng, K. Z. & Wu, Chia-Huei. (Eds). Emotion and Proactivity at Work: Prospects and Dialogues (pp.193–214). Bristol University Press.

Lee, J., & Shute, V. J. (2009). The Influence of Noncognitive Domains on Academic Achievement in K-12. Educational Testing Service.

Marinho, R. M. (2006). Liderança em Teoria e Prática. In J. F. Marinho, R. M. Marinho, A. I. Sugo, D. W. Rausch, J. A. Tucker, J. P. Neto, et al. (Eds.), *Liderança: Uma Questão de Competência*. Saraiva.

Moscon, D. C. B. (2015). As relações entre liderança e estabelecimento de vínculos do trabalhador nas organizações (tese de doutorado). Universidade Federal da Bahia. Salvador, Bahia, Brasil. Recuperado de http://repositorio.ufba.br/ri/handle/ri/17334

Meslec, N., Curseu, P. L., Fodor, O. C., & Kenda, R. (2020). Effects of charismatic leadership and rewards on individual performance. *Leadership Quarterly, 31*(6), [101423]. https://doi.org/10.1016/j.leaqua.2020.101423

Mo, S., & Shi, J. (2017). Linking ethical leadership to employee burnout,workplace deviance and performance: Testing the mediating roles of trust in leader and surface acting. *Journal of Business Ethics, 144*(2), 293–303. https://doi.org/10.1007/s10551-015-2821-z

Neider, L. L., & Schriesheim, C. A. (2011). The authentic leadership inventory (ALI): Development and empirical tests. *The Leadership Quarterly, 22*(6), 1146–1164. https://doi.org/10.1016/j.leaqua.2011.09.008

Pereira, M. M, & Ferreira, M. C. (2019). Propriedades Psicométricas da Escala de Liderança Servidora. *Avaliação Psicológica, 18*(3), 239–247. https://doi.org/10.15689/ap.2019.1803.14787.03

Pioli, B. L. T., Feuerschütte, S. G., Tezza, R., & Cancellier, E. L. P. L. (2020). Liderança autêntica: Análise da produção científica e de escalas de mensuração. *Revista de Administração Mackenzie, 21*(3), 1–30. https://doi.org/10.1590/1678-6971/eRAMG200126

Putra, I. K. S. W., Riana, I. G., & Surya, I. B. K. (2020). The influence of authentic leadership and work engagement over innovative work behavior. *Journal of Multidisciplinary Academic, 4*(5), 295-299. ISSN/e-ISSN: 2541 – 0369/2613 – 988X

Podsakoff, P. M., Bommer, W. H., Podsakoff, N. P., & MacKenzie, S. B. (2006). Relationships between leader reward and punishment behavior and subordinate attitudes, perceptions, and behaviors: A meta-analytic review of existing and new research. *Organizational Behavior and Human Decision Processes, 99*, 113–142. https://doi.org/10.1016/j.obhdp.2005.09.002

Peña-Sarrionandia, A., Mikolajczak, M., & Gross, J. J. (2015). Integrating emotion regulation and emotional intelligence traditions: a meta-analysis. *Frontiers in Psycholgy. 6*(160), 1–27. https://doi.org/10.3389/fpsyg.2015.00160

Robbins, S. P., Judge, T. A., & Sobral, F. (2010). *Comportamento Organizacional*. Pearson Prentice Hall.

Ronnie (Chuang Rang), Gao William H., Murphy Rolph E., Anderson (2020) Transformational leadership effects on salespeople's attitudes striving and performance. *Journal of Business Research 110*, 237–245. https://doi.org/10.1016/j.jbusres.2020.01.023

Rahmadani, V. G., & Schaufeli, W. B. (2020). Engaging leadership and work engagement as moderated by "diuwongke": an Indonesian study. *The International Journal of Human Resource Management*, 1–29. https://doi.org/10.1080/09585192.2020.1799234

Rahmadani, V. G., Schaufeli, W. B., Stouten, J., Zhang, Z., & Zulkarnain, Z. (2020). Engaging leadership and its implication for work engagement and job outcomes at the individual and team level: A multi-level longitudinal study. *International journal of environmental research and public health, 17*(3), 776. https://doi.org/10.3390/ijerph17030776

Rodríguez-Carvajal, R., de Rivas, S., Herrero, M., Moreno-Jiménez, B., & Van Dierendonck, D. (2014). Leading people positively: Cross-cultural validation of the Servant Leadership Survey (SLS). *The Spanish Journal of Psychology, 17*, E63. https://doi.org/10.1017/sjp.2014.73

Schaufeli, W. B. (2015). "Engaging leadership in the job demands-resources model", Career Development International, Vol. 20 No. 5, pp. 446–463. https://doi.org/10.1108/CDI-02-2015-0025

Sousa, M., & Van Dierendonck, D. (2014). Servant leadership and engagement in a merge process under high uncertainty. *Journal Organizational Change Manage. 27*(6), 877–899. https://doi.org/10.1108/JOCM-07-2013-0133

Sheehan, M., Garavan, T. N., & Morley, M. J. (2020). Transformational leadership and work unit innovation: A dyadic two-wave investigation. *Journal of Business Research, 109*, 399–412. https://doi.org/10.1016/j.jbusres.2019.10.072

Seligman, M. E., Ernst, R. M., Gillham, J., Reivich, K., & Linkins, M. (2009). Positive education: Positive psychology and classroom interventions. *Oxford review of education, 35*(3), 293–311. https://doi.org/10.1080/03054980902934563

Sobral, L.C.S. (2010). Emoções positivas e negativas na atividade da gestão. Dissertação de Mestardo. Programa de Pós-Graduação de Psicologia. Universidade Federal da Bahia.

Van Dierendonck, D. (2011). Servant leadership: A review and synthesis. *Journal of Management, 37*(4), 1228–1261. https://doi.org/10.1177/0149206310380462

Van Dierendonck, D., & Nuitjen, I. (2011). The servant leadership survey: Development and validation of a multidimensional measure. *Journal of Business Psychology, 26*, 249–267. https://doi.org/10.1007/s10869-010-9194-1

Vlachos, P. A., Panagopoulos, N. G., & Rapp, A. A. (2013). Feeling good by doing good: Employee CSR-induced attributions, job satisfaction, and the role of charismatic leadership. *Journal of business ethics, 118*(3), 577-588. https://doi.org/10.1007/s10551-012-1590-1

Walumbwa, F. O., Avolio, B., Gardner, W. L., Wernsing, T. S., & Peterson, S. J. (2008). Authentic leadership: Development and validation of a theory-based measure, *Journal of Management, 34*(1), 89–126. https://doi.org/10.1177/0149206307308913

Wei, H., King, A., Jiang, Y., Sewell, K. A., & Lake, D. M. (2020). The impact of nurse leadership styles on nurse burnout: A systematic literature review. Nurse Leader. https://doi.org/10.1016/j.mnl.2020.04.002

Weller, I., Süß, J., Evanschitzky, H., & von Wangenheim, F. (2020). Transformational leadership, high-performance work system consensus, and customer satisfaction. *Journal of Management, 46*(8), 1469–1497. https://doi.org/10.1177%2F0149206318817605

Wilderom, C. P., Van Den Berg, P. T., & Wiersma, U. J. (2012). A longitudinal study of the effects of charismatic leadership and organizational culture on objective and perceived corporate performance. *The leadership quarterly, 23*(5), 835–848. https://doi.org/10.1016/j.leaqua.2012.04.002

Walumbwa, F. O., Mayer, D. M., Wang, P., Wang, H., Workman, K., & Christensen, A. L. (2011). Linking ethical leadership to employee performance: The roles of leader–member exchange, self-efficacy, and organizational identification. *Organizational Behavior and Human Decision Processes, 115*(2), 204–213. https://doi.org/10.1016/j.obhdp.2010.11.002

Yukl, G. (2002). *Leadership in organizations*. Prentice-Hall.

Young, H. R., Glerum, D. R., Joseph, D. L., &McCord, M. A. (2020). A meta-analysis of transactional leadership and follower performance: Double-edge deffects of LMX and empowerment. *Journalof Management*, 0149206320908646.

Zehir, C., Müceldili, B., Altindağ, E., Şehitoğlu, Y., & Zehir, S. (2014). Charismatic leadership and organizational citizenship behavior: The mediating role of ethical climate. *Social Behavior and Personality: An International Journal, 42*(8), 1365–1375.

Zappalà, S., & Toscano, F. (2020). The Ethical Leadership Scale (ELS): Italian adaptation and exploration of the nomological network in a health care setting. *Journal of nursing management, 28*(3), 634-642. https://doi.org/10.1111/jonm.12967

Part II
Macro-organizational Measures and Future Perspectives

Chapter 7
Quality of Life at Work – Concepts, Models, and Measures

Laila Leite Carneiro and Maria das Graças Torres Paz

7.1 Introduction

Quality of life (QoL) has deserved attention in several contexts and has been related to the satisfaction of needs and interests of individuals toward a healthy and full life. The workplace is one of these contexts. It is of utmost importance, as for many, it is the reference to define their identities. In the scope of workplace, QoL started being tentatively discussed in the 1950s. However, the Industrial Revolution in the eighteenth century is likely to have kick-started the movement, raising awareness about the importance of seeking better ways to organize work in order to minimize its negative impacts on workers' health and well-being. Then, the systematization of production methods in the nineteenth century led to the scientific study on working conditions, their influence on productivity, and on the workers' readiness and, in the twentieth century, through the Taylorist theories, on motivation.

According to official records, the early reports of the term quality of life at work (QLW) date back to late in the 1960s (Nadler & Lawler, 1983; Easton & Van Laar, 2013). It was a hallmark of the increasing interest among scientists and organizations regarding the construct (Bagtasos, 2011; Martel & Dupuis, 2006). The relevance of the phenomenon by then was mainly boosted by instrumental reasons coupled with socioeconomic changes such as increase of inflation, emergence of new world powers, and the escalation of international competition resulting from globalization (Ferreira et al., 2012). This way, the investment in QLW, considered as a way to democratize and humanize the workplace (Bagtasos, 2011), aimed at providing better experiences to workers and also focused on productivity, thus

L. L. Carneiro (✉)
Federal University of Bahia, Salvador, BA, Brazil

M. das G. T. Paz
University of Brasília, Brasília, DF, Brazil

M. O. Macambira et al. (eds.), *Assessing Organizational Behaviors*,
https://doi.org/10.1007/978-3-030-81311-6_7

establishing a win-win relationship (Lau & Bruce, 1998). According to Walton (1980), look out the QLW means acknowledge that results can be improved both for the business and for people working in it, by including workers in the planning of work systems, focusing on issues related both to tasks contents and the workplace.

Since then, the term QLW has been arbitrarily used, sometimes considered in the individual's perspective, other times in a perspective of workplace, and even in the context of the individual's life. Moreover, it has been confused with satisfaction, stress, and other phenomena. The components of programs emerging from middle last century onward aimed at promoting QLW have proved to be little efficacious, maybe by virtue of the conceptual vagueness of the phenomenon. Therefore, the number of publications on the topic was reduced, coupled with the increased publications on related topics (e.g., mental health at work, or occupational stress) that are much better defined (Martel & Dupuis, 2006). Considering that the lack of consensus among scholars is a keynote with implications on the theoretical-methodological diversity that characterizes publications on the topic still these days, some issues are yet to be better answered such as what is QLW? What criteria define it? Who is responsible for promoting it? How can it be measured?

Researchers should invest in the pursue for these answers, even because the global changes being faced by humanity (e.g., new ways to communicate, technological development, actions on social inclusion, concern about nature and the planet) have affected the institutions, pushing them to adopt new forms of understanding and intervening on reality beyond their immediate economic needs. The concern about health, well-being, rights, social justice, worthy work, and human dignity becomes a keynote in the current century. It directly affects the dynamic of organizations that now face the need to be committed with the human, social, and ecological dimensions – which were less focused in the past – in their everyday lives.

Therefore, the movement toward QLW is strengthened in the world of organizational management. This movement is less intensive as work time and space dimensions play a more central role, and the existing frontiers between workplace and other important spheres of the individuals' lives become more fluid. As largely discussed in literature, the overall QoL of workers depends on the QoL they experience at work (Loscocco & Roschelle, 1991). Simultaneously, we consider that QLW is influenced by the overall QoL, including the social, political, and economic context of the individual. Therefore, the focus on the interaction of the different dimensions may be a path to be followed when outlining surveys to be developed, being attentive to avoid excessive expansion of the concept. The antecedents and consequents may be considered to better understand the phenomenon; however, some limits should be established to measure them.

Since 1948, the UN asserts that work is of utmost importance and centrality to the individuals' lives, being considered to be a right of all human beings. Concern about work is a primary issue in the current debates on establishment of policies and standards to ensure the security and health of workers (OIT, 1981). Therefore, thinking over the promotion of QLW in different workplaces is essential.

QLW management quality basically depends on understanding this phenomenon, and the instruments used to assess it prior to and after interventions aimed at improving it. Thus, the purpose of this chapter is to review the QLW measures existing in literature, discussing their coherence with theoretical contributions that support them, and establishing potential indications of use for specific contexts. To that, a brief conceptual overview of the QLW is presented, and some of the main existing theoretical models are described. Next, several instruments proposed more recently to measure QLW are described and reviewed, thus getting a picture of the measures being worked in literature since early in the twenty-first century. This is expected to provide a context of the evaluation strategies available for researchers and organizations that aim at improving QLW, managing its efficacy through reliable instruments.

7.2 Quality of Life at the Workplace: Concepts and Investigation Models

Despite the undeniable interest for QLW, in the last decades, researchers and managers have adopted different understandings about what this phenomenon means. In a classic criticism on the topic, Nadler and Lawler (193) pointed out the dangers entailed by the difficulty of clearly defining QLW, on the one hand leading it to be handled as a panacea – the everything that will solve all the problems of workers and organizations – and, on the other side, as a nothing – considering its imprecision, vagueness, and intangibility. As the authors have summarized, even the level of understanding about the QLW is quite variable. Some refers to it as a variable, others as an approach, a method, or even as a movement. Here, QLW should be considered as a variable that may be defined, broken down, measured, and managed.

In the same sense, Sashkin and Burke (1987) also warned about this exaggerate variability and vagueness resulting from excessive emphasis on the subjective perspective. They state that QLW is many times treated like as if it was not even the same phenomenon, being assigned different meanings by different people playing different roles, or meaning something different to the same person, depending on the role they play. The authors also add that the situation becomes even more complex when one thinks that people playing similar roles may also have different insights about QLW.

The challenge of defining QLW ensues from the conceptual chaos that follows the QoL phenomenon at large. The high degree of subjectivity inherent to those concepts make some authors advocate for the nonexistence of a single definition, arguing that such attempt would hurt the very nature of the phenomenon. However, embarking on that would mean denying the possibility of working with QLW on scientific grounds and would derail any possibility of measuring it. Although the existence of different concepts about organizational phenomena is quite usual, the excessive flexibility of this concept and the lack of definitions sharing the same essence prevent comparisons between studies and the accumulation of scientific evidence (Osigweh, 1989).

Despite this mismatch, the end of the twentieth century brings some advances both in the general and in the specific context of work. The World Health Organization (WHO) defines QoL as "an individual's perception of their position in life in the context of the culture and value systems in which they live and in relation to their goals, expectations, standards and concerns" (WHOQOL GROUP, 1994, p. 28). This perception is influenced by several factors intrinsic to the subject (e.g., physical and psychological health, degree of independence, social relations established, personal beliefs), as well as by the prominent characteristics of the respective environment (cultural, social) in which the subjective assessment of QoL takes place. As will be further shown, this definition is closely related with models/definitions of QoL in the workplace.

Few operational definitions of QLW are found in literature, as reported in previous reviews (e.g., Martel & Dupuis, 2006; Easton & Van Laar, 2013). In general, the prevailing definitions are those representing a compendium of its dimensions or interventional actions, thus reversing the logic of first understanding what the phenomenon is to further untangle it. These are different ways of establishing knowledge. One can either depart from general to the particular, or from particular to the general. What is really needed is to have a concept or definition of the construct and, for surveys on the construction of instruments, an operational definition. It is worth highlighting that describing dimensions or actions is not the same as operationally defining a construct. The lack of a robust definition implies weakness both in the assessment of the phenomenon and in the interventions oriented to management. Some conceptual weaknesses result from the initial construction and are strengthened by in-depth investigation. However, the concept of QLW may advance if added with more rigorous empirical surveys aimed at understanding the existing relations between its many components (Easton & Van Laar, 2013).

We do not intend to list all the concepts of QLW existing in literature. However, it is important to know the ideas of some of the most classic authors, spread in the 1970s and 1980s, before exploring how the phenomenon has been approached more recently. Figure 7.1 presents some of the main classic concepts of QLW.

As can be inferred from the summary provided by Klein et al. (2019), the seminal works define QLW exclusively focusing on the workplace scope, sometimes emphasizing the individual's experience reached through work (concepts of Lippitt and of Hackman and Suttle), other times emphasizing the organizational responsibility toward promoting such experiences (concepts of Westley and of Nadler and Lawler) from the construction of an organization-individual relation that leads to positive results for both parties (concepts by Walton, by Guest and by Werther and Davis).

Based on the foregoing, one could say that the classic models of QLW tend to fit into one of the two perspectives of analysis of the phenomenon: the organizational perspective that incorporates a set of context-related structural conditions that affect the worker's well-being and the subjective/individual perspective that emphasizes to what extent the workers' personal needs are satisfied, and how their personal

QUALITY OF WORKING LIFE CONCEPTS

Authors	Bases and understanding of QWL	Emphasis
Walton (1973)	Meeting needs and human aspirations, based on the idea of humanization and social responsibility of the company.	Humanization and social responsibility, focusing on the power of the company.
Hackman and Suttle (1977)	Describes how much people in the organization are able to meet their personal needs considered important through their work and life experiences in the organization.	Basic dimensions of the tasks.
Lippitt (1978)	Opportunity for the individual to satisfy the wide range of personal needs.	Work, personal growth, complete tasks, open systems.
Guest (1979)	A process by which an organization tries to reveal the creative process of its personnel, involving them in decisions that affect their lives at work.	Improved productivity and efficiency, as well as self-realization and self-aggrandizement.
Westley (1979)	Efforts focused on the humanization of work, seeking to solve problems generated by the very nature of productive organizations.	Way of thinking involving people, work and organization.
Werther and Davis (1983)	Efforts to improve the quality of life, seeking to make jobs more productive and satisfactory.	Valorization of positions, through analysis of organizational, environmental and behavioral elements.
Nadler and Lawler (1983)	Way to think about people including participation in problem-solving, enrichment of work and improvement in the work environment.	Humanistic vision in the work environment.

Source: Klein et al. (2019, p. 5).

Fig. 7.1 Summary of the classic concepts of QLW. (*Source:* Klein et al. (2019, p. 5))

characteristics influence the way they react to and perceive their work experiences (Loscocco & Roschelle, 1991; Paz et al., 2020). Definitely, the objective characteristics of QLW (e.g., workplace quality) shall be distinguished from the subjective characteristics (quality of life experienced by the individual) (Elyzur & Shye, 1990). Concurrently, it is worth noting that the latest models in the area have tried to integrate both perspectives. Therefore, QLW has been described as a construct made up both by objective and subjective characteristics (Hannif et al., 2008; Paz et al., 2020). For illustration purposes, some few models of each of these perspectives are presented below.

In the organizational perspective, the model by Walton (1973) stands out among the classic models. It is a turning point for the literature in this area, and one of the most widespread up to these days, subsidizing a large number of surveys. Walton (1973) devises QLW as the organization's emphasis on humanistic values and on social responsibility to promote the worker's development and satisfaction. To the author, autonomy and feedback to the worker's performance are crucial, so that the worker can participate in the process of enrichment and fitting of tasks. His model proposes eight indicators that organizations should consider to ensure the QLW. In practice, these are variables of context and are under the management responsibility: (1) fair and proper compensation, (2) healthy and safe work conditions, (3) immediate opportunity of use and development of capacities, (4) opportunity of continuous growth and security, (5) social integration in the workplace, (6) constitutionalism, (7) balance between work and full life space, and (8) social relevance of life at workplace.

The positioning focused on the organizational perspective remained being adopted by authors in the 1990s, as can be observed in Lau and Bruce (1998) who describe the QLW as "(...) the favorable conditions and environments of a workplace that support and promote employee satisfaction by providing employees with rewards, job security, and growth opportunities" (p. 213). These authors propose accessing the construct from four dimensions (job security, rewards system, training and career development opportunities, and openness to participate in decision-making) under the responsibility of the organization. Although dimensions are described in other words, the first three are also present in the model by Walton (1973). Still in the twenty-first century, that perspective remains present in studies as those by Nanjundeswaraswamy and Swamy (2015), Swamy et al. (2015), Fernandes et al. (2017), and Akter and Banik (2018), among many others that support the currentness of Walton's model by working with QLW indicators similar to those of the author. In other words, this approach remains strong in the baseline of studies on QLW.

Simultaneously to the stance of delimiting the organizational perspective in QLW promotion, literature outlines the subjective perspective of the approach to the phenomenon. Among the first classic authors to promote it, we could mention Hackman and Oldham (1976). Although these authors use the term "job enrichment" instead of "QLW," defining it as "conditions under which individuals will become internally motivated to perform effectively on their jobs" (p. 1), the dimensions they propose (task identity, task significance, skill variety, autonomy, and feedback) inspired many researchers that followed them to incorporate these factors related to content and working process into the QLW models' structure. This way, QLW starts being directly associated with the satisfaction of the individual's psychological growth needs. Under this premise, in the twenty-first century, some authors advocate that QLW refers to an intended and favorable interaction of three core elements: the worker, what the worker does (the task itself), and the context in which the worker performs the work. However, they highlight the influence of personal characteristics on the understanding of the phenomenon that would result from to what extent individuals believe to be satisfied in their workplace (Bagtasos, 2011).

In this sense, Martel and Dupuis (2006) pointed out three main characteristics of greater consensus in literature: (1) QLW is a construct of subjective order; (2) it gathers integrated and interactive elements of organizational, human, and social nature; and (3) it is a phenomenon inextricably linked to overall QoL. In this sense, the authors define QLW as:

> (…) a condition experienced by the individual in his or her dynamic pursuit of his or her hierarchically organized goals within work domains where the reduction of the gap separating the individual from these goals is reflected by a positive impact on the individual's general quality of life, organizational performance, and consequently the overall functioning of society (Martel & Dupuis, 2006, p. 356).

Although well operationalized, the excessive emphasis on subjectivity in this definition warns about the limitations imposed on management, which may hinder the application of interventional actions capable of promoting it. Despite the relevance of recognizing the individual objectives and expectations of its members, the organization cannot define customized policies and actions, as it would hardly satisfy all demands. Organizations should design guidelines and implement processes to ensure QLW to the organizational community. Although present in the literature on QLW since its beginning to these days, the subjective perspective of the analysis of this phenomenon has clear limitations that should be considered when proposing programs to promote it.

A third aspect of the analysis that is also emerging points out a tendency toward including the individual into the phenomenon's concepts in a more integral perspective, expanding attention previously focused exclusively on contextual and subjective aspects of the workplace toward factors that permeate the subject's life as a whole. Based on the classic theories of motivation and interface between work life and other areas of life, models that consider QLW as product of an interaction between needs satisfied in the workplace, life out of work, and the interaction between both levels are proposed. These models incorporate, in addition to the basic dimensions corresponding to work, dimensions such as worker's overall well-being, characteristics of the personality such as self-efficacy, and quality of the interaction between work-house/family (e.g., Sirgy et al., 2001; Van Laar et al., 2007; Easton & Van Laar, 2013; Hsu, 2016). Although this trend has been enhanced in the contemporary days, the expansion of these dimensions demands care in the sense of distinguishing what is effectively part of the QLW model and what is correlated. Stretching the concept to include dimensions that are not directly related to the work (e.g., general well-being) may give rise to inaccuracies in measures and the resulting interpretations.

Likewise, we understand that considering this integral (holistic) view is important to understand the phenomenon with its antecedents and consequents. However, organizations cannot be rendered liable for the individuals' QoL outside the organization. Many other variables external to the organization meddle with the general QoL, and the organization has no control over them. Likewise, the organization has no control over feelings, perceptions, characteristics of personality, and the worker's expectations. Thus, it seems coherent that studies about the phenomenon are limited to the workplace, setting the tone of QLW in the perspective of the collective, of policies, and organization guidelines. If organizations ensure QLW to their members by managing components in the workplace, they will be satisfactorily playing their role and are likely to give rise to a positive impact on the worker's QoL.

In a literature review comprising 91 publications from 2000 to 2017, Afroz (2019) used the strategy of "Pareto" analysis to identify the main QLW-related factors, regardless if components, antecedents, or consequents. After identification, factors with similar meanings were grouped based on semantic/linguistic adjustments and, then, accounted in terms of frequency of occurrence in publications. Of the 17 factors compiled, the 13 vital ones that together accounted for 79% of the occurrence were as follows: fair and proper compensation; growth opportunity; safe and healthy working conditions; social integration and cohesion; work relation and full life space; relationship with the supervisor; human progress capacities; constitutionalism, justice, and equity; award and recognition; job security; autonomy and control; participation in decision-making; and communication.

The results presented by the author highlight that the most recurrent factors in recent literature still date back to the main classic models. In his study Afroz (2019) considered articles of several natures: theoretical, qualitative, quantitative, etc. As we will see later, when we restrict the analysis to the factors that make up the measures of QWL today, we see that many of the classic dimensions are still in vogue. However, in another direction, the use of dimensions that emphasize the individual perspective grows, reinforcing the pulverization in the way the phenomenon has been treated in the literature.

7.3 Instruments to Measure Quality of Life at Work (QLW)

There are many approaches, proposals of models, and theoretical definitions to QLW, as well as great variety of practical actions aimed at promoting it. However, the interest on the theme did not echo with the same intensity regarding the construction of instruments to measure the phenomenon. Likewise, the links between the phenomenon definition, factors that make up the model, and the instrument itself are not always clear.

Martel and Dupuis (2006) criticized the lack of theoretical support to the measures proposed to evaluate the QLW, considering that many times they represent a compendium of dimensions not necessarily translated into an integrated construct. According to the authors, many instruments are created to identify factors part of the QLW without, a priori, starting from a robust operational definition of the phenomenon. This way, they fail in meeting some basic quality criteria such as present satisfactory validity indicators (i.e., effectively measure QLW); be objective and exempt from possible manipulation; and provide data that allow interpretations to support further intervention. These problems confirm the relevance of identifying scales adherent to these assumptions.

For the purposes of this analysis, a systematic review was performed on the Scorpus and Web of Science databases, using as keywords to search on title (qwl OR "quality of work life" OR "quality of working life" OR "quality of life at work" OR "work-related quality of life") AND (scale OR measur* OR instrument OR questionnaire), and limiting the materials found to the English, Spanish, and Portuguese languages. Duplicated texts, texts unavailable in full form, presented as book chapter or conference report, produced before the year 2000, and articles whose purpose did not match the process of proposal, validation, and/verification of QLW measures quality were excluded. By the end of the selection procedure, 26 articles were left to be reviewed. Of these, 13 were original proposals of instruments, while the other 13 are studies on adaptation and validation of measures existing in literature.

Among the original proposals on QLW measures, many still do not satisfy the minimal standards expected either due to the weakness or absence of theoretical grounding (e.g., Kimura & Carandina, 2009; Pedroso et al., 2015; Tabanejad et al., 2020) or for not detailing the psychometric data of the scale (e.g., Ventegodt et al., 2008; Subbarayalu & Al Kuwaiti, 2017). Especially regarding the "CVT-Gohisalo" (versión breve) (Moreno et al., 2018), although it reached good statistical indicators after the SFA, the items were not distributed among factors as expected by literature. Still, the authors fail in the discussion when they advocate for the quality of the scale version presented by them but do not justify the theoretical grounding. The Academics' Quality of Life at Work Scale (AQoLW) (Converso et al., 2018), in turn, although explicitly referring to QLW on its name, is a scale based on a theory that does not correspond to the traditions of the study on the phenomenon. In fact, the authors make clear that the theoretical ground to create the measure is the model of job demands-resources (JD-R), and the investigation axes making up the scale are the stimulating demands and the stressing demands of the workplace.

Because of this, only 6 of the 13 aforementioned scales will be reviewed in details. The following were the criteria to select them: presentation of theoretical grounding to propose the instrument and/or minimal psychometric data to validate it. The scales are Quality of Work Life Scale (QWLS) (Sirgy et al. (2001), Quality of Working Life Systemic Inventory (QWLSI) (Martel & Dupuis, 2006), Work-Related Quality of Life (WRQoL) scale (Van Laar et al., 2007), Nurses' Quality of Working Life (NQWL) (Hsu, 2016), Quality of Working Life Questionnaire for Cancer Survivors (QWLQ-CS) (de Jong et al., 2016a), and QWL scale (Beloor et al., 2019). The scales will be presented in chronological order, followed by studies identified in the literature review that contributed with additional data for validation. All studies and scale data may be consulted on Table 7.1.

7.3.1 *Quality of Work Life Scale (QWLS)*

The QWLS was proposed and validated by Sirgy and collaborators early in the twenty-first century (2001), based on the individual perspective of the phenomenon's conception. Three independent studies were conducted to validate the measure, all with samples of workers from the United States of America. Based on the confluence of two classic theoretical approaches in the area, that of need satisfaction and that of spillover, the authors define QLW as "(…) employee satisfaction with a variety of needs through resources, activities, and outcomes stemming from participation in the workplace." The satisfaction of needs arising from the workplace

Table 7.1 Summary of the QLW instruments mapped and their respective studies of validation

Authors	Measure	Country, target audience, and samples	Psychometric analyses performed	Internal consistency and goodness of fit of the model	Final composition of the scale (factors and items)
Sirgy et al. (2001)	Quality of Work Life Scale (QWLS)	The United States of America Several workers n1 = 180 n2 = 310 n3 = 73	EFA CFA Validity of the construct (convergent and discriminative) Predictive validity	$\alpha = 0.78$ $\chi^2(97) = 366.2$, $p = 0.0$; GFI = 0.92; AGFI = 0.88; CFI = 0.89; NFI = 0.86; hRMSEA = 0.07)	7 factors, 16 items Health and safety needs (3), e.g., “I feel physically safe at work” Economic and family needs (3), e.g., “I am satisfied with I’m getting paid for my work” Social needs (2), e.g., “I have enough time away from work to enjoy other things in life” Esteem needs (2), e.g., “I feel appreciated at work at this organization” Actualization needs (2), e.g., “I feel that my job allows me to realize my full potential” Knowledge needs (2), e.g., “This job allows me to sharpen my professional skills” Aesthetic needs (2), e.g., “There is a lot of creativity involved in my job”
Afsar and Burcu (2014)	Quality of Work Life Scale (QWLS) (Sirgy et al., 2001)	Turkey Higher education professionals $n = 254$	CFA	$\alpha = 0.84$ $\chi^2(93) = 191.53$, NC = 2.06, RMSEA = 0.064, SRMR = 0.049, CFI = 0.96	Idem original scale
Rastogi et al. (2018)	Quality of Work Life Scale (QWLS) (Sirgy et al., 2001)	India Several workers n1 = 380	CFA	$\alpha = 0.92$ $\chi^2(\text{df} = 61, n = 380) = 70.748$; $\chi^2/\text{df} = 1.160$; TLI = 0.997; NFI = 0.983; CFI = 0.998; RMSEA = 0.021	2 factors, 16 items Satisfaction of low-order needs (health and safety needs, economic and family needs) (6), e.g., “My job does well for my family” Satisfaction of high-order needs (social needs, esteem needs, actualization needs, knowledge needs, aesthetic needs) (10), e.g., “I have good friends at work”

Sinval et al. (2020)	Quality of Work Life Scale (QWLS) (Sirgy et al., 2001)	Portugal Several workers $n = 566$ Brazil Several workers $n = 597$	CFA Predictive validity	n1 $\alpha = 0.88$ $\chi^2(97) = 673.253$; 2/df = 6.94, $p < 0.001$; $n = 566$; CFI = 0.989; NFI = 0.987; TLI = 0.987; SRMR = 0.077; RMSEA = 0.103; P(rmsea) ≤0.05) <0.001, 90% CI]0.095; 0.110[n2 $\alpha = 0.90$ $\chi^2(97) = 479.314$; χ^2/df = 4.94, $p < 0.001$; $n = 597$; CFI = 0.992; NFI = 0.990; TLI = 0.990; SRMR = 0.063; RMSEA = 0.081; P(rmsea) ≤ 0.05) < 0.001, 90% CI]0.074; 0.089[	Idem original scale
Martel and Dupuis (2006)	Quality of Working Life Systemic Inventory (QWLSI)	Theoretical article presents the scale proposal	–	–	–
Voirol and Dupuis (2010)	Quality of Working Life Systemic Inventory (QWLSI) (Martel & Dupuis, 2006)	The authors do not report their own validation data, but those of Dupuis and Martel (2004)	–	$\alpha = 0.88$	8 factors, 34 items[a] Financial Career path Work schedule Climate with colleagues Climate with superiors Physical characteristics of the environment Factors influencing appreciation of tasks to do Support offered to employees

(continued)

Table 7.1 (continued)

Authors	Measure	Country, target audience, and samples	Psychometric analyses performed	Internal consistency and goodness of fit of the model	Final composition of the scale (factors and items)
Van Laar et al. (2007)	Work-Related Quality of Life (WRQoL) scale	The United Kingdom Healthcare workers n1 = 481 n2 = 472	EFA CFA	$\alpha = 0.91$ χ^2 (216, $n = 472$) = 642.15 $P < 0.01$, CFI = 0.93, GFI = 0.90, NFI = 0.89, RMSEA = 0.06	6 factors, 23 items Job and career satisfaction (JCS) (6), e.g., "I am satisfied with the career opportunities available to me at the organization" General well-being (GWB) (6), e.g., "Generally things work out well for me" Home-work interface (HWI) (3), e.g., "My current working hours/patterns suit my personal circumstances" Stress at work (SAW) (2), e.g., "I often feel under pressure at work" Control at work (CAW) (3), e.g., "I am involved in decisions that affect me in my own area of work" Working conditions (WCS) (3), e.g., "The working conditions are satisfactory"
Zeng et al. (2011)	Work-Related Quality of Life (WRQoL) scale (Van Laar et al., 2007)	Singapore Nurses $n = 811$	EFA Validity of the construct	$\alpha = 0.92$	5 factors, 21 items[a] Job and career satisfaction (JCS) General well-being (GWB) Home-work interface (HWI) Stress at work (SAW) Working conditions (WCS)

Duyan et al. (2013)	Work-Related Quality of Life (WRQoL) scale (Van Laar et al., 2007)	Turkey Several workers $n = 288$	CFA	$\alpha = 0.89$ χ^2 (129) = 278.213, RMSEA = 0.063, CFI = 0.93, SRMR = 0.058, GFI = 0.92, AGFI = 0.87	6 factors, 20 items[b] Job and career satisfaction (JCS) (4) General well-being (GWB) (5) Home-work interface (HWI) (3) Stress at work (SAW) (2) Control at work (CAW) (3) Working conditions (WCS) (3)
Lin et al. (2013)	Work-Related Quality of Life (WRQoL-2) scale 2 (adaptation of Van Laar et al., 2007)	China Nurses $n = 352$	EFA Test-retest	$\alpha = 0.94$	7 factors, 34 items General well-being (GWB) (8), e.g., "I am satisfied with my life" Home-work interface (HWI) (7), e.g., "My employer provides adequate facilities and flexibility for me to fit work in around my family life" Employee engagement (5), e.g., "I am proud to tell others that I am part of this University" Job and career satisfaction (JCS) (4), e.g., "I am satisfied with the career opportunities available for me here" Stress at work (SAW) (4), e.g., "I am pressured to work long hours" Working conditions (WCS) (3), e.g., "When I have done a good job it is acknowledged by my line manager" Control at work (CAW) (3), e.g., "I feel able to voice opinions and influence changes in my area of work"

(continued)

Table 7.1 (continued)

Authors	Measure	Country, target audience, and samples	Psychometric analyses performed	Internal consistency and goodness of fit of the model	Final composition of the scale (factors and items)
Sirisawasd et al. (2014)	Work-Related Quality of Life (WRQoL-2) scale 2 (adaptation by Lin et al., 2013 of Van Laar et al., 2007)	Thailand Nurses *n* = 374	EFA Test-retest Known-group validity	$\alpha = 0.97$	7 factors, 34 items Employee engagement (8), e.g., "I feel success/accomplishment from my work" Control at work (CAW) (5), e.g., "My employer provides me with what I need to do my job effectively" Home-work interface (HWI) (5), e.g., "In most ways my life is similar to ideal" General well-being (GWB) (7), e.g., "I have recently felt unhappy and depressed" Job and career satisfaction (JCS) (2), e.g., "I have an opportunity to use my abilities at work" Working conditions (WCS) (3), e.g., "I am happy with the physical environment of my workplace" Stress at work (SAW) (4), e.g., "I feel under pressure to increase my working hours"
Da Dai et al. (2016)	Work-Related Quality of Life (WRQoL) scale (Van Laar et al., 2007)	Taiwan Nurses n1 = 30 n2 = 213	Apparent validity Test-retest Concurrent validity Internal consistency	$\alpha = 0.88$	Idem original scale[c]

Kongsin et al. (2020)	Thai version of the Work-Related Quality of Life Scale (THWRQLS) (based on the adaptation by Lin et al., 2013 of Van Laar et al., 2007)	Thailand Healthcare professionals n1 = 320 n2 = 250	EFA CFA	$\alpha = 0.94$ $\chi^2 = 268.77$ ($n = 250$), p-value <0.01, CFI = 0.97, RMSEA = 0.04, SRMR = 0.05	7 factors, 24 items Job and career satisfaction (JCS) (6), e.g., "I have a clear set of goals and aims to enable me to do my job" Control at work (CAW) (3), e.g., "I have sufficient opportunities to question managers about change at work" Home-work interface (HWI) (3), e.g., "My current working hours/patterns suit my personal circumstances" Stress at work (SAW) (3), e.g., "I have unachievable deadlines" General well-being (GWB) (4), e.g., "In most ways my life is close to ideal" Working conditions (WCS) (3), e.g., "My employer provides me with what I need to do my job effectively" Employee engagement (2), e.g., "I would recommend this organization as a good one to work for"
Hsu (2016)	Nurses' Quality of Working Life (NQWL)	Taiwan Nurses $n = 619$	EFA	$\alpha = 0.95$	6 factors, 123 items[b] Organizational aspects (14) Work aspects (34) Self-actualization (15) Interrelationships (25) Self-efficacy (17) Vocational concepts (18)
de Jong et al. (2016a)	Quality of Working Life Questionnaire for Cancer Survivors (QWLQ-CS)	Theoretical article presents the scale proposal	–	–	–

(continued)

Table 7.1 (continued)

Authors	Measure	Country, target audience, and samples	Psychometric analyses performed	Internal consistency and goodness of fit of the model	Final composition of the scale (factors and items)
de Jong et al. (2016b)	Quality of Working Life Questionnaire for Cancer Survivors (QWLQ-CS) (de Jong et al., 2016a)	Netherlands Cancer survivors workers $n = 19$	Apparent validity	–	104 items
de Jong et al. (2018)	Quality of Working Life Questionnaire for Cancer Survivors (QWLQ-CS) (de Jong et al., 2016a)	Netherlands Cancer survivors workers n1 = 302 n2 = 130 n3 = 87	EFA Validity of the construct (convergent and discriminative)	$\alpha = 0.91$	5 factors, 23 items Meaning of work (4), e.g., "Working gives me structure in my life" Perception of the work situation (5), e.g., "I am suited to my work" Atmosphere in the work environment (5), e.g., "I have good relations with my colleagues" Understanding and recognition in the organization (5), e.g., "I consider that employees with health problems are treated well in my organization" Problems due to the health situation (4), e.g., "I am limited in my work by my health situation"
Beloor et al. (2019)	QWL scale	India Professionals of the textile sector $n = 341$	EFA CFA Validity of the construct (convergent and discriminative)	$\alpha = 0.87$ χ^2/df ratio = 10.40, GFI = 0.910, AGFI = 0.900, NFI = 0.899, IFI = 0.950, CFI = 0.908, TLI = 0.902 are more than 0.9 and RMSEA = 0.071	27 items 6 factors Compensation (6), e.g., "Fair salary" Work environment (6), e.g., "Working Conditions" Relation and co-operation (4), e.g., "Harmonious relationship" Job security/freedom (3), e.g., "Secured Job" Facilities (4), e.g., "Medical Facilities" Training and development (2), e.g., "Sufficient Training Programmes"

[a]Authors have not informed examples of items, neither the number of items per factor
[b]Authors have not informed examples of items
[c]Authors have not performed factor analyses but followed the same distribution as the original scale to perform their descriptive and correlational analyses
Source: Prepared by the authors

influences and is influenced by the satisfaction of needs in other life domains (home, family, leisure, etc.) (Sirgy et al., 2001, p. 242).

Using convergent, discriminating, and predictive analyses of construct validity, researchers present an instrument made up by 7 factors comprising 16 items corresponding to different types of needs to be satisfied to ensure the worker's quality of life. Each of them should be responded in a 7-point scale, ranging from "Very Untrue" to "Very True." The first two factors include items related to three dimensions each, while the other five factors include items corresponding to two dimensions each, as follows: factor 1, satisfaction of health and security needs (dimensions – protection from ill health and injury at work, protection from ill health and injury outside of work, and enhancement of good health); factor 2, satisfaction of family and economic needs (dimensions – pay, job security, and other family needs); factor 3, - satisfaction of social needs (dimensions – collegiality at work and leisure time off work); factor 4, satisfaction of esteem needs (dimensions – recognition and appreciation of one's work within the organization, recognition, and appreciation of one's work outside the organization); factor 5, satisfaction of actualization needs (dimensions – realization of one's potential within the organization, realization of one's potential as a professional); factor 6, satisfaction of knowledge needs (dimensions – learning to enhance job skills, learning to enhance professional skills); and factor 7, satisfaction of aesthetics needs (dimensions – creativity at work, personal creativity, and general aesthetics). It is worth mentioning that the needs mapped by the scale may be subdivided into lower-order needs for QLW (factors 1 and 2) and higher-order needs (factors 3 to 7) (Sirgy et al., 2001).

In addition to the fact that the scale evinces excellent psychometric indicators, the authors advocate that one of its advantages is that it briefly covers a large extension of dimensions that make up the QLW, thus facilitating its application with no damage to the analysis depth (Sirgy et al., 2001). The literature reviewed pointed out three additional studies (Afsar & Burcu, 2014; Rastogi et al., 2018; Sinval et al., 2020) that tried to validate the Quality of Work Life Scale (QWLS) proposed by Sirgy et al. (2001) for other contexts.

The first one was that by Afsar and Burcu (2014), based on the adaptation and further application of the instrument to 254 scholars (higher education professionals) in Turkey, which found evidence of validity that confirmed the suitability of the instrument's original structure to verify the QLW of Turkish workers. With alpha coefficient of 0.84 to the general scale and acceptable goodness-of-fit indexes (Chi-Square $\chi^2(93) = 191.53$, NC = 2.06, Root Mean Square Error of Approximation (RMSEA) = 0.064, Standardized RMR (SRMR) = 0.049, and Comparative Fit Index (CFI) = 0.96), the authors warn only that the level of reliability of the factors "health and safety needs" and "social needs" was lower than the expected. Therefore, it suggests that in Turkey, the instrument should be assessed only as a whole, rather than in details based on the assessment of each factor (Afsar & Burcu, 2014). However, it should be warned that shrinking factors may hinder the proposal of more directive interventions by any organization aiming at promoting enhanced QLW.

Rastogi et al. (2018) attempted to assess the psychometric indicators of the scale in an Indian sample of 380 intermediary-level employees working in several private and public companies from different regions of India. Although they have not made idiomatic changes to the items, since English is acknowledged as the official language of India jointly with Hindi, Rastogi et al. (2018) adapted the response scale that continued with seven points, but ranging from 1 for "strongly disagree" to 7 for "strongly agree." After the exploratory factor analyses (EFA) and confirmatory factor analyses (CFA), differently from the original validation, the authors found that the solution of two factors (higher-order satisfaction and lower-order needs) was superior to the seven-factor model in a first-order model. Considering that they recommend the instrument to be interpreted in India based on the simplified two-factor structure (χ^2(df = 61, n = 380) = 70.748; χ^2/df = 1.160; TLI = 0.997; NFI = 0.983; CFI = 0.998; RMSEA = 0.021).

Sinval et al. (2020) have translated the instrument of Sirgy et al. (2001) into Portuguese and validated it based on a sample made up by 1163 workers from several occupations, being 566 from Portugal and 597 from Brazil. Besides performing CFAs to verify the internal structure of the instrument, the authors sought evidence of external validity by reviewing the relation established between QLW, burnout, and engagement at work. The model tested with the scale original structure with seven latent factors in a second-order factor presented acceptable indexes both for the Brazilian sample (χ^2(97) = 479.314; χ^2/df = 4.94, $p < 0.001$; n = 597; CFI = 0.992; NFI = 0.990; TLI = 0.990; SRMR = 0.063; RMSEA = 0.081; P(rmsea) ≤ 0.05) < 0.001, 90% CI]0.074; 0.089[) and for the Portuguese sample (χ^2(97) = 673.253; χ^2/df = 6.94, $p < 0.001$; n = 566; CFI = 0.989; NFI = 0.987; TLI = 0.987; SRMR = 0.077; RMSEA = 0.103; P(rmsea) ≤ 0.05) < 0.001, 90% CI]0.095; 0.110[). With regard to predictive validity, Sinval et al. (2020) report results that point out that both the higher-order and lower-order satisfaction dimension are positively related to the engagement at work and negatively related to burnout in both samples.

In brief, the articles found that were focused in presenting evidence of validity of the QLW scale based on satisfaction of needs proposed by Sirgy et al. (2001) point out the quality of the scale's original proposal in different contexts, with integral maintenance of its structure and/or minor adjustments that do not conflict with the theoretical model that sustains the measure.

7.3.2 *Quality of Working Life Systemic Inventory (QWLSI)*

In 2006, Martel and Dupuis assume that QLW reflects the worker's dynamic experience in the pursue of their objectives in the workplace to present the proposal of an instrument named Quality of Working Life Systemic Inventory (QWLSI). To construct it, the authors refer to have simultaneously based on the four macro dimensions indicated by Turcotte (1988) as referring to QLW programs (nature of work itself, physical context, psychosocial context, and organizational context). These programs correspond to the 14 aspects listed by Kohl and Shooler (1982) (job complexity, routine, time pressure, environment cleanliness, work protection, feeling of belonging, empowerment level, supervision level, bureaucracy, hierarchical position, work security, stability at work, compensation, and work schedule). Therefore, the 33 domains of the instrument tried to specify each of these dimensions and were organized in 8 subscales as follows: financial, career path, work schedule, climate with colleagues, climate with superiors, physical characteristics of the environment, factors influencing appreciation of tasks to do, and support offered to employees (Dupuis & Martel, 2004).

The QWLSI stands out for its graphic and dynamic character of QLW measurement. Based on a nonlinear measurement strategy, each of the 33 domains is assessed based on 3 criteria/items: first, the worker should indicate what s/he considers to be the current situation and the ideal situation in relation to the domain being assessed (e.g., autonomy). Next, the worker should indicate if she perceives to be getting closer or farther from their ideal and the speed of this movement. Finally, the worker answers to what extent that domain is important or not, in his/her view, to his/her QLW. This measure allows evaluating not only each characteristic individually but also accessing a general QLW score calculated in relation to all domains together, based on the ratio of the difference between the worker's current and ideal situations, weighed by the dynamic of improvement or deterioration and by the ranking.

The great novelty of the QWLSI against other QLW instruments relies on its capacity of checking the phenomenon considering that it depends on the individual's perception on how close or far s/he is from the ideal parameters regarding different work domains, also considering that such domains may be more or less relevant to each worker. Therefore, among the advantages of the measure, the capacity of apprehending the dynamism and subjectivity inherent to the concept of QLW adopted by the authors is a highlight. Among disadvantages, one could mention the complexity of results interpretation that must consider the three aspects of the QLW variation: (1) the interval between current and ideal situations, (2) the speed of approximation or distancing in relation to the ideal situation, and (3) ranking of relevance of that aspect.

The literature review found only one subsequent study that mentioned the use of QWLSI. The study was performed by Voirol and Dupuis (2010) and applied the instrument to participants of public and private organizations in Switzerland and Canada in two moments: in the beginning of the survey and 17 weeks later. However, the authors do not add evidence of validity to that scale, as it is used only to gather evidence on other brief measures of psychosocial factors. This way, although the QWLSI was proposed to fill several gaps pertinent to the QLW assessment, up to now its repercussion in the scientific literature seems to be limited. Moreover, robust psychometric indicators are yet to be presented to advocate for it. The only reference (Dupuis & Martel, 2004) quoted by Martel and Dupuis (2006) and by Voirol and Dupuis (2010) with those data refers to a presentation in a congress, rather than to a peer-reviewed article. Therefore, based on the findings available according to the mapping performed, the QWLSI was not considered to be ready to be used in descriptive or correlational studies.

7.3.3 *Work-Related Quality of Life (WRQoL) Scale*

In 2007, Van Laar, Edwards, and Easton introduced the Work-Related Quality of Life (WRQoL) scale that, like the QWLSI, is also based on theoretical approaches of need satisfaction and spillover. To respond the instrument, workers should indicate on a 5-point Likert scale to what extent they agree or disagree with each statement, ranging from 1 (strongly agree) to 5 (strongly disagree). This scaling was inversed in some subsequent versions of validation (ranging from 1 – strongly disagree to 5 – strongly agree). Although being built to be applied to any group of workers, the authors focused on validating it specifically for workers in the healthcare field in the United Kingdom, including managers, administrative, and technical staff.

According to Van Laar et al. (2007, p. 325), QLW may be defined as "(...) the way in which work is good for you in the widest context in which an employee would evaluate their job," including specific job-related factors (e.g., job and career satisfaction, stress at work, control at work and working conditions), general life factors (general well-being), and factors connecting the life domains external and internal to job (home-work interface). These six factors make up the instrument proposed by the authors that, after the EFAs (with data of a 481 healthcare workers sample) and CFAs (with data of a 472 healthcare workers sample) confirmed its final structure with 23 items, distributed among factors as follows: factor 1, job and career satisfaction (JCS), with 6 items and $\alpha = 0.86$; factor 2, general well-being (GWB), with 6 items and $\alpha = 0.82$; factor 3, home–work interface (HWI), with 3 items and $\alpha = 0.82$; factor 4, stress at work (SAW), with 2 items and $\alpha = 0.81$; factor 5, control at work (CAW), with 3 items and $\alpha = 0.81$; and factor 6, working conditions (WCS), with 3 items and $\alpha = 0.75$. The goodness-of-fit indexes for the model were χ^2 (216, $n = 472$) = 642.15 $P < 0.01$, CFI = 0.93, GFI = 0.90, NFI = 0.89, and RMSEA = 0.06. According to Van Laar et al. (2007), the WRQoL also presents the possibility of being an instrument to measure the QLW in a unidimensional perspective, as the six factors are highly interrelated, mainly those specific to the workplace (JCS, WCS, and CAW).

Despite being welcome in the scientific world, considering it was subject to validation studies in several countries, the WRQoL has weaknesses that should be pointed out. The first one refers to the theoretical grounding. Van Laar et al. (2007) did not present an operational definition for QLW to subsidize the proposal of the instrument. The authors presented a comprehensive review of different models in literature and advocate for the inclusion of dimensions into the instrument by joining elements they consider relevant. However, they do not explain how these dimensions are integrated to the broader concept of QLW. It is also worth mentioning that, despite being based on the same theoretical framework as Sirgy et al. (2001), Van Laar et al. (2007) introduce in their instrument a factor that is not directly related to the field of work. This could reflect a stretching of the concept that damages its quality.

It is worth mentioning that all the six subsequent works found in the literature review that sought evidence to validate the WRQoL (Van Laar et al., 2007) were carried out in Asian countries such as China (Lin et al., 2013), Taiwan (Da Dai et al., 2016), Thailand (Sirisawasd et al., 2014; Kongsin et al., 2020), Singapore (Zeng et al., 2011), and Turkey (Duyan et al., 2013). One of them focuses on healthcare professionals in general (Kongsin et al., 2020), four approached only nursing professionals (Zeng et al., 2011; Lin et al., 2013; Sirisawasd et al., 2014; Da Dai et al., 2016), and only that with Turkish professionals comprised professionals of other segments (Duyan et al., 2013).

The large spectrum of studies to validate the scale may favor the comparison of QLW in professional groups of these different countries. However, it should be noticed that none of the validated versions of the scale has fully replicated the original proposal. The research conducted by Da Dai et al. (2016), although mentioning sound indicators of internal consistency and test-retest reliability, does not present detailed data on factor analyses, only descriptive and correlational data. Therefore, results cannot be reviewed in details in this study.

In the study performed with nurses in Singapore, based on the EFAs performed, the final model demanded excluding two items. The remaining items were distributed along the five original factors that explained 60% of the construct variation so that "control at work" was not maintained in the model (Zeng et al., 2011). For the study carried out with Turkish nurses, acceptable goodness-of-fit indexes were obtained in the CFA of the six-factor models of first and second order. However, three items had to be excluded from the scale (Duyan et al., 2013).

The survey conducted by Lin et al. (2013), in turn, proposes a Chinese version of the WRQoL named WRQoL-2, in which 12 items are added to the original 22 items. Some of the added items refer to a new factor named "employee engagement." After the EFAs, the authors identified issues such as the overlapping of the factors "job and career satisfaction," "working conditions," and "control at work." Nonetheless, they report the validation as consistent in relation to the original one (considering 22 items) and advocate for the applicability of the scale – composed of 34 items distributed along 7 factors (the 6 ones of the original scale, and the "employee engagement") – in the Chinese cultural context. However, the results presented showed that the items of different factors intermingled, and the authors did not present any theoretical discussion to support the scale's new configuration. Some examples, among many others, are the item "I am able to achieve a healthy balance between my work and home life" assigned to factor general well-being; the item "I am happy with the physical environment where I usually work" assigned to factor home–work interface; the item "I am encouraged to develop new skills" assigned to factor working conditions; and the item "I often feel under pressure at work" assigned to factor job and career satisfaction. The lack of theoretical grounds and operational definition to support the nomenclature of the factors considering the blending of items resulting from the statistical analyses suggest that this indication of use should be viewed with care.

It was this Chinese version of the WRQoL-2 (Lin et al., 2013) that Sirisawasd et al. (2014) translated into Thai, and to which they sought evidence of validity to assess the QLW of Thai nurses. Although they found good psychometric indicators to the internal consistency analyses of the scale and test-retest reliability, just like in the Chinese version, the authors found factors that shrank items referring to different theoretical dimensions of the phenomenon. Moreover, the items' organization across the seven factors has also widely varied in comparison to the validation made with the Chinese. Therefore, it should be considered that replicating scales without deepening this discussion is dangerous, since the proper interpretation of the tool demands sound reasoning in addition to statistical indexes.

Considering some points of improvement of the WRQoL-2 (Lin et al., 2013), such as the low factor loading of some items, the overlapping of content, and the total response time of the scale, Kongsin et al. (2020) tried to validate a brief version to the Thai context, which they named "Thai version of the Work-Related Quality of Life Scale" (THWRQLS). Thus, the authors came up with a model of 24 items distributed across 7 factors that presented acceptable goodness-of-fit indexes: $\chi^2 = 268.77$ ($n = 250$), p-value <0.01, CFI = 0.97, RMSEA = 0.04, and SRMR = 0.05. Although they did not bring up the discussion about the theoretical confusion in the previous studies on the scale's validation, the analysis criteria adopted by Kongsin et al. (2020) allowed all the seven factors of the final model to be made up by items corresponding to their definition, thus overcoming the difficulties found in the studies by Lin et al. (2013) and by Sirisawasd et al. (2014).

In face of the foregoing, consideration should be given to develop efforts to operationally describe each dimension making up the WRQoL (Van Laar et al., 2007) as a way to favor the interpretation of its results and more properly support discussions in further applications or validations. Despite its potential, this weakness is more visible in subsequent studies and may harm its use. Likewise interesting is to have the instrument tested in more varied audiences, as the prevailing audiences identified were those oriented to healthcare workers. Simultaneously, it is suggested that new surveys using this model as baseline could problematize the maintenance of the factor "general well-being" in the construct structure considering that, as previously discussed, we consider that the insertion of factors strange to the work to describe a phenomenon specific to this context may lead to a conceptual stretching that harms the understanding of the phenomenon as well as potential interventions aimed at promoting it.

7.3.4 Other Recent QWL Scales

More recently, three new instruments on QLW were developed. Each instrument was designed focused on a specific group, namely, nursing professionals (Hsu, 2016), cancer survivors workers (de Jong et al., 2016a), and professionals from textile industries (Beloor et al., 2019).

Hsu (2016) understands QLW as an indicator of to what extent professionals "(...) are satisfied with their jobs, how they feel in relation to opportunities as they see them, and how they find fulfillment in their work" (p. 87), while representing

"(…) a way of thinking about people, work, and the organization that involves a concern for employee well-being and organizational effectiveness" (p. 88). Although it neither operationalizes the phenomenon definition nor specifies the theoretical grounding, the author places his proposal in the latest perspective of understanding the phenomenon that includes organizational and individual aspects related to the workplace and also generic individual aspects not directly related to the workplace.

In an attempt to develop a specific measure to assess the QLW of nurses in Taiwan, Hsu (2016) relied on instruments preexisting in literature and focal groups to build and apply the Nurse's Quality of Working Life (NQWL) to 619 professionals. These professionals should point out their degree of agreement with each statement, (from 1 – strongly disagree to 5 – strongly agree). After the EFAs, he found a solution to the questionnaire composed of 123 items (α= 0.95) distributed across 6 factors, all with internal consistency higher than 0.80 and that, together, explained 63% of the total variance of the construct, as follows: organizational aspects (14 items), work aspects (34 items), self-actualization (15 items), interrelationships (25 items), self-efficacy (17 items), and vocational concepts (18 items).

Despite having complied with the initial stages required to build instruments and having associated self-efficacy with the mastery experiences at work that could favor the QLW, this factor should be reviewed in future applications of the instrument for both theoretical and empirical reasons. As aforementioned, this inclusion points out a likely conceptual stretching as there is no tradition of understanding it as part of the QLW. Moreover, the results found by the author evidence the low correlation between self-efficacy and QLW in the sample ($r = 0.355$, $p < 0.001$) if compared to the other factors that make up the scale. Likewise, future studies should focus on seeking evidence of confirmatory validation to the instrument.

In turn, anchored in an individual perspective of the QLW evaluation, the Quality of Working Life Questionnaire for Cancer Survivors (QWLQ-CS) is proposed by de Jong et al. proposal and the current literature review identified in three publications: the first on the process of developing the questionnaire (de Jong et al., 2016a); the second reporting the initial tests performed (de Jong et al., 2016b); and the third devoted to gathering evidence of validity per se (de Jong et al., 2018). The authors define the QLW of cancer survivor workers as "(...) the experiences and perceptions of cancer survivors in the work situation" (de Jong et al., 2018, p. 2), and after applying the QWLQ-CS to 302 participants and carrying out the EFAs, they advocate for the composition of 23 items ($\alpha = 0.91$) distributed across 5 factors, namely, meaning of work ($\alpha = 0.83$); perception of the work situation ($\alpha = 0.85$); atmosphere in the work environment ($\alpha = 0.86$); understanding and recognition in the organization ($\alpha = 0.85$), and problems due to the health situation ($\alpha = 0.84$). The authors also presented analyses of convergent and discriminative validity, indicating the quality of the proposed measure.

The authors suggest using the QWLQ-CS in both occupational health contexts and clinical contexts (de Jong et al., 2018), in order to favor the process of adaptation and return to work of individuals who developed cancer during their active labor lives. Although specifically delimiting the target audience, only the last factor more specifically represents the characteristics of that target audience, thus expanding the possibility of adapting and validating it to other groups of workers in further studies.

Finally, the last and more recent QLW measure identified was the QWL scale proposed by Beloor et al. (2019) that was developed to assess the phenomenon among professionals working in organizations of the textile sector in India. Assuming the concept of QLW as "(…) the standard of workers performing comfortably in an organization by satisfying their personal needs through the facilities provided to them by the management" (Beloor et al., 2019, p. 1736), the researchers rely on the organizational perspective of understanding the phenomenon to develop the instrument that was applied to 341 professionals of 40 Indian industries. After the EFAs and CFAs, they found a structure of 27 items ($\alpha = 0.875$) in 6 factors (all with internal consistency above 0.785) that reached the acceptable goodness-of-fit indexes to the model (χ^2/df ratio = 10.40, GFI = 0.910, AGFI = 0.900, NFI = 0.899, IFI = 0.950, CFI = 0.908, TLI = 0.902, RMSEA = 0.071) and that, together, explained 61% of the construct variance. The following were the factors: compensation (six items); work environment (six items); relation and co-operation (four items); job security (three items); facilities (four items); and training and development (two items).

It is worthwhile observing that among all instruments mapped in this review, that of Beloor et al. (2019) is the only one exclusively focused on job factors under the main responsibility of the organization's management to ensure a good level of QLW to its employees. This characteristic converges with the researchers' concern about developing an instrument that could serve as basis for the Indian textile industries to adjust their management to enable a more positive working experience to their employees and also improve the company's productivity indicators. In this sense, although the review found no study attempting to gather more evidence of validity of this measure in other contexts and/or occupational groups, this instrument is considered to be promising in the sense of enabling the proper measurement and management of QLW.

7.4 Final Remarks

The analysis presented herein about the instruments used to measure the QLW is expected to be useful to assist researchers and professionals in the selection of the most suitable scale, according to their purpose and target audience. Although the overview does not comprise all the recent measures existing in literature, the search criteria are very likely to have allowed the identification of the most relevant QLW scales validated in the last 20 years. It is worth mentioning that the keywords search restriction may have excluded articles that conducted analyses of validation of existing scales, however in a secondary way such as, for example, in a preliminary stage to test a correlational model.

With regard to the mapped scales, it draws attention to the large number of publications that does not meet or disseminate the minimal information expected for a study of proposal and validation of instruments, such as operational definition of the construct supported by sound theoretical framework, transparency and detailing of the methodology used to build the items and data analysis, and congruent interpretation of results in the theoretical and statistical light. This reality may be partially due to the huge interest in the theme by professionals in several fields of knowledge that may miss detailed training in psychometry. This could explain incompliance with the minimal requirements. We do not mean that good QLW measures can only be proposed by professionals of specific areas. We would only like to emphasize the need for deepening knowledge about the construction, adaptation, and/or validation of instruments by researchers devoted to conduct studies for that purpose.

Every attention is important when we recall that many users of the instruments are frontline professionals who, many times, miss the refined skill needed to identify whether a scale meets or not the quality standards. Therefore, managers and analysts working to promote QLW may end up by using insufficient or unsuitable standards for the diagnosis that should drive both the actions of intervention proposed and the interpretation of the efficacy or not of those actions.

In this sense, in the mapping performed, we warn more specifically about two issues that should be problematized. The first one is the theoretical stretching of the QLW concept translated into scales that gather a wide diversity of factors, including some with absolute no direct relation with the subject's experience at the workplace (e.g., WRQoL, WRQoL-2, THWRQLS, NQWL). The second one refers to the uncritical replication of instruments bearing theoretical weaknesses in studies that are robust in the statistical light, but that fails in supporting results of adaptation and validation on sound theoretical grounds.

On the other hand, the mapping also allowed to identify studies that aligned theory, instrument, models of validation, and interpretation of results, thus offering proper scales to measure the QLW and potential application to different workplaces. This is true to the QWLSI (Sirgy et al., 2001) that adopts the subjective perspective of analysis of the phenomenon, and of the QWL scale (Beloor et al., 2019) that adopts the organizational perspective.

With regard to the target audience, there is a clear interest in studying healthcare professionals, as this was the target audience of most studies of validation, including some instruments focused on specific professions. Differently from when the concept of QLW started gaining notoriety, the focus of evaluation in the twenty-first century seems to be much more on workers in the field of services than on workers of the industry.

However, there is an effort by the researchers in QLW toward building instruments applicable to a wide range of occupational groups. Most of the mapped scales are focused on workers at large. This flexibility is interesting, as it helps fighting the excess of subjectivity that many times follows the discussions on QLW, thus allowing comparisons on how QLW has been experienced by different professional segments. We encourage the adoption of this approach, as we understand that more investment should be made in instruments that operationalize a general definition of QLW applicable to a wide range of contexts and that allow for specific adjustments to dimensions and items whenever the scale needs to be adapted to new audiences.

We believe this practice enhances the accrual of scientific evidence on the phenomenon, what does not happen when it is assumed that QLW means something completely different for a professional group A and B.

As aforementioned, here the QLW is understood as a phenomenon that comprises both organizational/contextual and individual characteristics, and that occurs as a result of mutual responsibility of the management and the worker. In a sociopolitical perspective, in 2005, the United Nations Development Programme – UNDP (UNDP, 2005) – stated that one of the focuses considered to ensure QoL is that of rights that addresses how human rights are approached and how it may contribute to promote well-being in different contexts (Paz et al., 2012). The focus on human rights strongly emphasizes the relations of exchange and assumes a perception of human being as holder of rights rather than beneficiary of actions (Cyment, 2007).

Understanding and evaluating QLW in this light imply conversing the international principles of human rights into concrete actions. In this process, both workers and employers, chiefs and subordinates, inter- and intra-work team members should be aware of the rights and duties of each one, in order to build an organizational environment favorable to experiencing QLW. At the same time, it should be recalled that QLW cannot cope with the whole experience of satisfaction, expectations, and well-being of individuals. Therefore, we reaffirm the need for preventing a potential stretching of the concept in that sense. We expect this chapter contributed to shed light on instruments with theoretical grounds that are both solid and properly represented by the items that considers quality of life at workplace as a right of the collective, and that assists organizations and workers to identify how they can work toward improving the QLW.

References

Afroz, S. (2019). Quality of work life: A conceptual model. *Advances in Economics and Business Management (AEBM), 4*(8), 570–578.

Afsar, S. T., & Burcu, E. (2014). The adaptation and validation of quality of work life scale to Turkish culture. *Applied Research in Quality of Life, 9*(4), 897–910. https://doi.org/10.1007/s11482-013-9276-0

Akter, K. M., & Banik, S. (2018). Factors affecting the quality of work into the RGM industry of Bangladesh. *Journal of Human Resource Management, 6*(1), 26–36. https://doi.org/10.11648/j.jhrm.20180601.14

Bagtasos, M. R. (2011). Quality of work life: A literature review. *DLSU Business & Economics Review, 20*(2), 1–8.

Beloor, V., Nanjundeeswaraswamy, T. S., & Swamy, D. R. (2019). Quality of work life – Development and scale validation for textile sectors in India. *International Journal of Engineering and Advanced Technology, 8*(6), 1736–1747. https://doi.org/10.35940/ijeat.F8432.088619

Converso, D., Loera, B., Molinengo, G., Viotti, S., & Guidetti, G. (2018). Not all academics are alike: First validation of the academics' quality of life at work scale (AQoLW). *Frontiers in Psychology, 9*(DEC), 1–12. https://doi.org/10.3389/fpsyg.2018.02408

Cyment, P. (2007). Introducción al enfoque de derechos humanos en el desarrollo: guía conceptual y de recursos para utilizar los derechos humanos en las acciones de desarrollo de Intermóm Oxfam. *Cuaderno Temático para el cambio, 1*, 1–32.

Da Dai, H., Tang, F. I., Chen, I. J., & Yu, S. (2016). Taiwanese version of the work-related quality of life scale for nurses: Translation and validation. *Journal of Nursing Research, 24*(1), 58–67. https://doi.org/10.1097/jnr.0000000000000142

de Jong, M., Tamminga, S. J., de Boer, A. G. E. M., & Frings-Dresen, M. H. W. (2016a). Quality of working life of cancer survivors: Development of a cancer-specific questionnaire. *Journal of Cancer Survivorship, 10*(2), 394–405. https://doi.org/10.1007/s11764-015-0485-4

de Jong, M., Tamminga, S. J., De Boer, A. G. E. M., & Frings-Dresen, M. H. W. (2016b). The quality of working life questionnaire for cancer survivors (QWLQ-CS): A pre-test study. *BMC Health Services Research, 16*(1), 1–12. https://doi.org/10.1186/s12913-016-1440-4

de Jong, M., Tamminga, S. J., van Es, R. J. J., Frings-Dresen, M. H. W., & de Boer, A. G. E. M. (2018). The quality of working life questionnaire for cancer survivors (QWLQ-CS): Factorial structure, internal consistency, construct validity and reproducibility. *BMC Cancer, 18*(1), 1–14. https://doi.org/10.1186/s12885-017-3966-1

Dupuis, G., & Martel, J. P. (2004, August 26–29). Caracteristiques psychome'triques de l'ISQVT: Fidelite test-retest, coherence interne, validite de construit, validation transculturelle—La qualite de la vie au travail dans les annees 2000. Paper presented at the XIII ieme congres de l'Association internationale de psychologie du travail et des organisations de langue francaise (AIPTLF) [13th Congress of the International Association for Industrial = Organizational Psychology in French Language], Bologna, Italy.

Duyan, E. C., Aytaç, S., Akyildiz, N., & Van Laar, D. (2013). Measuring work related quality of life and affective well-being in Turkey. *Mediterranean Journal of Social Sciences, 4*(1), 105–116. https://doi.org/10.5901/mjss.2013.v4n1p105

Easton, S., & Van Laar, D. (2013). QoWL (quality of working life)—What, how, and why? *Psychology Research, 3*(10), 596–605.

Elyzur, D., & Shye, S. (1990). Quality of work life and its relation to quality of life. *Applied Psychology: An International Review, 39*(3), 275–291. https://doi.org/10.1111/j.1464-0597.1990.tb01054.x

Fernandes, R. B., Martins, B. S., Caixeta, R. P., Da Costa Filho, C. G., Braga, G. A., & Antonialli, L. M. (2017). Quality of work life: An evaluation of Walton model with analysis of structural equations. *Espacios, 38*(3), 5.

Ferreira, M. C., Souza, M. A., & Silva, C. A. (2012). Qualidade de vida e bem-estar no trabalho: principais tendências e perspectivas teóricas. In M. C. Ferreira, H. Mendonça, & (Org.) (Eds.), *Saúde e bem-estar no trabalho: dimensões individuais e culturais* (pp. 79–103). Casa do Psicólogo.

Hackman, J. R., & Oldham, G. R. (1976). Motivation through the design of work: Test of a theory. *Organizational Behavior and Human Performance, 16*(2), 250–279. https://doi.org/10.1016/0030-5073(76)90016-7

Hannif, Z., Burguess, J., & Cornell, J. (2008). Call centers and the quality of work life: Towards a research agenda. *Journal of Industrial Relations, 50*(2), 271–284. https://doi.org/10.1177/0022185607087902

Hsu, M. Y. (2016). A quality of working life survey instrument for hospital nurses. *Journal of Nursing Research, 24*(1), 87–99. https://doi.org/10.1097/jnr.0000000000000098

Kimura, M., & Carandina, D. M. (2009). Desenvolvimento e validação de uma versão reduzida do instrumento para avaliação da Qualidade de Vida no Trabalho de enfermeiros em hospitais. *Revista Da Escola de Enfermagem Da USP, 43*(spe), 1044–1054. https://doi.org/10.1590/s0080-62342009000500008

Klein, L. L., Pereira, B. A. D., & Lemos, R. B. (2019). Quality of working life: Parameters and evaluation in the public service. *RAM. Revista de Administração Mackenzie, 20*(3), 1–34. https://doi.org/10.1590/1678-6971/eramg190134

Kongsin, T., Chaiear, N., Thanomsieng, N., & Boonjaraspinyo, S. (2020). Validation of the brief Thai version of the work- related quality of life scale (brief THWRQLS). *International Journal of Environmental Research and Public Health, 17*(5). https://doi.org/10.3390/ijerph17051503

Lau, R. S. M., & Bruce, E. M. (1998). A win-win paradigm for quality of work life and business performance. *Human Resource Development Quarterly, 9*(3), 211–226. https://doi.org/10.1002/hrdq.3920090302

Lin, S., Chaiear, N., Khiewyoo, J., Wu, B., & Johns, N. P. (2013). Preliminary psychometric properties of the Chinese version of the work-related quality of life scale-2 in the nursing profession. *Safety and Health at Work, 4*(1), 37–45. https://doi.org/10.5491/SHAW.2013.4.1.37

Loscocco, K. A., & Roschelle, A. R. (1991). Influences on the quality of work and nonwork life: Two decades in review. *Journal of Vocational Behavior, 39*(2), 182–225. https://doi.org/10.1016/0001-8791(91)90009-B

Martel, J. P., & Dupuis, G. (2006). Quality of work life: Theoretical and methodological problems, and presentation of a new model and measuring instrument. *Social Indicators Research, 77*(2), 333–368. https://doi.org/10.1007/s11205-004-5368-4

Moreno, M. P., Baltazar, R. G., Beltrán, C. A., & Núñez, F. E. (2018). Fiabilidad y validez factorial del instrumento para medir calidad de vida en el trabajo "CVT-Gohisalo" (versión breve). *Salud Uninorte, 34*(1), 68–75.

Nadler, D. A., & Lawler, E. E. (1983). Quality of work life: Perspectives and directions. *Organizational Dynamics, 11*(3), 20–30. https://doi.org/10.1016/0090-2616(83)90003-7

Nanjundeswaraswamy, T. S., & Swamy, D. R. (2015). An empirical research on the relationship between quality of work life and leadership styles in SMEs. *Bangladesh e-Journal of Sociology, 5*(1), 65–78. https://doi.org/10.5267/j.msl.2014.12.006

OIT. (1981). *Convenção n°. 155 – Convenção sobre a segurança, a saúde dos trabalhadores e o ambiente de trabalho*. Genebra. Disponível em http://www.ilo.org/ilolex/portug/docs/convdisp1. htm. Acessado em 12/05/2009.

Osigweh, C. A. B. (1989). Concept fallibility in organizational science. *Academy of Management Review, 14*(4), 579–594. https://doi.org/10.2307/258560

Paz, M. G. T., Neiva, E. R., & Dessen, M. C. (2012). Bem-estar e felicidade nas organizações: um só fenômeno? In M. C. Ferreira, H. Mendonça, & (Orgs.) (Eds.), *Saúde e bem-estar no trabalho: dimensões individuais e culturais* (pp. 105–130). Casa do Psicólogo.

Paz, M. G. T., Fernandes, S. R. P., Carneiro, L. L., & Melo, E. A. A. (2020). Bem-estar pessoal nas organizações e qualidade de vida organizacional: O papel mediador da cultura organizacional. *Revista de Administração Mackenzie, 21*(1), 1–37. https://doi.org/10.1590/1678-6971/eRAMD200122

Pedroso, B., Pilatti, L. A., Gutierrez, G. L., & Picinin, C. T. (2015). Construção e validação do TQWL-42: um instrumento de avaliação da qualidade de vida no trabalho. *Revista de Salud Pública, 16*(6), 885–896. https://doi.org/10.15446/rsap.v16n6.30224

Rastogi, M., Rangnekar, S., & Rastogi, R. (2018). Psychometric evaluation of need-based quality of work life scale in an Indian sample. *Industrial and Commercial Training, 50*(1), 10–19. https://doi.org/10.1108/ICT-06-2017-0041

Sashkin, M., & Burke, W. W. (1987). Organizational development in the 1980's. *Journal of Management, 13*(2), 393–417.

Sinval, J., Sirgy, M. J., Lee, D. J., & Marôco, J. (2020). The quality of work life scale: Validity evidence from Brazil and Portugal. *Applied Research in Quality of Life, 15*(5), 1323–1351. https://doi.org/10.1007/s11482-019-09730-3

Sirgy, M. J., Efraty, D., Siegel, P., & Lee, D. (2001). A new measure of quality of work life (qwl) based on need satisfaction and spillover theories. *Social Indicators Research, 55*, 241–302.

Sirisawasd, P., Chaiear, N., Johns, N. P., & Khiewyoo, J. (2014). Validation of the Thai version of a work-related quality of life scale in the nursing profession. *Safety and Health at Work, 5*(2), 80–85. https://doi.org/10.1016/j.shaw.2014.02.002

Subbarayalu, A. V., & Al Kuwaiti, A. (2017). Development of a six sigma rating scale for measuring the quality of work life of teaching staff working in Saudi universities. *International Journal for Quality Research, 11*(2), 397–418. https://doi.org/10.18421/IJQR11.02-10

Swamy, D. R., Nanjundeswaraswamy, T. S., & Rashmi, S. (2015). Quality of work life: Scale development and validation. *International Journal of Caring Sciences, 8*(2), 281–295.

Tabanejad, Z., Oskouie, F., Ebadi, A., & Mesri, M. (2020). Development and psychometric evaluation of the police quality of work-life questionnaire. *Nursing and Midwifery Studies, 9*(3), 142–148. https://doi.org/10.4103/nms.nms_14_19

UNPD. (2005). *Los derechos humanos en el PNUD: nota práctica.* Disponível em http://www.undp.org/governance/docs/HRPN_Spanish.pdf. Acessado em 20/05/2009.

Van Laar, D., Edwards, J. A., & Easton, S. (2007). The work-related quality of life scale for healthcare workers. *Journal of Advanced Nursing, 60*(3), 325–333. https://doi.org/10.1111/j.1365-2648.2007.04409.x

Ventegodt, S., Andersen, N. J., Kandel, I., & Merrick, J. (2008). Scientific research in the quality of working-life (QWL): Generic measuring of the global working life quality with the SEQWL questionnaire. *International Journal on Disability and Human Development, 7*(2), 201–218. https://doi.org/10.1515/IJDHD.2008.7.2.201

Voirol, C., & Dupuis, G. (2010). Fluctuations in weekly brief measures of quality of working life and prediction of quality of working life systemic inventory (qwlsi) results after four months, using the internet. *Journal of Workplace Behavioral Health, 25*(4), 241–268. https://doi.org/10.1080/15555240.2010.518484

Walton, R. E. (1973). Quality of work life: What is it? *Sloan Management Review, 15*, 11–21.

Walton, R. (1980). Quality of work life activities: A research agenda. *Professional Psychology: Research and Practice, 11*(3), 484–493. https://doi.org/10.1037/0735-7028.11.3.484

WHOQOL GROUP. (1994). Development of the WHOQOL: Rationale and current status. *International Journal of Mental Health, 23*(3), 24–56.

Zeng, X., Chaiear, N., Klainin, P., Khiewyoo, J., Koh, D., Hien, P. W. H., & Lee, S. Y. (2011). Work-related quality of life scale among Singaporean nurses. *Asian Biomedicine, 5*(4), 467–474. https://doi.org/10.5372/1905-7415.0504.061

Chapter 8
Creativity Climate: An Analysis of Measurement Scales

Heila Magali da Silva Veiga and Pedro Afonso Cortez

8.1 Introduction

In the work context, creativity is considered a foundation for the survival and competitiveness of organizations in the current world (Amabile & Pratt, 2016; Anderson et al., 2014; Boso et al., 2017; Burbiel, 2009; Epstein et al., 2013; Zhou & Hoever, 2014; Zhou & Shalley, 2003). There is empirical evidence that a creativity-supporting organizational environment is positively related to introducing new products and services and to sales (Binnewies & Gromer, 2012; Dul & Ceylan, 2014).

Creativity is a complex construct with multiple dimensions, which have to be considered together for a more accurate analysis of an individual's creative ability. We may infer that the emergence of creativity is more likely when an individual has certain characteristics and skills, specific knowledge in a given area, intrinsic motivation, and perception of their work environment as a creativity-supporting one (Amabile, 1983; Burbiel, 2009; DiLiello & Houghton, 2008; DiLiello et al., 2011; Dixon et al., 2014; Mendonça et al., 2017). Creativity does not refer only to one concept; it designates a research domain in which there are numerous constructs (Montag et al., 2012). Therefore, delimiting creativity conceptually and operationally is fundamental, as well as properly specifying the measurement level of the construct studied.

Several studies have investigated the influence of individual and contextual aspects on the emergence of creativity (McLean, 2005; Oldham & Cummings, 1996; Shalley et al., 2004; Zhou et al., 2012). Egan (2005), in a literature review, analyzed over 100 articles and identified that the factors associated with creativity

H. M. da Silva Veiga (✉)
Federal University of Uberlândia, Uberlândia, MG, Brazil

P. A. Cortez
Methodist University of São Paulo, São Bernardo do Campo, SP, Brazil

M. O. Macambira et al. (eds.), *Assessing Organizational Behaviors*,
https://doi.org/10.1007/978-3-030-81311-6_8

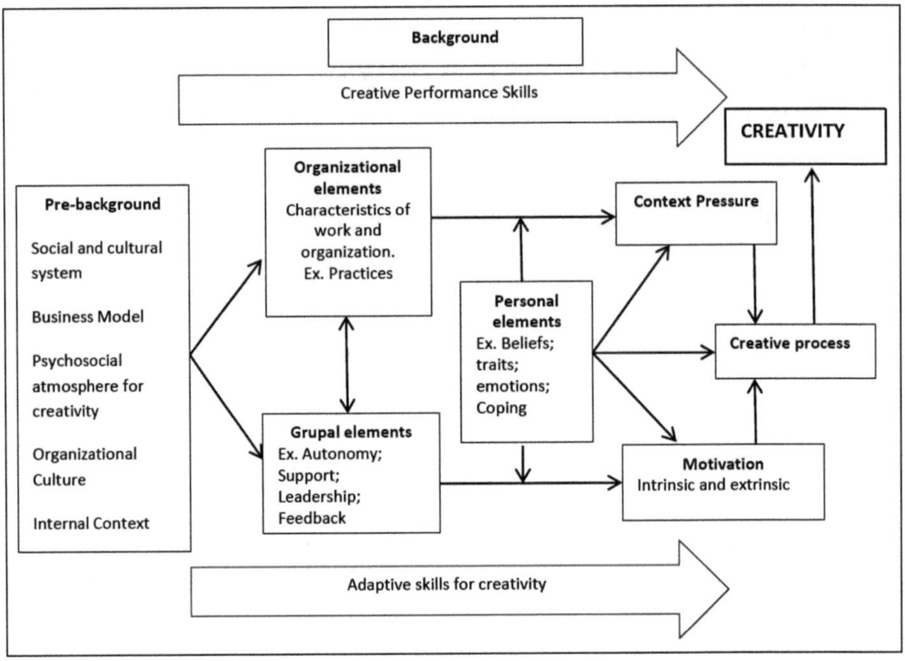

Source: Mendonça, Veiga, and Macambira, 2017, p. 39.

Fig. 8.1 Integrator Model and Potentializer of Work Creativity, MIPC. (Source: Mendonça et al., 2017, p. 39)

are classified as internal (general personality, big five personality) and external (creativity goal setting, evaluation and feedback, role models, leadership and supervision, and teamwork).

Based on the assumption that individual and contextual variables affect the emergence of creativity, Mendonça et al. (2017) proposed a theoretical model integrating the many variables that affect creativity in the work environment, the Integrator Model and Potentializer of Work Creativity, MIPC (Fig. 8.1).

In addition to pre-background elements, studies have shown that an individual's social context has a significant impact on the emergence of creativity, either directly or by interacting with other individual variables (Anderson et al., 2014). The present chapter focuses on the contextual variables, considering context as the interdependence between the aspects of a given environment, that is, "a context is defined as the particular set of personal, physical, and social aspects that come into play in the form of contextual factors and have an impact on focal variables, those immediately shaping behavior" (Glaveanu, 2014, p. 384). Therefore, creativity is a spatiotemporal psychological phenomenon.

In terms of the contextual background of creativity, the organizational climate variable has been highlighted. It concerns the perceptions of organizational policies, practices, and procedures (Wongtada & Rice, 2008). Several authors have recommended that, instead of studying the general organizational climate, it is more appropriate to investigate the concept with a specific focus, like creativity (Lin & Liu, 2012; Veiga et al., 2011). Therefore, this chapter focuses on creativity climate. Climate for creativity has also been named as conditions for creativity. Both concepts are related to contextual aspects that foster or hinder creative expression in the work context. Both constructs will be considered representations of contextual variables associated with creativity.

Creativity climate is positively associated with performance, creativity, innovation, and well-being. This variable also predicts positive bonds with work, as it depicts symbolically enriched and sociable work environments, capable of making work activity meaningful and, as a result, encouraging employees to be proactive and engage in sharing ideas to maximize the achievement of organizational goals (Amabile et al., 1996, 1999; Barrett et al., 2012; Olsson et al., 2019; Péter-Szarka, 2012; Veiga et al., 2020).

This chapter aimed to analyze measurement scales of creativity climate available in the literature in English and its psychometric characteristics to assist researchers and managers with these measures. To achieve this goal, this study analyzed (a) Creative Climate Questionnaire (CCQ) (Ekvall, 1996); (b) Situational Outlook Questionnaire, a measure of the climate for creativity (Isaksen et al., 1999); (c) KEYS, assessing the climate for creativity (Amabile et al., 1996); (d) Creative Environment Perceptions (CEP) (Mayfield & Mayfield, 2010); and (e) Indicators of Conditions to Create in the Workplace (ICCW) (Bruno-Faria et al., 2018).

8.2 Creativity Climate/Conditions for Work Creativity

Organizational climate is a perception about organizational policies, practices, procedures, and routines (Bowen & Ostroff, 2004). It is a descriptive concept (Patterson et al., 2004, 2005) that comprehends how the social environment is perceived by employees (Denison, 1996). This construct is "a shared perception of what the organisation is like in terms of practices, policies, procedures, routines and rewards, what is important and what behaviours are expected and rewarded" (Bowen & Stroff, 2004, p. 5). These perceptions of values and aspects of an organization's operation are possible predictors of economic, technological, commercial, and social performance (Patterson et al., 2004).

Climate perception is an individual-level measurement, but individuals are inserted in and exposed to the same context, so some analyses can ensure that there is a shared perception about organizational structure and practices. Therefore, climate perception is considered an organizational-level construct (Gohsh, 2015). This phenomenon is founded on inter-subjective agreement and interpretation (Schneider et al., 2013), once it is an organizational process-based phenomenon founded on inter-subjective agreement and interpretation (Glick, 1985).

Regarding this chapter's object, creativity climate, we seek to identify work environment aspects that may foster employee creativity (Amabile et al., 1996).

Measuring creativity climate includes contextual aspects, such as “enjoyable ambiance, openness of communication; emotional and functional support provided by supervisors to their staff, employees’ willingness to share expertise, ideas and responsibilities in the creative process; and risk-orientation” (Gohsh, 2015, p. 1131). Creativity-supporting work can be defined as “an overall work environment measure at firm level, consisting of several sources of creativity” (Dul & Ceylan, 2014, p. 5).

Regarding obstacles to creativity, there are also several variables listed in the literature. After analyzing a number of articles, Acar, Tarakci, and van Knippenberg (2019) proposed a theoretical model to summarize constraints to creativity. Their model shows a U-shaped relationship between motivational, cognitive, and social aspects that negatively affect the emergence of creativity. The constraints are divided in clusters. The first cluster has input constraints, which comprise unavailable financial and human resources and work overload. The second group is named process constraints and includes creativity-limiting procedures adopted by the organization, such as formalization and lack of autonomy. The third group is named output constraints and comprehends the organization’s regulations and quality standards. Acar, Tarakci, and van Knippenberg’s model (2019) assumes the existence of three distinct processes: (a) motivational (intrinsic motivation, creative self-efficacy), (b) cognitive (opportunity identification, cognitive search strategy), and (c) social routes (interpersonal conflict, internal knowledge sharing).

The Google Scholar database was used to identify articles to compose this chapter since it was the most comprehensive database when entering the descriptors of interest to this study. The keyword “measurement” was associated with other descriptors covering this study’s focus, namely, work environment measurement that specifically focuses on creativity at the organizational level ((a) “creativity climate,” (b) “conditions for workplace creativity,” (c) “conditions for creativity in the workplace,” (d) “social environment and creativity”) to locate measurement tools in the literature. Throughout the search, no time intervals were defined a priori to identify the studies. However, the identified measurements were published between 1996 and 2018.

In order to determine the tools to be analyzed, the following criteria were adopted: (a) availability of evidence on scales’ psychometric validity, (b) article published in a peer-review journal, and (c) availability of the full article in English. The following exclusion criterion was adopted: (d) complementary studies of previously published measurements that, although meeting the above inclusion criteria, only used a measurement proposed by another author. These contributions were only pointed out to the understanding of the psychometric properties of the tools previously created by another author.

The following scales were identified: (a) Creative Climate Questionnaire (CCQ) (Ekvall, 1996); (b) Situational Outlook Questionnaire, a measure of the climate for creativity (Isaksen et al., 1999); (c) KEYS, assessing the climate for creativity (Amabile et al., 1996); (d) Creative Environment Perceptions (CEP) (Mayfield & Mayfield, 2010); and (e) Indicators of Conditions to Create in the Workplace (ICCW) (Bruno-Faria et al., 2018). Next, these scales were thoroughly analyzed.

8.3 Creative Climate Questionnaire (CCQ) (Ekvall, 1996)

The Creative Climate Questionnaire is a 50-item tool encompassing 10 dimensions of creativity climate. According to Ekvall (1996, p. 105), creative "*climate is regarded as an attribute of the organization, a conglomerate of attitudes, feelings, and behaviours which characterizes life in the organization, and exists independently of the perceptions and understandings of the members of the organization.*" Ekvall (1996) argued about the importance of climate as an objective and realistic entity mediating the relationship between resources and results in work organizations, affecting aspects such as productivity, innovation, fulfillment, and well-being.

Ekvall (1996) tested the internal consistency of creative climates using Cronbach's alpha, which varied between 0.73 and 0.89 in the different scale factors. He also found positive correlations between the Creative Climate Questionnaire's scores and indicators of innovation and leadership styles oriented to organizational change and development. Overall, the analyzed indexes were appropriate. In the period he proposed the tool, Ekvall applied on the scale Laurer's (1994) theoretical model for creative climate, which approaches the ten dimensions of this variable and the importance of measuring it objectively ("It is common here for people to use their own initiative") as opposed to subjectively ("Most people here think [or agree] that it is possible to use initiative here") so that the scores could be aggregated in subsequent multilevel analyses of the phenomenon. The ten dimensions that comprise the measure are listed in Table 8.1.

In later work, Ekvall (1996) continued the development of the measure, maintaining the ten dimensions of his original study. By means of collaboration, Ekvall produced evidence of criterion validity, which made it possible to analyze the impact of creativity climate in universities. He concluded that "climate and resources seemed to exert the strongest influence on the creative outcome, and that climate operated in the organization as a lever for leadership and as a manifestation on the behavioral level of the organizations' culture, defined as basic values" (Ekvall & Ryhammar, 1999, p. 303). This measure was relevant to assess creativity climate in different types of institutions and audiences focusing on understanding climate as a major context variable mediating innovation-related organizational processes (Ling Tan & Yan Ho, 2015).

8.4 Situational Outlook Questionnaire (SOQ) (Isaksen et al., 1999)

The Situational Outlook Questionnaire is a tool with 9 factors and 52 items to assess creativity climate. It is a follow-up to Ekvall's proposition (1996). Comparing to the Creative Climate Questionnaire, the Situational Outlook Questionnaire advances on the first tool's theoretical and analytical properties, particularly concerning its internal structure and possibility of aggregating scores to assess creativity climate. The

Table 8.1 Creative Climate Questionnaire (CCQ)

Dimension	Definition (as proposed by Ekvall, 1996)
Challenge	The emotional involvement of the members of the organization in its operations and goals. A high-challenge climate is seen when the people are experiencing joy and meaningfulness in their job, and, therefore, they invest much energy. Low challenge means feelings of alienation and indifference; the common sentiment and attitude are apathy and lack of interest for the job and the organization
Freedom	The independence in behavior exerted by the people in the organization. In a climate with much of this kind of freedom, people make contacts and give and receive information, discuss problems and alternatives, plan and take initiatives of different kinds, and make decisions. The opposite climate would include people who are passive, rule-bound, and anxious to stay inside established boundaries
Idea support	The ways new ideas are treated. In a supportive climate, ideas and suggestions are received in an attentive and supportive way by bosses and workmates. People listen to each other and encourage initiatives. Possibilities for trying out new ideas are created. The atmosphere is constructive and positive. When idea support is low, the reflexive "no" prevails. Every suggestion is immediately refuted by a counter-argument. Fault finding and obstacle raising are the usual styles of responding to ideas
Trust/ openness	The emotional safety in relationships. When there is a strong level of trust, everyone in the organization dares to put forward ideas and opinions. Initiatives can be taken without fear of reprisal and ridicule in case of failure. Communication is open and straightforward. Where trust is missing, people are suspicious of each other and are wary of making expensive mistakes. They also are afraid of being exploited and robbed of their good ideas
Dynamism/ liveliness	The eventfulness of life in the organization. In the highly dynamic situation, new things are happening all the time and alterations between ways of thinking about and handling issues often occur. There is a kind of psychological turbulence which is described by people in those organizations as "full speed," "go," "breakneck," "maelstrom," and the like. The opposite situation could be compared to a slow jog-trot with no surprises. There are no new projects and no different plans. Everything goes its usual way
Playfulness/ humor	The spontaneity and ease that is displayed. A relaxed atmosphere with jokes and laughter characterizes the organization which is high in this dimension. The opposite climate is characterized by gravity and seriousness. The atmosphere is stiff, gloomy, and cumbrous. Jokes and laughter are regarded as improper
Debates	The occurrence of encounters and clashes between viewpoints, ideas, and differing experiences and knowledge. In the debating organization, many voices are heard and people are keen on putting forward their ideas. Where debates are missing, people follow authoritarian patterns without questioning
Conflicts	The presence of personal and emotional tensions (in contrast to conflicts between ideas) in the organization. When the level of conflict is high, groups and single individuals dislike each other, and the climate can be characterized by "warfare." Plots and traps are usual elements in the life of the organization. There is gossip and slander. In the opposite case, people behave in a more mature manner; they have psychological insight and control of impulses

(continued)

Table 8.1 (continued)

Dimension	Definition (as proposed by Ekvall, 1996)
Risk-taking	The tolerance of uncertainty in the organization. In the high risk-taking case, decisions and actions are prompt and rapid, arising opportunities are taken, and concrete experimentation is preferred to detailed investigation and analysis. In a risk-avoiding climate, there is a cautious, hesitant mentality. People try to be on the "safe side." They decide "to sleep on the matter." They set up committees and they cover themselves in many ways before making a decision
Idea time	The amount of time people can use (and do use) for elaborating new ideas. In the high idea-time situation, possibilities exist to discuss and test impulses and fresh suggestions that are not planned or included in the task assignment; and people tend to use these possibilities. In the reverse case, every minute is booked and specified. The time pressure makes thinking outside the instructions and planned routines impossible

Source: Elaborated by the authors based on Ekvall (1996, pp. 107–108)

Table 8.2 Situational Outlook Questionnaire

Factor	Definition
Challenge and involvement	The degree to which people are involved in daily operations, long-term goals, and visions
Freedom	The independence in behavior exerted by people in the organization
Trust/openness	The emotional safety in relationships
Idea time	The amount of time people can (and do) use for elaborating new ideas
Playfulness/humor	The spontaneity and ease displayed within the workplace
Conflict	The presence of personal and emotional tensions in the organization
Idea support	The ways in which new ideas are treated
Debate	The occurrence of encounters and disagreements between viewpoints, ideas, differing experiences, and knowledge
Risk-taking	The tolerance of uncertainty and ambiguity exposed in the workplace

Source: Elaborated by the authors based on Isaksen et al. (1999, p. 668)

internal structure of the Situational Outlook Questionnaire has nine measuring factors and 62.3% of explained variance. The internal consistency for the analyzed factors was also solid, with Cronbach's alpha indexes varying between 0.62 and 0.90, summarized in Table 8.2.

The possibility to aggregate scores occurred by means of a new answer and correction system based on situational questions, which optimized measurement stability between different evaluators. Nevertheless, managers and researchers should be cautious when doing so, since aggregation may be unfeasible when individuals experience different contexts or schooling levels (Isaksen & Lauer, 2002).

Recently, other studies have provided additional evidence on this tool, hence validating creativity climate as a variable of mediate (Isaksen, 2007; Isaksen & Akkermans, 2011) and immediate (Bertels et al., 2011) impact on leaders' behavior and innovation level. Thus, even in cases in which creativity climate has a direct impact on innovation, some useful indicators may be obtained by means of the Situational Outlook Questionnaire. In these situations, the analyst must observe that the statistics may present greater magnitude when compared to reality. Therefore, the analysis of creativity climate as a mediating variable is more appropriate to understand this variable and its effects on organizations.

8.5 Amabile's KEYS: Assessing the Climate for Creativity

KEYS assesses the perception of stimuli and obstacles in the work environment. It comprises 78 items, 66 of which relate to stimuli (six factors) and obstacles (two factors), 6 items assess creativity, and the remaining 6 measure productivity. This tool has a four-point answer scale, without a midpoint to avoid neutral answers. The reliability, Cronbach's alpha, varies between 0.66 and 0.91, and several indexes show the adjusted model with items loading on hypothesized factors (Amabile et al., 1996). The measurement has convergent and discriminant validity. Table 8.3 displays the factors for stimuli and obstacles to creativity, their definitions, and a sample item from KEYS.

KEYS' latest online version has 87 items arranged in 10 factors, 4 of which describe the managers' practices (freedom, challenging work, supervisory encouragement, and work group supports), 2 are related to organizational motivations for creativity (organizational encouragement and lack of organizational impediments), 2 relate to resources (sufficient resources and realistic workload pressures), and 2 factors focused on result perception (creativity and productivity). KEYS is cited by over 1225 papers in the literature (Culpepper, 2010). Although KEYS' structure has been observed in studies outside the United States, cultural distinctions must be considered by managers. For example, when comparing data of Taiwanese workers with American workers, the former perceived their organizations as having less freedom and more impediments and pressure compared to the latter (Lin & Liu, 2012).

In another investigation, Tseng and Liu (2011) tested KEYS' structure in a sample of Taiwanese workers and found a structure similar to the original one. First, the authors translated the tool from English into Chinese; then, they requested experts to translate it back to the source language. Tseng and Liu (2011) compared the two versions and followed the recommendations for tool validation by Hambleton et al. (2005). The scale was applied to a sample of 401 subjects. The results showed that the items loaded on the hypothesized factors. The items of realistic workload pressure and organizational impediments showed smaller factorial loads than those of the original study, some of them under 0.30. Additionally, the adjustment of the ten-factor structure by confirmatory factor analysis was not solid when compared to the original measurement. Such findings show that aspects related to the variation between cultures must be taken into account and indicate possibilities to enhance the scale from a transcultural perspective.

Table 8.3 KEYS

Scale name	Description	Cronbach's alpha
Stimulant scales		
Organizational encouragement	It concerns an organizational culture that encourages creativity through rewards, recognition for creative work, clear actions to develop new ideas, and a shared vision that creativity is valued in that context	0.91
Supervisory encouragement	The manager supports subordinates in proposing creative ideas, sets appropriate goals, and values individual contributions	0.91
Work group supports	Working group members have complementary skills, exchange information, and are open to new ideas and constructively challenge each other	0.86
Sufficient resources	People have the necessary resources (materials, equipment, financial support) to carry out their work	0.83
Challenging work	Tasks are perceived as challenging and require hard work to be performed	0.79
Freedom	The person assesses that he or she has can decide how to carry out his work and that he has a sense of control over his work	0.66
Obstacle scales		
Organizational impediments	It concerns an organizational culture that hinders the expression of creativity through a high degree of criticism of new ideas, excessive competitiveness, risk avoidance, and internal political problems	0.84
Workload pressure	Productivity expectations are unrealistic and there is high time pressure	0.77
Criterion scales		
Creativity	The organization or work unit endorses creativity, it takes a lot of creativity to perform the activities, and people perceive that they produce something creative	0.84
Productivity	An efficient, effective, and productive organization or unit	0.86

Source: Based on Amabile et al. (1996, p. 1166)

8.6 Creative Environment Perceptions (CEP)

Mayfield and Mayfield (2010) discuss that the measurements of organizational creativity have been primarily investigating skilled workers at the expense of garden variety creativity workers. They mention that skilled workers tend to have a greater level of internal motivation when joining an organization, and, as a result, they need less environment support as opposed to unskilled workers. Therefore, Mayfield and Mayfield (2010) defend the need for specific measurements to assess the conditions for creativity for garden variety creativity workers. Moreover, they point out that the expansion of existing measurements hinders studies with other professional categories.

Table 8.4 CEP item description

Factor	Alpha	Example of item
Creativity support	0.85	My supervisor encourages me to be creative
Work characteristics	0.71	My work is challenging
Creativity blocks	0.81	My organization's policies impede spontaneity in the workplace

Source: Elaborated by the authors based on Mayfield and Mayfield (2010)

In view of the above, Mayfield and Mayfield (2010) analyzed the literature and proposed the Creative Environment Perceptions (CEP) scale, which is comprised of nine items arranged in three factors: creativity support, work characteristics, and creativity blocks. To answer the items, a five-point Likert scale was used. The creativity support factor relates to the encouragement provided by the organization and managers. In turn, work characteristics address work structure and responsibilities. The creativity block factor refers to barriers and impediments to creativity. Table 8.4 lists CEP's factors and items.

The items developed for CEP were applied to a sample of 232 students who worked and met the criterion of having garden variety creativity. The results of the analyses showed an adjusted model with GFI 0.97, AGFI 0.94, and Bentler Bonnet 0.99, which tends to represent reasonably adequate psychometric indexes.

A Spanish version of CEP was also developed (Boada-Grau et al., 2014). For this purpose, the original measurement was translated and back-translated; then, its 9 items were applied to a sample of 975 Spanish workers. The results of this study validated the original scale's structure, composed of three factors – creativity support, work characteristics, and creativity blocks – with adequate indexes ($x^2 = 41{,}165$; gl = 24; P-value = 0.016; RMSEA = 0.03; CFI = 0.98; TLI = 0.98). The items' factorial load ranged from 0.47 to 0.91, and the internal consistency by Cronbach's alpha showed figures of 0.85, 0.71, and 0.81 for creativity support, work characteristics, and creativity blocks, respectively. Overall, the analyzed indexes were adequate.

8.7 Indicators of Conditions to Create in the Workplace (ICCW) (Bruno-Faria et al., 2018)

ICCW measures conditions for workplace creativity and is composed of two scales. The first assesses favorable conditions (physical environment, climate among coworkers, freedom to act, challenging activities, organizational strategies and actions, and leadership support), and the second assesses unfavorable conditions (workload pressure, inadequate leadership, communication problems, and rigidity of rules) to creative expression. The tool totals 60 items to be answered using a 5-point Likert scale. Table 8.5 describes ICCW's factors.

Table 8.5 Measurement models of the favorable and unfavorable conditions for creativity in the workplace

Factors	Operational definition	Cronbach's alpha
Favorable conditions for creativity in workplace		
Physical environment	It concerns the environmental aspects necessary for the production of creative ideas such as light, work space, equipment	0,70
Climate among coworkers	Support received from peers in the production of new ideas, such as encouragement, recognition and mutual support	0.81
Freedom to act	Feeling of being free to express different ideas at work and give an opinion on how to do the job	0.83
Challenging activities	The tasks performed by the worker require him to seek new knowledge and skills to be able to perform them	0.76
Organizational strategies and actions	It concerns the existence of different organizational strategies and actions that stimulate and/or facilitate the emergence of new ideas at work	0.81
Leadership support	It concerns the actions of the leader that encourages the expression of creativity of workers in their daily work	0.83
Unfavorable conditions for creativity in workplace		
Workload pressure	Relationship between time and the amount of activities to be performed at work, making it difficult for creative ideas to arise	0.73
Inadequate leadership	Manager's actions that hinder or prevent the emergence of creative ideas by workers	0.78
Communication problems	Difficulties and obstacles to the exchange of information between areas and/or sectors of the organization that hamper creativity	0.69
Rigidity of rules	High standardization in the way of carrying out activities and the excess of existing rules in the organization that make expression difficult of workers' creativity	0.73

Source: Elaborated by the authors based on Bruno-Faria et al. (2018)

According to Table 8.5, the reliability measured by Cronbach's alpha was greater than 0.70 in all dimensions, except for communications problems, which was 0.69. The greatest internal consistency indexes were obtained in the factors Freedom to act and Leadership support (alpha = 0.83). The first analysis of evidence based on ICCW's internal structure was carried out with a Brazilian sample (Bruno-Faria & Veiga, 2015). Afterward, these findings were cross-checked with an investigation carried out with a Portuguese sample (Bruno-Faria et al., 2018) and published in English. Considering both studies, the results show adequate adjustments in both samples. The adjustment indexes of the structural models for favorable factors in Brazil were $\chi^2 = 642.75$, df = 269, $\chi^2/df = 2.39$, GFI = 0.89, AGFI = 0.86, TLI = 0.92, CFI = 0.93; and RMSEA = 0.06 and in Portugal were $\chi^2 = 1303.935$, df = 269.00, $\chi^2/df = 4.85$, GFI = 0.78, AGFI = 0.73, TLI = 0.74, CFI = 0.77, and RMSEA = 0.09 (Bruno-Faria et al., 2018).

8.8 Critical and Comparative Analysis between Measurements

After presenting the measurements, we will critically and comparatively evaluate the potentials and limitations of each. Such evaluation is important since it can assist researchers and practitioners to overview the topic and clearly decide which scale they should use to measure creativity climate. The proposed critical observations do not constitute all of the potentials and limitations of the scales mentioned in the chapter. Authors in the field have been continuously incorporating new publications into the database; so, besides considering the information in this study, the reader should research the most recent information about these instruments whenever it is appropriate to select and use them.

The Creative Climate Questionnaire (Ekvall, 1996) can be applied with due regard to its limitations. There is evidence based on the measurement's content and criterion. However, the studies mentioned in this chapter did not gather validity evidence based on the construct or the internal structure, which may indicate the need to investigate further whether the dimensions represent an isolated or hierarchical factor, as well as whether the hypothesized internal structure is empirically replicable. Based on Ekvall (1996), the measurement is useful to track whether the content of the dimensions is related to innovation and organizational change-oriented leadership practices.

In relation to the Situational Outlook Questionnaire (Isaksen et al., 1999), studies with validity evidence based on content, construct, and criterion were identified, which shows adequacy in the measurement's analytical properties. In the practical aspect, the tool has two advantages: (i) the possibility of assessment by means of situational items that may decrease the evaluator's subjective bias and (ii) better conditions of score aggregation in different functional units or departments. As for the disadvantages, there is the fact that the items may not represent the existing conditions in the evaluated organizations, and they may be understood distinctly by different hierarchical and functional groups, which requires previous training to balance these aspects.

The scale developed by Amabile and collaborators (1996) is the most cited in the literature. Studies have published empirical validity evidence with samples from different countries and cultures, and adjustment indexes are solid. However, KEYS is not available for free; its use is restricted and managed by the Center for Creative Leadership. Therefore, despite the scale's considerable theoretical and analytical aspects, its limited rights of use and replication may hinder the implementation of the tool in organizational contexts due to budget restrictions to research and development. Either way, investing in this tool may result in improvements for the organizations that choose to use it to analyze the creativity climate.

The Creative Environment Perceptions (CEP) is a measurement with psychometric quality, and its adjustment indexes are adequate. CEP is a small scale, having only nine items, and is available in English (Mayfield & Mayfield, 2010) and Spanish (Boada-Grau et al., 2014). One weakness of this instrument is the sample used in the American study of empirical evidence for validity since only students and entry-level professionals were selected. This scale is a measurement for quick assessment. Other options may fit better for a more detailed creativity climate analysis.

The Indicators of Conditions to Create in the Workplace (ICCW) scale has the advantage of measuring factors that stimulate and block creative expression with independent scales. The psychometric indexes of both scales are adequate, and the measurement structure was tested in samples from two different countries, Brazil and Portugal. Another favorable point is that all items are available in the publication, which makes the socialization of knowledge for organizations free, transparent, and immediately available (Bruno-Faria & Veiga, 2015). One limitation of this scale is that it is in Portuguese. Therefore, to expand its use, developing an English version and applying it to other contexts and languages is recommended since the theoretical and analytical properties point to a high transcultural potential of the measurement's theorization and application to analyze and handle the creativity climate in the organizations. Table 8.6 displays a comparative analysis between the scales.

Some of the challenges of propositions developed so far include (a) theoretical clarification and convergence in relation to the content of representative dimensions of creativity climate (Hunter et al., 2005); (b) higher level of evidence for the climate's score aggregation and equivalence in three levels – individual, group, and organization (Luo et al., 2015); (c) differentiation of the situational items for distinct evaluation purposes, as in innovation management practices vs corporate innovation education (Péter-Szarka, 2012); (d) transcultural applications to analyze measurement invariance between organizations and contexts of different nationalities (French & Finch, 2008); and (e) proposition of computerized adaptive testing with contributions from IRT (Item Response Theory) and modern computational modeling (e.g., machine learning, deep learning, etc.) to reduce biases and maximize the level of the tools' predictive and explanatory evidence (Weiss, 2014). Including these conceptions as a possible investigation agenda on creativity climate may substantially enhance further studies on the topic and, consequently, increase the impact of handling this variable in the context of organizations and work management.

8.9 Final Considerations

We hope this chapter successfully demonstrated that, despite the complexity of analyzing creativity climate, fostering a context to enable creative expression is fundamental to adapt into a reality that actively demands innovation at all levels of an organization. In practice, besides following up and managing creativity climate using measurements – such as the ones presented in this chapter – managers must be aware that, in order to implement ideas, they need to specifically encourage

Table 8.6 Comparative overview of measurements of creativity climate

Measurement	Population	Validity evidence	Advantages	Disadvantages
Creative Climate Questionnaire (CCQ) (Ekvall, 1996)	Managers University students	Content Criterion	Evaluation of dimensions based on innovation and leadership-related content	Absence of evidence about internal structure
Situational Outlook Questionnaire (SOQ) (Isaksen et al., 1999)	Managers University students	Content Construct Criterion	Situational items capable of decreasing the evaluator's biases	Some items may not apply to specific contexts or certain hierarchy levels
KEYS (Amabile et al., 1996)	Over 12,500 workers in different countries, working on several job positions and in companies of varied industries	Content Construct Criterion	Specific scales for stimuli and blocks to creativity Evidence of empirical validity with samples from different countries Most cited scale related to the construct	Restricted access via the Center for Creative Leadership
Creative Environment Perceptions (CEP) (Mayfield & Mayfield, 2010)	USA: 232 students, many of them with professional experience	Content Construct	Reduced size Complete versions in English and Spanish	Students and entry-level professionals sample
Indicators of Conditions to Create in the Workplace (ICCW) (Bruno-Faria et al., 2018; Bruno-Faria & Veiga, 2015)	Brazil: 409 professionals from a large Brazilian company of agricultural and livestock research Portugal: professionals from various business industries, mainly with higher education	Content Criterion Construct	Independent scales to measure favorable and unfavorable conditions to creativity Complete version available	Scale available only in Portuguese

motivation and self-persistence so that individuals feel capable and valued to creatively contribute to the organization (Binnewies & Gromer, 2012).

Maintaining a creativity climate is an element of this process, but it does not total up the necessary conditions for creativity to lead to innovation and then add final value to organizations. Investment in human capital qualification, policies, and management practices that create positive bonds and reward employees for their innovation efforts should also be considered in the organizational strategic agenda, aiming to foster creativity as an organizational strength. Intervening in the creativity climate may be the first step of a process monitored by means of the measurements presented in this chapter.

References

Acar, O. A., Tarakci, M., & van Knippenberg, D. (2019). Creativity and innovation under constraints: A cross-disciplinary integrative review. *Journal of Management, 45*(1), 96–121. https://doi.org/10.1177/0149206318805832

Amabile, T. M. (1983). The social psychology of creativity: A componential conceptualization. *Journal of Personality and Social Psychology, 45*, 357–376.

Amabile, T. M., Burnside, R. M., & Gryskiewicz, S. S. (1999). *User's manual for KEYS, assessing the climate for creativity: A survey from the Center for Creative Leadership*. Center for Creative Leadership.

Amabile, T. M., Conti, R., Coon, H., Lazenby, J., & Herron, M. (1996). Assessing the work environment for creativity. *Academy of Management Journal, 39*(5), 1154–1184.

Amabile, T. M., & Pratt, M. G. (2016). The dynamic componential model of creativity and innovation in organizations: Making progress, making meaning. *Research in Organizational Behavior, 36*, 157–183.

Anderson, N., Potočnik, K., & Zhou, J. (2014). Innovation and creativity in organizations a state-of-the-science review, prospective commentary, and guiding framework. *Journal of Management, 40*(5), 1297–1333.

Barrett, H., Balloun, J. L., & Weinstein, A. (2012). Creative climate: A critical success factor for 21st century organisations. *International Journal of Business Innovation and Research, 6*(2), 202–219.

Bertels, H. M. J., Kleinschmidt, E. J., & Koen, P. A. (2011). Communities of practice versus organizational climate: Which one matters more to dispersed collaboration in the front end of innovation? *Journal of Product Innovation Management, 28*(5), 757–772.

Binnewies, C., & Gromer, M. (2012). Creativity and innovation at work: The role of work characteristics and personal initiative. *Psicothema, 24*(1), 100–105.

Boada-Grau, J., Vigil-Colet, A., Sánchez-García, J. C., & Prizmic-Kuzmica, A. (2014). Adaptación de la escala Creative Environment Perceptions al español. *Universitas Psychologica, 13*(4), 1357–1366.

Boso, N., Donbesuur, F., Bendega, T., Annan, J., & Adeola, O. (2017). Does organizational creativity always drive market performance? *Psychology & Marketing, 34*(11), 1004–1015. https://doi.org/10.1002/mar.21039

Bowen, D. E., & Ostroff, C. (2004). Understanding HRM-firm performance linkages: The role of the HRM system. *Academy of Management Review, 29*(2), 203–221.

Bruno-Faria, M. F., & Veiga, H. M. S. (2015). Indicadores de Condições para a Criatividade – ICCAT. *Revista de Administração (FEA-USP), 50*(4), 492–506. https://www.revistas.usp.br/rausp/article/view/108275

Bruno-Faria, M. F., Veiga, H. M. S., Carvalho, L. C., Torres, I., & Meireles, A. (2018). Analysis of conditions for creativity in the workplace: Validation of measures in Brazil and Portugal. *Business Creativity and the Creative Economy, 4*, 8–18. http://icscpress.com/journals/bcce/bcce-0401/bcce.2018.10.8.1.02/

Burbiel, J. (2009). Creativity in research and development environments: A practical review. *International Journal of Business Science and Applied Management, 4*(2), 35–51.

Culpepper, M. K. (2010). *KEYS to creativity and innovation: An adopt-a-measure examination*. The International Center for Studies in Creativity. Buffalo State College, US. Disponível em https://pdfs.semanticscholar.org/cb81/941253562bffcf2b6830144834cb52762c24.pdf?_ga=2.94143771.768160935.1578690764-860604206.1578690764

Denison, D. R. (1996). What is the difference between organizational culture and organizational climate? A native's point of view on a decade of paradigm wars. *Academy of Management Review, 21*(3), 619–654.
DiLiello, C., & Houghton, J. D. (2008). Creative potential and practiced creativity: Identifying untapped creativity in organizations. *Creativity and Innovation Management, 17*(1), 37–46.
DiLiello, T., Houghton, J. D., & Dawley, D. (2011). Narrowing the creativity gap: The moderating effects of perceived support for creativity. *The Journal of Psychology, 145*(3), 151–172.
Dixon, S., Meyer, K., & Day, M. (2014). Building dynamic capabilities of adaptation and innovation: A study of micro-foundations in a transition economy. *Long Range Planning, 47*(4), 186–205.
Dul, J., & Ceylan, C. (2014). The impact of a creativity-supporting work environment on a firm's product innovation performance. *The Journal of Product Innovation Management, 31*(6), 1254–1267.
Egan, E. (2005). Factors influencing individual creativity in the workplace: An examination of quantitative empirical research. *Advances in Developing Human Resources, 7*(2), 160–181.
Ekvall, G. (1996). Organizational climate for creativity and innovation. *European Journal of Work and Organizational Psychology, 5*(1), 105–123.
Ekvall, G., & Ryhammar, L. (1999). The creative climate: Its determinants and effects at a Swedish university. *Creativity Research Journal, 12*(4), 303–310.
Epstein, R., Kaminaka, K., Phan, V., & Uda, R. (2013). How is creativity best managed? Some empirical and theoretical guidelines. *Creativity and Innovation Management, 22*(4), 359–374.
French, B. F., & Finch, W. H. (2008). Multigroup confirmatory factor analysis: Locating the invariant referent sets. *Structural Equation Modeling: A Multidisciplinary Journal, 15*(1), 96–113.
Glaveanu, V. P. (2014). Theorising context in psychology: The case of creativity. *Theory and Psychology, 24*(3), 382–398. https://doi.org/10.1177/0959354314529851
Glick, W. (1985). Conceptualizing and measuring organizational and psychological climate: Pitfalls in multilevel research. *Academy of Management Review, 10*(3), 601–616.
Gohsh, K. (2015). Developing organizational creativity and innovation: Toward a model of self-leadership, employee creativity, creativity climate and workplace innovative orientation. *Management Research Review, 38*(11), 1126–1148.
Hambleton, R. K., Merenda, P. F., & Spielberger, C. D. (2005). *Adapting educational and psychological tests for cross-cultural assessment*. Erlbaum.
Hunter, S. T., Bedell, K. E., & Mumford, M. D. (2005). Dimensions of creative climate: A general taxonomy. *The International Journal of Creativity & Problem Solving, 15*(2), 97–116.
Isaksen, S. G. (2007). The Situational Outlook Questionnaire: Assessing the context for change. *Psychological Reports, 100*(2), 455–466. https://doi.org/10.2466/pr0.100.2.455-466
Isaksen, S. G., & Akkermans, H. J. (2011). Creative climate: A leadership lever for innovation. *The Journal of Creative Behavior, 45*(3), 161–187.
Isaksen, S. G., & Lauer, K. J. (2002). The climate for creativity and change in teams. *Creativity and Innovation Management, 11*(1), 74–86.
Isaksen, S. G., Lauer, K. J., & Ekvall, G. (1999). Situational Outlook Questionnaire: A measure of the climate for creativity and change. *Psychological Reports, 85*(2), 665–674.
Laurer, K. (1994). *The assessment of creative climate: An investigation of the Ekvall Creative Climate Questionnaire*. State University College Editors.
Lin, C. Y., & Liu, F. C. (2012). A cross-level analysis of organizational creativity climate and perceived innovation. *European Journal of Innovation Management, 15*(1), 55–76.
Ling Tan, C., & Yan Ho, M. (2015). Organizational creative climate in determining the work innovativeness among the knowledge workers. *Global Journal of Business and Social Science Review, 3*(2), 14–26.
Luo, L., Deng, X., & Zhou, C. (2015). The complexity of the assessment of creative climate and group creativity. *International Journal of Knowledge, Innovation and Entrepreneurship, 3*(3), 5–13.

Mayfield, M., & Mayfield, J. (2010). Developing a scale to measure the creative environment perceptions: A questionnaire for investigating garden variety creativity. *Creativity Research Journal, 22*(2), 162–169. https://doi.org/10.1080/10400419.2010.481511
McLean, L. D. (2005). Organizational culture's influence on creativity and innovation: A review of the literature and implications for human resource development. *Advances in Developing Human Resources, 7*(2), 226–246.
Mendonça, H., Veiga, H. M. S., & Macambira, M. (2017). Creativity at work: Trends and perspectives. In E. R. Neiva, C. Torres, & H. Mendonça (Eds.), *Organizational psychology and evidence-based management: What science says about practice* (1st ed., pp. 21–43). Springer.
Montag, T., Maertz, C. P., Jr., & Baer, M. (2012). A critical analysis of the workplace creativity criterion space. *Journal of Management, 38*(4), 1362–1386. https://doi.org/10.1177/0149206312441835
Oldham, G. R., & Cummings, A. (1996). Employee creativity: Personal and contextual factors at work. *Academy of Management Journal, 39*, 607–634.
Olsson, A., Paredes, B. K. M., Johansson, U., Olander Roese, M., & Ritzén, S. (2019). Organizational climate for innovation and creativity–a study in Swedish retail organizations. *The International Review of Retail, Distribution and Consumer Research, 29*(3), 243–261.
Patterson, M. G., Warr, P., & West, M. A. (2004). Organizational climate and company productivity: The role of employee affect and employee level. *Journal of Occupational & Organizational Psychology, 77*(2), 193–216.
Patterson, M. G., West, M. A., Shackleton, V. J., Dawson, J. F., Lawthom, R., Maitlis, S., Robinson, D. L., & Wallace, A. M. (2005). Validating the organizational climate measure: Links to managerial practices, productivity and innovation. *Journal of Organizational Behavior, 26*, 379–408. https://doi.org/10.1002/job.312
Péter-Szarka, S. (2012). El clima creativo como medio para promover la creatividad en el aula. *Electronic Journal of Research in Educational Psychology, 10*(3), 1011–1034. https://www.redalyc.org/pdf/2931/293124654004.pdf
Schneider, B., Ehrhart, M. G., & Macey, W. H. (2013). Organizational climate and culture. *Annual Review of Psychology, 64*, 361–388.
Shalley, C. E., Zhou, J., & Oldham, G. R. (2004). The effects of personal and contextual characteristics on creativity: Where should we go from here. *Journal of Management, 30*(6), 933–958.
Tseng, H. M., & Liu, F. C. (2011). Assessing the climate for creativity (KEYS): Confirmatory factor analysis and psychometric examination of a Taiwan version. *International Journal of Selection and Assessment, 19*(4), 438–441.
Veiga, H. M. S., Neiva, E. R., & Bruno-Faria, M. F. (2020). Proatividade: Influência das condições para a criatividade considerando a mediação da autoeficácia para criar. *Revista de Administração da UFSM, 13*, 602–624. https://periodicos.ufsm.br/reaufsm/article/view/31986
Veiga, H. M. S., Porto, J. B., & Laboissière, M. C. (2011). Comportamento pró-ativo nas organizações e sua relação com clima organizacional. *Contabilidade, Gestão e Governança, 14*(2), 98–113. https://www.revistacgg.org/contabil/article/view/263/pdf_163
Weiss, D. J. (Ed.). (2014). *New horizon testing: Latent trait test theory and computerized adaptive testing*. Elsevier.
Wongtada, N., & Rice, G. (2008). Multidimensional latent traits of perceived organizational innovation: Differences between Thai and Egyptian employees. *Asia Pacific Journal of Management, 25*(3), 537–562.
Zhou, J., & Hoever, I. J. (2014). Research on workplace creativity: A review and redirection. *The Annual Review of Organizational Psychology and Organizational Behavior, 1*, 11–27.
Zhou, J., & Shalley, C. E. (2003). Research on employee creativity: A critical review and directions for future research. *Research in Personnel and Human Resources Management, 22*, 165–218.
Zhou, Q., Hirst, G., & Shipton, H. (2012). Promoting creativity at work: The role of problem-solving demand. *Applied Psychology, 61*(1), 56–80. https://doi.org/10.1111/j.1464-0597.2011.00455.x

Chapter 9
Values in Organizations: Theory, Measurement, and Theoretical Reflections

Cláudio V. Torres, Elaine R. Neiva, and Sharon Glazer

9.1 Introduction and Contextualization of the Chapter

The concept of values has been of interest to scholars for quite a while now. Different and mainly complimentary definitions have been suggested in the psychology literature, all of them supporting different models or theories that try to explain the role of human values in the behaviors, attitudes, and choices of individuals. These definitions also agree on a common feature in the definition of values: its ability to transcend actions and situations. Based on this characteristic of the concept, it is plausible to inquire that if a single human value can be as relevant in the workplace as in any other environment or situation, then should we consider organizational values specifically or human values in general when examining organizational phenomena? Would models for organizational values bring a distinguishing aspect to the Industrial, Work, Organizational, and Personnel Psychology field, when compared to the human values theory? Are specific measures for organizational values really needed, or should we instead focus on basic human values of individuals within the workplace in order to predict and explain our variables of interest? And, what would be the level of analysis when we are studying values in organizations?

This chapter's main purpose is to address these questions by reflecting on the concept of values, specifically by reflecting on its theory and its measurement development. Therefore, the chapter begins with a brief historical review of the development of the human values concept. After presenting the definition of values, their levels of analyses, and a brief review of the values theory, we will discuss some evidence on the measurement of values, specifically, highlighting its use for the

C. V. Torres (✉) · E. R. Neiva
University of Brasília, Brasília, DF, Brazil

S. Glazer
University of Baltimore, Baltimore, MD, USA
e-mail: sglazer@ubalt.edu

M. O. Macambira et al. (eds.), *Assessing Organizational Behaviors*,
https://doi.org/10.1007/978-3-030-81311-6_9

investigation of the society and organizational contexts, and impact on organizational outcomes. We also present a debate on organizational values, based on the values theory, and forward propositions for how to think about organizational values and their use for organizational assessment purposes that might have implications on selection, socialization, and attrition, as well as predicting organizational performance and employee attitudes. We hope that our propositions will stimulate further research on values and practices in organizations.

We begin this discussion keeping in mind that the importance of values in psychology is an ever-growing topic of study, though it had already captured the imagination of several thinkers, such as Aristotle, who defined it as what everyone wants as opposed to what they should wish (Aristotle, 2001). It must be observed, though, that there was little consensus between Socrates, Plato, and the sophists on the meaning of value. For the sophists, values are subjective in essence and bring up the notion that the "human being is the measure of all things, of the things as they are and of the things they are not" (Waterfield, 2009, p. 213). According to *Protagoras of Abdera* (in Van Ophuijsen et al., 2007), the notion of having the human being as the center of all things results in the subordination of values to the judgment of the individual.

In psychology, the notion of values began to popularize in the 1980s and 1990s, as scholars began to explore how best to capture values through psychological assessments (Ros, 2006). Scholars of psychology developed and validated measures and attempted to demonstrate that values are a fundamental human concept. Values are conceptualized as fundamental principles that both shape a person's perspectives and motivate a person's actions. Schwartz's (1992, 2012) values theory suggests that values are desirable, trans-situational goals that carry different levels of importance for each person and serve as principles that guide people's interpretation of experiences, decisions, feelings, and behaviors. When shared at a group level, values may be evident in a family unit, a religious unit, a business unit, an organization, a nation, or even an industry culture (Erez & Gati, 2004). Each layer, as the group enlarges, shapes both the layer below and the layer above. Even across the globe, there are values that unify people, whether on the basis of religion, gender identity, language, or ethnicity or on the basis of values of in a profession (e.g., healthcare providers, e.g., Glazer & Beehr, 2005) or values in the global business arena (Erez & Shokef, 2008). In our increasingly globalizing world (i.e., whereby businesses and economies become more efficient with the promise of ensuring benefits of shared growth across all nations and people from around the world begin to overlap in knowledge and practices; Banerjee & Linstead, 2001; Brannen, 2004), where negotiations with foreign markets are crucial to national economic self-sufficiency, so is understanding national and individual values (Glazer et al., 2014). This comes with no surprise, as several theorists, such as sociologists (e.g., Williams, 1968/1983), anthropologists (Kluckhohn, 1951), and international business thinkers (Hofstede, 1980), have had already understood values as criteria that people use to evaluate their actions, other people, and events.

Origins of Cultural Values Through Organizational Research

Studies about differences in cultural values and practices and their relationships with different social structures, such as organizations, have been producing many significant findings in the social sciences. In the business and management area, one of the most influential of these studies has been that of Hofstede (1980), although it has also prompted some criticisms (Chinese Culture Connection, 1987; House et al., 2004). Using data from over 50 countries, Hofstede proposed a typology of 4 basic cultural dimensions: power distance, individualism-collectivism, masculinity-femininity, and uncertainty avoidance. Researchers associated with the Chinese Culture Connection (1987) identified an additional cultural value, *Confucian work dynamism*, which Hofstede (2001) adapted and renamed to long-term/short-term orientation.

After the seminal Hofstede (1980, 2006) research, House et al. (2004), using a database from 62 nations, proposed a typology of 9 dimensions of societal values (*what it should be*) and practices (*what it is*), some of which overlap with Hofstede's dimensions. House et al.'s Global Leadership Organizational Behavioral Effectiveness (GLOBE) study revealed the following cultural values and practices (as desired and as is): performance orientation, assertiveness, future orientation, humane orientation, institutional collectivism, in-group collectivism, gender egalitarianism, power distance, and uncertainty avoidance.

It is important to consider some features of international companies located in countries of different nationalities that might be affected by the values of their members. It is quite common to see in both public and private companies the presence of people of various nationalities, which inevitably increases intercultural encounters in the context of organizations. Generally, such encounters can bring on relationship difficulties between individuals who, to overcome them, seek strategies that may not always result in an optimal solution (Glazer, 2016). The identification of values of an individual that come into play during an intercultural encounter has, as a basic element, the recognition of indigenous aspects of a society or social group that influences individuals' affects, behaviors, and cognitions (Oyserman et al., 2002). This chapter explores theory that delves into and describes human values.

Smith and Bond (1999) point out that most of the research involving culture, such as those of Hofstede (1980) or House et al. (2004), relies on analyses of beliefs and behaviors of individuals who are believed to belong to a given national culture. These studies are conducted at the country level of analysis "in which the unit of analysis is the nation" (Smith et al., 1998; p. 358). Thus, the findings of those studies are applicable to cultures and not to individuals; within-culture (i.e., individual-level) sources of variance should not be discussed at the country level of analysis, leaving alone the organizational level for that matter. This is why some authors (e.g., Smith et al., 1994; Torres & Pérez-Nebra, 2015) recommend measuring cultural differences indirectly; that is, they can be inferred from data about collective behavior. However, it is not always clear how these indirect measures should be interpreted, and most of the information about individuals might be lost (Hofstede & Bond, 1988). This interpretation problem can be avoided by taking measures of culture through well-designed questions about people's values or beliefs.

Thus, although these aforementioned studies have had major influences in organizational science research and practice, Hofstede (1980) and House et al. (2004) focused primarily on managers and workers and were not systematically developed to be utilized for a broad general population nor at the individual level of analysis. On a regular basis, researchers were committing the ecological fallacy by assuming the factors that define and characterize nations could be used to characterize individuals. To remedy this ecological fallacy and employing methodological rigor, social psychologist Shalom Schwartz (1992) systematically developed a theory of human values that is assessed and meant to be used at the individual level of analysis. This theory has been validated time and again. Still, scholars employing his validated measure wanted to understand if the same individual-level values could be used to understand cultural values. Consequently, Schwartz (1999) extended the human values theory to assess cultural values. His measurement is the only values measure that has been shown to reliably and validly assess individuals' human values and group-level cultural values. This chapter focuses on Schwartz' values theory and proposes how the values measure may be used to study the under-tapped domain of organizational values, as well as link values with organizational behaviors.

Furthermore, a cultural perspective on organizational processes requires exploration not just of what happens but also of what people associated with the organization believe about what happens, how, and why (Archer & Fitch, 1994). Before measuring a culture, we must remember that in any culture the attitudes and values of the members are instilled in them by parents, church, and schools, long before they become members of a business organization (Schwartz, 2013). This socialization process does not mean, however, that researchers have to assess the cultural aspects that are reinforced by parents or churches before assessing the values of members of an organization. Rather, it means that in assessing the values of an employee, it is possible to assess the *cultural patterns* (Triandis, 1994) of the society of which the employee is a member (for a deepened discussion on cultural patterns, please see the concepts of *allocentrism-idiocentrism* in Triandis, 1994, 1995). Of course, in this case, assessment would be of those values that were reinforced by the organizational culture in which the employee is a member. However, one could argue (Pavett & Morris, 1995; Strohschneider & Güss, 1998) that the organizational culture is a reflection of the national culture of the country where the organization operates. At any rate, the concept of culture assumes that members of the same culture are subjected to similar social influences within that culture (Smith et al., 2012), because they perceive their society and the world in similar ways; they "share" the same perception in relatively similar values (Smith et al., 2011).

Level of Analysis

Level of analysis is a critical concept, requiring careful attention in order to avoid rampant errors found in published literature in which scholars fall prey to the ecological or reverse ecological fallacy. As noticed by Klein, Dansereau, and Hall

(1994), few theorists and researchers address level issues in their studies. Klein et al. (1994) believe that which levels of analysis were adopted in a study should be clearly stated in science, so that its strengths and weaknesses could be easily identified. Level issues necessitate alignment between "the level of the theory, the level of measurement, and/or the level of statistical analysis are incongruent" (Klein et al., 1994, p. 198). For Sackett and Larson (1990), every study is usually done in at least one of the three levels: individual, group, or organizational/cultural/systemic. A study finding focused at one level of analysis does not necessarily be generalized to another level. For Klein et al. (1994), the level of analysis adopted in a study influences the theoretical constructs used by the researcher, the data collection, the measurement, and the analysis of the data.

While discussing values of individuals within the organization, the present chapter or any other scientific product devoted to values typically attends to the individual level of analysis using Sackett and Larson's (1990) categorization. Furthermore, values within any organizational context – the target that this chapter aims to explain (i.e., the level of the theory, in Klein et al.'s, 1994, terminology) - is also within the limits of the individual-level of analysis, hence cannot expand its findings to the cultural and/or organizational differences found between the groups of people as relates to their values. "We should use characterizations of whole cultures (e.g., collectivist values) to explain specific attributes of that culture" (Smith & Bond, 1999, p. 60), such as preference for types of reward system in an organization, its leadership style, or strategic decisions, for instance. However, if we want to predict how individuals in an organization will behave, we shall use characterizations of values of those particular individuals. For Klein et al. (1994), as a condition for the group or organizational level of theory to be adopted in a study, a researcher should assume that the members of each group under investigation are homogeneous. Only a single characteristic is not sufficient to describe the group, as it is not feasible to assume that members of an organization are homogeneous in terms of their values. As Smith et al. (2011) mentioned, members of a culture or an organization share the same perception in *relatively similar values*: relatively similar, but not homogeneous. When the level of theory is established, Klein et al. suggest that the data should be collected "in a way that ensures the conformity of the data to the level of theory" (p. 209) and vice versa. The way data are collected refers to the level of measurement, which must be congruent to the level of theory. As we will present later in the chapter, data on organizational values are usually gathered using instruments administrated to individuals and, sometimes, are aggregated in order to obtain organizational differences or profile on values.

The fact that the measures are administered at the individual level and later discussed in the organizational level represents a threat to these studies. It was noted that "if the level of the theory is the homogeneous group, researchers are advised to use global scores" (Klein et al., 1994, p. 212). Finally, Klein's et al. (1994) last suggestion is that the treatment of the data during statistical procedures (i.e., the level of statistical analysis) should resemble the other two levels discussed above (i.e., the level of theory and of measurement). For these authors, statistical tests of the predicted homogeneity of a measure can be classified in two clusters: those that estimate the extent of agreement within individuals and those that estimate the extent of agreement by contrasting within- and between-group variance. When individual means are used in values research, and later on statistical tests of Klein et al.'s second cluster are employed, the reader should be aware that the statistical analyses are being performed at the group level jeopardizing the level of measurement – theory congruency in the entire study. The level of the theory, the level of measurement, and the level of statistical analysis must be considered to be congruent, which reduces the possibility of problems related to level issues in the discussion.

The Concept of Values: Background and Definition

The concept of values is central to psychology. Values are abstract concepts representing end states or attributes that transcend specific objects and specific positions (Feather, 1995). They are often expressed as personal norms, which are principles that individuals maintain for themselves, but influenced by societal presses (Schwartz, 1973). Moreover, values often connote virtues and morality or ethical stances (Lefkowitz, 2017) and thus generate a motivational influence over decision choices and behaviors (Feather, 1995; Schwartz, 1992). Indeed, in earlier works, Lewin (1942) discussed the influence of values on behaviors and considered that values define which activities are relevant, either negatively or positively, to an individual in a defined context. Allport (1955) too reinforced the idea that values influence behavior. As noticed by Rokeach (1973), "more than any other [the value concept can] unify the apparently diverse interests of all the sciences concerned with human behavior" (p. 3). Both for Rokeach (1973) and Feather (1995), individuals have infinite beliefs and attitudes; however, only a small number of values are considered of supreme importance, and those values vary between people. Thus, values represent attributes and end states that are important to a person and serve as the basis of an individual's framing of reality and motivate a person's actions, thoughts, and feelings.

As the aforementioned foundations indicate, societally shared conceptions of what is socially considered to be good or bad, and important or not, to our lives influence personal values. A few eminent scholars have developed models and theories which have become seminal in the study of values. The work of Thomas and Znaniecki (1918, as cited in Ros, 2006) can be seen as the landmark in the study of values. They differentiated the concepts of attitudes and values. In the case of attitudes, the concept comprises a process of individual consciousness that determines the actual or possible activity of the individual in the social world. Their definition of values is somewhat briefer, referring to any information that has an empirical content accessible to members of a social group and a meaning that can be the object of an attitude. Of these definitions, two aspects deserve to be emphasized: (1) attitudes and values are related, although they are different constructs, and (2) attitudes have an intra-subjective nature, while values are inter-subjective in nature, that is, their meaning must be shared by others.

Talcott Parsons (1949), who presented the theory of social action, was one of the important authors to shape the prevailing conception of values in psychology. He introduced the concept of motivated action, suggesting that an action takes place every time the person seeks to achieve certain goals – an idea that is inherent to the notion of human values as motivational principles. For him, the achievement of a value represents an underlying motivational goal (Schwartz, 1992). Parsons (1949) offers a definition of values when mentioning that "it is possible to call value an element of a shared symbolic system that serves as a criterion for the selection among the alternatives of orientation that are intrinsically open in a situation" (p. 443). Kluckhohn (1951) is credited with defining values as principles of what is desirable. For Kluckhohn, "a value is an explicit or implicit conception, characteristic of an individual or characteristic of a group, about the desirable, the which influences the selection of accessible modes, means and ends of actions" (p. 441). Hence, Kluckhohn (1951) made it clear that values should not be treated as objects or characteristics of objects (e.g., money). Values would not be the desired but desirable principles. Since their seminal work, the concept has been operationalized as general principles, whose meaning is shared by social groups and which guide people's actions (Schwartz et al., 2017). Inglehart (1977) was not interested in the study of individual values, but in those of national cultures, that is, average scores of people per country. Based on Maslow's (1954) typology of human needs, Inglehart (1977, 1989) presented a dimension of cultural variation that included of two poles: materialism, representing the most basic needs of physical and economic security, and post-materialism, which expresses higher needs, such as self-esteem, belonging, and aesthetic. The author starts from two main hypotheses to explain the importance of these two poles. The first is the scarcity hypothesis, which posits that the priorities of an individual reflect their socioeconomic environment. Things that are relatively scarce are given greater subjective importance. The second is the hypothesis of socialization, which suggests that individuals' values reflect the economic conditions of their society at the time they reach adulthood and are retained throughout adult life (Marks, 1997).

In his seminal work, Shalom Schwartz presented a perspective on the nature and structure and functions of human values which is undoubtedly one of the most influential in psychology, in general, and in cross-cultural psychology, in particular. Looking back at only the first decade of the 2000s in publications in the *Journal of Cross-Cultural Psychology* (*JCCP*), Knafo et al. (2011) found that about 20% of the articles published between the years 2007 and 2009 referred to values, while in the 1970s and 1980s, less than 8% of JCCP articles dealt directly with values. In Schwartz' (1992) theory, values are a motivational construct and motivational by nature. The theory stipulates that people are motivated by biological, social, and welfare needs (Schwartz, 1992; Schwartz & Bilsky, 1987). Thus, values are motivationally oriented because they propose a way of organizing the different needs. A primary content aspect of a value is the type of motivational goal it expresses.

Schwartz (*personal communication*, 2021) began his research on values with a study on changing teachers' behaviors with value self-confrontation items, in a format used by the Rokeach Value Survey (1973); that is, each value is named with a brief explanation of its content, and the respondent is expected to assign a score of how central that value is in his/her life. He then extended his research to 7 countries to test his initial theory of values circumplex, including a list of about 70 abstract values expanding on Rokeach's work. He both dropped and added values based on a literature review. All 70 items followed the same format of Rokeach's list. The list was intended to provide coverage of each of the values in a theoretical value motivational circumplex that he developed, and after further consulting with other scholars (see Helkama et al., 1992), he dropped 13 items as redundant or difficult to understand. With admirable patience and resilience, he then sent this list of 57 abstract items in the format of the first Schwartz Values Survey (SVS), together with a short description of his proto-theory of basic values, to 18 researchers in different countries whom he knew or who were suggested to him and invited them to join him in an international study of basic human values by administering this scale to a sample of school teachers and a sample of students in their country.

After several rounds of analysis and data collection, Schwartz finalized his values list, which consisted of the two subsets of terminal (end states) and instrumental (desirable motivational goals) values, and asked several scholars in the world to add any values they thought referred to important values that would be missing. These international researchers were also asked to explain the meaning of these values and to try to specify which, if any, of the broad basic values these specific values would fit under. He received very few (4 to 5) suggestions from the whole group, all of which clearly fit under one of the broad basic values already presented at the list. This procedure resulted in the 57-item Schwartz Values Survey (SVS; containing 30 nouns and 27 adjectives).

Throughout the early 2000s, there were many studies validating the measure (Schwartz, 1992, 1994, 2006a), adapting it to different populations, and eventually revamping it entirely to be useable with children and illiterate populations, though its psychometric properties are quite stronger among literate adults too (referred to as the Portraits Values Questionnaire or PVQ). The original SVS consisted of 10 motivationally distinct value orientations suggested by the values theory (Schwartz, 1992) and later a 19-values orientation of the refined values theory (Cieciuch et al., 2014; McQuilkin et al., 2016; Schwartz et al., 2012). In both, four high-order values emerge. These four higher-order values specify the dynamics of conflict and congruence among the values and include all the core values recognized in most national and societal groups around the world. They are conservation vs. openness to change and self-enhancement vs. self-transcendence. Designed in this way, human values are important constructs in the psychosocial concepts that are considered central to the prediction of attitudes and behaviors, including for the understanding of phenomena that humanities and social sciences are interested in studying.

9.2 The Values Theory

Knafo et al. (2011), in identifying Schwartz as a leader in understanding values, remind readers that Schwartz adopted a cross-cultural perspective both in the design of the theory and in its empirical test. Schwartz (1992) considers values as a universal requirement of human existence and, by proposing the theory, transformed the mere study of a list of values into a sound theory, which has been used to investigate behaviors, such as customer behavior (Voorn et al., 2021), political behavior (Tatarko, 2017), conservation behavior (Barbarossa et al., 2017), and participation in sports (Cabrera, 2008); to predict attitudinal variables, such as job satisfaction (Froese & Xiao, 2012) and organizational commitment (Glazer et al., 2004); and to study the relations with personality variables, such as social dominance (Fernandes et al., 2007), authoritarianism (Radkiewicz, 2016), Big-5 (Athota & O'Connor, 2014), and several other variables in the organizational context, like trust (Morselli et al., 2012) and well-being (Sagiv et al., 2015), to name a few. Thus, the contributions of this theory are essential for studying values in contemporary times and to the understanding of human behaviors in organizations.

Schwartz (1992)and Schwartz and Bilsky (1987) conceptualizes values along five characteristics that differentiate them from attitudes and behaviors, mainly in terms of generality and abstraction, as well as in their hierarchical ordering of importance. These are:

1. Values are beliefs linked to emotion intrinsically. They are not objective ideas and can generate positive or negative feelings.
2. Values are a motivational construct, related to the desirable objectives or goals that people strive to achieve and which guide people to act appropriately.
3. Values transcend specific actions and situations. They differ from concepts such as social norms and attitudes.
4. Values guide the selection or evaluation of actions, policies, people, and events. They serve as standards or criteria for judgments.
5. Values are ordered according to their importance in relation to each other. They form a system of priority that characterizes an individual.

In summary, values are characterized as desirable, trans-situational goals, varying in importance, that serve as guiding principles in people's lives. In addition, Schwartz and Bilsky (1987, 1990) proposed that the crucial content aspect that characterizes values is the type of motivational terminal and instrumental goal that they express. Following this rationale, and taking into account the cognitive representations of three types of universal human needs, biological needs of the organism, social interaction needs for the regulation of interpersonal relationships, and socio-institutional needs that seek the well-being and survival of the group, the authors derived ten motivational types of distinct values: *security*, *tradition*, *conformity*, *benevolence*, *universalism*, *self-direction*, *stimulation*, *hedonism*, *achievement*, and *power* (please see Fig. 9.1).

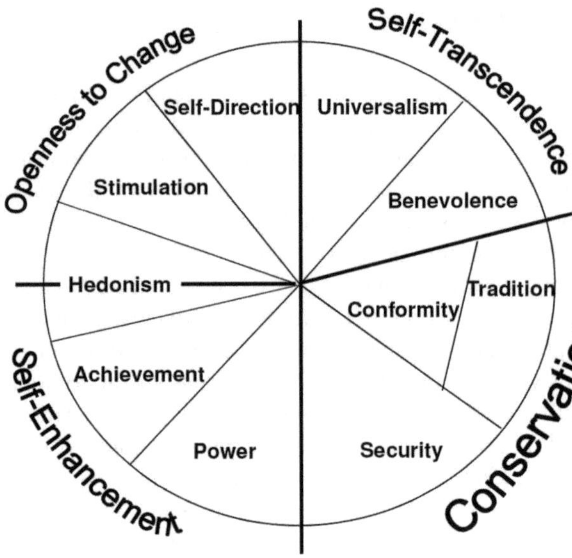

Elaborated by the authors based on Schwartz (2012).

Fig. 9.1 Theoretical structure of relations between values. (Elaborated by the authors based on Schwartz (2012))

Schwartz and Bilsky (1987) presented data on the theory of values from Australia, Finland, Hong Kong, Spain, and the United States and, later in 1990, with data from Germany, Israel, Australia, the United States, Hong Kong, Spain, and Finland. Initially, their studies presented a theory with universal types of values that included the values of pleasure, achievement, self-direction, maturity, security, prosocial, and restrictive compliance (Schwartz & Bilsky, 1987). They also described a bipolar dimension that allowed visualization of the position of opposite values and those with greater proximity. In 1990, Schwartz and Bilsky highlighted that the universality could only really be confirmed in a study involving more countries, as the diversity of samples could provide greater confidence in the universal structure values.

A theoretical improvement came in 1992, whereby Schwartz's samples, drawn from 20 different nations, empirically supported the expectation of the relationship between and among values. The results fortified the universality of the theory of values. Indeed, this 1992 study demonstrated that values are a universal requirement of human existence. Thus, in proposing the theory, Schwartz (1992) transformed what was previously seen as a mere study of a list of values and established a dynamic framework in which motivational goals predict or relate with different variables in different cultural groups. The typology of values was developed with the logic that individuals and groups express their basic needs through specific values, about which they adapt reality in a given social context (Schwartz, 2006a).

Through his proposal, Schwartz (2006a) provided a unifying theory of human motivation organizing different needs, motives, and objectives proposed by other theories. In empirical-based studies, Schwartz (1992) analyzed data of 210 samples from 67 countries across all continents, involving a total of 64,271 participants. Multiple culturally distinct samples allowed him to compare intra- and intercultural variations in the empirical context of values and the structure of value relationships. With this procedure, he was able to separate specific aspects of a culture from universal aspects with regard to the meaning and structure of values (Schwartz, 2006a).

Interrelationships Between and Among Values

Schwartz (2004, 2006b) forwarded that there is a psychological system representing underlying motivations. Those motivations are organized on a continuum of congruent or conflicting relationships, whereby some pairs of values are complementary (e.g., commitment to equality, justice, and protection of all people) and others compete (e.g., power by exercising control over other people). The theory predicts a dynamic structure between the motivational categories of these values, so that individuals may exhibit high priority for compatible types and low priority for antagonistic types (Schwartz & Bilsky, 1987). The structure of the relationships between motivational types is shown in Fig. 9.1. As the distance around the circular order increases, the values tend to be less compatible, until, if located in the opposite position, they indicate greater conflict and high negative correlations (Schwartz, 1992). Hence, values that express individual goals and interests (i.e., self-direction, stimulation, hedonism, achievement, and social power) occupy areas that oppose values that express collective goals and interests (i.e., benevolence, tradition, and conformity). Other values that express both collective and individual goals and interests (security and universalism) are located on the border of these two areas.

In addition, Schwartz's (1992) structure of values also has four high-order values, which form two basic conceptual dimensions: (1) *openness to change* versus *conservation*, where values that emphasize independent thinking and action (i.e., stimulation, self-direction and hedonism) oppose values that emphasize self-restraint, preservation of traditional practices, and protection of stability (i.e., security, conformity, and tradition), and (2) *self-promotion* versus *self-transcendence*, which presents in the first pole the values of power, achievement, and hedonism and, in the opposite, the values of universalism and benevolence. The latter dimension contrasts values that privilege the interests of the individual, even at the expense of others, to values which motivation refers to the concern for the well-being of others and nature. Hedonism is a component of both openness to change and self-promotion (Fig. 9.1).

The endorsement of values belonging to adjacent areas is predictable (e.g., security and tradition) as they satisfy similar interests, while the endorsement of values with opposite motivations (e.g., security and self-direction) can represent a conflict. Their relative importance to individuals differs because people have priorities or hierarchy of different values. In Schwartz's theory, the structure of the value system captures the dynamic relationship (compatible or antagonistic) between the ten values, allowing one to investigate the relationships of values with attitudes, behaviors, or other variables in an integrated manner (Nascimento, 2014).

By 2012, Schwartz et al. presented a refinement to the theory of values; instead of the 10 initial value types, the research team identified 17 value types (embedded within the 10), in addition to proposing 2 new value types, face and humility values. This 25-year period of research, from 1987 to 2012, therefore, improved the delimitation and conceptualization of values, better defining and describing the values previously presented by the theory and empirically increasing their predictive value (Schwartz et al., 2012). Still, it should be noted that the refined theory of values did not invalidate the proposed structure of the ten values discussed earlier. It presents the possibility of a refined value structure by grouping the values in a similar way to the original theory that proves to be more useful for the researcher, enhancing the values' prediction over other variables (Torres et al., 2016). These values are also based on the three basic requirements (biology, social interaction, and survival/welfare) and fulfill the various functions that had been previously proposed (Schwartz, 1992, 2006b). Thus, the 19 value types of the refined theory also focus on achieving personal or social results, promote growth and self-protection, express openness to change or preservation of the status quo, and promote self-interest or the transcendence of self-interest in the service of others (see Fig. 9.2).

The same continuous-circular logic with proximity and opposition between values is present in the refined theory. The greater the compatibility between two values, the closer they are to the circular ordering. The greater the conflict between the values, the more distant they are in the circle (Fig. 9.2). In addition to the 19 proposed values and the 4 higher-order values, the refined theory also specifies the values with a personal focus, that is, the concern with oneself, and on the opposite side, values with a social focus, or concern for others and/or established institutions. Finally, the values expressed at the top of Fig. 9.2 represent growth and self-expression, being more likely to motivate people when they are free from anxiety, whereas those expressed at the bottom of the figure are aimed at protecting the ego against anxiety and threat. A breakdown of the 19 values of the refined theory is presented in Table 9.1.

Since first presented, the refined theory of values has been validated in countries other than the ten countries (Germany, the United States, Finland, Israel, Italy, New Zealand, Poland, Portugal, Switzerland, and Turkey) from where Schwartz et al. (2012) drawn their data in the original sample, such as South Korea (Choi & Lee, 2014), Russia (Schwartz & Butenko, 2014), and Brazil (Torres et al., 2016), among other regions of the world (e.g., Schwartz et al., 2017).

Relationship Between Values and Other Variables

Hanel et al. (2020) developed a cross-cultural study linking values to well-being in 29 countries. They aimed to assess the extent to which people's well-being may be a function of greater value congruence between individuals' values and those of

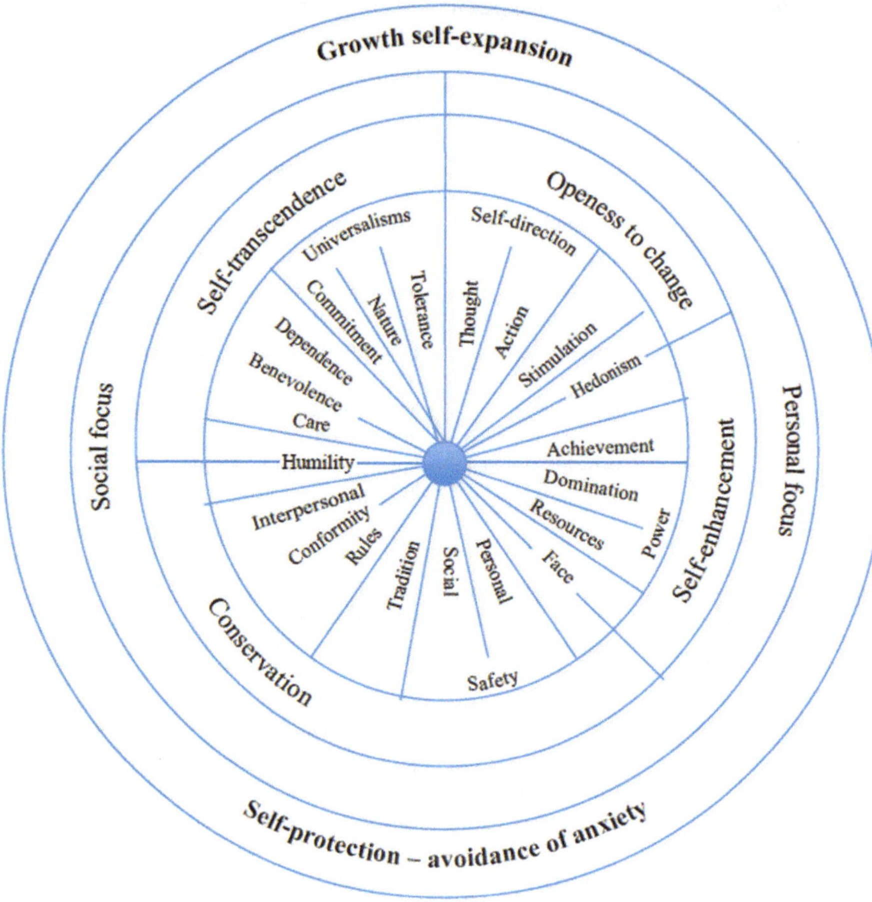

Elaborated by the authors based on Schwartz et al. (2012).

Fig. 9.2 Motivational circle according to the refined basic values theory. (Elaborated by the authors based on Schwartz et al. (2012))

their country, testing the hypothesis of whether the incongruence between these values is distressing. Thus, Hanel et al. (2020) designed a study to investigate if well-being is higher if people's values match with those of people living in the same country or region. They surmised that personal values that are similar to those who live in proximity, in the same region (i.e., person-region congruence) or country (i.e., person-country congruence), will have greater well-being than when values were incongruent. They found that the effects of "person-country" and "person-region" value congruence critically depend on the type of values that are endorsed. Value type is a moderator of whether person-country congruence is positively or negatively associated with well-being. People who endorse more openness-to-change values and live in countries and regions where people also endorse these values report lower well-being.

Table 9.1 Refined values theory in comparison

Originating value (1987/1990 theory)	Value in the refined theory	Definition components
Self-direction	Self-direction of thought	Freedom to cultivate your own ideas and skills
	Self-direction of action	Freedom to determine your own actions
Stimulation	Stimulation	Excitement, novelty, and change
Hedonism	Hedonism	Pleasure and sensual gratification for yourself
Achievement	Achievement	Success according to social standards
Power	Power dominance	Power by exercising control over other people
	Power resources	Power for control over social materials and resources
–[a]	Face	Maintaining public image and avoiding humiliation
Security	Security personal	Security in your immediate environment
	Security societal	Security and stability of wider society
Tradition	Tradition	Maintenance and preservation of culture, family, or religion
Conformity	Conformity rules	Comply with formal rules, laws, and obligations
	Conformity interpersonal	Avoid upsetting or hurting other people
–[a]	Humility	Recognition of one's own insignificance in a broad context
Benevolence	Benevolence dependability	Be a trusted and being a trusted member of the in-group
	Benevolence caring	Devotion to the Well-being of members of the in-group
Universalism	Universalism concern	Commitment to equality, justice, and protection of all people
	Universalism nature	Preservation of the natural environment
	Universalism tolerance	Acceptance and understanding of those who are different from themselves

Note. [a] No match in the 1992 Theory of Values; Elaborated by the authors based on Schwartz (2012)

The relationship with several other variables and values was also being studied. For instance, Youn and Lee (2016) investigated the difference in values between groups prone to primary and secondary psychopathic tendencies in South Korea. Tamir et al. (2016) demonstrated in eight countries the differences between the endorsement of preferred emotions and values, among other variables and relations. Specifically, in the organizational context, Mahmud et al. (2019) suggested the influence of individual values on organizational commitment, mediated by motivation at work, of employees of a large university in Indonesia.

Cultural Values

Schwartz (2006b) also proposed and tested a theory of cultural values that reflects basic issues that all societies must face. Cultural values reflect (1) the nature of the relationship between the group and the individuals, (2) the establishment of the appropriate behavior to preserve the social structure, and (3) the relationship between humanity and the social and natural environment. Cultural values arise from the desire to resolve these issues and comprise three bipolar dimensions. The first dimension defines autonomy, an emphasis on the tendency for individuals to independently seek their own ideas, intellectual directions, and positive affective experiences, as opposed to conservatism, or the maintenance of the status quo and restricting actions that may harm the group or traditions. The second dimension defines hierarchy (i.e., the legitimacy of the unequal distribution of power, roles, and resources) as opposed to egalitarianism (i.e., the transcendence of selfish interests in favor of voluntary commitment to promote the well-being of others). Finally, the third dimension places the domain (i.e., emphasizing success and predominance among other groups) in opposition to harmony (i.e., emphasizing harmonic adaptation to the environment).

Dominant Values in Relation to Work

As a final observation in our discussion about values theory, it is noteworthy that one of the formal features repeatedly mentioned in the theory and its refinement is that values transcend specific situations, actions, and people's roles in a situation, may this be of a manager or an employee. For example, the priority that a person attributes to power or achievement may be the same at work or at the home, with friends, co-workers, or complete strangers. This characteristic differentiates values from attitudes, which refer to a specific object, or norms that apply to a specific situation. This characteristic also serves as the basis for questioning a discussion that we will have in the following section, regarding organizational values. Now, if the same values can be relevant to both a workplace and a social gathering with friends, then what is the point of talking about specific values for the organizational context? Why develop specific measures and models for this context? That values permeate into the work and organizational domain and all the related activities is an undisputed claim. However, is it necessary to develop, for example, specific measures of organizational or work values, or would it not be just more appropriate (and logical) if we study the values of the group of individuals working in the same context, time period, and all seeking to achieve the same set of organizational goals? In the next section, we cover a brief revision of two of the most prominent measures of values used in psychology, before moving on to the measures specifically employed by the theory of human values. In doing so, we hope to stimulate dialog on how the aforementioned questions can be addressed in the organizational context, by reflecting on the nature of the values concept, the level of analyses of the investigation, and the definition and measures of the organizational values concept.

9.3 Values Measurements: *Foundational Measurements*

A couple of measures used to assess values have been well-known in psychology over the years. *The Allport-Vernon Study of Values* (SOV; Allport et al., 1951) is a noteworthy foundational work, as the first instrument for measuring values. They suggested that values guide the activities and aspirations of people and therefore play a fundamental role in our lives (Torres et al., 2016). Rokeach (1967, 1973) also classified values into terminal values, focusing on the need for human existence, and instrumental values, a mechanism to achieve the objectives and goals, presenting the functional relationship between values, attitudes, and behavior. His instrument – *Rokeach Values Survey* (RVS) – was widely used in the scientific field in the first half of the twentieth century (Ros, 2006) and is somewhat used in several areas including marketing and consumer behavior (Andrews et al., 2020). Rokeach suggested that human values are formed in three stages: a positive or negative experience in relation to an object that leads to the establishment of beliefs related to it, the organization of relative evaluative beliefs (i.e., establishing the attitude toward the object), and the conformity of all attitudes related to similar objects.

Schwartz's Values Survey

Several of the instruments developed in the context of the values theory have been later adapted by other authors (e.g., Oliveira & Tamayo, 2004) in order to measure values within the organizational context. In 1992, Schwartz proposed a theoretical-structural improvement to Rokeach's work, expanding the research to 20 countries and developing the SVS. Defending values as universal requirements of human life with potential for predicting other psychological phenomena in different cultures (Schwartz, 1992), it was observed with the SVS that values can be understood as conscious goals that connect to the needs of individuals in relation to their social context. The SVS is a list of values, in which each value is followed by an explanatory phrase, in order to specify its meaning. The guidelines in the instrument aim to define values in the broader context, asking respondents to assess how important each value is as "a principle that guides my life" (Schwartz, 2004). In this instrument, Schwartz used a 9-point scale, from "−1," *opposed* to the respondents' values; "0," *not important*; "6," *very important*; and "7," *of supreme importance*. Respondents are instructed to use ratings of −1 and 7 at the beginning of completing the instrument and, subsequently, to assign values from 0 to 6 according to the importance in their lives. The result should be a person profile showing a hierarchy of values.

Portrait Values Questionnaire

The fact that the SVS has a reasonable level of abstraction on the part of the respondents made the instrument ineffective in samples in which people have lower than high school levels of literacy, which led Schwartz to develop another measure to analyze the values, the Portrait Values Questionnaire (PVQ; Schwartz et al., 2001). The PVQ contains 40 sentences that indirectly describe goals, aspirations, or desires important to another person. Respondents are directed to indicate "How much does this person looks like me?" on a 6-point scale. A reduced version of the PVQ with 21 items was included in the European Social Survey due to the notoriety of the values theory and its international dissemination (Bilsky et al., 2011).

Portrait Values Questionnaire-Refined

Despite an increase in the volume of published research over the last two decades that involve the theory of values and the PVQ in its different formats, in a 2012 study, Schwartz and colleagues subjected the assessment of the values typology to greater statistical rigor and concluded that theory-based partitioning of the space was rather arbitrary. In other words, the boundary partitioning of the values represented in the motivational circumplex values could have been divided differently because values are not a discrete variable. The refinement of the values theory, however, resulted in more clearly bound values that are still ordered around the motivational continuum, but for which the boundaries are neither arbitrary nor fuzzy. In other words, the refined values theory forwards 19 conceptually "discrete values with greater universal heuristic and predictive power" (Schwartz et al., 2012, p. 342). The new division of the motivational continuum of values promotes greater explanatory and heuristic power than the theory of the ten original values. The Portrait Values Questionnaire-Refined (PVQ-R) has descriptions that vary by gender and represents a refinement of the original PVQ. The questionnaire also uses an ordinal scale with six points (1 = Not like me at all; 6 = Very much like me) and contains 57 items, 3 items for each of 19 motivational types described previously in the chapter (see Fig. 9.2). Results with this measure confirmed the ordering of the values in the motivational continuum predicted by the theory in different countries. Versions of the PVQ-R were validated by Schwartz and Butenko (2014) in Russia and by Torres et al. (2016) in Brazil, in New Zealand (Fischer & Karl, 2020), and in Italy (Vecchione & Alessandri, 2017), among other countries.

9.4 Organizational Values: A Dialog from the Perspective of Values Theory

The PVQ-R represents an innovative opportunity for assessing a finer set of meaningful and conceptually discrete values and then testing whether the distinctiveness of such values may predict substantive organizational phenomena. Most of the available research of values studied in relation to organizational behaviors, however, was done before the refined theory was widely known. Research focusing on values as measured with the SVS have been, and indeed are being, used to assess individual values in organizations and variables of interest to the organizational field. For instance, using the SVS, Glazer et al. (2004) observed that higher-order values (HOV) accounted for variance in affective organizational commitment in countries, such as the United States, Hungary, and Italy; the relationship between values and continuance commitment also appears to be homogenous across countries and cultures. These findings suggest that the type of values motivates the type of commitment individuals develop toward their organizations. When studying the profile of a specific occupation (i.e., nurses), self-transcendence and conservation were more prevalent for the success in this profession than other HOV, providing relevant information for recruitment and personnel selection procedures (Glazer & Beehr, 2002). Several other studies (e.g., Fernandes et al., 2007; Froese & Xiao, 2012; Morselli et al., 2012; Sagiv et al., 2015) also provided useful information while assessing individual values in the organizational context. In addition to connecting individual values to organizational attitudes and behaviors, this paper also considers the role of organizational values.

Organizational Values

Organizational values are understood as principles or beliefs, hierarchically organized, related to organizational goals and behaviors desirable, that guide the life of the company and are at the service of individual interests, group or societal interests, or mixed (Tamayo & Gondim, 1996). As a guide to the daily routine of the organization, values are perceived by members of the organization as a function of organizational integration of people to the environment, influencing the behavior of members of the organization (McNeely & Meglino, 1994). Studies on such values have a central place in several organizational phenomena (Bourne & Jenkins, 2013), including professional identity (Nascimento et al., 2016) and organizational culture (O'Reilly & Chatman, 1996). Nonetheless, it should be noticed that the definition of values adopted in such studies do not appear to identify and distinguish them from the concept of individual values. Hence, the concerns about level of analyses raised earlier apply here.

Organizational values are usually introduced by the company's creator or by individuals with strong power and influence within the organization (Bansal, 2003). However, the values of an organization are not necessarily identical, in terms of axiological priority, to those of the members of the organization, which can result in a conflictual relationship. For Veiga (2010), it is extremely important to share organizational values among the actors of the organization, due to the harmony or lack thereof that can occur between personal and organizational values. Compliance with the organization's values reflects the achievement of organizational socialization, which brings beneficial results (e.g., increased engagement) for both parties (Bourne & Jenkins, 2013).

The motivational, cognitive, hierarchical, and functional components of organizational values are present in both conceptual frameworks of individual and organizational values (Porto et al., 2012). The motivational component refers to the goals of organization, which implies that the attribution of importance to a given value is linked to the amount of effort to be undertaken by the organization's actors. The cognitive aspect refers to beliefs about what is desirable or not in the organization and represents a way of knowing the organizational identity, considering the role of values as a cognitive pattern for the selection of appropriate behaviors in the individual's environmental context. The hierarchical component reflects the existing differentiation between individuals and the organization (Tindale et al., 1996). From an axiological point of view, hierarchy is reflected in the priority given to each of the values and not to the values themselves, that is, in the continuum of importance that is assigned. Finally, the functional component emphasizes that the values guide the behavior of its members and the judgment made about the behavior, presenting itself as relevant to the day-to-day life of the organization. Thus, organizational values can be defined as collective mental representations (Tindale et al., 1996), shared by members of the organization, who live within the same environment, in a space of time, representing cognitions and principles that guide practices organizational (Bourne & Jenkins, 2013). They are hierarchically organized and transcend specific practices or standards.

From an organizational level of analysis, addressing organizational values is important if practitioners want to understand an organization's culture (Mendes & Tamayo, 2001), including diagnosing the organizational management (Dobni et al., 2000), as an alternative to bureaucratic control and an increase in service productivity (Ouchi, 1980). Other examples of values' influence on organizational issues include its prediction on strategic issues (Bansal, 2003), strategic change (Carlisle & Baden-Fuller, 2004), and organizational commitment (Ostroff et al., 2005). They play a role influencing critical organizational processes (Bourne & Jenkins, 2013), serve as implicit guides to action that are shared by individuals in the organization, and are the basis for individuals' attitudes and behaviors in organizations (Quenneville et al., 2010).

The scales and theoretical models most cited in the literature on organizational values were developed by Hofstede, Neuijen, Ohayv, and Sanders (1990), O'Reilly et al. (1991), Cameron and Quinn (2011), Oliveira and Tamayo (2004), and Tamayo et al. (2000). Each of these scales and models measures different phenomena and oscillates between specifying values (O'Reilly et al., 1991) and dimensions of values (Hofstede, Neuijen, Ohayv, & Sanders, 1990) and stipulating cultural typologies that are characterized by clusters of values (Cameron & Quinn, 2011). Hofstede, Neuijen, Ohayv, and Sanders (1990) proposed that national cultures differ mainly in terms of the sets of values people within the nation share, whereas organizational cultures differ more in terms of shared practices within the organizations. Members of different organizations within the same nation can share values, but they work for organizations that have developed different ways of implementing those values in practice. Hofstede, Neuijen, Ohayv, and Sanders (1990) used seven dimensions of practice to characterize the culture of each organization, regardless of the nation in which it operated. The dimensions included, for example, orientation toward processes or results, focus on the employee versus focus on work, and open versus closed systems. In analyzing data from his original study, Hofstede found six dimensions in organizational practices that refer to the ways in which organizations were perceived to vary according to their individual employees, namely, professionalism, distance from administration, trust in colleagues, order, hostility, and integration. Regardless of the type of organization or nation of the interviewees, women perceived more confidence, more order, and less hostility than men, and those who were lower in the organizational hierarchy perceived more distance from management and less integration than those higher in the organizational hierarchy, independent of sex.

O'Reilly et al.'s (1991) Organizational Culture Profile (OCP) was developed mainly to measure the individual-organization fit, with factors extracted empirically. The original version of the OCP, consisting of 54 value statements, was developed using exploratory factor analysis to establish 8 dimensions of organizational culture, including innovation, attention to detail, results orientation, aggressiveness, support, emphasis on rewards, team orientation, and determination. O'Reilly and colleagues labeled the factors in a way that best corresponded to the descriptions found. The authors reported in their original study an average reliability coefficient for the OCP of 0.88, whereas Vandenberghe (1999) established an average reliability of 0.86. Since then, the OCP has been revised and reduced by Cable and Judge (1996) to measure the orientations of organizational culture, but questions about the generalization of these dimensions between organizations and particular samples remain (Cable, 1999; Howard, 2000; Vandenberghe, 1999; Windsor & Ashkanasy, 1996).

Based on a survey designed to identify the main indicators of effectiveness in organizations, Quinn and Rohrbaugh (1983) presented a model of four quadrants and two main dimensions. The authors created descriptors (similar to value descriptions) to characterize the dimension of effectiveness in organizations. The Competing Values Framework (CVF) was initially based on research to identify indicators of organizational effectiveness (Quinn & Rohrbaugh, 1983, p. 363). Effectiveness is a central theme in the organizational literature, whereas its definition is perennially controversial. In a literature review, Campbell (1977) identified 30 different criteria of effectiveness. Quinn and Rohrbaugh (1983, p. 366) held that the choices of particular criteria usually reflect personal values about the appropriate emphases in the domain of effectiveness. They invited 52 organizational researchers to order the criteria listed by Campbell (1977) and then derived 3 value dimensions: internal-external, control-flexibility, and means-ends. They integrated the third dimension into the other two ones and established the CVF. One may certainly argue that it is insufficient to measure organizational culture values by only two or three dimensions. However, CVF does not attempt to explore the panorama of organizational culture. Rather, it looks at the value dimensions related to effectiveness. Moreover, this model can integrate most organizational culture dimensions proposed in the literature.

Scholars are debating the extent to which these descriptors translate into cultural dimensions and organizational values (Howard, 1998; Kwan & Walker, 2004; Porto & Ferreira, 2016; Yu & Wu, 2009). One dimension comprises poles that oscillate between flexibility and dynamism versus stability, order, and control, whereas the second dimension differentiates an internal orientation and integration versus an external orientation, differentiation, and rivalry (Cameron & Quinn, 2011). Each dimension forms a continuum of opposing central values (flexibility versus stability, internal versus external), and the quadrants are competing diagonally (Cameron & Quinn, 2011). For the authors, four defined quadrants represent a set of indicators of what people value about the organization's performance. Cameron and Quinn (2011) were also able to identify, from the quadrants, an organizational typology named the Competing Values Framework (CVF) that defines types of culture according to the cultural orientation of the organization, specifying primary values. The four cultural types involve culture of hierarchy, market culture, clan culture, and adhocracy culture.

Authors (e.g., Tamayo, 2008) suggested that values only exist effectively in minds of organization's members, making workers' acceptance and ratification essential for its existence. Thus, organizational values would only assume their status if they were shared by members of the company. Oliveira and Tamayo (2004), based on the values theory (Schwartz, 1992), proposed the inventory of organizational value profiles, composed of 48 items, arranged in 8 factors (i.e., autonomy, well-being, achievement, dominance, prestige or power, tradition, conformity, and concern for the community). Their results supported hypotheses of some motivational similarity between organizational and individual values, with their eight factors obtaining correspondence to nine of the individual values proposed by the theory. The inventory of organizational value profiles has been largely used (e.g., Canova & Porto, 2010; Guardani et al., 2009; Louback et al., 2009), and, in some cases, distinctions about factors in the model proposed by Oliveira and Tamayo were evidenced (Dias & Maestro-Filho, 2008). The main issue raised by literature and to be highlighted here concerns the extent to which the motivational content of the values has been properly transposed into organizational context or perspective (e.g., Guardani et al., 2009; Nascimento, 2014).

Wrestling with Levels of Analysis

Studies point to the relevance of Schwartz's (1992) theory of human values to understand organizational values (Bilsky & Jehn, 2004; Borg et al., 2011). Bilsky and Jehn (2004) and Borg et al. (2011) analyzed the structure of the OCP (O'Reilly et al., 1991) and concluded that there is support for the use of Schwartz's theory, since in the two theoretical dimensions the content of the OCP can be theoretically explained by the theory. Other authors (Porto & Ferreira, 2016; Sagiv & Schwartz, 2007; Tamayo et al., 2000) point out that a theory of cultural values would be more appropriate for understanding organizational values. Tamayo et al. (2000) adapted Schwartz's theory of cultural values to the context of organizations, proposing that organizations face the same three major problems as all societies: (1) resolving the tension between individuals and the group, (2) developing a structure that guarantees the functioning of the organization, and (3) defining the organization's relationship with the natural and social environment. These assumptions led to the creation of a three-dimensional model, with two opposite poles, which coincide with Schwartz's (1992) theory. However, the empirical data only partially corroborated the model proposed. The opposition between the poles was only confirmed for the dimension Hierarchy and Equalitarianism. Tamayo et al. (2000) justified the lack of opposition between the poles based on the hierarchy of values in Brazil and on the idea that differences in value priorities should not lead to differences in structure. Porto and Ferreira (2016) developed an instrument of organizational values based on the theory of cultural values by Schwartz (1992) in an attempt to overcome the limitations mentioned. These authors also suggest that the items created are not very consistent with the proposed structure.

Studies and measures of organizational values are surrounded by methodological issues. Over the past two decades, academic research on organizational values have developed measurement scales to explore the impact of culture (Cameron & Quinn, 2011; Hartnell et al., 2011; Oliveira & Tamayo, 2004; Sarros et al., 2005). Despite that, there is no consensus on dimensions of values to be used when comparing organizations (Sagiv & Schwartz, 2007). The concept of organizational values remains elusive, insofar as there are uncertainties regarding the applicability of this concept to specific objects or situations, as studies tend to treat organizational values as the equivalent to attitudes, except for pointing out the sharing aspect as a feature of their definitions. The motivational perspective of organizational values also raises questions about their applicability to the organizational context, as no studies were found that portrayed a clear impact of organizational values on different aspects of the organizations, such as those described in this chapter that did find a relationship between individual values and organization's interests (e.g., Mahmud et al., 2019).

Micro (Individual Level)

Concerning values and organizations, some questions need to be addressed. In the field of psychology, values measured at the individual level are predictors of various behaviors, attitudes, and other phenomena relevant to the organization, but all measured at the individual level of analysis, such as organizational commitment (Glazer et al., 2004; Ostroff et al., 2005; Wasti, 2010), work orientation (Lan et al., 2013), and job performance (Nascimento, 2014). Arieli, Sagiv, and Roccas (2020) pull together nearly 30 years of theoretical and empirical literature to explain possible implications of personal values on work (vocational interests and occupational interests) and organizations (e.g., creativity, proactive behaviors, organizational identity, response to organizational change, conflict resolution, competition, and cooperation). They further delve into 20+ years of scholarship that has attempted to link person-organization fit with worker health, well-being, and performance. Although the research could have implications on employee selection and training, Fischer and Karl (2020) expressed concern over an unclear causal mechanism and the lack of experimental research to confirm the currently available correlational research.

Meso (Group or Organizational Level)

Few studies have focused on proposing and evaluating organizational-level values (Porto & Ferreira, 2016). One research tendency is the study of organizational culture dimensions as predictors of innovation (Rinne et al., 2012), innovative behavior (Naranjo-Valencia et al., 2017), organizational strategy (Carlisle & Baden-Fuller, 2004), and critical organizational processes (Bourne & Jenkins, 2013). Basically, these studies assess cultural dimensions that primarily include beliefs, values, norms, and organizational practices – a wide spectrum of cultural components. These studies are also based on the Competing Values Framework which involves measurements of organizational typologies, dimensions, and indicators of organizational effectiveness (Porto & Ferreira, 2016). The Competing Values Framework predicts quality of work life (Goodman et al., 2001), organizational effectiveness (Grabowski et al., 2015), and leadership (Lavine, 2014).

Macro (Cultural Level)

At cultural level, Hofstede's (2001) dimensions are also predictive of attitudes and behaviors in organizations (Naranjo-Valencia et al., 2017; Rinne et al., 2012), including organizational strategy (Carlisle & Baden-Fuller, 2004). But these dimensions are not necessarily restricted to the organizational context (Hofstede, 1980; Hofstede, Neuijen, Ohayv, & Sanders, 1990; House et al., 2004). Here, it is important to highlight that Tamayo's instruments (Oliveira & Tamayo, 2004; Tamayo et al., 2000) have been used to evaluate different phenomena and levels of analysis, as well as organizational values (Oliveira & Tamayo, 2004; Tamayo et al., 2000). Porto and Ferreira (2016) also have proposed an instrument prepared with items from other scales (Ferreira et al., 2002; Oliveira & Tamayo, 2004; Quinn & Rohrbaugh, 1983). These instruments were created from adaptations of Schwartz's (1992) theory to the organizational context, focusing on individual level.

There is still a need for a clear definition of organizational values, how they are measured, and how they are distinguished from cultural values dimensions (or should they be?). The definition of values at the individual level of analysis is already clear, but at the collective level, its definition and differentiation from other cultural components deserve attention. Concerning organizational values, a study involving a list of possible organizational values and its application to a considerable contingent of organizations in various countries is recommended. Once a definition and application of values at the organizational level of analysis are clarified, then it is possible to address the existence of organizational values and their differentiation between organizations.

9.5 Final Comments

Criticism has been made regarding the difficulty to define which organizational actors should have their personal values measured (e.g., managers, employees) and how these values should be aggregated in order to compose organizational values indexes (Stackman et al., 2000). Measures of organizational values oscillate between cultural typologies, cultural dimensions, descriptors of general beliefs, and practices carried out in the organizational environment. Further, main measures of values were empirically developed without a consistent theoretical framework. In this sense, they may measure different elements of organizational culture (beliefs, norms, practices), as well as different dimensions of these elements without a clear definition of their concepts. Such hindrances make it quite difficult for a practitioner or scholar interested in the organizational field to compare results between studies. Previous studies have argued for convergence between research on organizational values and those on individual values (Bilsky & Jehn, 2004; Borg et al., 2011; Porto & Ferreira, 2016; Tamayo et al., 2000). This argument seems to be reasonable to defend.

The seminal works of Geert Hofstede (1980, 2001) and Shalom Schwartz (1992, 2012) have been used as guidance for the construction of models and measures of organizational values, but the question about the consistency of such models and instruments remains unaddressed. Studies found no differences in Hofstede's cultural dimensions between organizations (Hofstede, 1985; Hofstede, Neuijen, Ohayv, & Sanders, 1990; Nelson & Gopalan, 2003); yet organizational practices seem to be a better criterion to differentiate between organizations. Thus, we suggest that organizational values should be better characterized, defined, and measured for a better use in the organizational context. Or, perhaps, the assessment of individual values of organizations' members, understood as motivations that transcend specific situations, actions, and people's roles in a situation aligned with the measurement of organizational practices, may provide a better picture, understanding, and implication of these concepts to the successful solution of organizational challenges.

References

Allport, F. (1924). *Social psychology*. Houghton-Miffin.

Allport, G. W. (1955). *Becoming*. Yale University Press.

Andrews, C., Gardiner, K., Jain, T. K., Olomi, Y., & North, A. C. (2020). Culture, personal values, personality, uses of music, and musical taste. *Psychology of Aesthetics, Creativity, and the Arts*. Advance online publication. https://doi.org/10.1037/aca0000318.

Archer, L., & Fitch, K. (1994). Communication in Latin American multinational organizations. In R. L. Wiseman & R. Shuter (Eds.), Communicating in multinational organizations (pp. 75–93). Thousand Oaks, CA: Sage.

Arieli, S., Sagiv, L., & Roccas, S. (2020). Values at work: The impact of personal values in organisations. Applied Psychology: *An International Review, 69*(2), 230–275. https://doi.org/10.1111/apps.12181

Aristotle. (2001). *Nicomachean ethics* (4th ed.). Universidade de Brasília: UnB.
Athota, V. S., & O'Connor, P. J. (2014). How approach and avoidance constructs of personality and trait emotional intelligence predict core human values. *Learning and Individual Differences, 31*(4), 51–58. https://doi.org/10.1016/j.lindif.2013.12.009
Banerjee, S. B., & Linstead, S. (2001). Globalization, multiculturalism and other fictions. *Organization, 8*, 711–722. https://doi.org/10.1177/135050840184006
Bansal, P. (2003). From issues to actions: The importance of individual concerns and organizational values in responding to natural environmental issues. *Organization Science, 14*(5), 510–527. https://doi.org/10.1287/orsc.14.5.510.16765
Barbarossa, C., De Pelsmacker, P., & Moons, I. (2017). Personal values, green self-identity and electric car adoption. *Ecological Economics, 140*, 190–200. https://doi.org/10.1016/j.ecolecon.2017.05.015
Bilsky, W. & Jehn, K. (2004). Organizational culture and individual values: evidence for a common structure1. Miami ULB Münster: https://nbnresolving.de/urn:nbn:de:hbz:6-85659525375
Bilsky, W., Janik, M., & Schwartz, S. H. (2011). The structural organization of human values – Evidence from three rounds of the European Social Survey (ESS). *Journal of Cross-Cultural Psychology, 42*, 759–776. https://doi.org/10.1177/0022022110362757
Borg, I., Groenen, P. J. F., Karen A. J., Wolfgang B., & Schwartz, S. H. (2011). Embedding the Organizational Culture Profile into Schwartz'S Universal Value Theory Using Multidimensional Scaling with Regional Restrictions. *Journal of Personnel Psychology. 10*, 1–12. https://doi.org/10.1027/1866-5888/a000028
Bourne, H., & Jenkins, M. (2013). Organizational values: A dynamic perspective. *Organization Studies, 34*(4), 495–514. https://doi.org/10.1177/0170840612467155
Brannen, M. Y. (2004). When Mickey loses face: Recontextualization, semantic fit, and the semiotics of foreignness. *Academy of Management Review, 29*, 593–616. https://doi.org/10.2307/20159073
Cable, D. (1999). Paper JAP 82(4). Personal correspondence, 29 July (cabled@bschool.unc.edu).
Cable, D. M., & Judge, T. A. (1996). Person-organization fit, job choice decisions, and organizational entry. *Organizational Behavior & Human Decision Processes, 67*(3), 294–311. https://doi.org/10.1006/obhd.1996.0081
Cabrera, E. A. (2008). Sports and human values. *Journal of Human Sport and Exercise, 1*(1), 7–14. https://doi.org/10.4100/jhse.2006.11.02
Cameron, K. S., & Quinn, R. E. (2011). *Diagnosing and changing organizational culture: Based on the competing values framework* (3rd ed.). Jossey-Bass.
Campbell, L. E. (1977). The effects of different forms of feedback on the facilitative effectiveness of counselor trainees. University press: Indiana.
Canova, K. R., & Porto, J. B. (2010). O impacto dos valores organizacionais no estresse ocupacional: um estudo com professores de ensino médio. *RAM. Revista de Administração Mackenzie, 11*(5), 4–31. https://doi.org/10.1590/S1678-69712010000500002
Carlisle, Y., & Baden-Fuller, C. (2004). Re-applying beliefs: An analysis of change in the oil industry. *Organization Studies, 25*, 987–1019. https://doi.org/10.1177/0170840604045093
Chinese Culture Connection. (1987). Chinese values and the search for culture-fee dimensions of culture. *Journal of Cross-Cultural Psychology, 18*(1), 143–164. https://doi.org/10.1177/0022002187018002002
Choi, J. W., & Lee, Y. H. (2014). Validation of the Korean version of the Portrait Values Questionnaire-Revised (PVQ-R). *Korean Journal of Psychology: General, 33*, 533–590.
Cieciuch, J., Davidov, E., Vecchione, M., Beierlein, C., & Schwartz, S. H. (2014). The cross-national invariance properties of a new scale to measure 19 basic human values: A test across eight countries. *Journal of Cross-Cultural Psychology, 45*(5), 764–776. https://doi.org/10.1177/0022022114527348
Dias, D.V., & Maestro-Filho, A. (2008). Valores organizacionais e comprometimento: um estudo em empresas do setor siderúrgico mineiro. In: ENCONTRO DA ANPAD, XXXII, 2008, Rio de Janeiro, Anais... Rio de Janeiro, EnANPAD, p. 1–16.

Dobni, D., Ritchie, J. R. B., & Zerbe, W. (2000). Organizational values: The inside view of service productivity. *Journal of Business Research, 47*, 91–107. https://doi.org/10.1016/S0148-2963(98)00058-7

Erez, M., & Gati, E. (2004). A Dynamic, multi-level model of culture: From the micro level of the individual to the macro level of a global culture. Applied Psychology: *An International Review, 53*(4), 583–598. https://doi.org/10.1111/j.1464-0597.2004.00190.x

Erez, M., & Shokef, E. (2008). The culture of global organizations. In P. B. SmithM. F. Peterson, & D. C. Thomas The handbook of crosscultural management research (pp. 285-300). SAGE Publications, Inc., https://www.doi.org/10.4135/9781412982764.n17

Feather, N. T. (1995). Values, valences and choice: The influence of values on the perceived attractiveness and choice of alternatives. *Journal of Personality and Social Psychology, 68*(6), 1135–1151. https://doi.org/10.1037/0022-3514.68.6.1135

Fernandes, S., Costa, J., Camino, L., & Mendoza, R. (2007). Psychosocial values and social dominance orientation: A study about prejudice. *Psicologia: Reflexão e Crítica, 20*(3), 490–498. https://doi.org/10.1590/S0102-79722007000300017

Ferreira, M. C., Assmar, E. M. L., Estol, K. M. F., Helena, M. C. C., & Cisne, M. C. F. (2002). Desenvolvimento de um instrumento brasileiro para avaliação da cultura organizacional [Development of a Brazilian instrument for evaluation of organizational culture]. *Estudos de Psicologia (Natal), 7*(2), 271–280. https://doi.org/10.1590/S1413-294X2002000200008

Fischer, R., & Karl, J. A. (2020). The network architecture of individual differences: Personality, reward-sensitivity, and values. *Personality and Individual Differences, 160*(1). https://doi.org/10.1016/j.paid.2020.109922

Froese, F., & Xiao, S. S. (2012). Work values, job satisfaction and organizational commitment in China. *The International Journal of Human Resource Management, 23*(10), 2144–2162. https://doi.org/10.1080/09585192.2011.610342

Guardani, F., Teixeira, M. L. M., Bido, D. S., & Mazzon, J. A. (2009). A relação entre valores, práticas organizacionais e confiança de clientes no setor de serviços. Produção, 23(4), 806–817. https://doi.org/10.1590/S0103-65132013005000019

Glazer, S. (2016). One finger point toward the other, three are back at you. In J. L. Wildman & R. Griffith (Eds.), *Critical issues in cross cultural management.* Springer. https://doi.org/10.1007/978-3-319-42166-7

Glazer, S., & Beehr, T. A. (2002). Similarities and differences in human values between nurses in four countries. *International Journal of Cross Cultural Management, 2*(2), 185–202. https://doi.org/10.1177/14795802002002867

Glazer, S., & Beehr, T. A. (2005). Consistency of the implications of three role stressors across four countries. *Journal of Organizational Behavior, 26*, 467–487. https://doi.org/10.1002/job.326

Glazer, S., Daniel, S., & Short, K. (2004). A study of the relationship between organizational commitment and human values in four countries. *Human Relations, 57*(3), 323–345. https://doi.org/10.1177/0018726704043271

Glazer, S., Saner, L., Pavisic, I., & Barnes, M. (2014). Cross-cultural training and education for detection. In J. D. Egeth, D. Schmorrow, & G. L. Klein (Eds.), *Sociocultural behavior Sensemaking: State-of-the-art in understanding the operational environment.* McLean, VA. www.mitre.org

Goodman, E. A., Zammuto, R. F., & Gifford, B. D. (2001). The competing values framework: Understanding the impact of organizational culture on the quality of work life. *Organization Development Journal, 19*(3), 58.

Grabowski, L., Neher, C., Crim, T., & Mathiassen, L. (2015). Competing values framework application to organizational effectiveness in voluntary organizations: A case study. *Nonprofit and Voluntary Sector Quarterly, 44*(5), 908–923. https://doi.org/10.1177/0899764014546488

Hanel, P. H., Wolfradt, U., Wolf, L. J., Coelho, G. L. H., & Maio, G. R. (2020). Well-being as a function of person-country fit in human values. *Nature Communications, 11*(1), 1–9. https://doi.org/10.1038/s41467-020-18831-9

Hartnell, C. A., Ou, A. Y., & Kinicki, A. (2011). Organizational culture and organizational effectiveness: A meta-analytic investigation of the competing values framework's theoretical suppositions. *Journal of Applied Psychology, 96*(4), 677–694. https://doi.org/10.1037/a0021987

Helkama, K., Uutela, A., & Schwartz, S. (1992). Value systems and political cognition. In G. M. Breakwell (Org.), *Social psychology of political and economic cognition* (pp. 7–31). : Surrey University.

Hofstede, G. (1980). *Culture's consequences: International differences in work-related values*. Sage.

Hofstede, G. (1985). The interaction between national and organizational value systems. *Journal of Management Studies, 22*, 347–357. https://doi.org/10.1016/0361-3682(88)90026-8

Hofstede, G. (2001). *Culture's consequences: Comparing values, behaviours, institutions and organizations across nations*. Sage.

Hofstede, G. (2006). What did GLOBE really measure? Researchers' minds versus respondents' minds. *Journal of International Business Studies, 37*, 882–896. https://doi.org/10.1057/palgrave.jibs.8400233C

Hofstede, G. & Bond, M. (1988). The Confucius connection: From cultural roots to economic growth. *Organizational Dynamics, 16*, 4–21.

Hofstede, G., Neuijen, B., Ohayv, D. D., & Sanders, G. (1990). Measuring organizational cultures: A qualitative and quantitative study across twenty cases. *Administrative Science Quarterly, 35*, 286–316. https://doi.org/10.2307/2393392

House, R. J., Hanges, P. J., Javidan, M., Dorman, P. W., Gupta, V., & Globe Associates. (2004). *Leadership, culture and organizations: The GLOBE study of 62 nations*. Sage.

Howard, J. A. (2000). Social psychology of identities. *Annual Review of Sociology, 26*, 367–393. https://doi.org/10.1146/annurev.soc.26.1.367

Howard, L. W. (1998). Validating the competing values model as a representation of organizational cultures. *International Journal of Organizational Analysis, 6*(3), 231–250. https://doi.org/10.1108/eb028886

Inglehart, R. (1977). *The silent revolution: Changing values and political styles among Western publics*. Princeton University Press, NJ.

Klein, K. J., Dansereau, F., & Hall, R. J. (1994). Levels Issues in Theory Development, Data Collection, and Analysis. *Academy of Management Review, 19*, 195–229, https://doi.org/10.5465/amr.1994.9410210745

Kluckhohn, C. (1951). Values and value-orientations in the theory of action: An exploration in definition and classification. In T. Parsons & E. Shils (Eds.), *Toward a general theory of action*. Harvard University Press.

Knafo, A., Roccas, S., & Sagiv, L. (2011). The value of values in cross-cultural research: A special issue in honor of Shalom Schwartz. *Journal of Cross-Cultural Psychology, 42*(2), 178–185. https://doi.org/10.1177/0022022110396863

Kwan, P., & Walker, A. (2004). Validating the competing values model as a representation of organizational culture through inter-institutional comparisons. *Organizational Analysis, 12*(1), 21–39. https://doi.org/10.1108/eb028984

Lan, G., Okechuku, C., Zhang, H., & Cao, J. (2013). Impact of job satisfaction and personal values on the work orientation of Chinese accounting practitioners. *Journal of Business Ethics, 112*(4), 627–640. Retrieved April 12, 2021, from http://www.jstor.org/stable/23433672

Lavine, M. (2014). Paradoxical leadership and the competing values framework. *The Journal of Applied Behavioral Science, 50*(2), 189–205. https://doi.org/10.1177/0021886314522510

Lefkowitz, J. L. (2017). *Ethics and values in industrial-organizational psychology* (2nd ed.). Routledge.

Lewin, K. (1942). Field theory and learning. In D. Cartwright (Ed.), *Field theory in social science* (pp. 60–86). Harper & Row.

Louback, J., Teixeira, M. M. & Bido, D. (2009). Valores organizacionais e racionalidades: uma visita ao Terceiro Setor. O&S - Organizações & Sociedade. 16. 225–246. https://doi.org/10.1590/S1984-92302009000200002

Mahmud, A., Susilowati, N., & Tusyanah, T. (2019). Human values model analysis on organizational commitment in higher education. *JDM – Jurnal Dinamika Manajemen, 10*(1), 46–57. https://doi.org/10.15294/jdm.v10i1.17569

Marks, G. N. (1997). The formation of materialist and postmaterialist values. *Social Science Research, 26*(1), 52–68. https://doi.org/10.1006/ssre.1996.0585

Maslow, A. H. (1954). *Motivation and personality*. Harper & Row.

McNeely, B. L., & Meglino, B. M. (1994). The role of dispositional and situational antecedents in prosocial organizational behavior: An examination of the intended beneficiaries of prosocial behavior. *Journal of Applied Psychology, 79*, 836–844. https://doi.org/10.1037/0021-9010.79.6.836

McQuilkin, J., Garðarsdóttir, R. B., Thorsteinsson, T., & Schwartz, S. H. (2016). An Icelandic translation and validation of the revised 19-value portrait values questionnaire. *Personality and Individual Differences, 101*(1), 428–434. https://doi.org/10.1016/j.paid.2016.06.050

Mendes, A. M., & Tamayo, A. M. (2001). Valores organizacionais e prazer-sofrimento no trabalho. *Psico-USF, 6*(1), 39–46. https://doi.org/10.1590/S1413-82712001000100006

Morselli, D., Spini, D., & Devos, T. (2012). Human values and trust in institutions across countries: A multilevel test of Schwartz's hypothesis of structural equivalence. *Survey Research Methods, 6*(1), 49–60. https://doi.org/10.18148/srm/2012.v6i1.5090

Naranjo-Valencia, J. C., Jimenez-Jimenez, D., & Sanz-Valle, R. (2017). Organizational culture and radical innovation: Does innovative behavior mediate this relationship? *Creativity and Innovation Management, 26*(4), 407–417.

Nascimento, T. G. (2014). *Desempenho profissional: relações com valores, práticas e identidade no serviço policial. Performance compétente: Relations avec valeurs, pratiques et identité dans le service de police.* Tese de doutorado. Universidade de Brasília, Brasília. Université dÁix Marseille, Marselha, França.

Nascimento, T. G., Adaid-Castro, B. G., Carvalho, G. P., & Demo, G. (2016). Valores organizacionais: Uma análise bibliométrica da produção nacional do período de 2000 a 2013 na area de Administração [Organizational values: A bibliometric analysis of Brazilian national production from 2000 to 2013 in the Administration área]. *Revista Organizações em Contexto, 12*(1), 37–64.

Nelson, R. E., & Gopalan, S. (2003). Do organizational culture replicate national cultures? Isomorphism, rejection and reciprocal opposition in the corporate values of three countries. *Organization Studies, 24*, 1115–1151. https://doi.org/10.1177/01708406030247006

Oliveira, A. F., & Tamayo, A. (2004). Inventário de perfis de valores organizacionais. *RAUSP Management Journal, 39*(2), 129–140.

O'Reilly, C., Chatman, J., & Caldwell, D. F. (1991). People and organizational culture: A profile comparison approach to assessing person-organization fit. *Academy of Management Journal, 34*(3), 487–516. https://doi.org/10.2307/256404

O'Reilly, C. A., & Chatman, J. A. (1996). Culture as social control: Corporations, cults, and commitment. In B. M. Staw & L. L. Cummings (Eds.), *Research in organizational behavior: An annual series of analytical essays and critical reviews*, 18(1), 157–200. Elsevier Science/JAI Press.

Ostroff, C., Shin, Y., & Kinicki, A. J. (2005). Multiple perspectives of congruence: Relationships between value congruence and employee attitudes. *Journal of Organizational Behavior, 26*, 591–623. https://doi.org/10.1002/job.333

Ouchi, W. G. (1980). Markets, bureaucracies, and clans. *Administrative Science Quarterly, 25*(1), 129–141.

Oyserman, D., Coon, H. H., & Kemmelmeter, M. (2002). Rethinking individualism and collectivism: Evaluation of theoretical assumptions and meta-analyses. *Psychological Bulletin, 128*(1), 3–72. https://doi.org/10.1037//0033-2909.128.1.3

Parsons, T. (1949). *The structure of social action*. Harvard University Press.

Pavett, C., & Morris, T. (1995). Management Styles Within a Multinational Corporation: A Five Country Comparative Study. *Human Relations, 48*(10), 1171–1191. https://doi.org/10.1177/001872679504801004

Porto, J., & Ferreira, M. C. (2016). Uma escala de valores organizacionais com base na teoria de valores culturais de Schwartz [A scale of organizational values framed on Schwartz's theory of cultural values]. *Psicologia: Teoria e Pesquisa, 32*, 1–10. https://doi.org/10.1590/0102-3772e32ne222

Porto, J. B., Ferreira, M. C., Brandão, H. P., Freitas, I. A., & Pereira, S. C. M. (2012). *Valores Organizacionais: Evidências de adequação da Teoria de Valores Culturais de Schwartz.* Manuscrito Não-publicado. Instituto de Psicologia, Universidade de Brasília.

Quenneville, N., Bentein, K., & Simard, G. (2010). From organizational values to mobilization of human resources. *Canadian Journal of Administrative Sciences, 27*(2), 122–135. https://doi.org/10.1002/cjas.114

Quinn, R. E., & Rohrbaugh, J. (1983). A spatial model of effectiveness criteria: Towards a competing values approach to organizational analysis. *Management Science, 29*, 363–377. https://doi.org/10.1287/mnsc.29.3.363

Radkiewicz, P. (2016). Another look at the duality of the dual-process motivational model. On the role of axiological and moral origins of right-wing authoritarianism and social dominance orientation. *Personality and Individual Differences, 99*(1), 106–112. https://doi.org/10.1016/j.paid.2016.04.080

Rinne, T., Steel, G. D., & Fairweather, J. (2012). Hofstede and Shane revisited: The role of power distance and individualism in national-level innovation success. *Cross-Cultural Research, 46*(2), 91–108. https://doi.org/10.1177/1069397111423898

Rokeach, M. (1967). *Value survey*. Halgren Tests.

Rokeach, M. (1973). *The nature of human values*. The Free Press.

Ros, M. (2006). Valores, atitudes e comportamento: Uma nova visita a um Tema clássico [Values, attitudes and behavior: A new visit to a classic theme]. In M. Ros & V. V. Gouveia (Eds.), *Psicologia social dos valores humanos: Desenvolvimentos teóricos, metodológicos e aplicados [social psychology of the human values: Theoretical, methodological and applied developments]*. Senac.

Sackett, P. R., & Larson, J. R., Jr. (1990). Research strategies and tactics in industrial and organizational psychology. In M. D. Dunnette & L. M. Hough (Eds.), Handbook of industrial and organizational psychology (pp. 419–489). Consulting Psychologists Press.

Sagiv, L., Roccas, S., & Oppenheim-Weller, S. (2015). Values and well-being. In S. Joseph (Ed.), *Positive psychology in practice: Promoting human flourishing in work, health, education, and everyday life* (2nd ed., pp. 103–120). Wiley. https://doi.org/10.1002/9781118996874.ch7

Sagiv, L., & Schwartz, S.H. (2007). Cultural values in organisations: insights for Europe. *European Journal of International Management, 1*, 176.

Sarros, J. C., Gray, J. H., Densten, I. L., & Cooper, B. (2005). The organizational culture profile revisited and revised: An Australian perspective. *Australian Journal of Management, 30*(1), 159–182. https://doi.org/10.1177/031289620503000109

Schwartz, S. H. (1973). Normative explanations of helping behavior: A critique, proposal, and empirical test. *Journal of Experimental Social Psychology, 9*, 349–364. https://doi.org/10.1016/0022-1031(73)90071-1

Schwartz, S. H. (1992). Universals in the content and structure of values: Theoretical advances and empirical tests in 20 countries. *Advances in Experimental Social Psychology, 25*, 1–65. https://doi.org/10.1016/S0065-2601(08)60281-6

Schwartz, S. H. (1994). Are there universal aspects in the content and structure of values? *Journal of Social Issues, 50*(4), 19–45. https://doi.org/10.1111/j.1540-4560.1994.tb01196.x

Schwartz, S. H. (1999). A theory of cultural values and some implications for work. *Applied Psychology: An International Review, 48*, 23–47. https://doi.org/10.1111/j.1464-0597.1999.tb00047.x

Schwartz, S. H. (2004). Mapping and interpreting cultural differences around the world. In H. Vinken, J. Soeters, & P. Ester (Eds.), *Comparing cultures: Dimensions of culture in a comparative perspective* (pp. 43–73). Brill.

Schwartz, S. H. (2006a). Há aspectos universais na estrutura e no conteúdo dos Valores Humanos? [*Are there universal aspects in the structure and content of Human Values?*]. In M. Ros & V. V. Gouveia (Orgs). *Psicologia Social dos Valores Humanos: Desenvolvimentos teóricos, metodológicos e aplicados*. Cafalcchio, O. (Trad). São Paulo: Editora Senac.
Schwartz, S. H. (2006b). A theory of cultural value orientations: Explication and applications. *Comparative Sociology, 5*(1), 136–182. https://doi.org/10.1163/156913306778667357
Schwartz, S. H. (2012). An overview of the Schwartz theory of basic values. *Online Readings in Psychology and Culture, 2*(1). https://doi.org/10.9707/2307-0919.1116
Schwartz, S. H. (2013). Rethinking the concept and measurement of societal culture in light of empirical findings. *Journal of Cross-Cultural Psychology, 45*(1), 5–13. https://doi.org/10.1177/0022022113490830
Schwartz, S. H., & Bilsky, W. (1987). Toward a universal structure of human values. *Journal of Personality and Social Psychology, 53*(3), 550–562. https://doi.org/10.1037/0022-3514.53.3.550
Schwartz, S. H., & Bilsky, W. (1990). Toward a theory of the universal content and structure of values: Extensions and cross-cultural replications. *Journal of Personality and Social Psychology, 58*(5), 878–891. https://doi.org/10.1037/0022-3514.58.5.878
Schwartz, S. H., & Butenko, T. (2014). Values and behavior: Validating the refined value theory in Russia. *European Journal of Social Psychology, 44*(1), 799–813. https://doi.org/10.1002/ejsp.2053
Schwartz, S. H., Cieciuch, J., Vecchione, M., Davidov, E., Fischer, R., Beierlein, C., Ramos, A., Verkasalo, M., Lönnqvist, J.-E., Demirutku, K., Dirilen-Gumus, O., & Konty, M. (2012). Refining the theory of basic individual values. *Journal of Personality and Social Psychology, 103*(4), 663–688. https://doi.org/10.1037/a0029393
Schwartz, S. H., Cieciuch, J., Vecchione, M., Torres, C. V., Dirilem-Gumus, O., & Butenko, T. (2017). Value tradeoffs and behavior in five countries: Validating 19 refined values. *European Journal of Social Psychology, 47*(3), 241–258. https://doi.org/10.1002/ejsp.2228
Schwartz, S. H., Melech, G., Lehmann, A., Burgess, S., & Harris, M. (2001). Extending the cross-cultural validity of the theory of basic human values with a different method of measurement. *Journal of Cross-Cultural Psychology, 32*, 519–542. https://doi.org/10.1177/0022022101032005001
Smith, P. B., & Bond, M. H. (1999). Social psychology: Across cultures (2nd ed.). Allyn & Bacon.
Smith, P. B., Dugan, S., Peterson, M. F., & Leung, K. (1998). Individualism: Collectivism and the handling of disagreement: A 23 country study. International Journal of Intercultural Relations, 22, 351-367.
Smith, P. B., Peterson, M. F., Akande, D., Callan, V., Cho, N. G., Jesuino, J., D'Amorim, M. A., Koopman, P., Leung, K., Mortazawi, S., Munene, J., Radford, M., Ropo, A., Savage, G., & Viedge, C. (1994). Organizational event management in fourteen countries: A comparison with Hofstede's dimensions. In A. M. Bouvy, F. van der Vijver, P. Schmitz & P. Boski (Eds.), Journeys into cross-cultural psychology (pp. 364-373). Amsterdam: Swets & Zeitlinger.
Smith, P. B., Huang, H. J., Harb, C., & Torres, C. V. (2011). How distinctive are indigenous ways of achieving influence? A comparative study of *guanxi, wasta, jeitinho*, and "pulling strings". *Journal of Cross-Cultural Psychology*, 1–18. https://doi.org/10.1177/0022022110381430
Smith, P. B., Torres, C. V., Leong, C. H., Budhwar, P., Achoui, M., & Lebedeva, N. (2012). Are indigenous approaches to achieving influence in business organizations distinctive? A comparative study of guanxi, wasta, jeitinho, svyazi, and "pulling strings". *International Journal of Human Resource Management, 23*, 333–348. https://doi.org/10.1080/09585192.2011.561232
Stackman, R. W., Pinder, C. C., & Connor, P. E. (2000). Values lost: Redirecting research on values in the workplace. In N. M. Ashkanasy, C. P. Wilderom, & M. F. Peterson (Eds.), *Handbook of organizational culture and climate* (pp. 37–54). Sage.
Strohschneider, S., & Güss, D. (1998). Planning and problem solving: Differences between Brazilians and German students. *Journal of Cross-Cultural Psychology, 29*, 695–716. https://doi.org/10.1177/0022022198296002
Tamayo, A. (2008). Valores Organizacionais. In M. M. M. Siqueira (Org.). *Medida do comportamento organizacional: Ferramentas de diagnóstico e de gestão* (1st ed., pp. 309–340). Artmed.

Tamayo, A., & Gondim, M. G. C. (1996). Escala de valores organizacionais. *Revista de Administração, 31*(2), 62–72.

Tamayo, A., Mendes, M., & Paz, M. G. T. (2000). Inventário de valores organizacionais. *Estudos de Psicologia (Natal), 5*(2), 289–315. https://doi.org/10.1590/S1413-294X2000000200002

Tamir, M., Schwartz, S. H., Cieciuch, J., Riediger, M., Torres, C., Scollon, C., Dzokoto, V., Zhou, X., & Vishkin, A. (2016). Desired emotions across cultures: A value-based account. *Journal of Personality and Social Psychology, 111*(1), 67–82. https://doi.org/10.1037/pspp0000072

Tatarko, A. (2017). The relationship of basic human values and voting behavior. *Social Psychology and Society, 8*(1), 17–37. https://doi.org/10.17759/sps.2017080102

Thomas, W. I., & Znaniecki, F.. (1918). *The Polish peasant in Europe and America.* [Adobe Digital Editions version]. Retrieved in February 22nd 2021 from https://www.researchgate.net/profile/Ansgar_Weymann/publication/37927974_The_Polish_Peasant_in_Europe_and_America/links/563b178e08aeed0531dccdba.pdf

Tindale, R. S., Smith, C. M., Thomas, L. S., Filkins, J., & Sheffey, S. (1996). Shared representations and asymmetric social influence processes in small groups. In E. Witte & J. H. Davis (Eds.), *Understanding group behavior: Consensual action by small groups* (pp. 81–103). Erlbaum.

Torres, C. V., & Pérez-Nebra, A. R. (2015). Evaluación del individualismo-colectivismo vertical-horizontal en Brasil: Una propuesta de medida. *Perspectivas en Psicología, 12*(2), 9–21.

Torres, C. V., Schwartz, S. H., & Nascimento, T. G. (2016). A teoria de valores refinada: Associações com comportamento e evidências de validade discriminante e preditiva. *Psicologia USP, 27*(2), 341–356. https://doi.org/10.1590/0103-656420150045

Triandis, H. C. (1994). Cross-cultural industrial and organizational psychology. In H. C. Triandis, M. D. Dunnette, & L. M. Hough (Eds.), *Handbook of industrial and organizational psychology* (Vol. 4, 2nd ed., pp. 103–172). Consulting Psychology Press.

Triandis, H. C. (1995). *Individualism and collectivism.* Westview Press.

Van Ophuijsen, J. M., van Raalte, M., & Stork, P. (2007). *Protagoras of Abdera: The man, his measure.* Brill.

Vandenberghe, C. (1999). Organizational culture, person-culture fit, and turnover: A replication in the health care industry. *Journal of Organizational Behavior, 20*, 175–184. https://doi.org/10.1002/(SICI)1099-1379(199903)20:23.0.CO;2-E

Vecchione, M., & Alessandri, G. (2017). Validation of the Italian version of the portrait values questionnaire-revised (PVQ-R). *Giornale Italiano di Psicologia., 44*(1), 159–178. https://doi.org/10.1421/86906

Veiga, H. M. S. (2010). *Comportamento pró-ativo: relações com valores organizacionais, estímulos e barreiras à criatividade nas organizações e normas sociais. Tese de Doutorado não publicada.* Instituto de Psicologia, Universidade de Brasília.

Voorn, R., Van Rompay, T., Pruyn, A., Hegner, S., & van der Veen, G. (2021). Human values as added value(s) in consumer brand congruence: A comparison with traits and functional requirements. *Journal of Brand Management, 28*(1), 48–59. https://doi.org/10.1057/s41262-020-00210-w

Wasti, S. (2010). Organizational commitment, turnover intentions and the influence of cultural values. *Journal of Occupational and Organizational Psychology, 76*(3), 303–321. https://doi.org/10.1348/096317903769647193

Waterfield, R. (2009). *The first philosophers: The Presocratics and the sophists.* Oxford University Press.

Williams, R. (1983). *Culture and society, 1780–1950.* Columbia University Press. Retrieved from https://books.google.com.br/books?id=V3me7QWAZR0C

Windsor, C., & Ashkanasy, N. M. (1996). Auditor independence decision-making: The role of organisational culture perceptions. *Behavioural Research in Accounting, 8*(Supplement), 80–97.

Youn, H., & Lee, Y. H. (2016). Values of people with primary and secondary psychopathic tendency: Focused on Schwartz's value theory. *Korean Journal of Clinical Psychology, 35*(2), 473–497.

Yu, T., & Wu, N. (2009). A review of study on the competing values framework. *International Journal of Business and Management, 4*(7), 37–42. https://doi.org/10.5539/ijbm.v4n7p37

Chapter 10
Evaluation Tools of Social Support at Work and Contributions of Social Network Analysis

Elisa Maria Barbosa de Amorim-Ribeiro, Laila Leite Carneiro, Leonardo Fernandes Martins, and Ranna Carolina dos Santos Cunha

10.1 Introduction

Social support is a phenomenon studied since the 1950s by different fields of knowledge such as psychiatry, psychology, medicine, sociology, and anthropology. These areas were interested in investigating the relationship between social variables and physical and psychological responses of individuals (Wilcox & Vernberg, 1985). This movement echoed the significant increase in publications on the subject and spotlighted the construct in the scientific field from the 1970s onward. The multiplicity of disciplinary fields interested in the subject brought about a multitude of concepts, measurement strategies, and ways to analyze social support. Even in this context of conceptual diversity, the relational nature of social support that characterizes it as an essentially network-based phenomenon is always present in its many definitions (Caplan et al., 1975; Cobb, 1976; Wilcox & Vernberg, 1985).

Social support has been central in the field of studies in organizational and work psychology (OWP) and is considered to be a work resource. The many theories dedicated to study resources understand that these are factors (physical, psychological, social, organizational) that perform several functions, such as (1) mitigating the impact that job demands generate on workers; (2) enabling the achievement of goals/performance; (3) enhancing the worker's learning, growth, and development process; (4) protecting existing resources; and (5) facilitating the achievement of other valuable resources (Bakker & Demerouti, 2017). Social support is thus a resource of essentially relational nature that has been inserted into the testing of nomological network of many important constructs in the field, for example,

E. M. B. de Amorim-Ribeiro (✉) · L. F. Martins · R. C. dos S. Cunha
Salgado de Oliveira University, Niterói, RJ, Brazil

L. L. Carneiro
Federal University of Bahia, Salvador, BA, Brazil

M. O. Macambira et al. (eds.), *Assessing Organizational Behaviors*,
https://doi.org/10.1007/978-3-030-81311-6_10

engagement (e.g., Kiema-Junes et al., 2020), satisfaction (e.g., Côté et al., 2021), commitment (e.g., Xi et al., 2020; Gerich & Weber, 2020; Fazio et al., 2017), exhaustion (e.g., Woodhead et al., 2016), well-being (e.g., Kim et al., 2018), career development (e.g., Hou et al., 2019), innovation (e.g., Todt et al., 2018), pro-social voice (e.g., Loi et al., 2014), and organizational citizenship (Kapela & Pohl, 2020).

In studies about social support at work, the prevailing use of measures at the individual level by means of scales reflects the general trend of the science practiced within the scope of organizations and work. Despite the existing theoretical consensus that organizations and the phenomena studied in this and other work contexts are multilevel phenomena, the research designs favor the election of self-report scales that reflect only one of the levels, i.e., the individual level. The association of these traditional instruments with theoretical-methodological paradigms of a multilevel nature, such as social network analysis (SNA), is a promising way to understand the phenomena coming out from interactions, such as social support.

It is intriguing that the first argument put forward by Kozlowski and Klein (2000) about organizations as multilevel systems refers to seminal works and authors, such as Kurt Lewin and Elton Mayo, that attached great relevance to interpersonal relationships at the workplace. Although since the late 1990s authors such as Hall and Wellman (1985) have pointed to the promising use of network analysis in the social support research, this use is still limited, especially when it comes to social support at work.

Social network analysis (SNA) may be considered as a set of theories and strategies of analysis that elect interactions between actors and the structure emerging from these interactions as the core unit of analysis for understanding phenomena. Its potential as a multilevel analysis is anchored in elements such as simultaneity and interdependence between the different levels evaluated, as relations between two or three players are the baseline for groups that, in turn, make up a broader social structure with its own characteristics and dynamics. This very dynamic surrounds players and their groups and determines how resources shall circulate and the paths to access such resources. A mapping of a network, or of the interactions between a set of player, may reveal the nature of resources exchanged, degree of reciprocity, role played by players, and position held by those players in the web of interactions (Freeman, 2011). These characteristics of the SNA unveil its potential contribution to studies on social support and, more specifically, social support at work.

Considering the foregoing, in this chapter we intend to review the challenges related to measuring social support in surveys in the field of work and organizations. For contextualization purposes, we will discuss the conceptual issues surrounding the phenomenon. Next, we will present and discuss the weaknesses of some of the main scales used to measure it. Finally, we will discuss the specific theoretical and methodological contributions of the SNA toward understanding the phenomenon of social support in the work context.

10.2 Social Support at Work: Conceptual Issues and Main Characteristics

Although social support at work is one of the most researched topics in the field of OWP, its conceptualization remains quite unclear. As argued by Jolly et al. (2020), many scholars who include this construct in their research shy away from presenting its definition, maybe on the assumption that everyone knows what social support is. However, regardless how knowledge on the topic may seem intuitive, social support entails a wide variety of nuances. That is why it is essential to clearly define to what scope of the phenomenon the researcher is referring. Such an explicitness would allow studies to be better designed, be grounded on better-founded hypotheses, use assessment instruments more suitable to their objectives, and to have their results interpreted (and discussed in relation to existing findings) with greater certainty.

Some of the social support characteristics are consensual in the OWP literature and are also studied under names such as support at work and organizational support. For example, it is generally accepted that social support is a type of assistance that comes from ongoing or intermittent, direct or indirect links an individual establishes with members of his or her social network (Song et al., 2011). In the work context, social support will therefore broadly refer to resources (of psychological or material nature) that are provided to workers through their social relationships (Jolly et al., 2020). Importantly, social support is not something that provider passes on to recipient but rather something inherent in the process of interpersonal interaction (Gottlieb & Bergen, 2010).

Despite the consensual points about social support, as it is a complex and multifaceted phenomenon to be reviewed from multiple perspectives, its definition should be also operationalized based on its specificities. At least four peculiarities should be considered when working with social support in the work context: its nature/form, its type/content, its source, and its direction. Each of these characteristics may be responsible for important variations in the effects of social support on the variables of interest, whether these are of individual, group, or organizational order. When missing specifications, such variations may go unnoticed or lead to misinterpretations (Jolly et al., 2020).

As for its nature, social support can be either perceived, resulting from the individual's belief or assessment that support exists or is available if needed, or real – identified from observable behaviors that demonstrate mobilization and expression of assistance by the provider (Gottlieb & Bergen, 2010; Jolly et al., 2020). Thus, social support from coworkers can be identified based on the worker's belief (or not) that his or her coworkers help him or her, or can be identified based on the emission of concrete actions by those coworkers, such as helping him or her with work overload or comforting him or her after receiving a negative performance evaluation from a client.

More typically, studies are devoted to investigating perceived social support than actual social support. This may happen because perceived social support mirrors social support behaviors, thus presenting closer and stronger effect in relation to several factors of interest in the field of OWP, such as enhanced personal resources and work motivation and decreased worker's stress (Jolly et al., 2020; Gottlieb & Bergen, 2010).

Regarding source, social support can come both from interpersonal relationships in the workplace (coworkers, subordinates, supervisors, or the organization itself) and from outside that environment (family, community, friends, etc.), and its effects may vary depending on where it comes from. According to a systematic review conducted by Jolly et al. (2020), coworkers, supervisors, and the organization are the most commonly researched sources in the field of OWP, although many studies do not specify the reference source. The neglect of this information may greatly hinder the phenomenon interpretation since social support has different effects depending on who is issuing it. For example, comparatively, data show that supervisors influence workers more than coworkers in terms of work outcomes (such as attitudes and performance) and intrapersonal relationships (such as motivation and stress) (Jolly et al., 2020).

On the source side, it is also interesting to highlight the social support coming from the organization, better known as organizational support. Although the organization is not a person with whom workers can establish a social interaction, it is often personified and seen as a living being that has its own characteristics and drives that guide its intentional actions (Eisenberger et al., 2020). Therefore, organizational support is the result of the employee's perception of to what extent the company that employs him/her values his/her contribution and is concerned with promoting his/her well-being (Eisenberger et al., 2020; Siqueira & Gomide, 2008). This perception is influenced by organizational factors such as performance management practices, work demands and workload, material support offered and promotion, development, and salary practices of the organization (Queiroga et al., 2015; Siqueira & Gomide, 2008).

The type/content of support may also widely vary, with the four most frequently mapped in the organizations and work literature being instrumental, affective/socio-emotional, informational, and evaluative (Jolly et al., 2020). Instrumental support is the most tangible of the four. It is used to designate material resources that help workers deal with a specific demand, as in the case of help provided in the form of lending a faster computer so that the worker can finish his task faster. As for affective or socioemotional support, assistance comes in the form of psychological resources such as care, empathy, and encouragement. It is found, for example, when the worker is having trouble to match personal and work demands and finds in their social network people who listen to them, understand, and comfort them. Informational support, in turn, comprises information that helps the workers to develop their work. For illustration purposes, we may think of a worker who needs to perform a given type of data analysis but does not know some details of the required procedures, having access to the missing information through other people. Finally, evaluative support also encompasses information, but information that works as feedback as constructive criticism specifically aimed at helping the individual to improve his or her performance based on knowledge obtained by expanding their self-assessment.

The type of social support may differentially influence both the consequences for the worker and the quality of social interaction. Jolly et al. (2020) argue, for example, that, while instrumental support is better able to satisfy the worker's need for competence and to help him/her accomplish tasks, affective support tends to promote greater satisfaction of worker's need for relationships and construction of social exchanges that make the interpersonal relationship closer and of higher quality.

Finally, as regards direction, social support may be analyzed both from the receiver's and the provider's point of view. Despite the premise that social support is built on the expectation of reciprocity (Langford et al., 1997), in practice reciprocity is not always materialized. In the context of OWP, studies evaluating the impacts of social support received prevail. There is a still open agenda of research on social support provided and on the reciprocal (or not) support relations existing between individuals who are part of the same interaction network. Generally understood as a variable of positive consequences, social support also involves costs for those who provide it. However, little is known about this topic so far (Jolly et al., 2020).

As we will see later the measures used to assess social support commonly fail to explain each of these four core features that define the phenomenon (nature, type/content, source, and direction). When using analysis of information social network to assess social support at work these characteristics can be easily highlighted, helping the survey to comprise the whole complexity of the construct.

Social support at work encompasses resources (real or perceived) of different types (instrumental, affective, informational, evaluative, etc.) coming from various sources (coworkers, supervisors, subordinates, friends, etc.) established from social relationships, and may have different directions (given, received, or mutual), besides influencing the world of organizations and work at several levels. At the intra-individual level, it helps reduce stress and health impacts arising from work demands and increases well-being, engagement, and commitment to work. At the interpersonal level, it can improve quality of relationships and work climate. At the organizational level, it contributes toward performance improvements and decreased turnover and encourages extra-role collaborations (such as organizational citizenship behaviors). However, research and intervention on this phenomenon aimed to enhance its effects on all these positive consequences necessarily depend on its proper measurement.

10.3 Measures of Social Support at Work

The lack of agreement between measurements used to assess behaviors in the organizational context has important implications in relation to both production and application of knowledge (Munchinsky, 2004). Divergences between results and conclusions from measurement processes may have several origins. Most of these problems tend to result from the lack of care in the very construction of instruments.

Defining proper theoretical grounds and further operationalization of constructs to be measured by means of instruments are an important step in this regard. This, in turn, requires paying attention to several technical features that aim to produce a valid observation mode to record and analyze the phenomena of interest.

Manifestation of some phenomena is conditioned to complex aspects, especially when these are related to dynamic interactions and perceptions about these interactions thus demanding consideration of specific contextual aspects (Morgado et al., 2017). Measuring social support refers to characteristics present in complex phenomena. Especially important, for example, is to understand aspects related to the source of support, nature of support that may be related to a subjective experience or the observation of support behaviors in a given context, among other factors that should be present in the investigation process.

In an integrative literature review, Jolly et al. (2020) point to this measurement-related issue as a relevant component for understanding the phenomenon. Based on a systematic review covering part of this integrative review, those authors support the evidence pointed out by a previous systematic review by Halbesleben (2006) that suggests the presence of important challenges in measuring social support at work. Thus, both publications point out that the instruments for assessing social support lack good coordination with theoretical assumptions in the field. This entails important consequences that range from great diversity of instruments to substantive issues such as disregard of specific aspects present in the dynamics of interactions in which social support behaviors emerge and the subjective perception about them.

In the study conducted by Halbesleben (2006), literature mapping was restricted to surveys that assessed the relationship between social support and burnout, and 39 measures were found for assessing the former variable. Jolly et al. (2020), in turn, with a more comprehensive focus on social support regardless of its relationship with other variables, found 112 instruments in studies published up to 2018. The high number disclosed by both reviews is worth of notice. It unveils a worrying pulverization in literature accompanied by low quality of many of these instruments. Taken together, these findings disclose how advances in the field are still limited and how studies in the area frequently end up replicating problems of theoretical and methodological origin that hinder a broader understanding of the theme.

Considering those peculiarities and the relevance of the debate, this text is based on the database made available as a supplement to the text by Jolly et al. (2020). The database systematically reviewed the scales used in empirical studies published in the last 40 years in peer-reviewed journals that had social support at work as variable of interest. From 1978 to 2018, that database recorded 198 empirical articles reviewed measuring social support at work. Considering that time interval, the authors were able to disclose an overview of the most widely used scales to measure social support at work, as well as those that somehow reflect the universe of main measures of social support adopted by literature in recent decades. Despite the diversity of measures, one third of all production was related to three scales that will be presented below. Generally speaking, these instruments point to a common way of measuring social support at work. Limitations regard the operationalization of the construct and a wide range of versions resulting from adaptations that hinders integrating knowledge in the field and that clearly points out the need for new proposals.

According to Jolly et al. (2020), the most widely used scale in the literature on social support at work was developed by Caplan et al. (1975). The instrument was found in 27 studies, with 7 different adaptations of the original version. The measure, when considered in its integral form and with no adaptations, addresses the perception of social support from three sources: (1) immediate supervisor, (2) other people at work, and (3) friends, spouse, and family members. Each of these sources gave rise to the following items: (a) "how much people at workplace change their routine in order to make your work easier"; (b) "how easy it is to talk to those people"; (c) "how reliable these people are when work becomes difficult"; and, finally, (d) "to what extent these people are willing to listen to your personal problems." The measure reliability evaluated by Cronbach's alpha since its original study and in its different adaptations varied from the lowest alpha plateau equal to 0.73 (Varma et al., 2011) to alpha 0.95 (Sargent & Terry, 2000), indicating good internal consistency of the scale.

However, despite these good indicators of reliability, Caplan et al. (1975) measure clearly fails to capture some of the relevant characteristics to operationalize social support, particularly regarding its nature/form, type/content, source, and direction. A first example is related to how vague such items are by not specifying whether the support identified is related to instrumental or emotional resources, making that source of information to be confused, adding important noise to the assessment. In specific contexts, such as those with complex demands at the workplace, the provision of instrumental support to perform a task, if not accompanied by emotional support, is likely to echo on the health and well-being of the worker, just like the opposite scenario in which emotional support is not accompanied by instrumental support (Moeller & Chung-Yan, 2013).

Likewise, another relevant aspect that remains unclear is whether the perceived willingness to use such resources is being assessed or whether items actually refer to the observed behaviors, considering their frequency or concrete relevance. An additional pertinent aspect pointed out in this review and evidenced by the database analysis with the many applications of this instrument is related to its use as a way to evaluate general social support. This use considers that multiple sources of support when combined would allow measuring general social support at work, either by adding sources specifically related to work such as support from coworkers and supervisor, or as a general source, considering the role of external support to work. This would lead inferences about the phenomenon itself or even inferences about associated phenomena to be damaged by the low specificity of the measure. Although social support from internal and external sources to the workplace may jointly influence variables of interest in the field, it is considered that merging them in a measure based on a global indicator would impoverish information on the phenomena under investigation that could be extracted from the research.

The second most used instrument in the aforementioned literature review was the Survey of Organizational Support (SPOS; Eisenberger et al., 1986). It was originally aimed at assessing organizational support, but was adapted to the interpersonal context, emphasizing perceived aspects of the relationship between coworkers and supervisors. The SPOS was used in 25 studies comprised by the review, and, among these, 13 different versions of this measure were identified, resulting from adaptations that ranged from number of items to more extensive elements such as reformulation of some items. This observation is in consonance with what was identified in relation to Caplan's measure. Moreover, it denotes the existing variability even when a single instrument is considered in the analysis. It is a factor that greatly contributes to the difficulty of comparing social support among different studies, even when analytical interest is within the specific domain of a scale.

Based on this consideration, specifically for this instrument, the most frequent version and the one that better characterizes how most of versions are constructed is that defined as the eight-item short version (Jolly et al., 2020). This version refers to social support based on emotional support, consistent with the theory of organizational support (Eisenberger et al., 1986). An example of a typical item in this version is "My supervisor actually cares about my well-being," and a second one would be "My supervisor is proud of my accomplishments at work." As can be observed, these items are in line with a model that is operationalized based on the social exchange theory focusing on how individuals rule the flow of social support with others (Cropanzano & Mitchell, 2005).

It is worth noting that the full 36-item version captures aspects related to instrumental support, deviating from an emotional support-based approach. That emotional support prevails in the brief eight-item version, as evidenced by the item "My supervisor would meet my request for a change in my working conditions if the request was reasonable." Jolly et al. (2020) point out throughout the review how the application of the different versions of this instrument and consequent interpretation through different theoretical perspectives ends up bringing an additional challenge for understanding the phenomenon. Still, one can identify versions of the instrument with reliability values ranging from 0.93 (Lee & Ashforth, 1993) to 0.81 (Park & Jang, 2017).

The third most reported instrument was the Job Content Questionnaire (JCQ; Karasek et al., 1998), found in 12 studies, with 6 different adaptations. The scale's reliability indicators ranged from its lowest plateau 0.75 (Berkman et al., 2010) to higher levels, reaching 0.89 in the study by Samad et al. (2015). The scale, while also addressing other job characteristics, includes four important facets for measuring social support: two covering socioemotional support (one from coworkers and one from the supervisor) plus two more facets referring to instrumental support (one from coworkers and one from the supervisor). One example item is "My supervisor is worried about me" and another "My coworkers help me." Comparing the JCQ to Caplan's instrument, this scale is clearer regarding the source and type of support. Nonetheless, it is not as clear regarding how this support is expressed. This is something also found in the previous scales and that characterizes a great deal of the instruments for assessing social support. The distinction between perceived availability of support and observed support behaviors is, however, a crucial point, considering aspects related not only to perception but to the dynamics of interactions themselves.

In order to update the findings presented so far, we chose to replicate the strategy of Jolly et al. (2020) for the last 3 years, reviewing the literature published between the years 2018 to 2020 on social support in the context of work, as the specific focus on the instruments designed to measure the phenomenon. The initial search strategy returned 364 analyses that included the term work-related social support. After removing duplicates, 209 were selected that indicated to measure some component related to social support at work. After analysis of all the full texts, 94 instruments were found measuring the referred construct in different ways. The analysis of the three most frequently used instruments showed that they represented more than one third of all the production, totaling 42%. Among these, the most frequently used instrument in literature is the JCQ ($n = 59$) and the least used is the SPOS ($n = 9$), which used to be ranked second in the past. In this update, the Copenhagen Psychosocial Questionnaire (COPSOQ, Kristensen et al., 2005) appears and, although being the most recent of the three, it is now ranked second among the most frequently cited instruments ($n = 19$).

The COPSOQ scale assesses psychosocial risk factors at work and exposure to them. The instrument currently presents three versions developed from an international network, counting with validated versions in several countries around the world (Burr et al., 2019). It was conceptually designed to include the major dimensions predicted to be relevant to psychosocial theories of work (including the Job-Strain, Demand-Control-Support, and Effort-Reward-Imbalance models). Reported reliability indicators ranged from its lowest plateau at 0.70 (San Lin et al., 2018) to higher levels reaching 0.90 (Heinrichs et al., 2019). The full scale includes two facets for assessing social support: one in relation to coworkers' evaluation and one from the immediate superior's. Both scales assess how often the person is listened to or how often they receive assistance from this source. An example item is "How often do you get help and support from your colleagues?" and another would be "How often is your immediate superior willing to listen to your work-related problems?" Like the JCQ, this instrument presents a clearer source regarding support, and part of items seems to pursue a distinction between perceived availability of support and observed supportive behaviors. However, it still fails in making the dynamics of these interactions more evident.

The set of issues identified in measurement practices in the context of social support regarding form/nature, source, type, and direction of social support regards relevant aspects to measurement and for conclusions to be drawn from it. Therefore, it demands a more attentive approach to these aspects in literature. Another noteworthy aspect is the number of adaptations made to instruments, hindering considerations about replication and consistency of results over time. As a way to remedy these problems, Jolly et al. (2020) suggest researchers to always clearly justify the election of a specific measure of social support. To that, they should focus beforehand on how suitable the measure is, looking for the rationale for its use among conceptual rather than just psychometric aspects. Taking this suggestion into account, next we will analyze the contributions of the SNA as an alternative measure for assessing social support at work.

10.4 Social Network Analysis (SNA) to Understand Social Support at Work

This section aims to discuss potential uses of the social network analysis paradigm and tools to understand social support in the work context. General theoretical assertions are presented, and basic readings are indicated for readers to understand the specific measures of SNA. In the following, we describe studies that assess SNA-oriented social support at work. At the end of this section, we consider to what extent mapping workers' interaction networks can contribute to understanding the emergence or absence of social support at work.

A social network is defined as a set of players and the interaction patterns established by them. Social network analysis (SNA) is a scientific paradigm as it encompasses theories, methods, and an empirical corpus oriented toward understanding the dynamics of interaction among actors, the nature of their links, and the social structures constituting these interactions. It emphasizes the processes of players' insertion into associative spheres and how these insertions allow for more or less functional designs in the face of the concrete distribution of resources among different levels of the social fabric. In this light, social behavior is understood as a simultaneous consequence of both the possession of attributes and norms and the individual's involvement in the structure of social relations (Marin & Wellman, 2011).

Field theories define network as a space for the provision of resources that may be split into arrangements capable of preventing those resources from being unequally appropriated. In addition to resource coordination mechanisms, contagion mechanisms imply the idea that players are contaminated through flows moving through links. In the last mechanism proposed, that of adaptation, nodes respond to a contingent of environmental circumstances, such as sharing the same links with other nodes (Borgatti et al., 2018).

Thus, when research is developed in light of the SNA, the implicit premise is that relationships are the unit of analysis. Measures of networks evaluate distances, accesses, or obstacles resulting from how paths between players are set up, redundancies in connections, or gaps in relationships. Assessing how these paths are distributed in the network provides information about "who" players are, i.e., their positions and roles in the network (Scott & Carrington, 2011). Multilevel in nature, the SNA offers a wide range of interdependent measures at the macro-, meso-, and microlevels of the network that can be used to investigate a set of links. Measures at the macro level express characteristics of the broader social structure. Density and overall centralization are commonly used macro measures. The first informs about the ratio of existing links in relation to the possible ones. The second informs about the degree to which there are players centralizing the ratio of links in the network.

The meso-level measures, on the other hand, refer to the metrics of subgroups and can inform, for example, about the degree of cohesion and endogeneity present in these subgroups. Finally, the microlevel metrics inform about how much the player have cited or been cited, how close they are to influential players, or even how much they are bridges between others. To learn more about theoretical assertions and measures in social network analysis, we recommend reading the Handbook of Social Network Analysis, organized by Scott and Carrington (2011).

Research conducted by Zagenczyk et al. (2010) assessed the relationship between workers' informal social network structure and perceptions of organizational support (POS). The main argument of the study is centered on the idea that perceptions of organizational support are not due exclusively to individual evaluations of resources offered by the organization but by the social context. This social context was expressed by the web of interactions of counseling, friendship, and workflows among 183 workers in a medium-sized feed industry. The study associated measures of perceived organizational support with measures of networks, primarily those relating to cohesive subgroups and structural equivalence positions. Results indicated positive associations between counseling (but not friendship) links and similarity in perceived organizational support (POS) (= 0.10, $p < 0.05$); structural equivalence positions of friendship and counseling networks also positively associated with POS (= 0.16, $p < 0.05$). The authors point out the importance of paying attention not only to the consequences of perceptions on organizational support but also to antecedents that influence the process of building these beliefs that within the realm of social processes integrated with psychological ones. As a future agenda, the authors suggest studies that take into account one-way links, emphasize relationships established with emphasis on seeking counseling, and include relationships external to the workplace (friends and family).

Kowalewski and Ruschoff (2019) developed a study in SNA approaching the role of the variables work engagement and exhaustion on the worker's health. Social support, coming from friendship links and interaction with supervisors, is considered not only as a predictor of low levels of exhaustion and higher levels of engagement but mainly as a work resource. Ninety nurses belonging to four teams in a general hospital participated in the study. The links needed to perform the work, named the instrumental network and friendship links setting up the expressive network, were mapped. The Copenhagen Psychosocial Questionnaire, the Utrecht Burnout Scale, and the Utrecht Work Engagement Scale were applied jointly with this mapping. Associations were found between engagement and friend's links. The authors associated this finding with the degree of social support provided by the links. Among those who mentioned many colleagues, association was in the opposite direction. To explain this apparent contradiction, authors interpret it as a structural dependency, associated with the non-reciprocity of the links and an attempt to compensate for low work engagement through expansion of friendship links. The instrumental network showed no association with engagement or burnout data. The pattern of different association between links surveyed draws attention and led authors to question whether instrumental links are part of social support or only the friendship links.

A study on the power of social support for teachers in their first year of professional activity was conducted by Thomas et al. (2019). The choice of the network approach to understand support for beginning teachers is justified because this is an approach that allows for more refined analysis of the phenomenon regarding its presence or absence, frequency, usefulness, and scope of relationships. A total of 446 teachers, mostly women, participated in the study. A questionnaire was applied with information about the career, key factors of retention in the activity, and three types of egocentric support networks, namely, professional, emotional, and social. Data on frequency of interaction and use of support were also collected. The authors used measures of homogeneity (degree of similarity between the participant and others) and homophily (tendency to relate to similar players) regarding experience and gender. In addition, the variables job satisfaction, intrinsic motivation, and self-efficacy were measured using scales. The quality of support relationships evaluated through degree of instrumentality showed positive association with the aforementioned variables, what did not occur with data on frequency of relationships. Among the types of support studied, social support best explained the variability of intrinsic motivation. Social support and professional support better explained job satisfaction, to the detriment of emotional support. The authors conclude by emphasizing how the evidence on the role of social support in teacher retention should encourage interventions at management level oriented to create collaborative spaces among these professionals, making up cohesive teams with long-lasting relationships (Thomas et al., 2019).

A survey conducted by Amorim-Ribeiro et al. (in press) evaluated the role of informal social networks in the well-being of workers in organizations undergoing change. The study included 151 professionals belonging to a road transportation holding company. These professionals answered the scale of well-being at work and the network mapping questionnaire, generated based on the instruction: name the coworkers (including managers) with whom you get in touch to find out information about change. This consignment characterizes the establishment of a link in search of informational support, in this case, the information about the change. In the study, explanatory models were tested for each of the three factors that make up well-being at work: fulfillment, positive affect, and negative affect.

Results indicated that increase in well-being at work was associated with proximity of central players (eigenvector centrality), that is, those workers connected to coworkers who provide the most support through the sharing of information about change. Furthermore, being part of a subgroup with high degree of cohesion, indicated by the clustering coefficient, could predict the increase of the fulfillment factor in the network. For the network mapped, a cohesive subgroup represents high reciprocity in information exchanges, i.e., players belonging to this cohesive group provide and receive support in similar proportions.

The results expressed in this study regarding support-providing workers are noteworthy. The need to expand information about provision of social support is an important gap pointed out in the literature of the area (Jolly et al., 2020). The study indicated reduced well-being at work for players who bridged two subgroups. In the context of the study on seeking information in organizational change processes, bridging is likely to have implied high burden associated not only with the frequency of information seeking, but with managing ambivalent attitudes and beliefs in the face of change.

Another example of a study using SNA evaluated the role of social support as a protective factor against the occurrence of vicarious trauma in professionals assisting victims of sexual violence (Cunha, 2021). The survey was a case study of the interpersonal and inter-institutional networks established by a psychologist (Network A) and a social worker (Network B) as a function of their work with victims of sexual violence. Participants were chosen according to the degree of vicarious trauma presented among 20 professionals, with the psychologist presenting the lowest level and the social worker the highest. Vicarious trauma refers to unfavorable consequences to the health of professionals resulting from empathic listening to victims of violence (McCann & Pearlman, 1990). Mapping employed the tone of an interview, and professionals could mention any person (friends, coworkers, family members, etc.) or organization with which they had contact by virtue of their professional activity or content. For each interaction established, it was assigned the degree of contribution of that relationship toward solving the case and the quality of that relationship. Free comments and evaluations on reasons associated with the degree of contribution and quality of the relationship were encouraged. The type of network mapped was egocentric, as each professional identified the relationships established by them and characterized how players mentioned by them relate to each other.

The networks mapped by Cunha (2021) considerably differed in most of the indicators present at the three levels of analysis, as well as in the quality, nature, and dynamics of the relationships expressed in the reports that accompanied the mapping. Although similar in size, network A (associated with less vicarious trauma) had almost twice the density of network B (38% and 22%, respectively), as well as lower overall degree centralization (68% and 88%). At the meso-level, for example, network A shows integration between players belonging to different network niches (family, friendship, work, and self-care) and players who overlap these roles by being both coworkers and friends. A friend and coworker obtained high degree of betweeness centrality, which is related to lower degree of general centralization of network A and may indicate greater division of "load" in daily work, as it is a relationship that materializes both affective and technical support. In Network B, no relationships were found between subgroups, not even players playing friendship roles. The quality and contribution of the relationships present in network A were substantially better against those of network B, besides associating formal and informal contacts in counterpoint to the predominance of formal contacts in network B. It is also worth mentioning the variety of institutional relationships present in network A, and the quality of relationship with management and the team, reported as sources of technical and affective support.

The studies described aimed to understand social support at work based on the links established between workers. By electing links as the central unit of analysis, they recognize theoretically and empirically the inherent imbrication between the micro (player)-, meso (subgroups)-, and macro (general network)-levels. Moreover, they offer a wide range of options for the use of SNA in research on social support at work. Workers from several contexts have answered questions yielding networks of friendship or expressive, counseling, information, instrumental, and emotional, professional, and social support. Among the measures employed at the different levels there are: 1) density, size, and overall network centralization - macro-structural level; 2) structural equivalence; homogeneity; and homophily - meso level; and 3) degree centrality, betweenness centrality, and eigenvector centrality - micro level. As for the type of network mapped, both complete networks and egocentric networks were used. In general, we can say that the studies bring evidence that, beyond the contact with place that provide support, the place they occupy in the network and how they relate to each other may potentialize the emergence and constant offering of social support.

10.5 Contributions of SNA in the Understanding and Measurement of Social Support

The reflection on the existing measures of social support at work and the possible contributions of social network analysis in understanding the phenomenon slides toward reflections on the nature of the construct. Social support at work is usually defined as beliefs regarding the social support perceived by the worker at the workplace. There seems to be a common tendency in the area of organizational behavior to circumscribe the definition and operationalization of the construct to the possibilities of measuring it at the individual level. The very emphasis on perceived social support as the core of the investigation on social support at work may be overlapping with what is available both in terms of instruments and feasible research designs in terms of time and access to the field. In this sense, is social support the belief that social support exists, or what we are able to measure are the beliefs regarding access to that support?

As an essentially relational phenomenon, we can think that analyses at the level of the individual inform about beliefs related to social support. In this sense, and only in this sense, can we think of it as a phenomenon of psychological nature. It is unquestionable the relevance of studying the beliefs that individuals build about social support, conforming the perceived social support and its measurement at the microlevel. However, part of the existing limitations in the studies of this theme can be overcome with relational theoretical premises and measures compatible with these premises.

At first, we can think of network as the place, the space in which social support can be manifested. However, considering our tendency toward reasoning in the light of the individual or of the other with whom they relate, we need to make an effort to understand that support is either present or absent in the interaction between players. In addition to being the place where social support manifests itself, it is also in this structure arising from the network of relationships that the individual's beliefs about having or not social support at work are built, maintained, or extinguished. Far from putting an end to this complex range of issues concerning the nature, origin, and maintenance of social support at work, these reflections suggest to what extent we should consider them and cope not only with methodological but also with conceptual challenges inherent to the phenomenon of social support at work.

After unveiling these hard issues, the studies on social support anchored on the social network analysis approach bring contributions that can help to overcome problems and fill gaps related to this theme pointed out by the literature. In general, studies on social support at work anchored in the SNA contribute to understanding the phenomenon by showing how given interaction patterns can favor the emergence of social support.

Considering some limitations imposed by the use of social support scales, mapping networks allows identifying the direction of relationships, makes clear the sources of support, and qualifies the support as to its intensity. For example, regarding direction, the SNA allows researchers to identify the direction of relationships, making explicit in what social interactions support is given, received, or mutually exchanged. Likewise, in line with direction, the source of social support becomes clear, and it is possible to identify whether the player-provider plays a role of coworker, supervisor, subordinate, or even friend or family member. It is worth noting that there is no standard network mapping. While there is potential for gathering and reviewing the aforementioned elements, the researcher's outlines and strategies may vary, even limiting the potential volume of information and degree of potential data coordination.

Given the multitude of strategies for mapping interactions, we believe that some of these may offer more powerful data regarding the power of understanding the dynamics of social support. For example, considering the options of mapping a specific type of support or the relationships established in a broad way as a function of work, we believe the second option ensures the assessment of balance of forces of relationships that express social support jointly with non-supportive relationships. In addition to this, the comprehensiveness of the term for relations inside and outside the workplace, as well as intra- and inter-institutional relations, although making the analysis complex, comes closer to the worker's everyday dynamics. This follows a trend of studies in the scope of organizational behavior that reduces the dichotomy between the spheres through which workers move, considering their full life space.

A focus of analysis yet to be explored in the light of social support and its interfaces with organizational support is related to the nature of links in terms of their degree of formality. Future studies should explore aspects concerning the level of organizational support and social support underlying it, through experiments comparing the prescribed formal network and the informal social network. Objective similarities and discrepancies between these (measured by macro-, meso-, and micro-metrics) along with explanatory narratives elaborated by the network players themselves may contribute to understanding processes of formation, consolidation, and alteration of beliefs regarding organizational support. Besides that, efforts in this sense would enable a diagnostic look to design interventions to build a structure of relationships at work more favorable to the emergence of social support.

The selection of the type of network to be mapped, whether complete networks or egocentric ones, also poses questions to explore about perceived and "real" social support. Complete network is built based on the quotes from a group of players delimited by a well-defined criterion (a specific team or department, or even everyone in an organization). If link directions are considered, one can identify non-reciprocal links suggesting difference in the expectations of exchanges between two players. It could be an indication of a search for support that is not mutual or not reciprocated. Is this type of mapping closer to the status of identifying "real" social support? Or put another way, would non-reciprocal links indicate discrepant beliefs from what "really" happens in the dynamics of relationships? Or are these not discrepancies but indicative of a possible dynamic of relationships in which some people are support-seeking and others are support-providing? This debate can also be coupled with other hypotheses concerning the position of players as central providers, such as whether the presence of too many non-reciprocal relationships is responsible for states of attrition and overload.

The egocentric networks formed by the respondent, their direct connections, and, in turn, how they perceive relationships between the players they mentioned can be considered a perceived network. However, this is not to be confused with perceived social support measured by self-report instruments, because the interpretation about the degree of social support present in the egocentric network depends on the overall structure of interactions, the roles and positions occupied by the players. This is likely to point to the fact that the discussion on real and perceived support may be less relevant when support is located in the flow of relationships rather than on the individuals involved in such relationships.

The set of hypotheses and discussions raised here should be argued over time through a larger contingent of studies on social support at work, under the viewpoint of social network analysis. We believe that the increase of studies with longitudinal designs will favor the empirical testing of measurement concepts in social support. The effort to distinguish network-based antecedents of social support and to compare its effects with other phenomena is a necessary step in the understanding of this phenomenon.

References

Amorim-Ribeiro, E. M. B., Neiva, E. R., Macambira, M. O., & Martis, L. (in press). Bem-estar no trabalho em processos de mudança organizacional: o papel das redes sociais informais. *Revista de Administração Mackenzie, 23*(1), 1–26. https://doi.org/10.1590/1678-6971/eRAMG220125

Bakker, A. B., & Demerouti, E. (2017). Job demands-resources theory: Taking stock and looking forward. *Journal of Occupational Health Psychology, 22*(3), 273–285. https://doi.org/10.1037/ocp0000056

Berkman, L. F., Buxton, O., Ertel, K., & Okechukwu, C. (2010). Managers' practices related to work–family balance predict employee cardiovascular risk and sleep duration in extended care settings. *Journal of Occupational Health Psychology, 15*(3), 316. https://doi.org/10.1037/a0019721

Borgatti, S. P., Everett, M. G., & Johnson, J. C. (2018). *Analyzing social networks*. Sage.

Burr, H., Berthelsen, H., Moncada, S., Nübling, M., Dupret, E., Demiral, Y., … Pohrt, A. (2019). The third version of the Copenhagen Psychosocial Questionnaire. *Safety and Health at Work, 10*(4), 482–503. https://doi.org/10.1016/j.shaw.2019.10.002

Caplan, R. D., Cobb, S., French, J. R., Harrison, R. U., & Pinneau, S. R. (1975). *Job demands and work health. U. S. Department of Health, Education, and Welfare Publication No. 75-160*. Institute for Social Research.

Cobb, S. (1976). Social support as a moderator of life stress. *Psychosomatic Medicine, 38*(5), 300–314. https://doi.org/10.1097/00006842-197609000-00003

Côté, K., Lauzier, M., & Stinglhamber, F. (2021). The relationship between presenteeism and job satisfaction: A mediated moderation model using work engagement and perceived organizational support. *European Management Journal, 39*(2), 270–278. https://doi.org/10.1016/j.emj.2020.09.001

Cropanzano, R., & Mitchell, M. S. (2005). Social exchange theory: An interdisciplinary review. *Journal of Management, 31*(6), 874–900. https://doi.org/10.1177/0149206305279602

Cunha, R. C. S. (2021). *Trauma Vicário: o suporte social no trabalho com vítimas de violência sexual*. Dissertação de mestrado, Universidade Salgado de Oliveira, Niterói, RJ, Brasil.

Eisenberger, R., Huntington, R., Hutchison, S., & Sowa, D. (1986). Perceived organizational support. *Journal of Applied Psychology, 71*, 500–507. https://doi.org/10.1037/0021-9010.71.3.500

Eisenberger, R., Rhoades Shanock, L., & Wen, X. (2020). Perceived organizational support: Why caring about employees counts. *Annual Review of Organizational Psychology and Organizational Behavior, 7*, 101–124. https://doi.org/10.1146/annurev-orgpsych-012119-044917

Fazio, J., Gong, B., Sims, R., & Yurova, Y. (2017). The role of affective commitment in the relationship between social support and turnover intention. *Management Decision, 55*(33), 512–525. https://doi.org/10.1108/MD-05-2016-0338

Freeman, L. C. (2011). The development of social network analysis–with an emphasis on recent events. In J. Scott & P. J. Carrington, (Eds.). *The sage handbook of social network analysis* (pp. 40–54). Sage Publications.

Gerich, J., & Weber, C. (2020). The ambivalent appraisal of job demands and the moderating role of job control and social support for burnout and job satisfaction. *Social Indicators Research, 148*(1), 251–280. https://doi.org/10.1007/s11205-019-02195-9

Gottlieb, B. H., & Bergen, A. E. (2010). Social support concepts and measures. *Journal of Psychosomatic Research, 69*(5), 511–520. https://doi.org/10.1016/j.jpsychores.2009.10.001

Halbesleben, J. R. B. (2006). Sources of social support and burnout: A meta-analytic test of the conservation of resources model. *Journal of Applied Psychology, 91*(5), 1134–1145. https://doi.org/10.1037/0021-9010.91.5.1134

Hall, A., & Wellman, B. (1985). Social networks and social support. In S. Cohen & S. L. Syme (Eds.), *Social support and health* (pp. 23–41). Academic Press.

Heinrichs, K., Hummel, S., Gholami, J., Schultz, K., Li, J., Sheikh, A., & Loerbroks, A. (2019). Psychosocial working conditions, asthma self-management at work and asthma morbidity: A cross-sectional study. *Clinical and Translational Allergy, 9*(1), 25.

Hou, C., Wu, Y., & Liu, Z. (2019). Career decision-making self-efficacy mediates the effect of social support on career adaptability: A longitudinal study. *Social Behavior and Personality: An International Journal, 47*(5), 1–13.

Jolly, P. M., Kong, D. T., & Kim, K. Y. (2020). Social support at work: An integrative review. *Journal of Organizational Behavior, 42*(2), 1–23. https://doi.org/10.1002/job.2485

Kapela, D. T., & Pohl, S. (2020). Organizational support, leader membership exchange and social support as predictors of commitment and organizational citizenship behaviour: Poverty as moderator. *Pratiques Psychologiques, 26*(1), 19–30.

Karasek, R., Brisson, C., Kawakami, N., Houtman, I., Bongers, P., & Amick, B. (1998). The Job Content Questionnaire (JCQ): An instrument for internationally comparative assessments of psychosocial job characteristics. *Journal of Occupational Health Psychology, 3*(4), 322–355. https://doi.org/10.1037/1076-8998.3.4.322

Kiema-Junes, H., Saarinen, A., Muukkonen, H., Väyrynen, S., Ala-Mursula, L., & Hintsanen, M. (2020). Dimensions of social support in the experience of work engagement in middle age: A Northern Finland Birth Cohort 1966 Study. *Scandinavian Journal of Psychology, 61*, 679–689. https://doi.org/10.1111/sjop.12640

Kim, D., Moon, C. W., & Shin, J. (2018). Linkages between empowering leadership and subjective well-being and work performance via perceived organizational and co-worker support. *Leadership & Organization Development Journal, 39*(7), 844–858. https://doi.org/10.1108/LODJ-06-2017-0173

Kowalewski, T., & Ruschoff, B. (2019). Engagement and exhaustion in healthcare: A network approach. *Career Development International, 24*(4), 383–394. https://doi.org/10.1108/CDI-01-2019-0021

Kozlowski, S. W. J., & Klein, K. J. (2000). A multilevel approach to theory and research in organizations: Contextual, temporal, and emergent processes. In K. J. Klein & S. W. J. Kozlowski (Eds.), *Multilevel theory, research and methods in organizations: Foundations, extensions, and new directions* (pp. 3–90). Jossey-Bass.

Kristensen, T. S., Hannerz, H., Høgh, A., & Borg, V. (2005). The Copenhagen Psychosocial Questionnaire – a tool for the assessment and improvement of the psychosocial work environment. *Scandinavian Journal of Work, Environment & Health, 31*(6), 438–449.

Langford, C. P. H., Bowsher, J., Maloney, J. P., & Lillis, P. P. (1997). Social support: A conceptual analysis. *Journal of Advanced Nursing, 25*(1), 95–100. https://doi.org/10.1046/j.1365-2648.1997.1997025095.x

Lee, R. T., & Ashforth, B. E. (1993). A further examination of managerial burnout: Toward an integrated model. *Journal of Organizational Behavior, 14*(1), 3–20.

Loi, R., Ao, O. K. Y., & Xu, A. J. (2014). Perceived organizational support and coworker support as antecedents of foreign workers' voice and psychological stress. *International Journal of Hospitality Management, 36*, 23–30. https://doi.org/10.1016/j.ijhm.2013.08.001

McCann, I. L., & Pearlman, L. A. (1990). Vicarious traumatization: A framework for understanding the psychological effects of working with victims. *Journal of Traumatic Stress, 3*(1), 131–149. https://doi.org/10.1007/BF00975140

Marin, A., & Wellman, B. (2011). Social network analysis: An introduction. *The SAGE handbook of social network analysis*, 11, 25.

Moeller, C., & Chung-Yan, G. A. (2013). Effects of social support on professors' work stress. *International Journal of Educational Management, 27*(3), 188–202. https://doi.org/10.1108/09513541311306431

Morgado, F. F., Meireles, J. F., Neves, C. M., Amaral, A., & Ferreira, M. E. (2017). Scale development: Ten main limitations and recommendations to improve future research practices. *Psicologia: Reflexão e Crítica, 30*(3), 1–20. https://doi.org/10.1186/s41155-016-0057-1

Munchinsky, P. M. (2004). When the psychometrics of test development meets organizational realities: A conceptual framework for organizational change, examples, and recommendations. *Personnel Psychology, 57*(1), 175–209.

Park, R., & Jang, S. J. (2017). Mediating role of perceived supervisor support in the relationship between job autonomy and mental health: Moderating role of value–means fit. *The International Journal of Human Resource Management, 28*(5), 703–723.

Queiroga, F., Brandão, H. P., & Borges-Andrade, J. E. (2015). Escala de percepção de suporte organizacional – versão reduzida. In K. Puente-Palacios, A. A. Peixoto, & (Orgs.) (Eds.), *Ferramentas de Diagnóstico para Organizações e Trabalho: Um Olhar a Partir da Psicologia* (pp. 272–283). Artmed.

Samad, A., Reaburn, P., & Di Milia, L. (2015). The contribution of job strain, social support and working hours in explaining work–family conflict. *Asia Pacific Journal of Human Resources, 53*(3), 281–295.

San Lin, K., Zaw, T., Oo, W. M., & Soe, P. P. (2018). Burnout among house officers in Myanmar: A cross-sectional study. *Annals of Medicine and Surgery, 33*, 7–12.

Sargent, L. D., & Terry, D. J. (2000). The moderating role of social support in Karasek's job strain model. *Work & Stress, 14*(3), 245–261.

Scott, J., & Carrington, P. J. (2011). *The SAGE handbook of social network analysis*. SAGE Publications.

Siqueira, M. M. M., & Gomide, S. (2008). Suporte no Trabalho. In M. M. M. Siqueira & (Org.) (Eds.), *Medidas de Comportamento Organizacional: Ferramentas de Diagnóstico e de Gestão* (pp. 283–286). Artmed.

Song, L., Son, J., & Lin, N. (2011). Social Support. In J. Scott & P. J. Carrington (Eds.), *The SAGE handbook of social network analysis* (pp. 116–128). SAGE Publications Ltd..

Thomas, L., Tuytens, M., Moolenaar, N., Devos, G., Kelchtermans, G., & Vanderlinde, R. (2019). Teachers' first year in the profession: The power of high-quality support. *Teachers and Teaching, 25*(2), 160–188.

Todt, G., Weiss, M., & Hoegl, M. (2018). Mitigating negative side effects of innovation project terminations: The role of resilience and social support. *Journal of Product Innovation Management, 35*(4), 518–542.

Varma, A., Pichler, S., & Budhwar, P. (2011). The relationship between expatriate job level and host country national categorization: An investigation in the UK. *International Journal of Human Resource Management, 22*(1), 103–120.

Wilcox, B. L., & Vernberg, E. M. (1985). Conceptual and theoretical dilemmas facing social support research. In *Social support: Theory, research and applications* (pp. 3–20). Springer.

Woodhead, E. L., Northrop, L., & Edelstein, B. (2016). Stress, social support, and burnout among long-term care nursing staff. *Journal of Applied Gerontology, 35*(1), 84–105. https://doi.org/10.1177/0733464814542465

Xi, Y., Xu, Y., & Wang, Y. (2020). Too-much-of-a-good-thing effect of external resource investment—A study on the moderating effect of psychological capital on the contribution of social support to work engagement. *International Journal of Environmental Research and Public Health, 17*(2), 437.

Zagenczyk, T. J., Scott, K. D., Gibney, R., Murrell, A. J., & Thatcher, J. B. (2010). Social influence and perceived organizational support: A social networks analysis. *Organizational Behavior and Human Decision Processes, 111*(2), 127–138.

Chapter 11
Organizational Effectiveness: A Critical Review of the Proposals for Conceptualization and Measurement of the Construct

Sinésio Gomide Júnior, Diogo Freitas Pereira Gomes, Susiley Correa Costa, and Áurea de Fátima Oliveira

11.1 Introduction

One of the main challenges of contemporary people management is the management of human performance. The word performance is used in everyday language in diverse situations, such as in educational or sport institutions; however, it is perhaps more common to hear it in the organizational context (Gomes, 2020). In general, human performance in corporate environments is defined as the skills and knowledge applied in the work environment during the implementation of a task, as well as the commitment determined by the employee to behave efficiently, contributing to the achievement of organizational results through a conscious purpose or prior motivation (Bensassoli & Malvessi, 2013). For this reason, studies on job performance and the variables related to the construct have been developed for decades. The large number of publications on performance is certainly related to its importance within organizations that need the good performance of individuals to achieve their goals, to deliver products and services, and to gain a competitive advantage.

While human performance in organizations has received great attention in publications, notably those dealing with organizational behavior, the space dedicated to the performance of the organizations themselves is more limited. Conceptualized by organizational effectiveness, the global performance of corporations is traditionally associated with the degree to which an organization "achieves its goals": an accomplishment that was one of the organizational effectiveness criteria most widely used by researchers (Gomide Jr. and Fernandes (2008)). This proposition considered the organization to be effective as long as it fulfills its proposed objectives. However,

S. Gomide Júnior (✉) · D. F. P. Gomes · S. C. Costa · Á. de F. Oliveira
Federal University of Uberlândia, Uberlândia, MG, Brazil
e-mail: aurea.oliveira@ufu.br

M. O. Macambira et al. (eds.), *Assessing Organizational Behaviors*,
https://doi.org/10.1007/978-3-030-81311-6_11

with the emergence of systems theory, organizational effectiveness took on a new focus: organizations came to be seen as open systems in which effectiveness and the environment would be interconnected, that is, an organization would be effective if it were able to obtain the necessary resources from the external environment to carry out its activities and services (Harrison, 1994).

The literature has shown that organizational effectiveness is a complex construct, related to different domains of organizational activities, and that it involves multiple approaches or models. This variety of approaches and the lack of integration between theories seem to be due to the fact that the criteria that define organizational effectiveness are the result of individual values and preferences (value judgments) or the fact that individuals evaluate effectiveness with the criteria that are available or easily identifiable by them.

From the 1980s, these various criteria of organizational effectiveness were brought together in different models or approaches, in an attempt to promote a greater integration of the literature on the construct (Jaffe, 1995; Nascimento and Gomide Jr., 2011) and favor its management (Gerasimov & Gerasimov, 2015). One of the most accepted models covers three groups of criteria or dimensions. The first is understood as the ability of the organization to achieve production goals in a given period of time, in terms of the proposed quantity and quality. The second refers to the internal state of the system, which concerns the organization's internal processes – costs of production or services, human results, consensus and conflict, workflow and information, interpersonal relationships, and employee participation in decisions and adjustments – that facilitate the achievement of production goals. Finally, there is the group of dimensions that deal with the adaptation and positioning of resources that would indicate the organization's ability to strategically manage its elements (material and human) in order to adapt to the demands of the external environment. This last group includes criteria related to legitimacy, competitiveness and strategic position, impact on the environment, adaptation, and innovation.

With regard to the issue of measuring organizational effectiveness, international studies have focused on two aspects. In the first, the instruments were guided by the grouping of four dimensions of effectiveness: social, economic, systemic, and political (Cameron, 1986). The social dimension comprised the value of an organization's human resources and encompassed four criteria: morale, income, development, and the mobilization of employees. The economic dimension referred to the notion of productivity and was expressed by the relationship between quality and quantity of production and the resources used to achieve it, encompassing the criteria of internal economy and productivity. The systemic dimension reflected the degree of stability and growth of the organization, with the financial performance criteria being the most used. The political dimension, in turn, concerned the reputation of the organization and the relationships it maintains with groups of investors, partners, customers, and regulatory bodies in order to guarantee their support. The second aspect suggested that effectiveness was a construct consisting basically of three dimensions: socio-technical orientation, market orientation, and economic-financial or competitive orientation. The first dimension corresponded to the management and economic and social viability of the organizational system. The second dimension focused on product quality and external customer satisfaction. Finally, the third dimension was associated with the competitiveness of the organizational system, focusing on maintaining and acquiring market advantage.

In Brazil, the measures were also preferably guided by two aspects. In the first, the concept of organizational health was explored (Gomide Jr., Moura, Cunha, & Sousa, 1999). In this aspect, the measures were composed of two dimensions: organizational policies to promote worker health and the organization's capacity to manage all its internal components, to adapt, develop, and present a favorable external image, maximizing its positive impacts on the market. The second aspect explored the classic effectiveness models and was guided by two dimensions: the organization's ability to achieve production goals in a given period of time, in terms of the proposed quantity and quality, and its capacity for human and strategic planning (Gomide Jr. & Fernandes, 2008).

Accordingly, this chapter aims to examine international and Brazilian literature on the theoretical/conceptual development and empirical investigations related to the organizational effectiveness construct, also focusing on measurement models. To achieve this, the chapter is structured in four sections. The first discusses the concept of human performance and its relationship with organizational performance. In this section, a historical retrospective on the concept of effectiveness is discussed. The second section discusses the evolution of the concept of effectiveness that started in the 1970s and continues today. The following sections present the instruments for measuring effectiveness found in Brazilian and international literature and a critical analysis of them.

11.2 Human Performance and Organizational Performance: Historical Retrospective of the Effectiveness Concept

The contemporary corporate environment presents new challenges, leading organizations to seek ways to deal with the growing competitiveness, with their survival depending on achieving performance above the market average, this being one of the main challenges of contemporary corporate management (Gomes, 2020). Organizations, when concerned with the achievement of organizational goals, consider the performance of individuals as a basis for management decisions for reward/punishment procedures and alignment of employee-organization expectations, in obtaining the desired organizational results (Vaz, 2013). The performance of an organization is consolidated through the results achieved by it, in a certain period of time, where the evaluation occurs through quantifiable criteria (called indicators), the functions of which would indicate a desirable stage of development for the company. The actions of people at work contribute to the generation of results, which collaborate for the organization to achieve certain objectives and, then, generate value (Bensassoli & Malvessi, 2013). From this perspective, the authors define job

Performance ▼	❖ Behavior or actions guided by the intention of transforming reality. ❖ Focus on the process of performance production.
Results ▼	❖ Consequences of the behavior or actions. ❖ Changes caused in the environment, things or people.
Efficiency ▼	❖ Evaluation of performance results based on certain standards or criteria.
Productivity ■	❖ Ratio between the efficiency and the costs of the inputs used in the process of generating results (effectiveness). ❖ Relationship between what is produced as a result (outputs) and everything that is used in the production process (inputs).

Fig. 11.1 Conceptual distinctions between performance, results, efficiency, and productivity. (Elaborated by the authors based on Bensassoli and Malvessi (2013))

performance as "behaviors or actions that are relevant to the organization's objectives and that can be measured in terms of the level of proficiency (or contribution to the objectives) that is represented by a particular action or set of actions." The authors emphasize that, when defining performance, it is important to differentiate it from other concepts such as results, efficiency, and productivity (Fig. 11.1).

Bensassoli and Malvessi (2013) stated that the result is a concept different from performance, this being defined as states or conditions of people or things that are changed through performance and, consequently, collaborate or not to achieve the institutional objectives. In other words, the results are products of the performance. Unlike performance, which is regulated by psychosocial, cognitive, and affective aspects, the result is influenced by broader factors, such as fluctuations in input supply, consumer demand, economic crisis, and technological innovations. Efficiency refers to the evaluation of the performance result, based on and determined by the standards and criteria by which the results will be evaluated (e.g., production time, quality of services, and number of errors or defects). As with the result, efficiency is also influenced by other factors that are often beyond the individual's control.

Finally, according to Bensassoli and Malvessi (2013), productivity refers to the relationship between what is produced as a result and everything that enters the production process as an input, being the efficiency ratio and the costs of the inputs used in the generation of results process.

Organizations, sensitive to numerous pressures, seek criteria that guide the interventions necessary to achieve the desired objectives, seeking the best results. Therefore, obtaining valid indicators for measuring the achievement of objectives would seem simple if there were no other implications in the conceptual history of organizational effectiveness.

According to Gomide Jr., Fernandes, and Moraes (2008), when setting parameters of effectiveness for an organization, issues such as values, decision-making processes, and normal operations would be criteria commonly used in its conceptual definition. Also according to the authors, organizational effectiveness is a complex concept within the theory of organizations and includes a myriad of approaches.

In 1948, Selznick published one of the first studies on the criteria used in the conceptualization of organizational effectiveness, based on economic-financial indicators, such as the human quality of the organization and its adaptation to the environment. The basis of the proposal was the relationship between human behavior and a presumably fixed system of needs (economic organization/results) that would be considered to have basic needs, related to their subsistence. The organization, by developing means of self-defense for survival, would be effective. Effectiveness would then be defined as the daily defense in achieving this survival (Selznick, 1948). There would be five criteria of effectiveness: the security of the organization as a whole in relation to the social forces of its environment, the stability of lines of authority and communication, the stability of informal relations within the organization, the continuity of the policy and its sources, and, finally, homogeneity in the internal vision regarding the meaning and role of the organization (economic and human).

Parsons (1956) conceptualized effectiveness, based on the reasoning that organizations differ in relation to the scope of their strategies and that they can be differentiated analytically in terms of goal orientation.

Georgopoulos and Tannembaum, in 1957, reported the existence of a general tendency in the literature to accept productivity, profitability, the extent to which the organization performs its various missions, the success of the organization in maintaining or expanding, and, to a lesser extent, morale, commitment to the organization, staff turnover, absenteeism, and member satisfaction as criteria of organizational effectiveness. Some criteria of effectiveness were, however, criticized for not referring to the nature of the system itself, that is, they were the result or products of the organizational system. In order to circumvent these criticisms, Georgopoulos and Tannenbaum (1957) proposed the definition of organizational effectiveness with a focus on the path that the organization should follow in order to achieve these objectives.

The authors covered the concept of organizational effectiveness of (1) productivity, (2) internal organizational tension (verified in the incidence of tension and conflict between subgroups of the organization), and (3) organizational flexibility, defined as the ability to adjust to external or internal changes. That is, considering the organization as a social system, the authors defined organizational effectiveness as the extent to which an organization achieves its results without exhausting its means and resources or generating tension among the participating groups.

In 1958, Likert proposed the "multiple objective criterion" based on the hypothesis that organizations have more than one objective and the interaction of these objectives will produce a different scheme of values in different organizations, which would define effectiveness. The author stated that few organizations obtained a measure that would reflect the quality and capacity of their human resources. This was due to the *shadow* of traditional theory, which tended to neglect the human variables and motivation, and to the progress, at that time, of social science, regarding measures of this type.

In the 1960s, the concept of organizational effectiveness was conceived, primarily, through dependence on resources. Burns and Stalker (1961) define it as the level of adaptation of the organization to the environment and the comparison of the results obtained with the objectives set by the organization. Seashore (1962) does this by defining an effective organization as one that aims to store, transform, manipulate, and interpret information. Effectiveness would then be the achievement of goals or progress toward achieving those goals.

Argyris (1964), in turn, states that effectiveness is based on the problem of integration between the individual and the organization, when both must think about profit and seek balance that provides satisfaction in their relationships. The organization, therefore, would focus on three core activities to achieve its effectiveness: the organization manages to (1) achieve its internal objectives, (2) maintain its internal system, and (3) adapt to its external environment. Relating the three principles, the author states that organizations increase their effectiveness by constantly performing these three core activities, increasing their level of involvement with the environment and decreasing energy inputs.

Schein, in 1965, sought a definition of organizational effectiveness in terms of criteria at the systemic level due to the numerous organizational objectives and the unpredictability of the environment in which the organization is inserted. He then proposed that organizational effectiveness would be the organization's ability to survive, adapt, maintain, and grow, regardless of the particular functions performed.

For Schein (1965), the term effectiveness refers to the speed in reaching the organizational objectives, which, like any human system, would be varied. Progress toward objectives can be measured, and this measure has generally been defined as organizational effectiveness, understood from the identification of the objectives measured by the variations in the means used to arrive at the final results of the organization. The author (Schein, 1965) states that two factors undermined these evaluation criteria: (1) the fact that rational organizations behave in ways that seem inefficient if the sole and exclusive criterion is to increase profits or productivity and (2) real organizations have multiple functions and varied objectives and some of these objectives may come into conflict with each other. The attempt to resolve this dilemma was to define organizational effectiveness in terms of criteria at the systemic level, recognizing that each system has numerous functions and objectives and that it exists within an environment that provides unpredictable inputs. The author expands his definition of organizational effectiveness, conceiving it as the system's capacity to survive, to adapt, and to maintain and grow, regardless of the particular functions it performs.

In 1966, Bennis reported that, in studies on effectiveness, there have been two types of conceptualizations: (1) those that deal with some index of organizational functioning such as profit, cost, productivity rate, or individual production and (2) those related to human resources, such as morale, motivation, mental health, work commitment, rapport, or attitudes toward with the employer or the company.

Organizations differ in relation to their objectives and that these can be differentiated analytically in terms of result orientation. However, according to the author, it is necessary to have the definition of valid criteria to measure the effectiveness of each type of organization to which they refer.

Bennis (1966) also criticized the inadequacies of the previous models of effectiveness that provided static evidence of some production characteristics without clarification about the process through which the organization seeks, adapts, and solves its changing objectives. It would be necessary to simultaneously focus on production, changes, and people (Bennis, 1966).

Another important definition of organizational effectiveness starts from the concept of organization as an open and dynamic system (Katz & Kahn, 1966) dependent on its environment for the absorption of its products or services and for the necessary supply of inputs for its processes and transformations. For the authors (Katz & Kahn, 1966), organizations survive only as long as they are able to maintain the processing of information and energy necessary for their growth. Organizational effectiveness would then be related to the organization's growth and survivability.

The authors considered effectiveness as the extent to which all forms of income for the organization are maximized, which would be determined by a combination of the organization's success and its ability to obtain the inputs it needs under advantageous conditions, increasing its successes as a viable system, seeking its growth and survival (Katz & Kahn, 1966).

In the 1970s, within the perspective of the organization as an open system, some authors focused on subsystems and no longer the exchange with the environment. Goodman and Pennings (1977) stated that the organization is effective if the requirements that make up each subsystem are met; Kanter (1977) defined effectiveness as a "political field," a place where each sector will defend its own criteria as being the most reliable to achieve the results; Steers and Spencer (1977) proposed the adoption of a multidimensional approach where flexibility, productivity, job satisfaction, and profitability would be supported by the optimization of the objectives, by the understanding of the employees' perception of the organization and by the emphasis on human behavior. Fulfilling these criteria, the organization would be effective. Pfeffer and Salancik (1978) proposed that organizations become effective when they have interdependence among the resources and respond to the needs of the groups that control these resources.

In the 1980s, the authors turned their attention to the conceptualization of effectiveness summarized in models that emphasized how to survive, despite the scarcity of resources, also involving the figure of the leader/supervisor. Weick and Daft (1983) stated that organizational effectiveness depends on the ability of managers to interpret and understand indices (messages) provided by workers and the organizational environment in which they perform their tasks, as well as on the acumen to detect and recognize the limits of their actions.

Quinn and Rohrbaugh (1983) proposed four models of measures/criteria for organizational effectiveness: human relations, open system, internal process, and rational goal. The first model of Quinn and Rohrbaugh (1983) is that of human relations (internal focus), directed toward the development of human resources. The second model refers to growth goals, resource acquisition, and external support (open system). The third model proposes information management and communication seeking stability and process control. The final model is the rational goal (external focus), implemented through planning and seeking productivity aiming for the achievement of the organizational objectives.

Cameron (1986) conceptualized organizational effectiveness as productivity and organizational success, recognizing the presence of value judgments for the concept of effectiveness, with the judgments, directly or indirectly, affected by the organization.

Beginning in the 1990s, new authors proposed further investigations regarding the organizational effectiveness construct, although they recognized the difficulty in defining it in a way that is universally accepted, recognized, and used in any type of organization.

Ostroff and Schmitt (1993) highlighted that organizations operate in multiple domains and can perform well only in a limited number of them. This multidimensional view of performance implies that there would be different patterns or configurations of relationships between organizational performance and its determinants. The authors suggested that researchers should seek an internally consistent configuration of organizational attributes relevant to different domains of organizational performance.

Harrison (1994) defined organizational effectiveness as the ability of the organization to achieve production goals, to manage the processes related to the human and material resources available to achieve the production goals and to manage its internal resources in order to adapt to external influences. The author highlighted the following criteria for organizational effectiveness: (a) Production Goals (achievement of objectives, quantity, and quality of results), (b) Internal State of the System (costs of production or services (efficiency), human results (employee satisfaction, motivation, low absenteeism, and turnover), consensus/conflict, information flow, interpersonal relationships, and employee participation), and (c) Adaptation and Positioning of Resources (quantity and quality of resources, legitimacy, competitiveness, impact on the environment, adaptability, innovation, and integration or fit among organizational systems) (Harrison, 1994). The author also emphasized that the Internal State of the System can contribute to the achievement of the organization's objectives, and its criteria can be indicators of a more global state, which he called "organizational health."

Lusthaus et al. (2002) reported that organizational effectiveness can be defined as the extent to which an organization is able to achieve its goals. The authors highlighted the lack of standardized instruments in the literature capable of evaluating effectiveness due to the various definitions and dimensions proposed and that there is no common instrument to evaluate all organizations in a standard way. For this it would be necessary to comprehend the dynamic yet stable strategic objectives of the organization. Lusthaus et al. (2002) stated that an evolution of the conceptualization of effectiveness would be the influence of the external environment on the organization, which directly affects its dynamics of adapting to external or internal changes.

In 2007, organizational effectiveness was defined by Fernandes, Barale, Santos, Costa, and Gomide Jr. as the capacity of organizations to fulfill their mission, achieve their objectives, and adapt to changes in the environment. According to the authors, this definition is consistent with the conceptual models presented by the international literature that propose, as criteria of effectiveness, the analysis of internal procedures (harmony of interpersonal relationships, consensual establishment of production goals, and investments in employee training) and the analysis of organizational impacts on the surrounding environment (quality of production, customer satisfaction, and environmental impact).

The works that followed over the next decade seem to have opted for diversification in the conceptualization of the effectiveness of organizations, sometimes adopting a set of indicators of achievement of objectives as definitions and sometimes multidimensional definitions.

In the first case, Gerasimov and Gerasimov (2015) adopted the concept of "organizational development" as a criterion for effectiveness. According to the authors, an organization would be successful if it responded to the contemporary challenges demanded by market trends. They proposed a model composed of numerous criteria that would make up the notion of development, including the managerial practices, adequate choice of technologies, development of new products, adequate planning of the workforce, and satisfaction of the organizational actors involved. In 2016, Gogan, Artene, Sarca, and Draghici defined organizational performance linked not to macroeconomic policies or financial statements but to technological progress, innovation and quality of human resources, and the influence of investment in knowledge (education and research). The authors argue that organizational performance requires the proper management of knowledge and what they call "intellectual capital"; management aimed at all areas of organizational performance, such as market share. Subramony et al. (2018) postulated that organizational effectiveness is linked, solely, to its final objective (e.g., sales) measured by financial statements that would describe the organizational performance of a given period when compared to previous performances. An organization would be effective when its financial balance was positive.

Shanker, Bhanugopan, van der Heijden, and Farrel are among the authors that adopted a multidimensional definition of effectiveness conceptualizing, in 2017, effectiveness as composed of two dimensions measured through the perception of managers. The first is related to operational performance (customer satisfaction) and the second to market performance (market share). El-Kassar and Singh (2017) considered organizational effectiveness to be composed of three dimensions measured through the perception of the organization's employees: environmental performance (reduction of gas emissions in the environment and decrease in fuel consumption), competitive advantages (quality of the products or services and costs), and organizational performance (increase in market position and increase in production). In turn, Rehman et al. (2019) conceptualized effectiveness as the achievement of organizational objectives in three areas: market share, financial performance, and return (satisfaction) of stakeholders.

The breadth of the conceptualizations of effectiveness has, since the 1960s and 1970s, led to attempts at conceptual unification and, simultaneously, the search for more comprehensive definitions of the construct that would not only involve the financial or market performance of the construct. With the advent of the systemic view of organizations, the proposals that originated conceptualized effectiveness with dimensions related to internal and external aspects of the organizations: the internal being linked to health promotion policies and the training of employees and the external to the organization's ability to adapt to environmental demands and project a positive image in the marketplace. The next section will discuss these attempts.

11.3 Evolution of the Concept of Organizational Effectiveness

Considering the diversity of criteria and definitions of organizational effectiveness, Bennis (1962, 1966), Fordyce and Weil (1971), and Mello (1978) tried to resolve these divergences, through the transposition of the criteria for the development and renewal of open systems.

Bennis (1962) stated that the conceptualization and forms of assessing organizational effectiveness were inadequate and often misleading, since the criteria used would be insensitive to the needs of individuals and would be out of harmony with the needs of the conjuncture of organizations, and that in order to understand the organizational context it would be necessary to consider organizations as adaptable and organic structures that would solve problems, seeking competence, mastery, and aptitude in resolving their conflicts. In an attempt to circumvent the problems listed by him, Bennis (1962) introduced the organizational health concept into the literature, proposing multiple criteria for the organizational effectiveness concept, involving adaptability, sense of identity, ability to test reality, and the integration of people.

The author presented three criteria that served as a basis for the organizational health concept: adaptability that concerns the organization's ability to solve problems and its flexibility (freedom to learn through experience) to change simultaneously with internal and external circumstances, the reality test (when the organization must understand its business and the internal and external environment of its reality, being aware of its main limitations), and the sense of identity, when the organization must know what it is and what it must do, that is, it needs to have a clearly defined identity. Identity can be analyzed in two ways: (1) determining the extent to which the organization's objectives are understood and accepted and (2) determining to what extent the organization is being truly perceived by the employees.

In defining these criteria, Bennis (1962) stated that the basic characteristics of a healthy organization are supported by the appropriate methods to solve problems. The problem-solving process involves the organization's ability to assimilate and communicate information in a reliable and valid manner; internal flexibility and creativity to effect the changes that are imposed by the environment; integration of the numerous objectives of the organization and commitment to them; willingness to change when necessary; internal climate of support and absence of threats, the ability to continuously redesign its structure so that it is consistent with its objectives and tasks; and, finally, the integration of people into the organization, understood as an integration in the sense that the parties do not function with cross-purposes, but interdependently.

Some authors in the 1970s discussed what a healthy organization would be faced with changes arising in the environment. Fordyce and Weil (1971) presented a view of organizational health according to which a healthy organization would be one that efficiently achieves its goals in a changing environment, having a strong representation of its identity and mission, while also having the ability to adapt quickly and change. Furthermore, a highly adaptable organization is more likely to seek, in the external environment, more effective methods to conduct its business. According to Fordyce and Weil (1971), for the organization to be perceived as healthy, it would be necessary that in it the power games of the bosses did not obstruct the talented people from unlocking their potential, that there was availability to learn from their own experience, and that they find innovative ways to confront difficulties.

Based on the diagnosis by Fordyce and Weil (1971), an expanded view of the organizational health criteria was formulated by Mello (1978) who postulated that the individual health requirements are the same as those necessary for the development and renewal of open systems (groups, families, companies, communities, and societies), expanding the criteria of organizational health in seven relevant topics: identity (how the organization sees its past, its achievements, and how it identifies itself), orientation (the objectives that construct the organization), realistic sensitivity (perception and identification of internal and external changes), creativity (ability to renew, innovate, and adapt), flexibility (adaptation to changes, modification of attitudes, behaviors, activities, tasks, structures, methods, and goals), integration (alignment between the organization's goals and the needs of individuals), and energy reserve (capacity to obtain the necessary supplies for its results in the external environment and existence of reserves of energy resources in the internal environment).

In the midst of the propositions of the literature on the concept of organizational health in the 1990s, Williams (1994) sought to interrelate four factors for the definition of healthy organization: environmental factors, physical health, mental health, and social health. The author again introduced the notion of employee health, linking it to the health of the organization, reporting that it is necessary to understand the interactions and associations between the environmental factors that surround the organization and the physical, mental, and social health of the worker, to define a healthy organization.

In 1995, Jaffe defined organizational health as an expanded notion of organizational effectiveness. This expanded notion concerns the needs of customers, suppliers, shareholders, and members of the community that are connected to the organization. A healthy organization would be one that creates health for its employees and the community to which it belongs (Jaffe, 1995). The author proposed the perspective of a healthy organization as an entity. Therefore, the organization must be seen as having needs, movements, and integrations, just like a person.

The author, in a review of the literature in the area, identified four theoretical models that contributed to the concept of organizational health: (1) work stress, (2) organizational redesign or development, (3) human resources or organizational policies that promote health, and (4) psychodynamics of the leaders.

The first model refers to work stress. According to Jaffe (1995), stress is a psycho-physiological variable that interferes in the workplace, in the physical and emotional health of individuals. According to the author, organizations, in order to seek the well-being and health of individuals, should select employees whose style of stress response suits their organizational climate. The second model presented by Jaffe (1995) is that of organizational redesign. According to the author, organizational redesign or development refers to an approximation between organizational structures, processes, and models and the employee, as this action will directly influence motivation, satisfaction, and effectiveness at work. When the work environment undergoes a restructuring, creating more opportunities for all workers to exercise control and experience social support, this action would provide support for personal health, implementing greater health in the organization.

In the third model, Jaffe (1995) sought greater employee participation through organizational policies. The construction of policies that encourage workers to participate and control the environment in a responsible way constructs a participatory and cooperative culture. A healthy organization, in terms of its human resources policy practices, seeks, with its workers, to make time more flexible and to influence the new characteristic of how to work well without rigid structures. In the fourth model, Jaffe (1995) focused on the figure of the managers. From this perspective, healthy organizations are seen as manifestations of the development level of their leaders.

For Jaffe (1995) the organization must be healthy for its own growth, being efficient, adaptable, and coherent; be healthy for shareholders, increasing the value of products/services, offering them a positive image of the company; be healthy for employees, offering a suitable place to work, meeting their highest needs for growth, knowledge, and participation; be healthy for suppliers and customers, implementing excellence in their services with values compatible with the market, honest and useful interactions, and good products and partnerships; and also be healthy for the community, examining its responsibility towards social resources.

Within the context of healthy organization presented by Jaffe (1995), Keyes et al. (2000) postulated the concept of positive organizations. For the authors, positive organizations have their definition linked to companies that do not only think about business, strictly seek profit, or only implement actions to increase the values of their shares in the market. These organizations also seek to promote the provision of well-being at work, seek to legitimize autonomy for the leaders, and give consistency to the relationship at work.

Peterson and Wilson (2002), in turn, recommended a multilevel approach to the health of the organization that covers the health of the employee. Multilevel analysis incorporates individual and cultural factors to determine organizational and individual health. With this, they proposed the "culture-work-health" theoretical model. According to the proposed model, the culture would have an impact on organizational health and employee health. Therefore, the health of the organization and the health of workers would determine the quality of life at work. The authors argued that the crux of the matter is to attribute the same value to individual and organizational health, considering them simultaneously in the investigations. The argument used by the authors is that the exclusive emphasis on workers' health can impose restrictions and regulations that end up compromising the company's health, whereas the exclusive emphasis on the organization's health can, in turn, create a negative environment that encourages immediate success but which, in the long run, induces chronic illnesses, worker stress, and poor performance.

Also in the first decade of the century, Assmar and Ferreira (2004) studied the influence of organizational culture and justice on the effective functioning of organizations and their repercussions on health at work, considering the same concepts of organizational health and individual health used by Peterson and Wilson (2002). They concluded by discussing how extremely conflicting interpersonal relationships can cause serious losses in the performance of workers and organizations. The authors stated that culture reflects the organizational orientation regarding the outlined values and the practices to implement those values.

Wilson et al. (2004) characterized organizational health as the institutional capacity to make intentional efforts to confront the market, carried out systematically and with the collaboration of employees in obtaining increased productivity with consequent greater worker well-being. For these authors, a healthy organization is one that provides social support, highlighting equal and accessible opportunities and promotions for all, seeking to have workers with productive and, at the same time, healthy performances.

In the Brazilian context, Gomide Jr. and Fernandes (2008) sought to reinforce the concepts with more theoretical consistency present in the literature and proposed a definition of the health of organizations based on the perception of employees in Brazilian public and private organizations. According to the authors, the construct is multidimensional, defined as the organization's ability to encourage the sharing of organizational objectives and the integration of its members with its work teams, in addition to having flexible work policies and procedures aimed at adapting the organization to the demands of the external environment. This definition proposed by the authors was ratified in 2011 by Nascimento and Gomide Jr.

New definitions of organizational health have been proposed by Fridrich et al. (2020) and by Dagonay and Dagli (2020). For the former, organizational health would be closely linked to the capacity of organizations to undertake changes in order to adapt to internal and external demands. The authors (Fridrich et al., 2020) stated that, to achieve this, interventions in all areas of the organization (e.g., structure and personnel) should aim to change the expectations and personal satisfaction of the organizational actors regarding the organizational performance.

In a more complex definition, Dagonay and Dagli (2020) assumed that organizational health is a concept that addresses the harmony of the organization with all its internal components and the environment as well as the ability to achieve its goals and objectives. At the same time, organizational health addresses the state of the organization's physical environment and the appropriate tools to accomplish its purpose, the state of communication between the organization and senior management, and the potential for problem-solving, development, growth, and innovation. Organizational health also deals with the quality of inputs and the safety of raw materials, with the organization's management and decision-making activities, with the moral, psychological, and physical health, and with the well-being and performance of its employees. They also claimed that an organization could not be considered healthy if it exists only within its own limits for a certain period of time. The healthy organization is one that has existed, continuously, for a long time, possessing survival and resilience skills, establishing and maintaining its internal integrity and its value (Dagonay & Dagli, 2020).

Although the concept of organizational health has emerged in the literature as a more comprehensive alternative for organizational effectiveness that sought to respond to the difficulties and breadth of its definition, both concepts are still present in diverse contemporary works. The studies found in the international literature, as well as (to a lesser extent) in the Brazilian literature, either used the concepts as isolated indicators of organizational performance or used multidimensional concepts that generated measures that are still scarce in the investigations. It is these measures that will be discussed in the next section.

11.4 Organizational Effectiveness/Health Measurement Instruments

The search undertaken in the literature comprised the first two decades of this century, with eight instruments for measuring constructs related to organizational performance being identified. These instruments deal with the perception of effectiveness or organizational health and differ from performance measures used in investigations where the performance criterion was unique, normally focused on the financial aspects of organizations (e.g., sales).

In chronological order of publications, the first conceptually consistent instrument found, which was empirically validated, was that of Fernandes et al. (2007). The authors constructed and validated a measure of perceived organizational effectiveness, the theoretical parameters of which were based on the work of Harrison (1994). This measure is composed of two factorially identified factors, denominated by the authors as "production goals" (17 items) and "internal state of the system" (9 items), with factor loadings that vary between 0.40 and 0.69 for the first and between 0.42 and 0.79 for the second. The percentages of explained variance are 27.91% and 5.27%, respectively. The authors report that the reliability (Cronbach's alpha) is 0.90 for "production goals" and 0.87 for "internal state of the system."

The second instrument found was proposed by Gomide Jr. and Fernandes (2008), who reported the validation of an organizational health perception measure composed of two factors. The first, the authors called "the employees' beliefs that the organization is capable of encouraging the sharing of organizational objectives and the integration of its members into their work teams." The authors reported factor loadings between 0.42 and 0.80 and reliability (Cronbach's alpha) of 0.92 for this factor. The second factor was named "employees' beliefs that the organization has flexible work policies and procedures aimed at adapting the organization to the demands of the external environment" with reported factor loadings between 0.43 and 0.80 and reliability of 0.84 (Cronbach's alpha).

The third measurement instrument found in the literature was proposed by Nascimento and Gomide Jr. (2011), who validated a measure of perception of organizational health, based on the theoretical assumptions of Peterson and Wilson (2002). Validated factorially, the measure is composed of two factors. The first, referred to by the authors as the "employees' beliefs in the organization's ability to provide support and maintenance for their physical and mental health," has factor loadings between 0.44 and 0.83, with reliability (Cronbach's alpha) of 0.91 and explained variance of 27.18%. The second factor concerns the "employees' beliefs about the organization's ability to manage its internal components, to adapt, develop, and present a favorable external image, maximizing its positive impact on the market," with loadings between 0.42 and 0.62, with reliability (Cronbach's alpha) of 0.87 and explained variance of 2.50%.

In 2015, Muterera, Hemswoth, Baregheh, and Garcia-Rivera presented a measure of organizational effectiveness (Organizational Performance), composed of 16 items in a single factor. The authors did not provide validation data in relation to this measure. They only stated that the items cover four dimensions of effectiveness: the organization's rational goals (RG), the degree to which it is an open system (OS), its internal process (IP), and human relations (HR).

In a study on the construction and validation of a scale of expectations for the organizational future, Vasconcellos and Neiva (2017) reported that one of the factors concerns organizational effectiveness. The final instrument consists of two factors, with factor loadings between 0.75 and 0.80 for the first factor (management and organizational environment, with four items) and 0.81 and 0.90 for the second (organizational effectiveness, with five items). The reported reliability is 0.92 and 0.93, respectively. The authors reported that the two-factor model surpasses the single-factor model, tested for the measure, in all fit indicators. The chi-square difference between the models ($\Delta\chi^2 = 363.10$, $p < 0.01$) was very high and significant.

The sixth instrument found was validated by El-Kassar and Singh, in 2017. The instrument presents a single factor and is composed of four items, with factor loadings between 0.75 and 0.84 and a reported reliability (Cronbach's Alpha) of 0.84. Named by the authors as Organizational Performance, the items conceptually cover the definition of effectiveness that addresses market share, increased sales, profit, and reputation in the marketplace.

Organizational Performance was also the name given to the instrument of Rehman et al. (2019). The instrument has a single factor, factorially validated, and consists of nine items that cover financial and non-financial aspects of the organization. The factor loadings are between 0.60 and 0.86, with reliability (Cronbach's alpha) of 0.90.

In the study period, the most recent instrument refers to organizational health (Dagonay & Dagli, 2020). The study of construction and validation of the measure, aimed at educational institutions, resulted in an instrument composed of 23 items distributed in 4 factors. The validation procedures included exploratory factor analysis; reliability, measured through Cronbach's alpha; and confirmatory factor validation, through structural equation modeling (confirmatory factor analysis (CFA)). The first factor was named by the authors as Academic Emphasis and consists of seven items with factor loadings between 0.60 and 0.85 with a reported reliability of 0.91. The second factor (Supportive Leadership) consists of six items with factor loadings between 0.63 and 0.89 with a reliability of 0.92. The third factor is composed of five items, the loadings of which ranged from 0.72 to 0.86, with a reliability of 0.92. According to the authors, this factor, named "Morale," is related to the institution's moral aspects such as support provided by superiors and organizational climate. The authors named the final factor extracted Environmental Factors, which is also composed of five items that are related to the physical conditions of the institution and external support received. The loadings of these items are between 0.57 and 0.77, with reliability of 0.87. The model was confirmed through CFA, with satisfactory parameters ($\chi^2 = 626.46$, $N = 429$, $df = 221$, $p = 0.00$; CFI = 0.98; RMSEA = 0.065).

Table 11.1 summarizes the characteristics of the instruments reported.

The eight conceptually consistent and empirically validated instruments found in the Brazilian and international literature present similarities and differences, as well as advantages and disadvantages in their application. This is what the next section will analyze.

11.5 Critical Analysis of the Organizational Effectiveness Measuring Instruments

Organizational performance occupies a large space in the literature due to its evident importance for the life and survival of organizations. In the 1960s, Katz and Kahn (1966) already emphasized that the primary objective of any organization would be its survival, which would depend on the capacity of that organization to generate financial surpluses. Therefore, for the authors, organizational effectiveness would be the organization's ability to profit and survive in the medium term.

In the 1970s, the authors highlighted the difficulty of defining and measuring effectiveness due to the numerous criteria that could be adopted considering the fact that organizations have multiple objectives and goals, which would make it difficult to adopt a single criterion, profit, and survival therefore not being sufficient.

Table 11.1 Authorship, construct evaluated, and instrument validation data

Authors/year of publication	Construct evaluated	No. of items/ factors	Reliability	Validation
Fernandes, Barale, Santos, Costa, and Gomide Jr. (2007)	Organizational effectiveness	26 items/2 factors	0.90 and 0.87	Exploratory factor analysis
Gomide Jr. and Fernandes (2008)	Organizational health	27 items/2 factors	0.92 and 0.84	Exploratory factor analysis
Nascimento and Gomide Jr. (2011)	Organizational health	32 items/2 factors	0.91 and 0.86	Exploratory factor analysis
Muterera, Hemswoth, Baregheh, and Garcia-Rivera (2015)	Organizational performance	16 items/ unifactorial	Not reported	Not reported
Vasconcellos and Neiva (2017)	Expectations of organizational future	9 items/2 factors	0.92 and 0.93	Confirmatory factor analysis
El-Kassar and Singh (2017)	Organizational performance	4 items/ unifactorial	0.84	Exploratory factor analysis
Rehman, Mohamed, and Ayoup (2019)	Organizational performance	9 items/ unifactorial	0.90	Exploratory factor analysis
Dogonay and Dagli (2020)	Organizational health	23 items/4 factors	0.91, 0.91, 0.91, and 0.87	Confirmatory factor analysis

In an attempt to circumvent the problem, the proposal arose, designed by Bennis (1966) and developed by Jaffe (1995) for a new construct: organizational health. This construct would cover not only the achievement of financial goals but also the internal functioning of the organizations, notably the existence of policies aimed at the physical and mental integrity of their employees. This proposal took on new dimensions when new health criteria were incorporated, such as the organization's commitment to the environment (Dagonay & Dagli, 2020) and the projection of the organizational image in the marketplace (Peterson & Wilson, 2002). However, as shown in the literature, the two concepts continued to be investigated in parallel, mainly in the literature of non-psychological areas. This dichotomy reflects directly on the instruments found in the last two decades. On one hand, they are scarce, while on the other, they present, for the most part, evidence of validity which, today, is insufficient.

The low quantity of the instruments would be expected, considering that most of the studies on effectiveness investigate it through single criteria, usually of a financial nature, or with a "gross" criterion, such as an increase in sales. In the eight instruments found, a characteristic that is common to them is the configuration of a self-applicable instrument, being configured as measures of attitudes (Pasquali, 1999). They all investigate the assessments of the organizations' employees regarding corporate results and use Likert-type scales.

Of the eight instruments, six were restricted to exploratory factor validation, which makes them outdated, considering current requirements. Two were submitted to confirmatory factor analysis (CFA). This characteristic makes them more valid for use in institutional investigations and diagnoses. In one of them (Vasconcellos & Neiva, 2017), the measure of effectiveness is one of the factors of a scale validated for other purposes. This characteristic does not invalidate the use of this factor as a single factor measure, as it presents, according to the authors, consistent construct validity. Regarding the other instrument submitted to CFA, the problem lies in the fact that its validation is directed toward a specific corporate nature, educational institutions. This characteristic raises the need for revalidation of the measure, when investigating its suitability for other organizational environments.

A characteristic that unites the eight instruments found is the consistency in their construct validities, as measured by exploratory factor analysis. In them, the authors report robust psychometric characteristics (factor loadings and reliability) that enable their use in academic investigations. A research agenda that seeks to investigate the "organizational effectiveness" construct cannot do without new validation updates of the instruments available, such as the use of confirmatory analyses, which would substantially improve their measurement parameters.

11.6 Final Considerations

This chapter aimed to examine the international and Brazilian literature regarding the theoretical/conceptual development of the organizational effectiveness construct, with a focus on models and measurement instruments. The conceptualizations of effectiveness proved to be quite diversified, covering single criterion and multiple criteria as definitions, and, even with a proposal for the evolution of the concept having been presented in the literature, they continue to be used. The forms of measurement reflect this diversity. There are two forms present in the literature: the so-called gross criteria, when mainly financial indices are used to measure the achievement of organizational objectives, and the self-applicable instruments, with their characteristic being the affectivity measured through the perceptions of the organizational actors. Considering these, the chapter sought to show that, in addition to being scarce, most of them are not very current or are too specific for widespread use considering what is expected from a validated instrument.

As an antithesis to these findings, organizational performance is a very current, attractive, and necessary topic in a competitive scenario such as the present one. Including it in the investigation guidelines of Organizational and Work Psychology is an urgent need, with this chapter hopefully contributing to this.

References

Argyris, C. (1964). *Integration the individual and the organization*. Wiley.
Assmar, E. M. L., & Ferreira, M. C. (2004). Cultura, justiça e saúde no trabalho. In A. Tamayo (Ed.), *Cultura e saúde nas organizações*. Artmed.

Bennis, W. G. (1962). Toward a truly scientific management: The concept of organizational health. *General Systems Yearbook, 7*, 269–282.

Bennis, W. G. (1966). *Changing organizations: Essays on the development and evolution of human organization*. McGraw-Hill Book Company.

Bensassoli, P. F., & Malvessi, S. (2013). Desempenho no trabalho: definições, modelos teóricos e desafios à gestão. In L. de Oliveira Borges & L. Mourão (Eds.), *O trabalho e as organizações: Atuações a partir da Psicologia*. Ed. Artmed.

Burns, T., & Stalker, G. M. (1961). *The management of innovation*. Tavistock.

Cameron, K. S. (1986). Effectiveness as paradox: Consensus and conflict in conceptions of organizational effectiveness. *Management Science, 32*, 539–553.

Dagonay, E., & Dagli, A. (2020). Organizational health scale: A scale development study. *International Education Studies, 13*(7), 128–144.

El-Kassar, A., & Singh, S. K. (2017). Green innovation and organizational performance: The influence of big data and moderating role of management commitment and H.R. practices. *Technological Forecasting & Social Change*. https://doi.org/10.1016/j.techfore.2017.12.016

Fernandes, M. N., Barale, R. F., Santos, T. G. C., Costa, T. P. A., & Gomide, S., Jr. (2007). Percepção de Efetividade Organizacional: construção e validação de uma medida do construto. *Revista Psicologia: Organizações e Trabalho, 7*(2), 115–132.

Fordyce, J. K., & Weil, R. (1971). *Managing with people: A managers handbook methods*. Addison Wesley.

Fridrich, A., Bauer, G. F., & Jenny, G. J. (2020). Development of Generic Workshop Appraisal Scale (WASC) for organizational health interventions and evaluation. *Frontiers in Psychology, 11*, 1–11.

Georgopoulos, B. S., & Tannenbaum, A. S. (1957). A study of organizational effectiveness. *American Sociological Review, 22*, 534–540.

Gerasimov, B. N., & Gerasimov, K. B. (2015). Modeling the development of organization management system. *Asian Social Science, 11*(20), 82–89.

Gogan, L. M., Artene, A., Sarca, I., & Draghiei, A. (2016). The impact of intellectual capital on organizational performance. *Procedia – Social and Behavioral Sciences, 221*, 194–202.

Gomes, D. F. P. (2020). *Impacto das Políticas e Práticas de Gestão de Pessoas no Desempenho no trabalho e o papel mediador do Capital Psicológico: Um estudo de caso em empresas certificadas como um GPTW.* Dissertação, Universidade Federal de Uberlândia, Uberlândia, MG.

Gomide, S., Jr., & Fernandes, M. N. (2008). Saúde Organizacional. In M. M. M. Siqueira (Ed.), *Medidas do comportamento organizacional: Ferramentas para diagnóstico e gestão*. Artmed.

Gomide Jr., S., Moura, O. I., Cunha, W. B., & Sousa, W. M. V. (1999). Explorando o conceito de Saúde Organizacional: construção e validação de um instrumento de medida para o ambiente brasileiro [Resumos]. Sociedade Brasileira de Psicologia (Org.), Resumos da XXIX Reunião Anual. Campinas, 43.

Gomide Jr, S., Fernandes, M. N. & Moraes, E.R. (2008). De Efetividade à Saúde das Organizações: a evolução os critérios de desempenho organizacional. In D. H. Helal, F. C. Garcia & L. C. Honório (Eds). *Gestão de Pessoas e Competência: Teoria e Pesquisa*. Curitiba: Juruá.

Goodman, P. S., & Pennings, J. M. (1977). *New perspectives on organizational effectiveness*. Jossey-Bass.

Harrison, M. I. (1994). *Diagnosing organizations: Methods, models and processes*. Sage Publications.

Jaffe, D. T. (1995). The healthy company: Research paradigms for personal and organizational health. In S. L. Sauter & L. R. Murphy (Eds.), *Organizational risk factors for job stress*. American Psychological Association.

Kanter, R. M. (1977). *Men and women of the corporation*. Basic Books.

Katz, D., & Kahn, R. L. (1966). *The social psychology of organizations*. Wiley.

Keyes, C. L. M., Hysom, S. J., & Lupo, K. L. (2000). The positive organization: Leadership legitimacy, employee well-being, and the bottom line. *The Psychologist-Manager Journal, 4*(2), 143–153.

Likert, R. (1958). Measuring organizational performance. *Harvard Business Review, 36*, 41–60.
Lusthaus, C., Adrien, M. H., Anderson, G., Carden, F., & Montalván, G. P. (2002). *Organizational assessment: A framework for improving performance*. IDRC/IDB (210p.). Disponível em: www.idrc.ca/en/ev-23987-201-1-DO_TOPIC.html. Acessado em: 20/01/2021.
Mello, F. A. F. (1978). *Desenvolvimento das organizações: uma opção integradora*. Livros Técnicos e Científicos.
Muterera, J., Hemswoth, D., Baregheh, A., & Garcia-Rivera, B. R. (2015). The leader-follower dyad: The link between leader and follower perceptions of transformational leadership and its impact on job satisfaction and organizational performance. *International Public Management Journal*. https://doi.org/10.1080/10967494.2015.1106993
Nascimento, J. O., & Gomide, S., Jr. (2011). Percepções de Saúde e Efetividade Organizacionais: Construção, Validação e Discriminação das Medidas dos Construtos. *Horizonte Científico, 5*, 72–76.
Ostroff, C., & Schmitt, N. (1993). Configurations of organizational effectiveness and efficiency. *Academy of Management Journal, 36*(6), 1345–1361.
Parsons, T. (1956). Suggestions for a sociological approach to the theory of organizations. *Administrative Science Quarterly, 1*, 63–85.
Pasquali, L. (1999). *Instrumentos Psicológicos: Manual Prático de Elaboração*. LabPAM/IBAPP.
Peterson, M., & Wilson, J. F. (2002). The culture-work-health model and work stress. *American Journal of Health Behavior, 26*(1), 16–24.
Pfeffer, J., & Salancik, G. R. (1978). *The external control of organizations*. Harper and Row.
Quinn, R. E., & Rohrbaugh, J. (1983). A spatial model of effectiveness criteria: Towards a competing values approach to organizational analysis. *Management Science, 29*, 363–377.
Rehman, S., Mohamed, R., & Ayoup, H. (2019). The mediating role of organizational capabilities between organizational performance and its determinants. *Journal of Global Entrepreneurship Research, 9*, 30. https://doi.org/10.1186/s40497-019-0155-5
Schein, E. H. (1965). *Organizational psychology* (Foundations of Modern Psychology series). Prentice-Hall.
Seashore, S. E. (1962). *The assessment of organizational performance*. Survey Research Center.
Selznick, P. (1948). Foundations of the theory of organizations. *American Sociological Review, 13*, 25–35.
Shanker, R., Bhanugopan, R., van der Heijden, B. I. J. M., & Farrel, M. (2017). Organizational climate for innovation and organizational performance: The mediating effect of innovative work behavior. *Journal of Vocational Behavior, 100*, 67–77. https://doi.org/10.1016/j.jvb.2017.02.004
Steers, A., & Spencer, D. G. (1977). *Organizational effectiveness: A behavioral view*. Goodyear.
Subramony, M., Segers, J., Chadwick, C., & Shyamsunder, A. (2018). Leadership development practice bundles and organizational performance: The mediating role of human capital and social capital. *Journal of Business Research, 83*, 120–129.
Vasconcellos, V. C., & Neiva, E. R. (2017). Escala de Expectativas de Futuro Organizacional: Desenvolvimento e Evidências de Validade. *Read, 86*(3), 58–82.
Vaz, C. M. F. R. (2013). *O impacto do capital psicológico e da confiança organizacional sobre o desempenho no trabalho*. Dissertation, Universidade Federal de Uberlândia, Uberlândia, MG.
Weick, K. E., & Daft, R. L., (1983) The effectiveness of interpretation systems. In: K. S. Cameron & D. A. Whetten (Eds). *Organizational effectiveness. A comparison of multiple models*. : Academic Press.
Williams, S. (1994). Ways of creating healthy work organizations. In C. L. Cooper & S. Williams (Eds.), *Creating healthy work organizations*. Wiley.
Wilson, M. G., Dejoy, D. M., Vandenberg, R. J., Richardson, H. A., & McGrath, A. L. (2004). Work characteristics and employee health and well-being: Test of a model of healthy work organization. *Journal of Occupational and Organizational Psychology, 77*(4), 565–588.

Chapter 12
The Next Challenges for Measuring Organizational Behavior Constructs

Ronald Fischer and Johannes Alfons Karl

12.1 Introduction

The current volume brings together an impressive statement of the state of the art in organizational behavior measurement. These instruments are typically applied in the format of a self- or other-report. In some cases, 360-degree feedback options are available in which information on a target person is collected from superiors, peers, and subordinates. The data generated for different dimensions is then typically aggregated at the dimensional level across the whole sample and compared to previously established norms. The dimensions themselves are based on modern psychometric theory, which often specify latent variable models, which imply a true underlying latent variable that causes the behavioral expression of scores on individual items (Everett, 2013). These latent variables are derived and validated through the application of complex multivariate statistics, including confirmatory factor analysis or item response theory models. In this chapter, we are looking forward to the next big challenges and opportunities on the horizon. We will focus on three interrelated areas that connect with each other in often interesting and intriguing ways to offer both exceptional opportunities and challenges to both our mode of research and theoretical models. The three areas that we will focus on are (1) big data, (2) network science, and (3) cross-cultural equivalence and bias. Importantly, all questions are discussed against a backdrop of substantial moral and ethical considerations raised by novel approaches, but these issues are outside the scope of the

R. Fischer (✉)
Instituto D'Or of Research and Teaching, Rio de Janeiro, RJ, Brazil

Victoria University of Wellington, Wellington, New Zealand
e-mail: Ronald.Fischer@idor.org

J. A. Karl
Victoria University of Wellington, Wellington, New Zealand
e-mail: Johannes.Karl@vuw.ac.nz

M. O. Macambira et al. (eds.), *Assessing Organizational Behaviors*,
https://doi.org/10.1007/978-3-030-81311-6_12

current work (for explorations of the ethical issues, see Crawford (2021), Crawford et al. (2014) and Nunan and Di Domenico (2013)). The moral issues of big data in particular are discussed in much detail elsewhere (Herschel & Miori, 2017).

12.2 Big Data

We are living in a moment in which technology is transforming our lives to such an extent that workplaces themselves will be largely unrecognizable within a few years from what we knew. Central to this revolution is the advance of information technology in nearly all areas of human life (e.g., internet of things) and work. The pervasiveness of sensors and data recording devices in our environment has created opportunities for an unprecedented amount of information that can be harvested from these devices, from obvious sources such as your cellular or computer and their usage patterns to your car or refrigerator to CCTV cameras capturing images of us 24 hours a day. Traditionally, such high-volume data recording in areas such as economics (e.g., stock exchange performance) or health (e.g., EEG recordings of electric activities on the surface of our skull) were limited to a single type of variable and often generated and recorded on a single device. Today, it is increasingly possible to link up previously unconnected data sources and types of variables across various dimensions and formats with much greater ease. There are clear logistical and ethical challenges involved in these endeavors (Herschel & Miori, 2017); however, here we will focus more on the possibilities of big data for changing how we think about organizational behavior constructs themselves.

Big data may be derived from various sources. As highlighted by George et al. (2014), a big data perspective shifts the perspective and use of data rather than specifying a number of individuals that count as big data. Hence, fine-grained analysis of a single individual collected with high sensitivity sensors across multiple behavioral dimensions which generates unprecedented details at fine temporal detail is a core feature of what is commonly called big data. In contrast, a survey of 1000 individuals responding to a single customer satisfaction item run during a long holiday weekend may not qualify, because it does not capture information at great behavioral, spatial, or temporal scale and it does not allow more detailed insights into success or failure of a product or campaign just by itself.

Big data comes in different forms and shapes, including public and private data, passively collected data with no information value for the data collection agent, community data available in various forms, and data available via self-quantification devices. Public data is probably the data that has been collected for the longest time by governments and authorities on issues such as birth or death registers, transportation patterns, energy use, or usage patterns of hospitals or doctors. Private data in contrast is held by private companies or individuals, including customer purchase profiles, private energy consumption, website browsing information, or mobile phone usage.

The third class is quite interesting in that it captures an important source of big data which often creates substantive ethical and moral concerns. To provide an example, new technology such as GPS signals in mobile phones provide better information to individual users about their position (e.g., maps) and close-by points of interest (e.g., restaurants, garages, museum displays), but this technology feature now allows generating data on the individual as a side-product using a wide range of user-carried GPS sensors (Ehrlich & Blankenbach, 2019; Zafari et al., 2019). Similarly, our use of search engines facilitates and improves our research by providing access to the latest publications. At the same time, us searching on our work computer allows others to infer that we are positioned in a research institute given highly similar research focused searched by others nearby. Hence, the usage of devices can create information that is harvested automatically and becomes available for further analyses. For example, this information may be used to direct targeted ads to users. The second author regularly receives advertisement about joining the university – which is based on matching information on his age saved in his profile with search behavior. Therefore, different pieces of information are linked and used to provide targeted advertisements. This however also shows some of the limitations, as the co-author is already a PhD student at this institution; hence, it means marketing budgets are wasted, and, without options to update this information, the models continue offering these ads.

Fourth, consumer data are similar but different in an important aspect. They include any kind of unstructured data that individuals consciously create when engaging with online and social media sources in public, for example, button clicks, public twitter feeds, or consumer reviews. For example, us leaving a comment about an academic event that we attended is an active act of ours and creates information that can be harvested and further analyzed.

The final source is self-quantification data, which is collected through conscious decisions by individuals to quantify their own behavior to obtain feedback on their personal actions and behaviors (e.g., wearable sensors such as Fitbits measuring exercise behavior, heart rate monitors to capture training levels, and an increasing integration of a new generation of sensors) (George et al., 2014).

Psychological research focusing on the psychometric properties of scales and instruments have a relatively long tradition and well-established criteria for judging the quality of the information (Cronbach, 1951; Nunnally & Bernstein, 1994). As with many emerging fields, the field of big data analysis is moving fast ahead, fueled by technological advances at an unprecedented scale. OB and allied areas such as psychological research typically work on much longer time cycles compared to the possibilities for data harvesting and data visualization that emerge within the ongoing technological transformation. Hence, validity information on these techniques and approaches may not be well understood. In addition, at the point where the validity of techniques are better understood by potential users, these algorithms and technologies might have been phased out of use or replaced by newer methods or algorithms. Similarly, validity criteria in computer science and engineering may not align with our expectations of validity. Psychological research aims for a maximum of validity and precision in measurement to make individual decisions (e.g., personnel selection, entry into academic institutions); in an applied big data context, a balance often may be struck between measurement quality and feasibility to provide information fast. These are important issues to consider further and require transdisciplinary teams examining these issues together.

These different types of data can be combined and integrated (which can pose substantial hurdles, Sharples, 2018), creating potentially very powerful sets of information if information on individuals or communities can be linked at a deep level. One of the most interesting aspects of such data sources is that they often provide high-density information on the same individual over time, creating a behavioral record which can be analyzed in real time. This allows shifting the level of analysis from the population between-person level to the within-person level.

This aspect provides one of the most interesting challenges and opportunities for OB researchers. Psychological research is typically focused on sample-level characteristics, which may or may not describe dynamics for any single individual (Beckmann & Wood, 2017; Brose et al., 2015; Fisher et al., 2018), since our constructs are in the large majority developed and validated on population samples that focus on average between-individual relationships. Hence, they are describing an average individual that does not exist in the real world. With near unlimited information on behavior across different dimensions, it now becomes possible to shift from static analyses that have characterized previous psychometric analyses to dynamic within-person level analyses for specific individuals (Bak et al., 2016). Therefore, the availability of high-density information at the individual level across different behaviors and across time now allows more fine-grained analyses of variability within individuals. A few points are important here to note.

First, recent research has highlighted that within-person and between-person information is not necessarily leading to the same insights (Beckmann et al., 2010; Beckmann & Wood, 2017; Fisher et al., 2018) and substantial developments have occurred in this area in recent years (Hamaker et al., 2015; Mulder & Hamaker, 2020; Zyphur, Allison, et al., 2020; Zyphur, Voelkle, et al., 2020). By examining how behavioral dynamics change within individuals over time, we can start to understand both individual and sample level dynamics, bridging the gap from describing average statistical features at the sample level to understanding temporal and within-person dynamics of individuals as agents embedded within a cultural system (Epskamp, 2020).

The diversity of data and recording devices also opens new opportunities but also new challenges. Core to these challenges are issues such as differences in reliability of indicators and the need to prioritize some information as more important than other information (J. Liu et al., 2016). Some of the data are based on physiological data (e.g., heart rate dynamics in Fitbits) or subtle behavioral data (e.g., attention focus as captured by eye tracking) which is typical outside of conscious awareness and therefore is difficult to reflect on and respond to in self-report measures. These sensors may also be differentially sensitive across different devices, leading to substantive measurement variability.

These analyses based on such devices nevertheless can provide new and exciting insights into individual differences. Combined with contextual analyses, this can allow for interesting opportunities to expand the construct space. For example, with physiological data, it is possible to examine temporal variability in response to emotional stressors. To what extent does the body system respond to the stressor and how long does it take for the activated system to return to baseline levels? Such information is of exceptional value in professions that involve high stress but also high risk of failure (e.g., medical profession, security personnel). The extent to which the system responds to stressors is sometimes described as stress reactivity. In contrast, if previous states are the best predictors of current states, then the emotional system is not changing strongly, which is called inertia (Kuppens et al., 2010). Combining these insights can provide important new insights that are relevant for measuring organizational behavior (Beal, 2015).

In addition to the possibility of examining variability and covariation with individual in greater detail, it also allows a more nuanced investigation of extreme cases. These are typically excluded as outliers in population-focused analyses as they bias the overall mean effects. In contrast, with temporal dynamics, outliers can become highly diagnostic and interesting. Rare events captured by these "outliers" can be of vital importance at every level of occurrence. For an example at macro level, in foreign relations, transitions of countries to new systems of governance are rare but can substantially reshape the overall system leading major transition of world order in some instances (King & Zeng, 2001). Similarly, at an individual level, some rare or even just unique events such as birth of the first child can have substantial impact on individual's subsequent behavior (Lanzendorf, 2010).

Much of the promise of this research is that by examining human behavior across different domains it becomes possible to study "revealed preferences," that is, psychological insights that are not available from self-reports or other psychological data analysis methods. In some ways, this is the behavioral equivalent to implicit association tests (Oswald et al., 2013), geared to bring out hidden preferences that nevertheless are important for understanding behavior and decisions made by individuals.

Focusing on some of the challenges to sort out with big data, first of all, it is important to remember that major transitions often result in truly innovative and valid resolutions but also a much larger number of products, models, and innovations that ultimately fail. Additionally, technological advance can result in paradigm-shifting solutions but more commonly advance is defined by gradual evolutionary improvement of solutions that necessitate consistent validity recalibration. This is one of the important points to keep in mind: many opportunistic providers in such a dynamic and unregulated environment are going to offer solutions of questionable value and validity. Given the much higher complexity, including the use of technological devices to record data with limited information on quality and often unsupervised machine learning algorithms will make it more difficult for users to understand the applicability and validity of the solutions for their problems. The appeal of big data is to make better decisions, yet unsupervised algorithms may just replicate bad human decision making in disguise (Courtland, 2018) and stakeholders have called attention to risks both in implementation and failure to live up to expectations (Ciocca et al., 2021; Vinci, 2020).

Second, the focus to uncover hidden psychological information is questionable if (a) the "wrong" behavior is captured or an incomplete behavioral profile is tracked or (b) if the construct of interest is only indirectly expressed in overt behavior. The former deals with some of the obvious questions such as whether online behavior is predictive of offline behavior or whether the trackable behavior is of value or concern for organizational issues. Would the online behavior of an individual in their private life (e.g., search words, social media posts) predict work behavior? From what we know about personality expressions in social media posts (Schwartz et al., 2013), the answer is probably more complex and depends on the specific personality trait and work behaviors of interest. Swearing or cursing in online posts may indicate lack of emotional stability and, hence, may contain some informative value. In contrast, manga- or game-related posts that indicate low extraversion may not actually be informative for many contexts. Furthermore, the validity of these indicators might shift in the personality network as sociocultural factors change over time. For example, recent studies investigating the role of extraversion and problem game use show a positive relationship, which is further increased by perceived loneliness (Ok, 2021). This might be due to the shift in the wider media landscape in which games have an increasing social focus and are used as tools of social connection (Marston & Kowert, 2020). Again, extreme values may be more informative than variation in the typical range, which presents opportunities for OB researchers to creatively think about validity criteria in the future. These questions raise many interesting opportunities for OB researchers, including the question to what extent and which online behaviors have closer correspondence to offline behavior than others or whether there are individual differences in online-offline correspondence.

Focusing on the second issue related to the behavioral expression of underlying psychological states or traits, the work on emotion expression in particular has created a lot of interest and buzz in the business community. The promise to track emotional states in real time via sensors or cameras has created a multimillion dollar business, based on observations that it is possible to detect basic emotions across cultures from facial expressions (Cowen et al., 2021). Again, this industry is poorly regulated, and the validity of any such analysis system can be of unproven validity and scientifically questionable. Other issues that have created validity concerns are the widespread use of unsupervised machine learning algorithms, which often tend to replicate human biases, as mentioned above. There have been calls for regulation (Crawford, 2021), but it is unclear how fast and how effective such regulations might be in the short run.

There are big underlying questions to be solved, in which OB scholars should have a strong voice. What are the appropriate criteria for training machine learning algorithms? What training data is available that does not include human biases and can be used for training unbiased algorithms? What thresholds are deemed acceptable for assessing the success of a model? Is a criterion of 70% accuracy sufficient, considering the time and cost savings when using machine-based learning algorithms? Or should we expect the same or even higher accuracy from models compared to what we would expect from humans (e.g., research on self-driving cars indicates a consistent bias against automatic models (P. Liu et al., 2019))? Ultimately, these questions come back to core issues that have been the main concern of organizational researchers for decades, but open new interesting conceptual and empirical opportunities with these much enriched data worlds. The core questions remain – what is validity and how do you measure good performance (Pritchard, 1990).

12.3 Network Science

The most common methods for test development are based on variations of a latent variable model, either within an item response theory tradition or with a structural equation modeling approach (Fischer & Karl, 2019). The underlying assumption is that there is a latent concept which is causally responsible for the behavioral responses recorded on self-report measures. The observed indicators or items included in the survey are thought to be conditionally independent given the latent variable. In other words, the items or indicators need to measure only one latent variable and should not be contaminated with other content. The items themselves are interchangeable. What is interesting here is that this approach assumes the presence of a latent variable that is causally responsible for behavioral observations. The important task for organizational researchers is to identify the relevant latent variable and then select individuals with favorable traits on that variable. Similarly, for training and development initiatives, the focus is on these presumed latent variables. These questions are not trivial, as the numerous research traditions attest. Identifying the relevant number and composition of underlying latent variable(s) and the best measurement has occupied researchers for nearly a century, across fields as diverse as leadership (Yukl, 2013), intelligence (Eysenck, 1979; Lubke, 2003), and extra role behavior (Van Dyne & LePine, 1998).

In recent years, a different approach has gained traction which is building on a movement within the wider research environment towards complexity science and based on insights gained from the big data revolutions (Barabási, 2012). This network science perspectives provides an alternative form to think about constructs and has already shifted thinking in health, neuroscience, and clinical research (Bertolero & Bassett, 2020; Borsboom & Cramer, 2013; Cramer et al., 2010; Fried et al., 2016). Network approaches organize variables in relation to each other, which allows to uncover possible relationships between constructs in observational research without making assumptions about the ontological status (Costantini et al., 2015; Epskamp et al., 2018; Golino et al., 2020). It consists of mapping the relationship between observed indicators (nodes) and the relationship with other nodes (edges). Due to the highly interconnected nature of psychological systems, networks modeled on psychological data tend to be fully saturated including many edges (capturing correlations between observed indicators) that are close to but not exactly zero. The *Least Absolute Shrinkage and Selection Operator* (*LASSO*) and in particular the *Extended Bayesian Information Criterion Gaussian Least Absolute Shrinkage and Selection Operator* (*EBICglasso*; Foygel & Drton, 2010) are regression-based approaches that have been shown to more faithfully represent the overall network while preserving parsimony by constraining close to zero edges to exactly zero. Furthermore, with cross-sectional data, it allows to identify central nodes (variables) within the overall network and nodes which link so-called communities (Costantini et al., 2015; Epskamp et al., 2018), clusters of tightly connected variables which could be conceptualized similar to latent variables. Using such community detection methods via exploratory graph analysis (Epskamp & Fried, 2018) with a clustering method such as Walktrap algorithm (Yang et al., 2016), it is possible to overcome problems with latent confounding (Hallquist et al., 2019). These methods are empirically superior to other factor analytical techniques for identifying optimal number of clusters, which are then often interpreted as latent variables (Golino et al., 2020).

One of the interesting statistics available for networks is a so-called small-worldness index (Humphries & Gurney, 2008; Watts & Strogatz, 1998) which provides an index of the overall clustering of the network. Many processes in the real world at various scales and levels of complexity are highly clustered. The original work by Watts and Strogatz (1998) identified small-world properties in the appearance of actors in feature films as a proxy of social networks, but it has also been identified as six degrees of separation in human relational networks (Travers & Milgram, 1969), the power grid of the Western United States, and the completely mapped neural network of a tiny nematode worm. In other words, social networks, power grids based on settlement patterns, and neurons in a brain seem to all show sparse networks with high clustering, where a small number of shortcuts allow connecting all nodes with each via intermediate nodes. Similar properties have been reported in network structures tested with items from personality, social psychology, and psychopathology domains (Borsboom et al., 2011; Borsboom & Cramer, 2013; Costantini et al., 2015; Fischer & Karl, 2020).

It is possible to derive various additional statistical properties about both the individual nodes and network properties. Most commonly reported are network centrality indicators such as strength, betweenness, and closeness centrality of the individual nodes (Costantini et al., 2015). Strength centrality is a measure of the overall connectedness, that is, the sum of all edges connected to a node. This can be thought of as a kind of popularity within a social network – how many people select a person as a friend or how many items are positively (or negatively) correlated with an item. Put in other words, nodes (items or people) high in strength can be expected to have a direct impact to (or be impacted by) many different nodes (items or people) without the mediating effect of other nodes (items or people) (Barrat et al., 2004). The second indicator betweenness captures the average shortest path length between two other nodes passing through the item of interest. Conceptually, this could be conceptualized as similar to a "middlemen" or "broker" within a network structure (Epskamp et al., 2018). A third type we are discussing here is closeness centrality. This is similar to flow speed through the network (Borgatti, 2005; Freeman, 1978; Sabidussi, 1966), the extent to which a specific node acts like "superconductor" connecting other nodes either directly or indirectly. Other forms of centrality can be computed. These various indicators can provide complementary information on the centrality and importance of an item within the network. For the three coefficients discussed here, they can be thought of as capturing the popularity, the quality, and speed of those connections within a network.

Based on network characteristics, it is possible to identify clusters within the network. Above we briefly commented on exploratory graph analysis (Golino & Epskamp, 2017). The basic idea is to identify groups of strongly linked edges that show stronger links with each other than with other nodes. These clusters can point toward possible latent variables – but this is a theoretical question that requires additional inferences, which we will discuss in a bit more detail below.

If such clusters have been identified, a further interesting question is which nodes within communities identified in the EGA provide links to other nodes in other communities (Jones et al., 2019). One statistic that can be computed is bridge strength, which is calculated as the sum of the absolute value of all edges that exist between a specific node within a community and all nodes that are not in the same community as the focal node. Therefore, bridge strength reports which node within a network community is most strongly connected overall to any other communities within the network. Other forms of bridge strength can be computed that examine expected influence either directly or indirectly. Such bridge network statistics can provide important information on how major clusters within network (which could indicate possible latent variables) are linked and connected within a larger network. Importantly, these techniques shift the focus to the linkages and the emergent structure, rather than abstract latent constructs.

In short, network statistics provide information on links between observed indicators instead of specifying and testing unmeasured latent variables. However tight clustering can provide pointers toward sets of variables that may operate akin to latent variables. Moreover, the ability of network statistics to identify possible latent variables appears more powerful than standard techniques (Golino et al., 2020; Golino & Epskamp, 2017) while also providing additional information on how such presumed latent variables may be related to each other via linking nodes.

However, it is important to emphasize that mathematically network models and latent variable models are interchangeable: a network model can be mathematically translated into an IRT or CFA model and vice versa (Christensen & Golino, 2021; Kruis & Maris, 2016). The interesting point is that these new approaches based on network science also show the mathematical equivalence of other operationalizations such as formative models, a discussion which has plagued organizational research for years (Edwards, 2011; Podsakoff et al., 1986). Hence, the emergence of the network science approach promises to resolve various longstanding debates based on mathematical principles. The powerful empirical approach embedded with network psychometrics provides important additional information on item relationships that may not be apparent through other approaches, without presupposing assumptions about causal directions. Longitudinal network models also have the additional advantage that they allow possibilities for separating temporal within-person and between-person dynamics (Epskamp, 2020). Yet, the demonstrated mathematical equivalence of these models with cross-sectional data then also shifts the responsibility squarely back to the researchers. The conceptualization of theoretical processes and the status of variables now take on a new importance and cannot be resolved simple through a one-point cross-sectional survey. One recent option is the use of approaches such as directed acyclic graphs to support researchers' decision-making (Textor et al., 2016).

To provide a more tangible example and demonstrate the practical implications, let's consider the case of depression. Traditionally, symptoms such as fatigue, sleeping problems, and depressed mood are thought to be caused by an underlying conceptual variable called depression. There are a number of interesting questions here. First, even though many of these observed indicators correlate with each other, the relationship between these indicators is often uneven. Similarly, clinical diagnoses of depression require the presence of at least five different behavioral symptoms over a period of 2 weeks, and two of these have to be depressed mood and loss of interest (Fried et al., 2016). From a latent variable perspective, we would expect that that all criteria should be present to at least some degree. Cross-cultural work also suggests that the indicators of depression can be variable across different cultural communities, with depressed mood or loss of interest not necessarily being the most important indicators.

The development of depression over time would also possibly show different trajectories from a latent variable vs network perspectives (Borsboom, 2017). Latent variable models would likely predict a linear and gradual change over time, with increasing deterioration of the person's well-being and functioning over time with increasing levels of depression at a latent level. In contrast, a network perspective allows nonlinear and even rapid transitions from healthy to depressive states. If a central node such as depressive mood receives negative input from a number of related nodes (e.g., observed indicators such as lack of sleep, concentration problems, fatigue, and increased guilt) simultaneously, the overall state of the network system may deteriorate suddenly, and when a certain threshold is reached, the system may show sudden jumps (e.g., clinical depression). Such an analysis of network parameters may also allow greater predictability compared to a latent variable model. For example, it may be possible to examine the performance of individual nodes and whether there are warning signals within specific parts of the network associated with key nodes. These warning signals could alert clinicians about the overall fragility of the system and improve access to professional help earlier and more efficiently. Furthermore, intervention options are quite different from a network vs a latent variable perspective. If each of the indicators is thought to be a result of the underlying variable, from a clinical perspective, it is important to improve the levels of the underlying variable via specific medical or therapeutic interventions. With improvements in the levels of the underlying variable, the observed indicators such as fatigue, sleeping problems, or depressed mood are then thought to be improving. In contrast, in a network perspective, it is important to intervene at the weakest nodes or at central nodes that affect multiple other nodes. Hence, it allows for more directed and focused interventions that shift the overall system.

As all these examples hopefully show, the theoretical implications of a network and latent variable perspective are quite different, even though mathematically the correlational data can be analyzed from either perspective and may show equivalent fit (e.g., fit indices approximate network strengths) (for an example, see Fischer et al. (2020)). This requires greater theoretical attention about the conceptual nature of the phenomenon. It also opens up interesting new research questions. Experiments could be designed to test whether the manipulation of one observed indicator affects other observed indicators associated with the same latent variable. From a latent variable perspective, we would not necessarily expect that the manipulation of one indicator affects another one, because conceptually it does not make sense to expect that the effects of the manipulation travel from the observed indicator to the latent variable, change the state of the latent variable which in turn affects other observed indicators. However, this is what would be expected from a network perspective because individual nodes are causally connected; hence, manipulations at one node should spread through the network in predictable ways. In contrast, in a latent variable perspective, the manipulation should target the latent variable and the effectiveness of the manipulation should be observed to similar degrees across all the measured observed indicators causally affected by the latent variable. We show an example of this in Fig. 12.1. In this example, both the latent construct and the network cover the same construct: depression. The construct is measured with five items (I1–I5) with the first item measuring sleep problem. In a network perspective, if a shock factor (e.g., consistent building noise) impacts this indicator/behavior, over time the activation can percolate through the network, first impacting energy levels and later mood, even if the initial disruption and the sleep issues are resolved. In contrast, in a latent variable perspective for something to impact all measures indicators, it would need to impact the latent variable (depression). The latent approach (because the responses to items are reflections of an underlying construct) conceptually does not allow for an effect on an item to affect other variables because this would require for activation to travel "up" to the latent variable and "down" again to a different item.

Translating this back to the area of organizational behavior, let's focus on a specific example such as extra-role behavior. Organ (1988) and Organ et al. (2005) first popularized the concept of organizational citizenship behavior as a form of discretionary work behavior which goes beyond explicit role descriptions and therefore cannot be legally enforced but is essential for the smooth functioning of work organizations. A long line of research has demonstrated that it is conceptually possible to differentiate at least five different dimensions (which are often tested with confirmatory factor analysis – a latent variable method) (Organ et al., 2005). At the same, a long line of research has failed to identify differential relationships between these five dimensions and other antecedents or consequences (LePine et al., 2002). To the best of my knowledge to date, no research has explicitly focused on extra-role behavior instruments from a network perspective, even though social networks are recognized to be important for OCB behavior (Brass, 2018). Researchers routinely identified five clusters of tightly connected items, but the lack of differential relationships at the construct level suggests that a latent variable perspective may not be the best option to conceptualize this construct. Let us examine some of the items from Podsakoff et al.'s initial OCB instrument (Podsakoff et al., 1986). The highest loading item in their sample was "help each other out if someone falls behind with

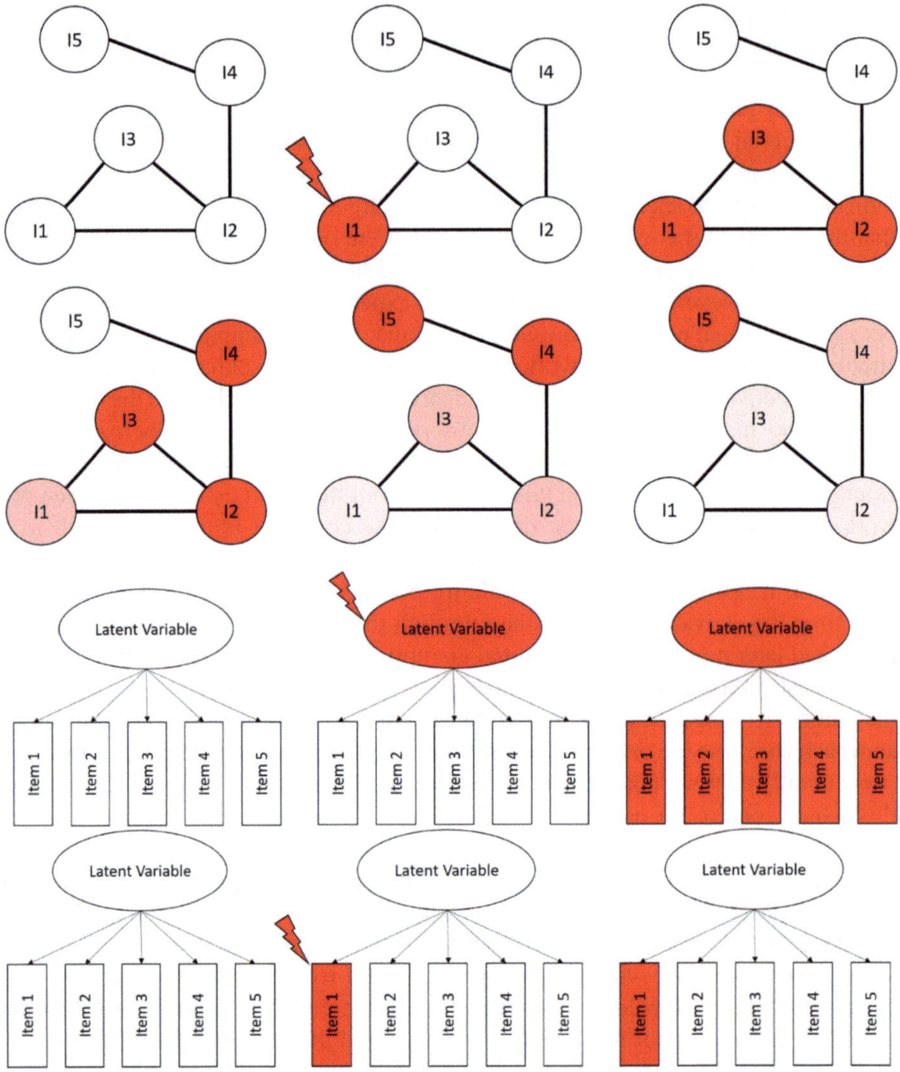

Fig. 12.1 Activation in latent variable and network models over time. Note: Six time points are displayed for network models (top) and latent variable models (bottom). For network models, starting from the top left, activation in one node (I1) will activate neighboring nodes over time in a serial direction. Activation will phase out gradually over time without new activation. Individual nodes are differentially affected over time. For latent variable models in contrast, activation at the latent variable will simultaneously activate all observed indicators. In contrast, activation of one of the observed indicators will not result in any changes at the latent variable level and should not influence other observed indicators (under the assumption of conditional independence)

his/her work," whereas the second lowest loading item was "touch base with other crew members before initiating activities that may affect them." From a network perspective, we may expect that the first item is quite central, whereas the second item is probably more peripheral in the network. The behavioral node of helping others out if there are delays is probably quite important for meeting work targets; hence, we could expect that this item predicts work outcomes over and above other items. The latter item on the other hand might be an important node connecting the helping cluster to the civic virtue cluster within the larger OCB network. From a network perspective, the overall clusters could be rethought of as connected behavioral syndromes, with individual nodes within the network having differential effectiveness on other clusters and on important work outcomes. Similarly, training of behavior related to individual nodes instead of emphasizing overall OCB may have flow through effects through the larger system, which could shift how training initiatives are conceptualized and initiated.

In summary, the data-based revolution driven by big data has also led to the emergence of new ways of thinking about data. One of the most exciting developments in recent years has been the emergence of network science, including network psychometrics. Recent advances have demonstrated that classic psychometrics including latent variable models are mathematically equivalent to networks and can be mathematically transformed into networks and vice versa. The implication of these recent insights is that the onus is on the researcher to correctly specify whether a construct works more like a latent variable or more like a network. We demonstrated with examples from clinical work that this has important conceptual and practical ramifications. In the next section, we discuss one more area of great importance for the next generation of OB research.

12.4 Taking Culture Seriously

Today, we interact with greater facility and greater frequency than ever in human history with other members of our own species which do not share our own cultural background, based on shared socialization experiences, values, and norms. At some level, these frequent interactions nicely demonstrate that we are one species and that no cultural divide is too large to not be successful bridged. Yet, on the other hand, our global working village is rife with conflicts and misunderstandings that also highlight that cultural issues cannot be ignored. As summaries of decades of research have demonstrated, intercultural teams face increased conflict and productivity losses and only limited process gains (Stahl et al., 2010). Culture needs our attention for improving organizational performance.

One of the less appreciated implications of culture is that our research lenses that we use to examine work processes also need attention. We will briefly review the statistical options that researchers are probably more familiar with, which is the invariance testing framework. We will also briefly discuss some concerns of cultural bias from a network perspective. However, our goal is to highlight the conceptual questions, issues for which there are no direct statistical tests available but which bring us back to these central themes of constructs and validity.

The majority of research instruments continue to originate in English-speaking countries. Researchers interested in applying any of these instruments or tests need to go through a number of validation steps before the instrument can be used and scores be interpreted in a different sample. One of the first and key steps is to translate and, if necessary, adapt instruments for a new cultural and linguistic context. Modern translation guidelines and checklists such as the TRAPD methodology (Translation, Review, Adjudication, Pretesting, and Documentation (Harkness et al., 2003)) have been described that overcome many of the shortcomings of commonly used translation-backtranslation, which remain the dominant translation method in major international business journals despite the noted limitations and flaws of this method (Chidlow et al., 2014). Luckily, there are excellent guidelines and checklist which can be used free of charge for research purposes (International Test Commission, 2018; Jowell & Centre for Comparative Social Surveys (Great Britain), 2007; Translation | European Social Survey (ESS), n.d.).

Once instruments have been translated, researchers need to carefully collect data and in this process control and rule out various types of biases. Statistical tools are available that can be used to examine whether the collected data is comparable or not across cultural groups. These standards have developed within the context of psychometric testing, but these ideas are also more broadly applicable (e.g., for experiments, Fischer and Karl (2020)) and can even be considered for trainings or organizational interventions in cross-national contexts more broadly. The idea of the unified bias and equivalence framework is that it helps to define criteria to identify the target problem to be addressed and guides thinking of how a specific organizational behavior may manifest across cultural contexts. Importantly, this unified bias and equivalence framework (see Fischer and Karl (2019), Fontaine (2005), and Van de Vijver and Leung (2021)) is conceptually independent of the latent variable framework, even though it is often associated with or tested through latent variable processes (Vandenberg & Lance, 2000). There are at least three major steps to go through in a typical cross-cultural validation process. First, researchers need to define their variable of interest and consider how the conceptual status of the variable may differ within and across cultural groups. What is extra-role performance or how do you define intrinsic motivation? The aim is to identify the functional equivalence of concepts to be compared and measured across cultural contexts. If there is no functional equivalence of concepts at even some minimal level (Patel, 2015), no comparisons can be made. If functional level can be demonstrated, the next step is to generate indicators that can measure the concept of interest. If the concept has different components in addition to a shared core, it is important to use indicators that represent both the culture-specific as well as the culturally shared components. For example, in what way would intrinsic motivation manifest itself across different cultural contexts? This step typically requires identifying culturally specific and relevant items or indicators of the construct through collaborative work. Are all relevant domains and expressions of intrinsic motivation captured in the new instrument? This second step in the process is labeled structure equivalence. These two steps are sometimes discussed in conjunction under the label of construct equivalence (although we believe it makes conceptually sense to distinguish between the philosophical and the operational steps as low quality operationalization does not hold implications on the ontology of a concept across cultures). These operational processes are typically conducted using qualitative and ethnographic methods.

Statistical procedures become important once data has been collected. Statistically, it is important to analyze both (a) the strength of the relationship between each indicator and the overall construct (e.g., factor loading or item discrimination) and (b) the purity of the item (does the indicator capture other construct content distinct from the construct of interest?). If the first analytical process shows that an instrument shows similar relationships between each indicator and the intended theoretical construct across cultural samples, the condition of metric equivalence is being met. The second analysis examines the extent to which an indicator only captures variance due to the construct of interest (e.g., no intercept differences or differences in item difficulty). If this condition is met, then the researcher has identified conditions of full score or scalar equivalence. This is often the primary aim because, if met, mean scores from the instruments can be directly compared across samples and groups. In recent years, significant statistical progress has been made in improving techniques to address these questions (Boer et al., 2018; Fischer & Karl, 2019). Unfortunately, despite the importance of these steps for drawing appropriate conclusions about the data, these steps are still being ignored in a large number of studies (Boer et al., 2018; Hult et al., 2008). This implies that results in many published studies cannot be interpreted with confidence due to possible biases because invariance was not demonstrated. This remains a major area for further improvement. This is also an important area of development for network approaches, and some recent progress has been made for testing the equivalence of network structures (Williams & Mulder, 2019). These issues are equally important for the emerging big data approaches, because big data analytics are often ignorant of the origin of data and this can significantly bias any results, leading to further discrimination and marginalization of certain groups. Nowadays, easy-to-use and very powerful tools are available, and there are little excuses that can be made for not checking these important steps before using instruments or methods developed in different cultural contexts.

12.5 Conclusions

In this chapter, we looked forward to major opportunities and challenges lying ahead for organizational behavior theory and practice. In our view, the three points approached here – big data, network psychometrics, and focus on cultural bias and equivalence – are intrinsically linked. The transformation of modern workplaces will require more and more intercultural contact, while the form of interaction is likely to be technology mediated and technology assisted. This will allow organizations over the world to gain access to measurable performance and behavioral indicators at an unprecedented scale and detail. These data-driven approaches have already resulted in major breakthroughs such as network science, which are likely to increase in popularity. As discussed here, all these issues will push the theorizing and conceptualization about variables back to the researcher (and practitioner). How can we interpret the output of an unsupervised machine learning algorithm? How do we decide on valid criteria that can identify performance issues as captured by wearable devices in real time? How do we make sure that any kind of measurement process does not unfairly discriminate against any group or individuals? The intersection between smart big data, network thinking, and attention to cultural bias and equivalence issues is the new conceptual frontier for OB researchers. We are fairly confident that our field will look quite different, possibly even radically transformed in two or three decades from now. In some ways, we might be a few steps away from achieving some of the old dreams of the philosophy of science, namely, developing a theory of consilience that allows integrating different levels of explanations across different and independent data sources to arrive at much stronger conclusions than any single theoretical framework will permit (Wilson, 1999).

References

Bak, M., Drukker, M., Hasmi, L., & van Os, J. (2016). An n=1 clinical network analysis of symptoms and treatment in psychosis. *PLoS One, 11*(9), e0162811. https://doi.org/10.1371/journal.pone.0162811

Barabási, A.-L. (2012). The network takeover. *Nature Physics, 8*(1), 14–16. https://doi.org/10.1038/nphys2188

Barrat, A., Barthélemy, M., Pastor-Satorras, R., & Vespignani, A. (2004). The architecture of complex weighted networks. *Proceedings of the National Academy of Sciences, 101*(11), 3747–3752. https://doi.org/10.1073/pnas.0400087101

Beal, D. J. (2015). ESM 2.0: State of the art and future potential of experience sampling methods in organizational research. *Annual Review of Organizational Psychology and Organizational Behavior, 2*(1), 383–407. https://doi.org/10.1146/annurev-orgpsych-032414-111335

Beckmann, N., & Wood, R. E. (2017). Editorial: Dynamic personality science. Integrating between-person stability and within-person change. *Frontiers in Psychology, 8*. https://doi.org/10.3389/fpsyg.2017.01486

Beckmann, N., Wood, R. E., & Minbashian, A. (2010). It depends how you look at it: On the relationship between neuroticism and conscientiousness at the within- and the between-person levels of analysis. *Journal of Research in Personality, 44*(5), 593–601. https://doi.org/10.1016/j.jrp.2010.07.004

Bertolero, M. A., & Bassett, D. S. (2020). On the nature of explanations offered by network science: A perspective from and for practicing neuroscientists. *Topics in Cognitive Science, 12*(4), 1272–1293. https://doi.org/10.1111/tops.12504

Boer, D., Hanke, K., & He, J. (2018). On detecting systematic measurement error in cross-cultural research: A review and critical reflection on equivalence and invariance tests. *Journal of Cross-Cultural Psychology, 49*(5), 713–734. https://doi.org/10.1177/0022022117749042

Borgatti, S. P. (2005). Centrality and network flow. *Social Networks, 27*(1), 55–71. https://doi.org/10.1016/j.socnet.2004.11.008

Borsboom, D. (2017, January 27). The meaning of model equivalence: Network models, latent variables, and the theoretical space in between. *Psych Networks*. https://psych-networks.com/meaning-model-equivalence-network-models-latent-variables-theoretical-space/

Borsboom, D., & Cramer, A. O. J. (2013). Network analysis: An integrative approach to the structure of psychopathology. *Annual Review of Clinical Psychology, 9*, 91–121. https://doi.org/10.1146/annurev-clinpsy-050212-185608

Borsboom, D., Cramer, A. O. J., Schmittmann, V. D., Epskamp, S., & Waldorp, L. J. (2011). The small world of psychopathology. *PLoS One, 6*(11), e27407. https://doi.org/10.1371/journal.pone.0027407

Brass, D. J. (2018, August 25). A social network perspective on organizational citizenship behavior. *The Oxford Handbook of Organizational Citizenship Behavior*. https://doi.org/10.1093/oxfordhb/9780190219000.013.25.

Brose, A., Voelkle, M. C., Lövdén, M., Lindenberger, U., & Schmiedek, F. (2015). Differences in the between-person and within-person structures of affect are a matter of degree. *European Journal of Personality, 29*(1), 55–71. https://doi.org/10.1002/per.1961

Chidlow, A., Plakoyiannaki, E., & Welch, C. (2014). Translation in cross-language international business research: Beyond equivalence. *Journal of International Business Studies, 45*(5), 562–582. https://doi.org/10.1057/jibs.2013.67

Christensen, A. P., & Golino, H. (2021). On the equivalency of factor and network loadings. *Behavior Research Methods*. https://doi.org/10.3758/s13428-020-01500-6

Ciocca, J., Horowitz, M. C., & Kahn, L. (2021, April 6). *The Perils of Overhyping Artificial Intelligence*. https://www.foreignaffairs.com/articles/united-states/2021-04-06/perils-overhyping-artificial-intelligence

Costantini, G., Epskamp, S., Borsboom, D., Perugini, M., Mõttus, R., Waldorp, L. J., & Cramer, A. O. J. (2015). State of the aRt personality research: A tutorial on network analysis of personality data in R. *Journal of Research in Personality, 54*, 13–29. https://doi.org/10.1016/j.jrp.2014.07.003

Courtland, R. (2018). Bias detectives: The researchers striving to make algorithms fair. *Nature, 558*(7710), 357–360. https://doi.org/10.1038/d41586-018-05469-3

Cowen, A. S., Keltner, D., Schroff, F., Jou, B., Adam, H., & Prasad, G. (2021). Sixteen facial expressions occur in similar contexts worldwide. *Nature, 589*(7841), 251–257. https://doi.org/10.1038/s41586-020-3037-7

Cramer, A. O. J., Waldorp, L. J., van der Maas, H. L. J., & Borsboom, D. (2010). Comorbidity: A network perspective. *The Behavioral and Brain Sciences, 33*(2–3), 137–150. discussion 150–193. https://doi.org/10.1017/S0140525X09991567

Crawford, K. (2021). Time to regulate AI that interprets human emotions. *Nature, 592*(7853), 167–167. https://doi.org/10.1038/d41586-021-00868-5

Crawford, K., Gray, M. L., & Miltner, K. (2014). Big datal critiquing big data: Politics, ethics, epistemology I special section introduction. *International Journal of Communication, 8*, 10.

Cronbach, L. J. (1951). Coefficient alpha and the internal structure of tests. *Psychometrika, 16*(3), 297–334. https://doi.org/10.1007/BF02310555

Edwards, J. R. (2011). The fallacy of formative measurement. *Organizational Research Methods, 14*(2), 370–388. https://doi.org/10.1177/1094428110378369

Ehrlich, C. R., & Blankenbach, J. (2019). Indoor localization for pedestrians with real-time capability using multi-sensor smartphones. *Geo-Spatial Information Science, 22*(2), 73–88. https://doi.org/10.1080/10095020.2019.1613778

Epskamp, S. (2020). Psychometric network models from time-series and panel data. *Psychometrika, 85*(1), 206–231. https://doi.org/10.1007/s11336-020-09697-3

Epskamp, S., Borsboom, D., & Fried, E. I. (2018). Estimating psychological networks and their accuracy: A tutorial paper. *Behavior Research Methods, 50*(1), 195–212. https://doi.org/10.3758/s13428-017-0862-1

Epskamp, S., & Fried, E. I. (2018). A tutorial on regularized partial correlation networks. *Psychological Methods, 23*(4), 617–634. https://doi.org/10.1037/met0000167

Everett, B. (2013). *An introduction to latent variable models*. Springer Science & Business Media.

Eysenck, H. J. (1979). *The structure and measurement of intelligence*. Springer Berlin Heidelberg. https://doi.org/10.1007/978-3-642-67075-6

Fischer, R., & Karl, J. A. (2019). A primer to (cross-cultural) multi-group invariance testing possibilities in R. *Frontiers in Psychology, 10*. https://doi.org/10.3389/fpsyg.2019.01507

Fischer, R., & Karl, J. A. (2020). The network architecture of individual differences: Personality, reward-sensitivity, and values. *Personality and Individual Differences, 160*, 109922. https://doi.org/10.1016/j.paid.2020.109922

Fischer, R., Mattos, P., Teixeira, C., Ganzerla, D. S., Rosa, R. G., & Bozza, F. A. (2020). Association of Burnout with depression and anxiety in critical care clinicians in Brazil. *JAMA Network Open, 3*(12), e2030898–e2030898. https://doi.org/10.1001/jamanetworkopen.2020.30898

Fisher, A. J., Medaglia, J. D., & Jeronimus, B. F. (2018). Lack of group-to-individual generalizability is a threat to human subjects research. *Proceedings of the National Academy of Sciences, 115*(27), E6106–E6115. https://doi.org/10.1073/pnas.1711978115

Fontaine, J. (2005). Equivalence. In K. Kempf-Leonard (Ed.), *Encyclopedia of social measurement* (Vol. 1, pp. 803–813). Elsevier.

Foygel, R., & Drton, M. (2010). Extended Bayesian information criteria for Gaussian graphical models. *Proceedings of the 23rd International Conference on Neural Information Processing Systems – Volume 1*, pp. 604–612.

Freeman, L. C. (1978). Centrality in social networks conceptual clarification. *Social Networks, 1*(3), 215–239. https://doi.org/10.1016/0378-8733(78)90021-7

Fried, E. I., Epskamp, S., Nesse, R. M., Tuerlinckx, F., & Borsboom, D. (2016). What are "good" depression symptoms? Comparing the centrality of DSM and non-DSM symptoms of depression in a network analysis. *Journal of Affective Disorders, 189*, 314–320. https://doi.org/10.1016/j.jad.2015.09.005

George, G., Haas, M. R., & Pentland, A. (2014). Big Data and Management. *Academy of Management Journal, 57*(2), 321–326. https://doi.org/10.5465/amj.2014.4002

Golino, H., & Epskamp, S. (2017). Exploratory graph analysis: A new approach for estimating the number of dimensions in psychological research. *PLoS One, 12*(6), e0174035. https://doi.org/10.1371/journal.pone.0174035

Golino, H., Shi, D., Christensen, A. P., Garrido, L. E., Nieto, M. D., Sadana, R., Thiyagarajan, J. A., & Martinez-Molina, A. (2020). Investigating the performance of exploratory graph analysis and traditional techniques to identify the number of latent factors: A simulation and tutorial. *Psychological Methods, 25*(3), 292–320. https://doi.org/10.1037/met0000255

Hallquist, M. N., Wright, A. G. C., & Molenaar, P. C. M. (2019). Problems with centrality measures in psychopathology symptom networks: Why network psychometrics cannot escape psychometric theory. *Multivariate Behavioral Research, 56*, 199–223. https://doi.org/10.1080/00273171.2019.1640103

Hamaker, E. L., Kuiper, R. M., & Grasman, R. P. P. P. (2015). A critique of the cross-lagged panel model. *Psychological Methods, 20*(1), 102–116. https://doi.org/10.1037/a0038889

Harkness, J. A., van de Vijver, F. J. R., & Mohler, P. P. (Eds.). (2003). *Cross-cultural survey methods*. Wiley.

Herschel, R., & Miori, V. M. (2017). Ethics & big data. *Technology in Society, 49*, 31–36. https://doi.org/10.1016/j.techsoc.2017.03.003

Hult, G. T. M., Ketchen, D. J., Griffith, D. A., Finnegan, C. A., Gonzalez-Padron, T., Harmancioglu, N., Huang, Y., Talay, M. B., & Cavusgil, S. T. (2008). Data equivalence in cross-cultural international business research: Assessment and guidelines. *Journal of International Business Studies, 39*(6), 1027–1044. https://doi.org/10.1057/palgrave.jibs.8400396

Humphries, M. D., & Gurney, K. (2008). Network 'small-world-ness': A quantitative method for determining canonical network equivalence. *PLoS One, 3*(4), e0002051. https://doi.org/10.1371/journal.pone.0002051

International Test Commission. (2018). ITC guidelines for translating and adapting tests (second edition). *International Journal of Testing, 18*(2), 101–134. https://doi.org/10.1080/15305058.2017.1398166

Jones, P. J., Ma, R., & McNally, R. J. (2019). Bridge centrality: A network approach to understanding comorbidity. *Multivariate Behavioral Research*, 1–15. https://doi.org/10.1080/00273171.2019.1614898

Jowell, R., & Centre for Comparative Social Surveys (Great Britain) (Eds.). (2007). *Measuring attitudes cross-nationally: Lessons from the European Social Survey*. SAGE.

King, G., & Zeng, L. (2001). Explaining rare events in international relations. *International Organization, 55*(3), 693–715.

Kruis, J., & Maris, G. (2016). Three representations of the Ising model. *Scientific Reports, 6*(1), 34175. https://doi.org/10.1038/srep34175

Kuppens, P., Allen, N. B., & Sheeber, L. (2010). Emotional inertia and psychological maladjustment. *Psychological Science, 21*(7), 984–991. https://doi.org/10.1177/0956797610372634

Lanzendorf, M. (2010). Key events and their effect on mobility biographies: The case of childbirth. *International Journal of Sustainable Transportation, 4*(5), 272–292. https://doi.org/10.1080/15568310903145188

LePine, J. A., Erez, A., & Johnson, D. E. (2002). The nature and dimensionality of organizational citizenship behavior: A critical review and meta-analysis. *Journal of Applied Psychology, 87*(1), 52–65. https://doi.org/10.1037/0021-9010.87.1.52

Liu, J., Li, J., Li, W., & Wu, J. (2016). Rethinking big data: A review on the data quality and usage issues. *ISPRS Journal of Photogrammetry and Remote Sensing, 115*, 134–142. https://doi.org/10.1016/j.isprsjprs.2015.11.006

Liu, P., Du, Y., & Xu, Z. (2019). Machines versus humans: People's biased responses to traffic accidents involving self-driving vehicles. *Accident Analysis & Prevention, 125*, 232–240. https://doi.org/10.1016/j.aap.2019.02.012

Lubke, G. (2003). On the relationship between sources of within- and between-group differences and measurement invariance in the common factor model. *Intelligence, 31*(6), 543–566. https://doi.org/10.1016/S0160-2896(03)00051-5

Marston, H. R., & Kowert, R. (2020). What role can videogames play in the COVID-19 pandemic? *Emerald Open Research, 2*. https://doi.org/10.35241/emeraldopenres.13727.2

Mulder, J. D., & Hamaker, E. L. (2020). Three extensions of the random intercept cross-lagged panel model. *Structural Equation Modeling: A Multidisciplinary Journal, 28*, 1–11. https://doi.org/10.1080/10705511.2020.1784738

Nunan, D., & Di Domenico, M. (2013). Market research and the ethics of big data. *International Journal of Market Research, 55*(4), 505–520. https://doi.org/10.2501/IJMR-2013-015

Nunnally, J. C., & Bernstein, I. H. (1994). *Psychometric theory* (3rd ed.). McGraw-Hill.

Ok, C. (2021). Extraversion, loneliness, and problematic game use: A longitudinal study. *Personality and Individual Differences, 168*, 110290. https://doi.org/10.1016/j.paid.2020.110290

Organ, D. W. (1988). *Organizational citizenship behavior: The good soldier syndrome* (pp. xiii, 132). Lexington Books/D. C. Heath and Com.

Organ, D. W., Podsakoff, P. M., & MacKenzie, S. B. (2005). *Organizational citizenship behavior: Its nature, antecedents, and consequences*. SAGE Publications, Inc.

Oswald, F. L., Mitchell, G., Blanton, H., Jaccard, J., & Tetlock, P. E. (2013). Predicting ethnic and racial discrimination: A meta-analysis of IAT criterion studies. *Journal of Personality and Social Psychology, 105*(2), 171–192. https://doi.org/10.1037/a0032734

Patel, T. (2015). Crossing disciplinary, epistemological and conceptual boundaries in search of better cultural sense-making tools: A review of principal cultural approaches from business and anthropology literatures. *Journal of Organizational Change Management, 28*(5), 728–748. https://doi.org/10.1108/JOCM-03-2015-0049

Podsakoff, P. M., Williams, L. J., & Todor, W. D. (1986). Effects of organizational formalization on alienation among professionals and nonprofessionals. *The Academy of Management Journal, 29*(4), 820–831. JSTOR. https://doi.org/10.2307/255948.

Pritchard, R. D. (1990). *Measuring and improving organizational productivity: A practical guide*. Greenwood Publishing Group.

Sabidussi, G. (1966). The centrality index of a graph. *Psychometrika, 31*(4), 581–603. https://doi.org/10.1007/BF02289527

Schwartz, H. A., Eichstaedt, J. C., Kern, M. L., Dziurzynski, L., Ramones, S. M., Agrawal, M., Shah, A., Kosinski, M., Stillwell, D., Seligman, M. E. P., & Ungar, L. H. (2013). Personality,

gender, and age in the language of social media: The open-vocabulary approach. *PLoS One, 8*(9), e73791. https://doi.org/10.1371/journal.pone.0073791
Sharples, L. D. (2018). The role of statistics in the era of big data: Electronic health records for healthcare research. *Statistics & Probability Letters, 136*, 105–110. https://doi.org/10.1016/j.spl.2018.02.044
Stahl, G. K., Maznevski, M. L., Voigt, A., & Jonsen, K. (2010). Unraveling the effects of cultural diversity in teams: A meta-analysis of research on multicultural work groups. *Journal of International Business Studies, 41*(4), 690–709. https://doi.org/10.1057/jibs.2009.85
Textor, J., van der Zander, B., Gilthorpe, M. S., Liśkiewicz, M., & Ellison, G. T. (2016). Robust causal inference using directed acyclic graphs: The R package 'dagitty'. *International Journal of Epidemiology, 45*(6), 1887–1894. https://doi.org/10.1093/ije/dyw341
Translation | European Social Survey (ESS). (n.d.). Retrieved April 12, 2021, from https://www.europeansocialsurvey.org/methodology/ess_methodology/translation/
Travers, J., & Milgram, S. (1969). An experimental study of the small world problem. *Sociometry, 32*(4), 425–443.
Van de Vijver, F. J. R. R., & Leung, K. (2021). In V. H. Fetvadjiev, J. Fontaine, J. He, & Y. H. Poortinga (Eds.), *Methods and data analysis for cross-cultural research* (Vol. 1, 2nd ed.). Cambridge University Press.
Van Dyne, L., & LePine, J. A. (1998). Helping and voice extra-role behaviors: Evidence of construct and predictive validity. *Academy of Management Journal, 41*(1), 108–119. https://doi.org/10.5465/256902
Vandenberg, R. J., & Lance, C. E. (2000). A review and synthesis of the measurement invariance literature: Suggestions, practices, and recommendations for organizational research. *Organizational Research Methods, 3*(1), 4–70. https://doi.org/10.1177/109442810031002
Vinci, A. (2020, October 7). *The Coming Revolution in Intelligence Affairs*. https://www.foreignaffairs.com/articles/north-america/2020-08-31/coming-revolution-intelligence-affairs
Watts, D. J., & Strogatz, S. H. (1998). Collective dynamics of 'small-world' networks. *Nature, 393*(6684), 440–442. https://doi.org/10.1038/30918
Williams, D. R., & Mulder, J. (2019). BGGM: A R package for Bayesian Gaussian graphical models. *PsyArXiv*. https://doi.org/10.31234/osf.io/3b5hf
Wilson, E. O. (1999). *Consilience: The unity of knowledge* (1st Vintage books Ed). Vintage Books.
Yang, Z., Algesheimer, R., & Tessone, C. J. (2016). A comparative analysis of community detection algorithms on artificial networks. *Scientific Reports, 6*(1), 30750. https://doi.org/10.1038/srep30750
Yukl, G. A. (2013). *Leadership in organizations* (8th ed.). Pearson.
Zafari, F., Gkelias, A., & Leung, K. K. (2019). A survey of indoor localization systems and technologies. *IEEE Communications Surveys Tutorials, 21*(3), 2568–2599. https://doi.org/10.1109/COMST.2019.2911558
Zyphur, M. J., Allison, P. D., Tay, L., Voelkle, M. C., Preacher, K. J., Zhang, Z., Hamaker, E. L., Shamsollahi, A., Pierides, D. C., Koval, P., & Diener, E. (2020). From data to causes I: Building a general cross-lagged panel model (GCLM). *Organizational Research Methods, 23*(4), 651–687. https://doi.org/10.1177/1094428119847278
Zyphur, M. J., Voelkle, M. C., Tay, L., Allison, P. D., Preacher, K. J., Zhang, Z., Hamaker, E. L., Shamsollahi, A., Pierides, D. C., Koval, P., & Diener, E. (2020). From data to causes II: Comparing approaches to panel data analysis. *Organizational Research Methods, 23*(4), 688–716. https://doi.org/10.1177/1094428119847280

Index

M. O. Macambira et al. (eds.), *Assessing Organizational Behaviors*,
https://doi.org/10.1007/978-3-030-81311-6

MIX
Papier aus verantwortungsvollen Quellen
Paper from responsible sources
FSC® C105338

If you have any concerns about our products,
you can contact us on
ProductSafety@springernature.com

In case Publisher is established outside the EU,
the EU authorized representative is:
Springer Nature Customer Service Center GmbH
Europaplatz 3, 69115 Heidelberg, Germany

Printed by Libri Plureos GmbH
in Hamburg, Germany